Corporate Accountability under Socio-Economic Rights

In recent decades, corporations have increasingly accepted that they have obligations to respect the socio-economic rights of individuals whose rights to livelihoods, education, food, health, housing and water are affected by the actions of corporations on a daily basis. Despite this, it is often difficult for victims to bring corporations to court for violations of their socio-economic rights. Domestic constitutional systems provide, at best, fragile and limited protections against adverse corporate activities, while international responses have been lacking in creating obligations and accountability for corporations under socio-economic rights. The urgency of bolstering corporate accountability for socio-economic rights is therefore apparent.

In light of this, this book asks whether corporations are required to observe socio-economic rights and if they are accountable for any violations. In doing so, it identifies and analyzes the theoretical foundations and the existing scope of corporate accountability arising from socio-economic rights at both national and international levels. Through careful analysis, Jernej Letnar Černič exposes the stark need for greater clarity in the obligations and accountability of corporations, advocating a normative framework for corporate accountability for socio-economic rights in national legal orders which builds on existing mechanisms.

Jernej Letnar Černič is Associate Professor of Human Rights Law at the Graduate School of Government and European Studies, Senior Research Associate at gLAWcal – Global Law Initiatives for Sustainable Development (United Kingdom) and Senior Research Fellow at the University Institute of European Studies – IUSE, Turin (Italy). He graduated from University of Ljubljana with the France Prešeren award. He completed his Ph.D. in Human Rights Law at the University of Aberdeen and holds a Diploma in Human Rights Law from the European University Institute and Diplome de droit international et de Droit compare des Droits de l'Homme (merit) from René Cassin Institut International des droits de l'homme. He has written extensively in the past on business and human rights law and on the European Human Rights Law. His works have been cited in reports by the United Nations, European Parliament and the Council of Europe and in academic studies from around the world.

Transnational Law and Governance

Series Editor: Paolo Davide Farah

West Virginia University, USA and gLAWcal – Global Law Initiatives for Sustainable Development, UK

In recent years the concepts of "transnational law" and "governance" have been explored by both scholars and practitioners with the terms taking on new meaning and significance, particularly in light of the ongoing economic crisis and a corresponding critical reappraisal of global institutional structures and governance. This multidisciplinary series aims to provide a home for research exploring these issues.

Transnational law covers a broad theoretical definition which includes studies emerging from disciplines such as international law, comparative law, international economic law and administrative law undertaken by legal scholars but also features extensive research undertaken by scholars from other disciplines, including but not limited to, political sciences, international relations, public administration, sociology, history, philosophy and geography. Governance in particular is now seen as important when we refer to the general stability of the markets, to good faith and other key principles which are fundamental to the notion of a fair market which is responsive to the needs of governments and citizens as well as businesses.

This series features cutting-edge works which critically analyse the relationship between governance, institutions and law from a variety of disciplinary perspectives.

Available titles in this series include:

Business and Human Rights in Europe
International Law Challenges
Angelica Bonfanti

Corporate Accountability under Socio-Economic Rights
Jernej Letnar Černič

A Radically Democratic Response to Global Governance
Dystopian Utopias
Margaret Stout and Jeannine M. Love

Sustainability and Peaceful Coexistence for the Anthropocene
Pasi Heikkurinen

Forthcoming titles:

Administrative Appeals in EU Law
Giacomo Gattinara and Alessandro Di Mario

Corporate Accountability under Socio-Economic Rights

Jernej Letnar Černič

Routledge
Taylor & Francis Group
LONDON AND NEW YORK

First published 2019
by Routledge
2 Park Square, Milton Park, Abingdon, Oxon OX14 4RN

and by Routledge
52 Vanderbilt Avenue, New York, NY 10017, USA

First issued in paperback 2020

Routledge is an imprint of the Taylor & Francis Group, an informa business

British Library Cataloguing-in-Publication Data
A catalogue record for this book is available from the British Library

Library of Congress Cataloging-in-Publication Data
Names: Cernic, Jernej Letnar
Title: Corporate accountability under socio-economic rights / Jernej Letnar Cernic.
Description: New York : Routledge, 2019. | Series: Transnational law and governance | Includes index.
Identifiers: LCCN 2018018194 | ISBN 9781138288782 (hbk)
Subjects: LCSH: Tort liability of corporations. | Social responsibility of business. | Social rights. | Human rights.
Classification: LCC K1329.5 .C475 2018 | DDC 346/.066—dc23
LC record available at https://lccn.loc.gov/2018018194

ISBN 13: 978-0-367-58682-9 (pbk)
ISBN 13: 978-1-138-28878-2 (hbk)

Typeset in Galliard
by Apex CoVantage, LLC

Contents

Foreword vii
Acknowledgements xiv

PART I
Fundamental concepts and historical context 1

1 Corporate accountability for socio-economic rights: introductory remarks 3

2 The historical development of corporate accountability for socio-economic rights 21

3 Globalization, investment and the socio-economic environment 40

4 Business, socio-economic rights and good practices 64

PART II
Corporate accountability for socio-economic rights 85

5 Corporate human rights obligations under socio-economic rights 87

6 Corporate human rights obligations under specific socio-economic rights 125

7 Access to justice for victims of socio-economic rights violations 153

PART III
Corporate accountability for socio-economic rights and case studies 193

8 Corporate accountability concerning socio-economic rights in Cambodia 195

9 Corporate accountability concerning socio-economic rights in China 220

10 Corporate accountability concerning socio-economic rights in Colombia 247

PART IV
Proposals for reform 277

11 Conclusions and recommendations 279

Index 288

Foreword

Paolo Davide Farah[1]

Corporate Accountability under Socio-Economic Rights by Jernej Letnar Černič represents an important contribution to the broader discussions about non-state actors in the economic globalization and their roles, impacts and contributions to better govern free trade and the regulation of the global expansion of world trade with the objective of reducing or eliminating the related risks and damages occurring to Non-Trade Concerns (NTCs).

As Founder, President and Director of gLAWcal – Global Law Initiatives for Sustainable Development, I can say that the theoretical frameworks and conceptualization of NTCs – which are at the centre of the gLAWcal book series on "Global Law and Sustainable Development" and "Transnational Law and Governance", both published by Routledge Publishing (New York/London) – include some of the core societal values such as good governance, human rights, right to water, rights to food, social, economic and cultural rights, labour rights, access to knowledge, public health, social welfare, consumer interests, animal welfare, climate change, energy, environmental protection and sustainable development, product safety, and food safety and security.[2]

1 Paolo Davide Farah, West Virginia University, John D. Rockefeller IV, School of Policy and Politics, Department of Public Administration and College of Law; West Virginia University, Energy Institute and Center for Innovation in Gas Research and Utilization (CIGRU); West Virginia University, Institute of Water Security and Science (IWSS). Founder, President, Director and Principal Investigator at gLAWcal – Global Law Initiatives for Sustainable Development. Senior Fellow at the IIEL – Institute of International Economic Law, Georgetown University Law Center. Editor-in-Chief for the gLAWcal Book Series "Global Law and Sustainable Development" and for the gLAWcal Book Series "Transnational Law and Governance" published by Routledge Publishing (New York/London). The research leading to this result has received funding from People Programme (Marie Curie Actions) of the European Union's Seventh Framework Programme (FP7/2007–2013) under REA grant agreement no. 318908, acronym of the project: POREEN (2013–2016) entitled 'Partnering Opportunities between Europe and China in the Renewable Energies and Environmental Industries', within the results of the Research Team at gLAWcal – Global Law Initiatives for Sustainable Development (United Kingdom).

2 Paolo Davide Farah, 'Trade and Progress: The Case of China', 30 *Columbia Journal of Asian Law* 97–107 (2016); Paolo Davide Farah, Elena Cima (eds.), *China's Influence on Non-Trade Concerns in International Economic Law*, Global Law and Sustainable Development Book Series (New York/London: Routledge), ISBN 978-1-4094-4848-8, September 2016, pp. 1–584.

Jernej Letnar Černič's latest book focuses on how civil society and corporations have become increasingly aware of corporate impacts on local and global socio-economic environments in the past few decades.

Jernej Letnar Černič has been working over fifteen years in the field of human rights and business. For these reasons, he has become aware of the importance of establishing a better understanding of how to improve governance, rule of law and human rights protection against often adverse corporate conduct. He has been actively involved in recent years in promoting those values in Europe and at the global level. This book illustrates his belief that it is necessary to paint a clearer picture on how to effectively protect socio-economic rights of ordinary individuals against adverse business activities.

Jernej Letnar Černič is Associate Professor of human rights law at the Graduate School of Government and European Studies, Senior Research Associate at gLAWcal–Global Law Initiatives for Sustainable Development (United Kingdom) and Senior Research Fellow at the University Institute of European Studies–IUSE, Turin (Italy).

I met Jernej Letnar Černič at one of the European Society of International Law (ESIL) conferences. Following our encounter, as I was aware of the work he was implementing in China, I decided to invite him to join two of the initiatives I have been leading in China in the last few years, in collaboration with different Chinese Universities, academic and research institutions, and NGOs. During the summer 2014, I had the pleasure to collaborate with him in Beijing, China, when Jernej Letnar Černič accepted my invitation as Guest Lecturer in the framework of the 9th Edition of the Summer Institute in China held at Peking University, School of Government (China), academic programme, which I have been leading for the last thirteen years. The programme is composed of two curricula: the "Summer Institute on Climate Change, Energy and Environmental Protection" (SICCEP) and the "Summer Institute on Intellectual Property Rights and China" (IP-China). Letnar Černič taught a class on "Corporate Social Responsibility and Sustainable Development in China". During the additional time he spent in China, he was also involved in the People Programme (Marie Curie Actions) of the European Union's Seventh Framework Programme (FP7/2007–2013) under REA grant agreement n° 318908 (acronym of the project: POREEN [2013–2016]), entitled "Partnering Opportunities between Europe and China in the Renewable Energies and Environmental Industries". Some of the research and case studies in China leading to this book have received funding and were implemented in the framework of the POREEN project, within the results of the Research Team I lead as Principal Investigator at gLAWcal–Global Law Initiatives for Sustainable Development and in my capacities as POREEN Vice-Coordinator and POREEN Legal Workpackage Leader. Moreover, Jernej Letnar Černič has also contributed with a supplementary paper, "Business, Sustainable Development and Human Rights in China", which is forthcoming in another outlet I am editing.

Letnar Černič has invested a lot of effort and determination in researching and writing the book by not merely dissecting the normative frameworks, but also exploring the real-life context on the ground in Cambodia, China, Colombia and beyond. Those experiences from local milieus have opened his eyes to striking the inequality of much of the Global South and deepened his understanding and approach to corporate accountability for socio-economic rights. Poverty – for example in the form of inadequate access to water, food, decent living conditions, health care and education – has been somewhat common in many urban and rural environments in the Global South. It has particularly affected vulnerable groups such as Indigenous peoples, women, children and elderly. He finds that in many parts of the Global South there exists no equality of initial opportunities and of basic capabilities, as states and even business actors cannot provide even the minimum of socio-economic rights. If the state is absent and does not guarantee basic socio-economic rights such as those listed above, it (in)directly affects the ability of individuals to achieve self-fulfilment. In this way, he notes that corporations have become powerful actors in much of the Global South and are often reported to contribute to the denial of those socio-economic rights. He strongly and persuasively argues that corporations have obligations under socio-economic rights and should be held accountable for their abuses. Therefore, his book illustrates the search for justice, respect, compassion and forgiveness to the benefit of everyday peoples.

The guarantees and the protection of human rights, in particular socio-economic rights, are shifting more and more from the public sphere, from the governmental, supra-governmental and intergovernmental level, towards the private, where corporations and various other private entities are directly or indirectly assuming public commitments and constructive undertakings; wherein they have the objective to provide possible solutions and actions in guaranteeing welfare and the respect of these rights to a growing sphere of the citizens, targeting primarily the most powerless and fragile groups within the population.

The expansion and extent of the process of globalization is unquestionable and has gained tremendous dimensions and vast scale in recent times. There is a part of the public opinion and civil society which is vehemently against globalization and is afraid of its negative effects on NTCs, local societal values and traditions. These communities are making the equalization between the role of the states and international organizations responsible for adopting adequate governance, precautionary principles, and rules concerning human rights and social justice and multinational corporations. Private entities are indeed active on the market and directly capable of putting these rights at stake or independently protecting these rights in practice through strict compliance as well as through voluntary actions. This means that if multinational companies operate in such a way that they undermine societal values, public opinion, instead of simply accusing the private ownership of these actions, might consider both the states and governments accountable, along with international organizations, for not complying with their supposed duties to prevent actions that could put human life and health in danger and also for their eventual omission to act, to take positive and incremental measures.

For this reason, the paradigm shift towards the pivotal role and significance of corporate social responsibility fostering sustainable development and facing challenges, such as poverty, climate change and environmental degradation, should not mean that the role of public good governance must decrease and the general level of trust in the private sector should automatically increase. On the contrary, the pursuit of profit and power is still strongly present in today's business models and a solid corporate accountability approach is inevitable to reinforce domestic and international supervisory systems able to step in, whenever the holders of these socio-economic rights suffer violations.

The eleven chapters of this book describe the current reality of how to secure these socio-economic rights using domestic and international legal provisions and good governance. Some of the chapters focus on the historical developments and conceptualization of the origins of the current "state of the art" regarding corporate behaviour, governance and ethics, while some other chapters try to offer tangible solutions and strategies, which are feasible in the light of specific domestic law and regulations as well as in the light of the international legal system.

Some chapters try to present the full picture of protecting socio-economic rights, while others take a closer look to the particularities and distinctiveness between the substantial elements and focus of these rights such as the right to water, housing, education, food and health. The specific case studies in China, Colombia and Cambodia put the final touches on the complexity and interest of this publication, pointing out specific deficiencies or limits in these legal, political and administrative systems being only local manifestations of a broader global governance problem: vagueness.

Letnar Černič argues that vaguely formulated (and rarely assessed) and fragmented international legal frameworks, as well as the lack of a coordinated, reconciliated and harmonious domestic system related to corporate accountability, regulated under multiple branches of civil, criminal and administrative rules, make the enforcement of socio-economic rights problematic and ineffective.

Many countries rely mainly on the companies' altruism to shape their internal rules in conformity with public fundamental values of general common interest and having in mind the priority of the protection of global public goods and global commons opposed to the profit and otherwise benefit for their own shareholders. Without underestimating the positive and constructive role that private companies play in the society and the benefits and service that they provide to the community as a whole, independently from the action of the states and government, in particular with the creation of jobs, opportunities of growth and many other important inputs, it is still of utmost importance that states govern and oversee whether the private decision-making preserve and continue consistently to protect important societal values.

States should not interfere excessively in economic activities and we should preserve the core of the economic systems in which private business operates in competition and largely free of state control. But at the same time, it is necessary to acknowledge that in a globalized world predominantly dominated by economic and financial transactions, free-trade and liberal principles, multinationals might take advantage of the loopholes and of the fragmentation of international and domestic law against human rights or the protection of the environment. States should be ready, unhesitant and equipped to go against companies that endanger fundamental values, global public goods and global commons.

In developed democracies, private entities must respect and abide by domestic and international human rights obligations which might show contrast, depending on the different judicial systems. An important and essential tool in any democracy is to empower more and more the public opinion, the civil society and all types of stakeholders with the granting of high-level access to justice to guarantee more severe and scrupulous company accountability. Having in mind the needs and the necessary balance between national security and individual liberties, the citizens should play the role of onlookers and surveillance of the powers, should be vigilant of both public agencies and private entities.

However, this requires actions going beyond the individuals, involving a broader cooperation of the civil society. It could be in a form of various organizations representing rights and stakeholders, public platforms open for constructive discussions and information sharing, etc. Additionally, the author of the book largely reflects on how to ensure a higher rate of cases where a harmful effect (one-time or ongoing) can be eliminated and responsibility drawn in a timely and efficient manner. Such an effective service of justice in sensitive cases would not only fulfill the repressive function of regulations and legal provisions, but also widely contribute to the prevention of further violations in a Thomas Aquinas sense of the term.

Unfortunately, several developing and least-developed countries are still behind in this pathway. Corporate governance principles and the notion of a company being a separate entity from its leaders, shareholders and employees in general makes it even more difficult to prevent the effect of corporate accountability. The possibility for individuals to separate themselves from corporate actions at least, but not only, in civil and administrative terms, ensure the decision-makers and the instigators of the actual perpetuators walk away without any responsibility and charges related to their actions in violation of human rights. In other words, the combination of company law and corporate governance rules might have a tendency of limiting and hindering the repressive function of the law from otherwise having a direct impact on a company representative or group of representatives. As Thomas Aquinas has written in his well-known *Summa Theologica* about the effects of law, stating that "it is not always through perfect goodness of virtue that one obeys the law, but sometimes it is through fear of punishment", the system of modern corporate accountability cannot simply entrust private companies with the duty to self-regulate through voluntary actions supported by an insufficient, sometimes non-binding, framework of provisions either.

Different chapters of the book analyze and take into account all these aspects and angles, while pointing out the fundamental primacy of human dignity over merely economic interests. The recommendations and conclusions presented in this book highlight the obstacles not only for ascribing real significance and meaning to the term "dignity", but also the complications and shortcomings when it comes to enforcement and the real potential to shield such an essential human value and human status from any attempts towards transactional relations and commodification.

At the beginning of our modern times, certain areas have been considered too sacred and too essential for the public good to be a subject of revenue maximization. Unfortunately, we have seen the clock being turned back, rather than being speeded up to keep pace with human developments, when few representatives of the corporate society have slowly shifted away from the acceptance of the full protection of global commons and global public goods without negotiations or step-backs. Devastation as well as the plundering of resources have become opportunities to gain influence, power and secure economic strength in the form of market shares.

Now is the time to go back to the original boundaries, which were already the eventual achievements after centuries of slavery and subjugations, in order to overcome new social, humanitarian, economic and environmental frustrations worldwide. It is compelling, inevitable and absolutely crucial to lead our society towards sustainability, global welfare, fairness and equity to all for rebuilding-up of the social pact between human beings and for the creation of a harmonious society among humans and the Earth.

This book calls for a more holistic approach related to corporate accountability, ending the fragmentation between systems – some more lenient, some more strict but most of them opaque and hardly approachable by individuals; the call for a more pluralistic approach operating on multiple levels of accountability so that investigations may be able to hold liable not only the companies themselves, but also the states and individuals, are all evidence of this book's relevance.

Besides the importance of a holistic approach, it is essential not only to determine, enumerate and at the same time to consolidate the range of socio-economic rights, as well as the procedural and legal framework of their protection, but it is equally relevant to construe a clear formulation of corporate obligations. Only when companies know exactly what society expects from them and makes those commitments binding and enforceable, we might count on a change in corporate accountability, we might observe significant shifts in how business decisions are made, and we might realize transformations in companies' operations, procedures and activities.

Under the current circumstances of global governance and development, this book can be a useful tool for paving the way towards the necessary transition to a more sustainable society. Technological and scientific development will mainly accelerate the process of global value chain creations and the exploitation of natural and human resources for economic development during the upcoming decades. New challenges, which need to be taken into consideration by legislators and policymakers, and the additional need of efforts arise on an annual basis. The latest outlook warns about the increased vulnerability of privacy and data protection, which will also have to be at the top of the corporate responsibility agenda in the upcoming years. States and governments must act for preserving also these human rights or eventually be considered equally accountable for failure to act and omissions.

Consumer expectations are steadily increasing in terms of quality and availability of different products, and these buyer demands place growing strains on the business sector. These thrusts are unfortunately incapable of keeping pace towards the current increased awareness and sensitivity of some companies, when it comes specifically to protection of socio-economic rights, which are still seen as too broad, too demanding and at odds with corporate interests.

Therefore, a dilemma is present in the current debate about corporate activities, which requires a sensitive balance between consumer welfare, thriving economies, and business interests on one hand, and sustainability and the protection of individual rights on the other. This book has great potential to contribute to the forming of such a balanced approach of policies, global governance and good governance; thus at the end these values and principles are intertwined and cannot exist without one another.

Professor Paolo Davide Farah
Editor-in-Chief for the gLAWcal Book Series "Transnational Law and Governance" published by Routledge Publishing (New York/London).
West Virginia University, USA and gLAWcal–Global Law Initiatives for Sustainable Development, United Kingdom

Acknowledgements

This project has taken many years and great effort and sacrifice to finish. First, I would like to thank my family, without whom this book would not have come to light. More specifically, I am particularly grateful to Miren Cabada Rodriguez, Marjeta Černič, Tara van Ho, Surya Deva, Nicolás Carrillo-Santarelli, Ago Shinchi, Felipe Gómez Isa, Larry Catá Backer, Manoj Kumar Sinha, Wouter Vandehole, Derek Fincham, Beatriz Eugenia Sánchez Mojica and Humberto Cantú Rivera for their support and advice in completing this research project. I am grateful to the editor of this book series, Professor Paolo Davide Farah, for all his support, advice and patience. I would also like express my gratitude to the following institutions, which over the years provided me stimulating intellectual space during my research stays: City University of Hong Kong, University of Deusto, Indian Law Institute, South Texas College of Law, University of Los Andes and Pontifical Javeriana University. Further, I would like to thank my home institution, the Graduate School of Government and European Studies, and the Slovenian Research Agency for giving me opportunity to embark on this project. Some of the research and the case studies in China leading to this book have received funding from the People Programme (Marie Curie Actions) of the European Union's Seventh Framework Programme (FP7/2007–2013) under REA grant agreement n° 318908 (acronym of the project: POREEN [2013–2016]), entitled "Partnering Opportunities between Europe and China in the Renewable Energies and Environmental Industries", within the results of the Research Team at gLAWcal–Global Law Initiatives for Sustainable Development (United Kingdom), coordinated by Professor Paolo Davide Farah. Finally, I would like to thank the editorial team at Routledge Publishing for their work, patience and support.

Ljubljana, 22 January 2018

Part I

Fundamental concepts and historical context

1 Corporate accountability for socio-economic rights

Introductory remarks

Introduction	3
Illustrations of alleged corporate abuses of socio-economic rights	7
Literature review	9
Brief overview of the nature of the work	11
Methodology of the research	14
Roadmap of the book	15

Introduction

Rights-holders around the world have for decades suffered daily violations of their socio-economic rights due to inadequate and weak domestic and international supervisory systems, a lack of access to justice, or an absence of effective remedies to the wrongful behaviour of state actors and/or non-state actors such as corporations. The book therefore has the overall aim to investigate corporate accountability for socio-economic rights and propose ways to bolster its respect and enforcement. Socio-economic rights are essential for the individual's welfare, comfort and self-realization. Every day, corporations affect local and global environments via the enjoyment of vulnerable individuals' socio-economic rights. Business operations therefore bring both negative and positive effects, as this book illustrates. Corporations generate economic growth, jobs, investment and a higher standard of living, yet some are involved in breaches of human rights, including socio-economic rights. Are corporations required to observe socio-economic rights and are they accountable for any violations? Where can rights-holders find a place to enforce corporate accountability for socio-economic rights violations?

Individuals whose socio-economic rights have been violated by corporations encounter several obstacles to enforcing corporate accountability in judicial, quasi-judicial and non-judicial mechanisms.[1] This volume attempts to answer

1 Jernej Letnar Černič and Tara Van Ho, 'Introduction', *in* Jernej Letnar Černič and Tara Van Ho (eds.), *Human Rights and Business: Direct Corporate Accountability for Human Rights*, Oisterwijk: Wolf Legal Publishers (2015), pp. 1–23.

the above questions and analyses how to make progress in the area of business and socio-economic rights by making proposals for reform. In this way, it comprehensively establishes and analyzes the current scope and nature of corporate human rights obligations and corporate accountability deriving from economic and social human rights.

This book focuses on economic and social rights. Economic and social rights include rights to adequate housing, food, education, water, health, work and social security. States are primarily responsible for ensuring the respecting of socio-economic rights, although corporations have certain obligations concerning the exercise of socio-economic rights that derive from the domestic constitutional system or indirectly under international law. Several alleged violations of socio-economic rights have occurred in the last few decades. Corporations can, for instance, directly affect individuals' rights to adequate housing, through pollution endanger their right to health, engage in land grabbing, contaminate land and water, cause starvation and breach the right to food in local communities, limit children's access to primary and secondary schools and thus interfere with the right to education, or disconnect individuals and communities from water resources for personal use and violate their right to health and water.

For individuals to enjoy equality in a given area, they must at least have access to basic commodities like education, food, health, adequate housing and water. Accordingly, this book focuses on the rights to education, food, health, adequate housing and water.[2] Without such basic goods, an individual cannot be placed on an equal footing. Sen argues that "deprivation ability . . . is more important than the measure of disadvantage, such as low income, since it is only instrumentally important, with its implementing value conditioned by many social and economic circumstances".[3] If one does not have these fundamental commodities available for their survival and that of their children, their ability to achieve basic human development is limited, if not completely undermined. If a family of five sleeps on the street and the children wander around naked, drinking dirty water and eating food scraps from landfills, it is clear they will be largely guided by their survival instinct and everything else will be seen as an unnecessary luxury. It is only when the individual achieves a certain level of human development that they acquire personal freedom and can make independent decisions about how to lead their life and will continue to invest in raising the living standards of both themselves and their children.

Economic and social rights have long been considered inferior to civil and political rights, chiefly due to difficulties in enforcing them. They have been described as non-enforceable, programmatic in nature and non-genuine human rights. However, several national legal orders allow for the enforcement of socio-economic rights, which runs against the idea of "gradually implementing" their

2 Asbjørn Eide, 'Economic, Social and Cultural Rights as Human Rights', *in* Asbjørn Eide, Catarina Krause and Allan Rosas (eds.), *Economic, Social and Cultural Rights: A Textbook*, Dordrecht: Martinus Nijhoff Publishers (2001), pp. 9–28, pp. 21 and 22.

3 Amartya Sen, *Development as Freedom*, Oxford: Oxford University Press (1999), p. 131.

features at the international level. They have been employed as a tool in ideological battles, often forgetting the reasons and contents of their existence. Yet in recent decades the normative background and enforceability of socio-economic rights have grown in recognition in domestic and international settings. Nonetheless, civil and political rights and socio-economic rights are equal and indivisible, and should be treated as a whole in order achieve the full enjoyment of all human rights. Economic and social rights depend on a state's available financial resources.[4] Yet it is contended that "maximum available resources" not only include those of the state or international community,[5] but also of local and global business actors.[6]

However, socio-economic rights are often found in national constitutions in a separate chapter to civil and political rights, often the difference being in their potential mandatory nature.[7] Likewise, they often differ in legal nature from civil and political rights by being described as programmatic and non-enforceable. Scheinin observes that "the problem relating to the legal nature of economic and social rights does not relate to their validity but rather to their applicability".[8] The challenges of their enforceability are often seen on the domestic level, with only a few isolated examples in the world of the highest national courts recognizing their applicability.[9] As the case studies in this book show, such problems are exacerbated in proceedings against corporations where only a few have been successfully prosecuted. This observation is even less valid at the international level, where the only forum is the United Nations Committee on Economic, Social and Cultural Rights under the Optional Protocol of the International Covenant

4 UN, International Covenant on Economic, Social and Cultural Rights, GA res 2200A (XXI), 21 UN GAOR Supp (No. 16) at 49', UN Doc. A/6316, Treaty Series, vol. 993, 16 December 1966. See for a detailed discussion, Jernej Letnar Černič, 'Sovereign Financing and Corporate Responsibility for Economic and Social Rights', *in* Juan Pablo Bohoslavsky and Jernej Letnar Černič (eds.), *Making Sovereign Financing and Human Rights Work*, Oxford and Portland: Hart Publishing (2014), pp. 139–162. See, Robert E. Robertson, 'Measuring State Compliance with the Obligation to Devote the "Maximum Available Resources" to Realizing Economic, Social and Cultural Rights"' 16 *Human Rights Quarterly* 694 (1994).

5 See, Magdalena Sepulveda, *The Nature of the Obligations Under the International Covenant on Economic, Social and Cultural Rights*, Antwerp, Oxford and New York: Intersentia (2003), pp. 370–377. See also, Phillip Alston and Gerard Quinn, 'The Nature and Scope of States Parties' Obligations Under the International Covenant on Economic, Social and Cultural Rights', 9(1) *Human Rights Quarterly* 156 (1987).

6 See, Chapter 3.

7 Martin Scheinin, 'Economic and Social Rights as Legal Rights', *in* Asbjørn Eide, Catarina Krause and Allan Rosas (eds.), *Economic, Social and Cultural Rights: A Textbook*, Dordrecht: Martinus Nijhoff Publishers (2001), pp. 29–54, pp. 41 and 53.

8 Ibid., p. 41; See also, Christian Courtis, 'Standards to Make ESC Rights Justiciable: A Summary Exploration', 2 *Erasmus Law Review* 379 (2009).

9 Fons Coomans (ed.), *Justiciability of Economic, Social and Cultural Rights*, Antwerp: Intersentia (2006). See also, Malcom Langford, 'Justiciability of Social Rights: From Practice to Theory', *in* Malcom Langford (ed.), *Social Rights Jurisprudence: Emerging Trends in International and Comparative Law*, Cambridge: Cambridge University Press (2008), pp. 3–45.

on Economic, Social and Cultural Rights (ICESCR).[10] Therefore, provisions on socio-economic rights have depended internally on states being the primary duty-holder. Alston therefore argues

> it is important to recognize that the promotion of economic and social rights as human rights . . . does not imply that there is a universal one-size-fits-all approach that will secure the realization of economic and social rights in countries with very different histories, legal systems, traditions and cultures.[11]

Yet, corporations exert a daily impact on the provision of socio-economic rights. In addition, Aguirre observes that corporations "have considerable influence on ESCR through their control over governmental economic and social policy".[12] Corporate accountability arising from economic and social rights is thus not simply an abstract consideration.

This book therefore holds direct relevance for rights-holders, society, the economy, governments and corporations, both national and transnational, that do business in the Global South and elsewhere where they may be involved in breaching economic and social human rights. The way in which national and international legal systems provide answers to the enforcement of corporate accountability for socio-economic rights is important. The book thus not only holds theoretical value, but also practical value for those whose social and economic rights are violated. It is thus directly and highly important for global civil society.

Socio-economic rights have traditionally been best protected in the domestic human rights system. The regional and international human rights systems often step in where the domestic system fails or is unwilling to protect socio-economic rights. Victims' limited access to justice is still a major obstacle to realization of their socio-economic rights. Thus, corporate accountability for socio-economic rights is best enforced by suitable domestic mechanisms. However, the normative framework for enforcing corporate accountability for socio-economic rights at national and international levels remains quite weak not only in the Global South but also in the Global North. Difficulties enforcing corporate accountability arise not only from the incompleteness of regulatory safeguards in supervising these corporations' activities, but from their lack of enforcement as well. This is

10 UN, 'Optional Protocol to the International Covenant on Economic, Social and Cultural Rights', UN Doc. A/63/435, C.N.869.2009.TREATIES-34, 11 December 2009. See, Matthew Craven and Malcolm Langford, *The International Covenant on Economic, Social and Cultural Rights*, Oxford: Oxford University Press (2014); Katharine G. Young and Julieta Lemaitre, 'The Comparative Fortunes of the Right to Health: Two Tales of Justiciability in Colombia and South Africa', 26 *Harvard Human Rights Journal* (2013); Fons Coomans, 'Justiciability of the Right to Education', 2(4) *Erasmus Law Review* 427 (2009).

11 UN, Human Rights Council, 'Report of the Special Rapporteur on Extreme Poverty and Human Rights, Philip Alston', 28 April 2016, para 71.

12 Daniel Aguirre, 'Multinational Corporations and the Realisation of Economic, Social and Cultural Rights', 35 *California Western International Law Journal* 53, 54 (2004).

apparent from the vague institutional framework regulating companies in several local environments where the rule of law is often abused. Therefore, building a stronger system to protect socio-economic rights at both national and international levels is a *condition sine qua non* for successfully supervising corporations in the human rights field. The book is the first to address these challenges comprehensively on both the theoretical and practical level and advocates specific ways to reform corporate accountability for socio-economic rights.

Illustrations of alleged corporate abuses of socio-economic rights

The corporate sector directly affects the socio-economic rights of individuals. It can infringe them in various manners. First, corporations can violate their negative obligations not to interfere with socio-economic rights. Second, they can infringe their positive obligations to ensure a minimum level of socio-economic rights, particularly in the case of state-owned corporations, corporate groups and global supply chains, or when corporations exercise public functions through concessions and licenses. The question arises: Can corporations affect all of socio-economic rights, or only some of them? As Ruggie, the former UN Special Representative on Business and Human Rights, argued concerning the responsibilities of transnational corporations: "businesses can affect virtually all internationally recognized human rights". As such, "any limited list will almost certainly miss one or more rights that may turn out to be significant in a particular instance".[13] In line with Ruggie's assertion, corporations can potentially impact all human rights, including economic and social rights, noting that some (elements of) rights are more relevant than others. However, there is a gap in research regarding corporate accountability for economic and social rights. This book seeks to address this gap.

In recent decades a growing body of evidence has shown that corporate activities can result in socio-economic rights abuses of vulnerable communities and individuals. For instance, FIDH and Lawyers for Human Rights report negative impacts of state and corporate behaviour on socio-economic livelihoods in the Blyvooruitzicht Mine Village in South Africa.[14] Moreover, Unilever Hindustan Ltd recently admitted it had negatively affected its workers' human rights.[15] BHP Billiton accepted responsibility for an environmental disaster in Samarco, Brazil that upset the socio-economic livelihoods of thousands.[16] Further, there is much

13 UN, Human Rights Council, 'Protect, Respect and Remedy: A Framework for Business and Human Rights', Report of the Special Representative of Secretary-General: John Ruggie, UN Doc. A/HRC/8/5, 7 April 2008, para 6.

14 FIDH and Lawyers for Human Rights, 'Blyvooruitzicht Mine Village: The Human Toll of State and Corporate Abdication of Responsibility in South Africa', January 2017.

15 Sudeep Chakravarti, 'HUL Pays a Price for Toxic Legacy', *Live Mint*, 11 March 2016.

16 Australian Associated Press, 'BHP Billiton Reaches $1.55bn Settlement with Brazil Over Dam Collapse', London: *The Guardian*, 2 March 2016.

evidence of corporations' impacts on Indigenous peoples' socio-economic livelihoods around the world.[17] The alleged negative environmental and human rights impacts of Chevron's oil extraction in Ecuador are widely reported.[18] Moreover, individuals in Zambia alleged "their land and livelihood have been destroyed by water pollution caused by the Nchanga Copper Mine, which is owned by Vedanta through its subsidiary KCM".[19] Further, City Water Services Limited, a subsidiary of the British corporation Biwater, endangered the qualitative provision of water in Dar es Salaam, Tanzania.[20] Nestlé recently admitted forced-labour conditions at its coffee plantations in Brazil that were affecting the socio-economic rights of its population.[21] Similarly, socio-economic rights violations in India's tea plantation industry are widely reported.[22] Comparable reports come from Myanmar[23]

17 Gonzalo Aguilar Cavallo, 'Pascua Lama, Human Rights, and Indigenous Peoples: A Chilean Case Through the Lens of International Law', 5(1) *Goettingen Journal of International Law* 215 (2013); Ibironke T. Odumosu-Ayanu, 'Indigenous Peoples, International Law and Extractive Industry Contract', Symposium on international indigenous rights, financial decisions and local policy, 109 AJIL UNBOUND 220 (2015); Ibironke T. Odumosu-Ayanu, 'Governments, Investors and Local Communities: Analysis of a Multi-Actor Investment Contract Framework', 15 *Melbourne Journal of International Law* 473 (2014); Shalanda Baker, 'Why the IFC's Free, Prior and Informed Consent Policy Does Not Matter (Yet) to Indigenous Communities Affected by Development Projects', 30 *Wisconsin International Law Journal* 668 (2013); Nicholas Dorf, 'Making an Offer They Can't Refuse: Corporate Investment in Africa and the Divestment of Indigenous Land Rights', 38 *Boston College International and Comparative Law Review* 65 (2015).

18 *Maria Aguinda Salazar y otros v Chevron Corporation*, Judgment No. 174-2012, National Court of Justice, Civil and Corporate Division, Quito, Ecuador, 12 November 2013. See for example, for a detailed discussion: Kathia Martin-Chenut and Camila Perruso, 'El Caso Chevron-Texaco y el Aporte de los Proyectos de Convencion sobre Crimenes Ecológicos y Ecocidio a la Responsabilidad Penal de las Empresas Transnacionales', *in* Humberto Cantú Rivera (ed.), *Derechos Humanos y Empresas: Reflexiones desde Amé*rica Latina, San José: Instituto Interamericano de Derechos Humanos (2017), pp. 355–369. See also, Audrey Anne Crasson, 'The Case of Chevron in Ecuador: The Need for an International Crime Against the Environment?', 9 (3) *Amsterdam Law Forum* 29 (2017).

19 Barbara Lewis, 'Zambian Villagers Win Right to sue Vedanta in English Courts', London: *Reuters*, 13 October 2017.

20 Food and Water Watch, 'Biwater: A Civil Society Perspective' (2008). See also, Business and Human Rights Resources, Biwater-Tanzania arbitration, 18 February 2014. See also, Ashley Seager, 'Tanzania Wins £3m Damages from Biwater Subsidiary', London: *The Guardian*, 11 January 2008. See, *Biwater Gauff (Tanzania) Ltd v United Republic of Tanzania*, case No. ARB/05/22, ICSID, 24 March 2008. See, Jernej Letnar Černič, 'Sovereign Financing and Corporate Responsibility for Economic and Social Rights', *in* Juan Pablo Bohoslavsky and Jernej Letnar Černič (eds.), *Making Sovereign Financing and Human Rights Work*, Oxford and Portland: Hart Publishing (2014) for further discussion.

21 Kate Hodal, 'Nestlé Admits Slave Labour Risk on Brazil Coffee Plantations', London: *The Guardian*, 2 March 2016.

22 Human Rights Institute (Columbia Law School), 'The More Things Change: The World Bank, Tata and Enduring Abuses on India's Tea Plantations', January 2014.

23 Irene Pietropaoli, 'Corporate Accountability and Transitional Justice in Myanmar', *Justice Info.net*, 7 March 2016.

and Guatemala.[24] Further, it is reported that Lonmin Plc allegedly violated its employees' rights to adequate housing.[25] In such scenarios, corporations have failed to do no harm to the provision of socio-economic rights. What is more, South African gold miners and the transnational corporations Anglo American and AngloGold recently reached a settlement concerning their failure to comply with safety and health regulations that left several workers with lifelong diseases.[26] In 2007, a financial fund won the case before the High Court in London against the government of Zambia, thereby decreasing its financial capacity to guarantee economic and social rights.[27] The Economic and Social Rights Centre (Hakijamii) in Kenya observed in its study concerning activities of Base Titanium Corporation, in Kwale County (Kenya), that there is "no equitable benefit sharing in that context, with the mining host communities in Nguluku and Bwiti still experiencing dire socio-economic conditions despite the mining project minting billions from titanium exploitation in their backyards".[28] All of the above cases demonstrate how corporate activities can have a substantially negative impact on the enjoyment of economic and social rights.

Literature review

The international academic literature lacks scientific research with a specific, in-depth focus on business and socio-economic rights able to produce normative proposals for the necessary reforms. This gap is most notable and of greatest concern in the legal field. A lot has already been written on business and human rights, and the literature is growing, yet this book specifically examines the obligations and accountability for socio-economic rights corporations hold, an area that no research agenda has so far concentrated on. Where there is some literature, it mostly deals with specific dimensions of corporate accountability for socio-economic human rights.[29] There are not many of these works: They are

24 Guatemala Human Rights Commission, 'La Puya Protest at the Ministry of Energy and Mines', 3 March 2016.

25 Kevin Crowley, 'Govt. Threatens to Cancel Lonmin's Licence Over Failure to Meet Housing Commitment for Employees: Company Says Working to Find a Lasting Solution', Bloomberg Markets (South Africa), 19 December 2016.

26 Leigh Day, 'Victory at Last for South African Gold Miners as Anglo American and AngloGold Agree Landmark Silicosis Compensation Scheme', 5 March 2016.

27 BBC World, 'Zambia Loses "vulture fund" Case', 15 February 2007.

28 The Economic and Social Rights Centre (Hakijamii), *Titanium Mining Beneft Sharing in Kwale County: Comprehensive Analysis of the Law and Practice in the Context of Nguluku and Bwiti*, Nairobi: The Economic and Social Rights Centre (Hakijamii) (September 2017), p. 4.

29 See for example, Olivier De Schutter, 'Corporations and Economic, Social and Cultural Rights', *in* Eibe Riedel, Gilles Giacca and Christophe Golay (eds.), *Economic, Social, and Cultural Rights in International Law: Contemporary Issues and Challenges*, Oxford: Oxford University Press (2014), pp. 193–224, p. 217; Justine Nolan and Luke Taylor, 'Corporate Responsibility for Economic, Social and Cultural Rights: Rights in Search of a Remedy?', 87(2) *Journal of Business Ethics* 433 (2009); Chris Fletcher, 'Corporate Social Responsibility:

scattered, undertheorized and lack a holistic approach to the questions addressed above. A comprehensive treatment of businesses' accountability for socio-economic rights is thus clearly missing.

Determining corporate obligations concerning socio-economic rights has considerable practical utility for corporations, governments and civil society alike. Corporate obligations under socio-economic rights may level the playing field by limiting the competitive advantage of those corporations that avoid negative and positive obligations. Such obligations would also create more certainty and stability for corporations doing business around the globe, clarifying the expectations concerning the operations of a corporation. Moreover, effective national and international preventive and remedial structures for realizing socio-economic rights could help rights-holders to efficiently protect their human dignity. It appears that the essence of academic commentary is only a discussion of corporations' international human rights obligations or corporate social responsibility,[30] the UN Guiding Principles on Business and Human Rights[31] or the international human rights obligations of corporations, thereby not making any connection between corporate obligations and economic and social human

A Legal Framework for Socioeconomic Development in Tibet', 17 *Yale Human Rights and Development Law Journal* 120 (2014). Brigit C. Toebes and Jernej Letnar Černič, 'Corporate Human Rights Obligations Under Economic, Social, and Cultural Rights', *in* Jeffrey F. Addicott, Jahid Hossain Bhuiyan and Tareq M. R. Chowdhury (eds.), *Globalization, International Law, and Human Rights*, Oxford: Oxford University Press (2012), pp. 1–33; Robert Ashford, 'Socio-Economic Foundation of Corporate Law and Corporate Social Responsibility', 76 *Tulane Law Review* 1187 (2001); Rajat Panwar, Tommi Rinne, Eric Hansen and Heikki Juslin, 'Corporate Responsibility: Balancing Economic, Environmental, and Social Issues in the Forest Products Industry', 56(2) *Forest Products Journal* 4 (2006); Daniel Aguirre, 'Multinational Corporations and the Realisation of Economic, Social and Cultural Rights', 35 *California Western International Law Journal* 53 (2004); Maria McFarland Sanchez-Moreno and Tracy Higgins, 'No Recourse: Transnational Corporations and the Protection of Economic, Social and Cultural Rights in Bolivia', 27(5) *Fordham International Law Journal* 1663 (2003).

30 Tineke Lambooy, 'Legal Aspects of Corporate Social Responsibility', 30 *Utrecht Journal of International and European Law* 1 (2014); Ronen Shamir, 'Between Self-Regulation and the Alien Tort Claims Act: On the Concept of Corporate Social Responsibility', 38 *Law and Society Review* 635 (2004); David Scheffer and Caroline Kaeb, 'The Five Levels of CSR Compliance: The Resiliency of Corporate Liability Under the Alien Tort Statute and the Case for a Counterattack Strategy in Compliance Theory', 29 *Berkeley Journal of International Law* 334 (2011).

31 Jena Martin Amerson, '"The End of the Beginning?" A Comprehensive Look at the Business and Human Rights Agenda from a Bystander Perspective', 17 *Fordham Journal of Corporate and Finance Law* 871 (2012). David Bilchitz, 'The Ruggie Framework: An Adequate Rubric for Corporate Human Rights Obligations?', 12 *Sur – International Journal of Human Rights* 199 (2010). Susan Ariel Aaronson and Ian Higham, '"Re-righting Business": John Ruggie and the Struggle to Develop International Human Rights Standards for Transnational Firms' 35 *Human Rights Quarterly* 333 (2013). See, also Ruggie's explanation: John G. Ruggie, *Just Business: Multinational Corporations and Human Rights*, New York: W.W. Norton & Co. (2013); John G. Ruggie, 'Business and Human Rights: The Evolving Agenda', 101 *American Journal of International Law* 819 (2004).

rights.[32] On the other hand, a huge gap in the international legal literature can also be identified since most literature on economic and social rights considers state obligations[33] while hardly covering corporate obligations. Other than a few isolated scientific works, comprehensive scientific research is missing. This book seeks to rectify these gaps. It brings out these connections, focuses on their advantages and disadvantages and proposes a set of reforms. For this reason, the book adopts a holistic approach and therefore argues that corporate obligations and the field of economic and social rights are interconnected, interdependent and complementary. It thus seems especially important to establish the scope and nature of corporations' accountability and their human rights obligations under socio-economic rights.

This book investigates the nature of corporate accountability and obligations in relation to economic and social rights. It does so by adopting a comprehensive approach to corporate accountability and obligations under socio-economic rights, one that connects the fields of human rights and business with the field of economic and social rights. Such a holistic approach will be also employed with respect to corporate accountability for socio-economic rights. The chosen approach is distinct in the wider international environment which has so far, as indicated, neglected the specific challenges raised by the impact businesses have on individuals' socio-economic rights.

Brief overview of the nature of the work

This volume examines corporate accountability for socio-economic rights and its different dimensions.[34] In doing so, it applies a predominantly legal and normative approach. The Cambridge Dictionary defines accountability as "a situation in which someone is responsible for things that happen and can give a satisfactory

32 Steven R. Ratner, 'Corporations and Human Rights: A Theory of Legal Responsibility', 111 *Yale Law Journal* 443 (2001). Andrew Clapham, *Human Rights Obligations of Non-State Actors*, Oxford: Oxford University Press (2006); Nicola Jägers, *Corporate Human Rights Obligations: In Search of Accountability*, Antwerp: Intersentia (2002), pp. 75–95; Peter T. Muchlinski, *Multinational Enterprises and the Law*, Oxford: Oxford University Press (2nd Edition, 2007), pp. 519–524; David Kinley and Junko Tadaki, 'From Talk to Walk: The Emergence of Human Rights Responsibilities for Corporations at International Law', 44 *Virginia Journal of International Law* 931 (2004); Larissa Van den Herik and Jernej Letnar Černič, 'Regulating Corporations Under International Law: From Human Rights to International Criminal Law and Back Again', 8 *Journal of International Criminal Justice* 725 (2010).

33 Philip Alston and Gerard Quinn, 'The Nature and Scope of States Parties' Obligations under the International Covenant on Economic, Social and Cultural Rights', 9 *Human Rights Quarterly* 156 (1987). Asbjørn Eide, 'Economic, Social and Cultural Rights as Human Rights', *in* Asbjørn Eide, Catarina Krause and Allan Rosas (eds.), *Economic, Social and Cultural Rights: A Textbook*, Dordrecht: Martinus Nijhoff Publishers (2001), pp. 9–28, pp. 21 and 22; See also, Amnesty International, 'What Are Economic, Social and Cultural Rights?'.

34 See for a discussion of the definition of corporations, Jernej Letnar Černič, *Human Rights Law and Business*, Groningen: Europa Law Publishing (2010).

reason for them".[35] Joseph argues that "given the potential for [transnational corporations] to translate their economic power into potentially huge de facto political power, it is perhaps unrealistic to expect human rights accountability . . . to emanate exclusively from host States".[36] Corporate accountability in this book refers to a broader, inclusive and holistic concept of accountability that includes any possibility of rights-holders to bring responsible actors to justice for alleged abuses of socio-economic rights, including individual and state responsibility. Obviously, given the space limits of the book the focus is on corporate accountability for socio-economic rights. Yeshanew offers the following definition of accountability as referring to "judicial or quasi-judicial procedure of enforcement",[37] but also an increasing number of non-judicial mechanisms or several other bottom-up enforcement modes depending on the socio-economic context. In 2017, the UN Working Group on Business and Human Rights observed that:

> access to justice . . . is a concept that is more elastic than the notions of the right to an effective remedy and access to an effective remedy. In a narrow sense, access to justice can be equated with the right or access to effective judicial remedies and in this sense effective remedies should often result in justice being provided to rights holders.[38] (footnote omitted)

Access to justice is therefore a broader category that includes not only top-down modes but also bottom-up ones.[39] This work attempts to make a three-fold contribution to the field by:

- providing a theoretical and historical framework for corporate accountability for socio-economic rights;
- submitting that corporations are obliged to observe socio-economic rights deriving from national, international, regional, voluntary and other sources in their business operations, and arguing they have negative and positive

35 Cambridge Dictionary, definition of "accountability".

36 Sarah Joseph, 'An Overview of the Human Rights Accountability of Multinational Enterprises', *in* Menno T. Kamminga and Saman Zia-Zarifi (eds.), *Liability of Multinational Corporations under International Law*, The Hague: Wolters Kluwer (2000), pp. 75–93, 78.

37 Sisay Alemahu Yeshanew, *The Justiciability of Economic, Social and Cultural Rights in the African Regional Human Rights System*, Cambridge, Antwerp and Portland: Intersentia (2013), p. 37.

38 UN, Report of the Working Group on the Issue of Human Rights and Transnational Corporations and other Business Enterprises, 'Access to Effective Remedies Under the Guiding Principles on Business and Human Rights: Implementing the United Nations Protect, Respect and Remedy Framework', UN Doc. A/72/162, 18 July 2017, para 16.

39 Dinah Shelton, *Remedies in International Human Rights Law*, Oxford: Oxford University Press (2006); Juan José Álvarez Rubio and Katerina Yiannibas (eds.), *Human Rights in Business: Removal of Barriers to Access to Justice in the European Union*, Abingdon: Routledge (2017); Amnesty International, 'Injustice Incorporated: Corporate Abuses and the Human Right to Remedy', 7 March 2014.

obligations to strive to ensure their suppliers, contractors and business partners respect socio-economic rights through supply chains; and
- calling for improved access to justice in cases against corporations for alleged socio-economic rights violations and arguing for an inclusive, pluralistic, holistic and concurrent approach to corporate accountability for socio-economic rights.

The study of corporate accountability for socio-economic rights faces several challenges. First, human rights have traditionally been protected in the vertical relationships between the state and individuals and/or groups. Business and human rights question such an assumption, as it is argued that human rights also apply horizontally between corporations and individuals and/or groups, where corporations act as a duty-bearer and individuals as rights-holders. Second, business and socio-economic rights or corporate accountability for socio-economic rights contends that businesses can, in addition to states, act as a duty-holder in the remit of socio-economic rights, despite their particularities of their programmatic and weak-enforcement nature. The third challenge reflects the fact that the enforcement of such corporate accountability traditionally functions through a state-based enforcement mechanism such as courts or a human rights commissions. However, non-state non-judicial enforcement mechanisms have recently been emerging around the world.[40] This book therefore contends that states and not-state actors should work together to establish and strengthen local and global normative structures for corporate accountability for socio-economic rights, and those different mechanisms should reinforce and complement each other and work alongside each other in an inclusive, pluralistic and holistic manner. All the different mechanisms must ensure that victims have access to justice either through effective judicial, quasi-judicial or non-judicial remedies considered fairly, independently and impartially in local environments or, if necessary, in the corporation's home state.

Corporations are obliged to respect socio-economic rights and protect their minimum reasonable core. The book argues there is a strong need to clarify the different limbs of corporate obligations to observe socio-economic rights; in particular, the positive protect and fulfil obligations are desperate for greater clarity if they are to become full-fledged legal obligations. It is no longer controversial to claim that corporations have negative obligations with respect to socio-economic rights, meaning they are obliged to not directly interfere with the individual's enjoyment of their socio-economic rights. However, positive obligations remain a potential mine field, particularly their scope. Are corporations there to provide at least a minimum level of socio-economic services where governments are falling short? Such positive obligations are therefore difficult to define and context dependent. Yet, this book asserts that corporate obligations concerning

40 May Miller-Dawkins, Kate Macdonald and Shelley Marshall, 'Beyond Effectiveness Criteria: The Possibilities and Limits of Transnational Non-Judicial Redress Mechanisms', Corporate Accountability Research (2016).

socio-economic rights go beyond mere negative obligations to respect socio-economic rights.

Methodology of the research

The book follows basic principles, instruments and methods of legal or normative research. It is divided into three main parts: The first two are theoretical and the third is practical. The methods employed in the theoretical part are normative, deductive, analytical, comparative, historical and socio-legal. In this way, it follows the traditional way to conduct legal research.[41] Tlyer observes that "the field of legal scholarship has been most heavily dominated by normative analyses of the law" and that "such doctrinal analyses involve efforts to understand the best balance of rights and obligations under the framework defined by law".[42] Van Gestel, Micklitz and Maduro add that "What all legal scholars should have in common, though, is a scientific attitude".[43] Slaughter and Ratner observe that this entails "the application of a conceptual apparatus or framework – a theory of international law – to the concrete problems faced in the international community".[44] Accordingly this book examines one of the seminal concrete challenges of local and global environments through theoretical apparatus of human rights law.

This volume primarily adopts an analytical and deductive approach to researching corporate accountability and obligations arising under socio-economic rights. In this way, the study follows a non-complicated methodology which includes a review of primary and secondary official sources, academic literature, reports, national legislation, international treaties, jurisprudence of national and international courts, along with interviews with practitioners and professors engaged in work in the field of business and human rights. The materials used were selected based on the input and perspectives they were able to provide for the study. It was the author's intention to provide a critical analysis of the approaches, findings or conclusions of the material used. A socio-legal approach is adopted in Part III of the work to outline the domestic context for developing corporate accountability with respect to economic and social rights. It examines the socio-economic context of corporate conduct and its functioning in domestic environments. This part has benefited from field research in various contexts of the Global South, particularly in Cambodia, Colombia and China, where the deductive method was also employed. In addition, the study applies the historical approach as a basis for exploring corporate accountability for socio-economic rights and providing the context of the historical development of corporate accountability concerning socio-economic rights. In attempting to prove the existence of certain

41 Steven R. Ratner and Anne-Marie Slaughter, 'Appraising the Methods of International Law: A Prospectus for Readers', 93 *American Journal of International Law* 291 (1999).

42 Tom R. Tyler, 'Methodology in Legal Research', 13(3) *Utrecht Law Review* (2017), p. 1.

43 Rob van Gestel, Hans-W. Micklitz and Miguel Poiares Maduro, 'Methodology in the New Legal World', EUI Working Paper LAW 2012/13, p. 23.

44 Steven R. Ratner and Anne-Marie Slaughter, 'Appraising the Methods of International Law: A Prospectus for Readers', 93 *American Journal of International Law* 292 (1999).

human rights obligations of corporations, this book looks at the socio-legal context within which they operate. A main component of the legal methodology is the comparative approach. This comparative approach discerns general principles of national and international law common to states by examining the respective national law relating to how corporations are regulated concerning socio-economic rights and accountability. In order to formulate proposals for their reform and improvement, the existing national and international frameworks are studied. The aim is to identify failures in the functioning of corporate accountability for socio-economic rights in domestic and international settings and ways to improve such a normative regime.

Roadmap of the book

The book itself is divided into three main parts, where the first and last of the eleven chapters are an introduction and conclusion. Part I includes the introduction and three chapters on historical contexts, globalization and the socio-economic environment, and good practices of corporations. The first part introduces the theoretical framework and historical background of business and socio-economic rights with an introduction that sets out the theoretical conundrum and research question concerning corporate accountability arising from economic and social rights, including several instances where corporate activities have allegedly violated socio-economic rights. Chapter 3 defines some seminal foundational pillars of the concepts, while Chapter 4 explains certain good practices of businesses.

In the next step, an in-depth theoretical stage, the second part identifies corporate human rights obligations, first generally in Chapter 5 and then more specifically in Chapter 6, including rights to adequate housing, food, education, water and health. Both chapters attempt to theoretically demonstrate and analyze the existing scope and nature of corporate accountability and obligations arising from socio-economic rights. Chapter 7 thereafter offers a definition of corporate accountability for socio-economic rights, consider current possibilities for access to justice and devise solutions to improve them. In this way, it examines domestic and international mechanisms for enforcing corporate accountability and analyze new approaches such as internal corporate complaints mechanisms, arbitration and bottom-up approaches. It subsequently identifies failures and shortcomings of the current framework for access to justice in business-related socio-economic rights cases and argue for a holistic approach which, apart from corporate accountability, include individual and state responsibility in order for rights-holders to have several alternatives available for redressing corporate violations of socio-economic rights.

The third part examines corporate accountability for socio-economic rights in practice by studying three case studies. It synthesizes the results of the theoretical examination and uses them in a practical case study of Cambodia, China and Colombia where corporations allegedly breached the economic and social rights of individuals. The case studies were chosen due to, first, relevance for the topic of this book; second, both prevalence of violations of socio-economic rights by or involving business and protest by rights-holders in all three countries; and third, challenges arising from shortcomings in the domestic frameworks for corporate accountability for socio-economic rights. It studies corporate obligations concerning socio-economic rights and accountability for socio-economic rights in these three countries. It looks at access to justice for victims of socio-economic violations in all three practical contexts and also the general rule-of-law environment, which is important for securing access to an effective remedy.

The conclusion in Chapter 11 of Part IV summarizes the seminal parts of the concepts of corporate accountability for socio-economic rights by highlighting the book's original research contribution in the field of business and human rights. Finally, this part answers the main research question of the book; i.e. how can rights-holders enforce corporate accountability for socio-economic rights and how to improve corporate accountability for socio-economic rights. The conclusion thus includes proposals for eliminating shortcomings in domestic and international structures for corporate accountability under socio-economic rights, and suggests how to improve access to remedies and reform the existing frameworks.

Bibliography

Books

Alemahu Yeshanew, Sisay, *The Justiciability of Economic, Social and Cultural Rights in the African Regional Human Rights System*, Cambridge, Antwerp and Portland: Intersentia (2013).

Álvarez Rubio, Juan José and Yiannibas, Katerina (eds.), *Human Rights in Business: Removal of Barriers to Access to Justice in the European Union*, Abingdon: Routledge (2017).

Clapham, Andrew, *Human Rights Obligations of Non-State Actors*, Oxford: Oxford University Press (2006).

Coomans, Fons (ed.), *Justiciability of Economic and Social Rights*, Antwerp: Intersentia (2006).

Craven, Matthew and Langford, Malcolm, *The International Covenant on Economic, Social and Cultural Rights*, Oxford: Oxford University Press (2014).

Jägers, Nicola, *Corporate Human Rights Obligations: In Search of Accountability*, Antwerp: Intersentia (2002).

Letnar Černič, Jernej, *Human Rights Law and Business*, Groningen: Europa Law Publishing (2010).

Muchlinski, Peter T., *Multinational Enterprises and the Law*, Oxford: Oxford University Press (2nd Edition, 2007).

Ruggie, John G., *Just Business: Multinational Corporations and Human Rights*, New York: W.W. Norton & Co. (2013).

Sen, Amartya, *Development as Freedom*, Oxford: Oxford University Press (1999).

Sepulveda, Magdalena, *The Nature of the Obligations under the International Covenant on Economic, Social and Cultural Rights*, Antwerp, Oxford and New York: Intersentia (2003).

Shelton, Dinah, *Remedies in International Human Rights Law*, Oxford: Oxford University Press (2006).

Journal articles

Aaronson, Susan Ariel and Higham, Ian, '"Re-Righting Business": John Ruggie and the Struggle to Develop International Human Rights Standards for Transnational Firms', 35 *Human Rights Quarterly* 333 (2013).

Aguilar Cavallo, Gonzalo, 'Pascua Lama, Human Rights and Indigenous Peoples: A Chilean Case Through the Lens of International Law', 5(1) *Goettingen Journal of International Law* 215 (2013).

Aguirre, Daniel, 'Multinational Corporations and the Realisation of Economic, Social and Cultural Rights', 35 *California Western International Law Journal* 53 (2004).

Amerson, Jena Martin, '"The End of the Beginning?" A Comprehensive Look at the Business and Human Rights Agenda from a Bystander Perspective', 17 *Fordham Journal of Corporate and Finance Law* 871 (2012).

Alston, Philip and Quinn, Gerard, 'The Nature and Scope of States Parties' Obligations Under the International Covenant on Economic, Social and Cultural Rights', 9(4) *Human Rights Quarterly* 156 (1987).

Ashford, Robert, 'Socio-Economic Foundation of Corporate Law and Corporate Social Responsibility', 76 *Tulane Law Review* 1187 (2001).

Baker, Shalanda, 'Why the IFC's Free, Prior and Informed Consent Policy Does Not Matter (Yet) to Indigenous Communities Affected by Development Projects', 30 *Wisconsin International Law Journal* 668 (2013).

Bilchitz, David, 'The Ruggie Framework: An Adequate Rubric for Corporate Human Rights Obligations?', 12 *Sur – International Journal of Human Rights* 199 (2010).

Coomans, Fons, 'Justiciability of the Right to Education', 2(4) *Erasmus Law Review* 427 (2009).

Courtis, Christian, 'Standards to Make ESC Rights Justiciable: A Summary Exploration', 2 *Erasmus Law Review* 379 (2009).

Crasson, Audrey Anne, 'The Case of Chevron in Ecuador: The Need for an International Crime Against the Environment?', 9(3) *Amsterdam Law Forum* 29 (2017).

Dorf, Nicholas, 'Making an Offer They Can't Refuse: Corporate Investment in Africa and the Divestment of Indigenous Land Rights', 38 *Boston College International and Comparative Law Review* 65 (2015).

Fletcher, Chris, 'Corporate Social Responsibility: A Legal Framework for Socioeconomic Development in Tibet', 17 *Yale Human Rights and Development Law Journal* 120 (2014).

Kinley, David and Tadaki, Junko, 'From Talk to Walk: The Emergence of Human Rights Responsibilities for Corporations at International Law', 44 *Virginia Journal of International Law* 931 (2004).

Lambooy, Tineke, 'Legal Aspects of Corporate Social Responsibility', 30(78) *Utrecht Journal of International and European Law* 1 (2014).

McFarland Sanchez-Moreno, Maria and Higgins, Tracy, 'No Recourse: Transnational Corporations and the Protection of Economic, Social and Cultural Rights in Bolivia', 27(5) *Fordham International Law Journal* 1663 (2003).

Nolan, Justine and Taylor, Luke, 'Corporate Responsibility for Economic, Social and Cultural Rights: Rights in Search of a Remedy?' 87(2) *Journal of Business Ethics* 433 (2009).

Odumosu-Ayanu, Ibironke T., 'Governments, Investors and Local Communities: Analysis of a Multi-Actor Investment Contract Framework', 15 *Melbourne Journal of International Law* 473 (2014).

Odumosu-Ayanu, Ibironke T., 'Indigenous Peoples, International Law and Extractive Industry Contract', *Symposium on international indigenous rights, financial decisions and local policy*, 109 *AJIL UNBOUND* 220 (2015).

Panwar, Rajat, Rinne, Tommi, Hansen, Eric and Juslin, Heikki, 'Corporate Responsibility: Balancing Economic, Environmental and Social Issues in the Forest Products Industry', 56(2) *Forest Products Journal* 4 (2006).

Ratner, Steven R. and Slaughter, Anne-Marie, 'Appraising the Methods of International Law: A Prospectus for Readers', 93 *American Journal of International Law* 291 (1999).

Ratner, Steven R., 'Corporations and Human Rights: A Theory of Legal Responsibility', 111 *Yale Law Journal* 443 (2001).

Ratner, Steven R. and Slaughter, Anne-Marie, 'Symposium on Method in International Law: A Special Issue of the American Journal of International Law', 93 *American Journal of International Law* (1999).

Robertson, Robert E., 'Measuring State Compliance with the Obligation to Devote the "Maximum Available Resources" to Realizing Economic, Social and Cultural Rights', 16 *Human Rights Quarterly* 694 (1994).

Ruggie, John G., 'Business and Human Rights: The Evolving Agenda', 101 *American Journal of International Law* 819 (2004).

Scheffer, David and Kaeb, Caroline, 'The Five Levels of CSR Compliance: The Resiliency of Corporate Liability under the Alien Tort Statute and the Case for a Counterattack Strategy in Compliance Theory', 29 *Berkeley Journal of International Law* 334 (2011).

Shamir, Ronen, 'Between Self-Regulation and the Alien Tort Claims Act: On the Concept of Corporate Social Responsibility', 38 *Law and Society Review* 635 (2004).

Tyler, Tom R., 'Methodology in Legal Research', 13(3) *Utrecht Law Review* 130 (2017).

Van den Herik, Larissa and Letnar Černič, Jernej, 'Regulating Corporations Under International Law: From Human Rights to International Criminal Law and Back Again', 8 *Journal of International Criminal Justice* 725 (2010).

Young, Katharine G. and Lemaitre, Julieta, 'The Comparative Fortunes of the Right to Health: Two Tales of Justiciability in Colombia and South Africa', 26 *Harvard Human Rights Journal* (2013).

Book chapters

De Schutter, Olivier, 'Corporations and Economic, Social and Cultural Rights', *in* Eibe Riedel, Gilles Giacca and Christophe Golay (eds.), *Economic, Social and Cultural Rights in International Law: Contemporary Issues and Challenges*, Oxford: Oxford University Press (2014), pp. 193–224.

Eide, Asbjørn, 'Economic, Social and Cultural Rights as Human Rights', *in* Asbjørn Eide, Catarina Krause and Allan Rosas (eds.), *Economic, Social and Cultural Rights: A Textbook*, Dordrecht: Martinus Nijhoff Publishers (2001), pp. 9–28.

Joseph, Sarah, 'An Overview of the Human Rights Accountability of Multinational Enterprises', *in* Menno T. Kamminga and Saman Zia-Zarifi (eds.), *Liability of Multinational Corporations under International Law*, The Hague: Wolters Kluwer (2000), pp. 75–93.

Langford, Malcom, 'The Justiciability of Social Rights: From Practice to Theory', *in* Malcolm Langford (ed.), *Social Rights Jurisprudence: Emerging Trends in International and Comparative Law*, Cambridge: Cambridge University Press (2008), pp. 3–45.

Letnar Černič, Jernej, 'Sovereign Financing and Corporate Responsibility for Economic and Social Rights', *in* Juan Pablo Bohoslavsky and Jernej Letnar Černič (eds.), *Making Sovereign Financing and Human Rights Work*, Oxford and Portland: Hart Publishing (2014), pp. 139–162.

Letnar Černič, Jernej and Van Ho, Tara, 'Introduction', *in* Jernej Letnar Černič and Tara Van Ho (eds.), *Human Rights and Business: Direct Corporate Accountability for Human Rights*, Oisterwijk: Wolf Legal Publishers (2015), pp. 1–23.

Martin-Chenut, Kathia and Perruso, Camila, 'El Caso Chevron-Texaco y el Aporte de los Proyectos de Convencion sobre Crimenes Ecológicos y Ecocidio a la Responsabilidad Penal de las Empresas Transnacionales', *in* Humberto Cantú Rivera (ed.), *Derechos Humanos y Empresas: Reflexiones desde América Latina*, San José: Instituto Interamericano de Derechos Humanos (2017), pp. 355–369.

Scheinin, Martin, 'Economic and Social Rights as Legal Rights', *in* Asbjørn Eide, Catarina Krause and Allan Rosas (eds.), *Economic, Social and Cultural Rights: A Textbook*, Dordrecht: Martinus Nijhoff Publishers (2001), pp. 29–54.

Toebes, Brigit C. and Letnar Černič, Jernej, 'Corporate Human Rights Obligations under Economic, Social and Cultural Rights', *in* Jeffrey F. Addicott, Jahid Hossain Bhuiyan and Tareq M. R. Chowdhury (eds.), *Globalization, International Law and Human Rights*, Oxford: Oxford University Press (2012), pp. 1–33.

Treaties

UN, International Covenant on Economic, 'Social and Cultural Rights', GA res. 2200A (XXI), 21 UN GAOR Supp. (No. 16) at 49, UN Doc. A/6316, Treaty Series, vol. 993, 16 December 1966.

UN, 'Optional Protocol to the International Covenant on Economic, Social and Cultural Rights', Doc. A/63/435, C, N,869.2009.TREATIES-34, 11 December 2009.

Newspaper articles

Australian Associated Press, 'BHP Billiton Reaches $1.55bn Settlement with Brazil Over Dam Collapse', London: *The Guardian*, 2 March 2016.

Lewis, Barbara, 'Zambian Villagers Win Right to Sue Vedanta in English Courts', London: *Reuters*, 13 October 2017.

Hodal, Kate, 'Nestlé Admits Slave Labour Risk on Brazil Coffee Plantations', London: *The Guardian*, 2 March 2016.

Seager, Ashley, 'Tanzania Wins £3m Damages from Biwater Subsidiary', London: *The Guardian*, 11 January 2008.

Sudeep Chakravarti, 'HUL Pays a Price for Toxic Legacy', *Live Mint*, 11 March 2016.

Official documents

UN, Human Rights Council, 'Protect, Respect and Remedy: A Framework for Business and Human Rights', Report of the Special Representative of Secretary-General: John Ruggie, UN Doc. A/HRC/8/5, 7 April 2008.

UN, Human Rights Council, 'Report of the Special Rapporteur on Extreme Poverty and Human Rights, Philip Alston', UN Doc. A/HRC/32/31, 28 April 2016.

UN, Report of the Working Group on the Issue of Human Rights and Transnational Corporations and other Business Enterprises, 'Access to Effective Remedies Under the Guiding Principles on Business and Human Rights: Implementing the United Nations Protect, Respect and Remedy Framework', UN Doc. A/72/162, 18 July 2017.

Cases

Maria Aguinda Salazar y otros v Chevron Corporation, Judgement No. 174-2012, National Court of Justice, Civil and Corporate Division, Quito, Ecuador, 12 November 2013.

Biwater Gauff (Tanzania) Ltd v United Republic of Tanzania, No. ARB/05/22, ICSID, 24 March 2008.

Reports and miscellaneous

Amnesty International, 'Injustice Incorporated: Corporate Abuses and the Human Right to Remedy', 7 March 2014.

Amnesty International, 'What Are Economic, Social and Cultural Rights?'

BBC World, 'Zambia Loses "vulture fund" Case', 15 February 2007.

Business and Human Rights Resources, 'Biwater-Tanzania Arbitration', 18 February 2014.

Cambridge Dictionary, Definition of 'Accountability'.

Crowley, Kevin, 'Govt. Threatens to Cancel Lonmin's Licence Over Failure to Meet Housing Commitment for Employees: Company Says Working to Find a Lasting Solution', Bloomberg Markets (South Africa), 19 December 2016.

Economic and Social Rights Centre (Hakijamii), 'Titanium Mining Beneft Sharing in Kwale County: Comprehensive Analysis of the Law and Practice in the Context of Nguluku and Bwiti', Nairobi: The Economic and Social Rights Centre (Hakijamii) (September 2017).

FIDH and Lawyers for Human Rights, 'Blyvooruitzicht Mine Village: The Human Toll of State and Corporate Abdication of Responsibility in South Africa', January 2017.

Food and Water Watch, 'Biwater: A Civil Society Perspective' 2008.

Human Rights Institute (Columbia Law School), 'The More Things Change: The World Bank, Tata and Enduring Abuses on India's Tea Plantations', January 2014.

Guatemala Human Rights Commission, 'La Puya Protest at the Ministry of Energy and Mines', 3 March 2016.

Leigh Day, 'Victory at Last for South African Gold Miners as Anglo American and AngloGold Agree Landmark Silicosis Compensation Scheme', 5 March 2016.

Miller-Dawkins, May, Macdonald, Kate and Marshall, Shelley, 'Beyond Effectiveness Criteria: the Possibilities and Limits of Transnational Non-judicial Redress Mechanisms', Corporate Accountability Research, 2016.

Pietropaoli, Irene, 'Corporate Accountability and Transitional Justice in Myanmar', Justice Info.net, 7 March 2016.

Rob van Gestel, Micklitz, Hans-W. and Maduro, Miguel Poiares, 'Methodology in the New Legal World', EUI Working Paper LAW 2012/13.

2 The historical development of corporate accountability for socio-economic rights

Introduction	21
Corporations, slave trade and colonialism	22
Corporations during the Second World War	23
Interim conclusion	33
Corporate accountability and the post–Second World War period	34
Conclusion	36

Introduction

This chapter examines the developments that have taken place on national and international levels in relation to past socio-economic human rights violations by or involving corporations. It seeks to enhance our understanding of the role of corporations in the commission of human rights violations, including socio-economic rights, during the past century. Following on from these brief introductory comments, it will be maintained that both socio-economic violations by or involving corporations and the absence of an effective complaints mechanism are not new phenomena. It will be further maintained that in investigating the legal-historical development of corporate accountability, such examination illustrates a nice battleground for the theoretical approaches to responsibility for socio-economic rights violations by or involving corporations, as well as about the uniform standards of socio-economic rights protection to be applied against corporations when they operate with direct or indirect knowledge of socio-economic rights violations. Socio-economic rights have been often in history best enforced against corporations or their responsible persons through other categories of human rights such as civil and political rights and even through international crimes. This section also argues that the historical development itself brings forth an old-new issue of corporate accountability for socio-economic rights to regulate corporations in the contemporary legal order and offers rationale and guidance for such regulations.

In seeking to establish these propositions, the balance of this chapter is devoted to exploring three main issues on historical trends. First, the role of corporations during the slave trade and colonialism will be examined in relation to corporate responsibility for socio-economic rights. The second section analyzes post–Second World War German industrialists' cases, mostly before the US military courts. The third and final section turns to corporate responsibility for socio-economic violations during the Vietnam War and Apartheid regime in South Africa. The analysis hereunder begins with the role of corporations during the slave trade.

Corporations, slave trade and colonialism

To understand the rationale behind corporate responsibility, it is valuable first to recall the role corporations played during the period of the slave trade and colonialism. The transatlantic slave trade provided the needed labour for European economies and the period from 1496 to 1838 saw Africans as one of the major goods in triangle transatlantic international trade between Africa, the Americas and Europe. In other words, triangle transatlantic trade was trade in African slaves in exchange for luxury goods (coffee, cotton, gold, sugar) of Latin America.[1] Moreover, it is believed that several millions of persons from Africa died as a result of the slave trade.[2] The slave trade was conducted by private merchants under the aegis of chattered corporations such as the Portuguese Guinea Company, Company of Grão Pará and Maranhão, Company of Pernambuco and Paraíba, Royal African Company, Dutch West India company, Spanish Cadiz Slave Company, South Sea Company, German New Guinea Company, German East Africa Company, Danish West India Company and Danish African Company.[3] The aim of this part of the chapter is to demonstrate that corporations were in past centuries involved in the slave trade, which was arguably considered as a human rights violation even at that time.

Chartered corporations were formed by groups of merchants under the auspices of a particular state, which were issued the charter of the company. Royal charters were awarded particularly to corporations involved in overseas slave trade, exploration and colonization.[4] First, such corporations emerged in the sixteenth century to explore the territories of Africa, Asia and the Americas. Even more corporations were created during the colonization process of Africa. Corporations differed at that time in structure and legal nature from a contemporary

1 See generally, Hugh Thomas, *The Slave Trade: The History of the Atlantic Slave Trade 1440–1879*, London: Picador (1997). Boddy-Evans, Alistair, 'How Many Slaves Were Taken from Africa?' *ThoughtCo.*, "It is estimated that during the 4 1/2 centuries of the trans-Atlantic slave trade, Portugal was responsible for transporting over 4.5 million Africans" and "during the eighteenth century however, when the slave trade accounted for the transport of a staggering 6 million Africans, Britain was the worst transgressor – responsible for almost 2.5 million", https://www.thoughtco.com/the-trans-atlantic-slave-trade-44544 (last accessed 19 January 2018).

2 See generally, Milton Meltzer, *Slavery: A World History*, Boston: Da Capo Press (1993).

3 Ibid.

4 Derek French, Stephen W. Mason and Christopher L. Ryan, *Company Law*, Oxford: Oxford University Press (2007), 5. Paul Lyndon Davies and Laurence Cecil Bartlett Gower, *Gower and Davies Principles of Modern Company Law*, London: Sweet & Maxwell (2003).

corporation, ranging from entirely private to others that were completely controlled by the governments.[5] A number of chattered corporations, such as the Dutch West and East India Companies, the British East India Company and Hudson's Bay Company, helped to administer newly colonized territories in India, Indonesia, Canada and parts of Africa. For instance, there is evidence available that the Dutch East India Company had been during the period of colonization involved in human rights violations.[6] Those European corporations became the principal agents in the economic exploitation of resources and people of conquered territory.[7]

The regulatory latitude rendered the victims of the slave trade unable to access legal protection or access to justice. Part of the reason for this is that the concept of human rights was at that time only in embryonic form. Yet another problem was that slavery at that time was not perceived as illegal and there was no judicial support to deal with such violations. By all accounts, people in colonized territories enjoyed no or little socio-economic or any other rights in respect of corporations and to the governing elite of the states they were coming from. Local communities received few benefits for their work and were not allowed to complain.

With the development of an accountability mechanism at the national and international level, the role played by corporations during this period have begun to be scrutinized in much detail. A number of claims have been brought against corporations for their activities during the colonization period.[8] For example, the Hereros people of Namibia sued Deutsche Bank for complicity in genocide of more than 65,000 Hereros between 1904 and 1907 during German rule in Namibia.[9] However, victims have yet to succeed in their attempts to hold corporations responsible for socio-economic rights during this period of time. To sum up, it appears that in the discussed period there was no consistent systematic attempt to regulate the activities of corporations either at national or international levels.

Corporations during the Second World War

This section examines some of the numerous cases which were heard before post-war Military Tribunals relating to corporate complicity in crimes against humanity and war crimes. This section explores only the most relevant sections from the

5 See for a detailed discussion, Nadia Bernaz, *Business and Human Rights: History, Law and Policy – Bridging the Accountability Gap*, Oxford: Routledge (2017), chapter 2.

6 See, Kenniscentrum, www.voc-kenniscentrum.nl/themas.html#Jan (last accessed 19 January 2018).

7 See, Huw V. Bowen, *The Business of Empire: The East India Company and imperial Britain*, Cambridge: Cambridge University Press (2006); Hugh Thomas, *The Slave Trade: The history of the Atlantic Slave Trade 1440–1879*, London: Picador (1997); Pieter Emmer, *The Dutch in the Atlantic Economy 1580–1880*, London: Ashgate (1998).

8 Jeremy Sarkin, 'The Coming of Age of Claims for Reparations for Human Rights Abuses Committed in the South', 1(1) *Sur Journal of Human Rights* 91 (2004).

9 *Herero People's Reparations Corp. v. Deutsche Bank*, A.G., 370 F.3d 1192 (D.C. Cir. 2004).

cases against corporations and their officers before Military Tribunals. The London Charter of the International Military Tribunal provides in Article 6 that "leaders, organizers, instigators and accomplices participating in the formulation or execution of a common plan or conspiracy to commit any of the foregoing crimes are responsible for all acts performed by any persons in execution of such plan".[10]

Two months after the International Military Tribunal defendants were convicted and sentenced, the Allied Powers enacted Control Council Law No. 10 in order to "establish a uniform legal basis in Germany for the prosecution of war criminals and other similar offenders, other than those dealt with by the International Military Tribunal".[11] In this way, the Control Council Law No. 10 specifically provided that both private economic actors and could be convicted of crimes against peace, war crimes or crimes against humanity:

> Any person without regard to nationality or the capacity, in which he acted, is deemed to have committed a crime . . . . (f) . . . held a high political, civil or military (including General Staff) position in Germany or in one of its Allies, co-belligerents or satellites or held high position in the financial, industrial or economic life of any such country.[12]

The US Nuremberg Military Tribunal (USNMT) conducted twelve trials between 1946 and 1949.[13] Because of the USNMT's broad jurisdiction, at least three of the Industrialist cases (*Farben, Flick and Krupp*) addressed the first question, holding that private actors could indeed be convicted of crimes against humanity and other crimes.

In *United States of America v. Friedrich Flick, et al.*,[14] the defendants (Friederich Flick) and five other leading managers (Steinbrinck, Weiss, Burkart, Kaletsch and Terberger) of Flick Concern were charged *inter alia* with deportation, enslavement, use of prisoners of war for war production, and complicity in murders and other crimes by the Nazi Party and other Nazi organizations.[15] Friederich Flick was "the principal proprietor and active head of a large group of industrial enterprises, including coal and iron ore mines and steel producing and manufacturing plants".[16]

The tribunal held that "it is clear that the slave-labor program had its origin in Reich governmental circles and was a governmental program and that

10 Agreement for the Prosecution and Punishment of the Major War Criminals of the European Axis, London Charter of the International Military Tribunal, 8 August 1945, Article 6.

11 Control Council Law No. 10, Punishment of persons guilty of war crimes, crimes against peace and against humanity, Preamble, 20 December 1945.

12 Ibid., art. II.

13 See, Kevin Jon Heller, 'Retreat from Nuremberg: The Leadership Requirement in the Crime of Aggression', 18(3) *European Journal of International Law* 477, 482 (2007).

14 Law Reports of Trials of War Criminals, Selected and Prepared by the United Nations War Crimes Commission, vol. IX, The Flick Trial, London, 1949.

15 Ibid., p. 5.

16 Ibid., p. 1.

the defendants had no part in creating or launching this program".[17] It seems that Flick and others did not have any influence towards abolishing such a programme. The Tribunal observed that the criminal combinations that were generally present in Germany between industry and the slave-labour programme "did not prevail in the plants and establishments of the defendants".[18] The tribunal therefore acquitted four defendants as they only followed the German government's programme. It observed that:

> The defendants lived within the Reich. The Reich, through its hordes of enforcement officials and secret police, was always "present," ready to go into instant action and to mete out savage and immediate punishment against anyone doing anything that could be construed as obstructing or hindering the carrying out of governmental regulations or decrees.[19]

In this light, the prosecution, however, argued in the following way that:

> The defendants in this case, as they have repeatedly and plaintively told us, were not military men or government officials. None of the acts with which they are charged under any count of the indictment were committed under "orders" of the type we have been discussing. By their own admissions, it seems to us they are in no position to claim the benefits of the doctrine of "superior orders" even by way of mitigation.[20]

The Tribunal noted that the defence of superior orders may not be employed in respect of corporate defendants, but only the defence of necessity, which sufficed for acquittal of those defendants. With regard to individual criminal responsibility, the Court therefore held that "one who knowingly by his influence and money contributes to the support thereof must, under settled legal principles, be deemed to, if not a principal, certainly an accessory to such crimes" and that "we cannot believe that a man of Steinbrick's intelligence and means of acquiring information could have remained wholly ignorant of the character of the S.S.".[21] With regard to defendant Bernhard Weiss, the Tribunal noted that "it likewise appears that Weiss took an active and leading part in securing an allocation of Russian prisoners of war for use in the work of manufacturing such increased quotas".[22]

17 The Flick case, *Trials of War Criminals Before the Nuremberg Military Tribunals Under Control Council Law No. 10*, 1951, Vol VI, 1196.

18 Ibid., p. 1199.

19 The Flick case, *Trials of War Criminals Before the Nuremberg Military Tribunals Under Control Council Law No. 10*, 1951, Vol VI, 1201.

20 Ibid.

21 Law Reports of Trials of War Criminals, Selected and Prepared by the United Nations War Crimes Commission, vol. IX, The Flick Trial, London, 1949, p. 29.

22 The Flick case, *Trials of War Criminals Before the Nuremberg Military Tribunals Under Control Council Law No. 10*, 1951, Vol. VI, 1198.

Consequently, the Tribunal held that defendants Weiss and Flick (because of Flick's knowledge and approval of Weiss's plan) could not invoke the defence of necessity and were therefore convicted. Based on what has been examined up to now, it appears that corporate managers can be prosecuted and convicted on the basis of individual criminal responsibility for international crimes.

In *United States v. Carl Krauch*,[23] or the *I.G. Farben* case, twenty-four corporate officers, all from within corporate structure of I.G. Farben, were prosecuted before US Military Tribunal 6 "for acting through the instrumentality of Farben and otherwise"[24] on five counts of war crimes, including slavery (enslavement and deportation to slave labour) and mass murder (count three)[25] and participation in a common plan or conspiracy to commit war crimes and crimes against humanity (count five).[26] This was the sixth post-Nuremberg case in front of the US Military Tribunal. The prosecutor argued that officers of the Farben corporation were acting in tacit concert with Nazi leadership. It further alleged that Farben's industrial concern contributed to the "creation and equipment of the German military machine for war" and that without its contribution "Nazi Germany could not have initiated and waged aggressive war".[27] USNMT portrayed Farben as a criminal organization. The US Military Tribunal based much of its finding on the role of Farben as a corporate entity being involved in war crimes and crimes against humanity. The Tribunal did not have jurisdiction over legal persons and therefore could not render a verdict against Farben itself. However, it illustrates how individual actors were able to collectively engage in criminal acts. As the USNMT noted in a seminal paragraph:

23 See, *U.S. v Krauch, et al.*, The I.G. Farben case, 14 August–29 July 1948; Law Reports of Trials of War Criminals, Selected and Prepared by the United Nations War Crimes Commission, vol. X, The I.G. Farben and Krupp Trials, London, 1949, pp. 3–67. See for a detailed discussion, Kyle Rex Jacobson, 'Doing Business with the Devil: The Challenges of Prosecuting Corporate Officials Whose Business Transactions Facilitate War Crimes and Crimes Against Humanity', 56 *Air Force Law Review* 167 (2005); Matthew Lippman, 'War Crimes of German Industrialists: The 'other Schindlers', 9 *Temple International Law & Comparative Law Journal* 173 (1995).

24 Law Reports of Trials of War Criminals, *Selected and Prepared by the United Nations War Crimes Commission*, vol. X, The I.G. Farben and Krupp Trials, London, 1949, p. 1.

25 Law Reports of Trials of War Criminals, Selected and Prepared by the United Nations War Crimes Commission, vol. X, The I.G. Farben and Krupp Trials, London, 1949, pp. 4–5. See for a detailed account, Anita Ramasastry, 'Corporate Complicity: From Nuremberg to Rangoon: An Examination of Forced Labor Cases and Their Impact on the Liability of Multinational Corporations', 20 *Berkeley Journal International Law* 91 (2002), and Anita Ramasastry, 'Secrets and Lies? Swiss Banks and International Human Rights', 31 *Vanderbilt Transnational Law Journal* 325 (1998).

26 Law Reports of Trials of War Criminals, Selected and Prepared by the United Nations War Crimes Commission, vol. X, The I.G. Farben and Krupp Trials, London, 1949, p. 5.

27 Ibid., p. 16. See also, *Trials of the Major War Criminals Nuremberg Military Tribunal*, vol. VII, p. 19.

> While the Farben organization, as a corporation, is not charged under the indictment with committing a crime and is not the subject of prosecution in this case, it is the theory of the prosecution that the defendants individually and collectively used the Farben organization as an instrument by and through which they committed the crimes enumerated in the indictment. All of the members of the Vorstand or governing body of Farben who were such at the time of the collapse of Germany were indicted and brought to trial.[28]

The Court was also of the opinion that different rules should be used to examine the actions of corporate entities. It went on to conclude that

> certainly where the action of private individuals, including juristic persons, is involved, the evidence must go further and must establish that a transaction, otherwise apparently legal in form, was not voluntarily entered into because of the employment of pressure. Furthermore, there must be a causal connection between the illegal means employed and the result brought about by employing such intimidation.[29]

It also held that Farben as a corporation had been directly committing war crimes and crimes against humanity. This tribunal, amongst others, stated that

> Auschwitz was financed and owned by Farben . . . In 1942, at the instigation of Farben, a separate labour camp known as Monowitz was built adjacent to and across the road from the plant site . . . The Auschwitz construction workers furnished by the concentration camp lived and labored under the shadow of extermination.[30]

With respect to slave labour, the USNMT observed that:

> the use of concentration camp labour and forced foreign workers at Auschwitz with the initiative displayed by the officials of Farben in the procurement and utilization of such labour, is a crime against humanity and, to the extent that non-German nationals were involved, also a war crime, to which the slave labour programme of the Reich will not warrant the defence of necessity.[31]

28 See, *U.S. v. Krauch et al.*, The I.G. Farben Case, Allied Control Council Law No. 10, 20 December 1945, Preamble, 15 Trials of War Criminals before the Nuremberg Military Tribunals under Control Council Law No. 10 (1951), 1108.

29 *Trials of War Criminals*, vol. VIII, p. 1136.

30 Law Reports of Trials of War Criminals, Selected and Prepared by the United Nations War Crimes Commission, vol. X, The I.G. Farben and Krupp Trials, London, 1949. pp. 55–57.

31 Ibid., p. 63.

In this way, the USNMT held that Krauch "did and, we think, knowingly participate in the allocation of forced labor to Auschwitz and other places where such labor was utilized within the chemical field".[32] It further noted that:

> in view of what he clearly must have known about the procurement of forced labor and the part he voluntarily played in its distribution and allocation, his activities were such that they impel us to hold that he was a willing participant in the crime of enslavement.[33]

The USNMT concluded that "Krauch, by his activities in connection with the allocation of concentration-camp inmates and forced foreign laborers, is guilty under count three".[34]

Similarly, in the Krupp case, twelve officials from the Krupp firm were prosecuted before the US Military Tribunal (No. 3 of the Nuremberg Military Tribunals).[35] Like the Farben defendants, they were charged *inter alia* with enslavement.[36] The lead defendant was Alfried Krupp, the "sole owner, proprietor, [and] active and directing head" of the company.[37] Along the same lines as Farben, Krupp Corporation was led by the board, "at least one member of the Vorstand was on the Aufsichtsrat of each of the principal subsidiary companies".[38] It was identified that Krupp Corporation as a whole had employed, between 1940 and 1945, "a total of 69,898 foreign civilian workers and 4,978 concentration camp inmates, the great majority of whom were forcibly brought to Germany and detained under compulsion throughout the period of their services, as well as 23,076 prisoners of war".[39] For example, in August 1943, 2412 prisoners of war (in violation of the 1907 Hague Regulations) and 11,557 foreign workers were forced to produce war materials at the firm's main plant (Krupp Gustahlfabrik) in Essen.[40] The Tribunal noted

32 *Trial of War Criminals Before the Nuremberg Military Tribunals*, vol. VIII, p. 1189.
33 Ibid.
34 *Trial of War Criminals Before the Nuremberg Military Tribunals*, Vol. VIII, p. 1190.
35 *Trial of Alfried Felix Alwyn Krupp von Bohlen und Halbach and eleven others*, United States Military Tribunal, Nuremberg, 17 November 1947–1930 June 1948, Law Reports of Trials of War Criminals, Selected and Prepared by the United Nations War Crimes Commission, vol. X, The I.G. Farben and Krupp Trials, London, 1949.
36 Ibid., pp. 74–75. Count three of the indictment (war crimes and crimes against humanity – employment of prisoners of war, foreign civilians and concentration camp inmates in armament production under inhuman conditions), ibid.
37 Ibid., pp. 76.
38 The Krupp Trial, *Trial of War Criminals Before the Nuremberg Military Tribunals*, Vol. IX., p. 1336.
39 *Trial of Alfried Felix Alwyn Krupp von Bohlen und Halbach and Eleven Others*, United States Military Tribunal, Nuremberg, 17 November 1947–1930 June 1948, Law Reports of Trials of War Criminals, Selected and Prepared by the United Nations War Crimes Commission, vol. X, The I.G. Farben and Krupp Trials, London (1949), p. 93.
40 Ibid., p. 93.

> (1) that Russian prisoners of war were put to heavy work when, due to undernourishment, they were totally unfit physically and (2) that not only was there no official requirement that this be done, but it was directly contrary to the orders of the competent officials.[41]

In this light, there was enough evidence that Krupp Corporation participated directly in the German forced labour programme. Consequently, the defendants Krupp, Loeser, Houdremont, Mueller, Janssen, Ihn, Eberhardt, Korschan, von Buelow, Lehmann and Kupke were convicted and sentenced by the USMT under the count of enslavement as a crime against humanity.

Further, Carl Rasche was prosecuted in the Ministries[42] case for war crimes and crimes against humanity relating to ill treatment, enslavement, imprisonment and slave labour, and looting and slavery (counts four, five, six and seven).[43] Rasche was a member of the management board of Dresdner Bank, a private bank in Germany that served in many respects as the bank for the Third Reich.[44] USNMT noted that "the evidence clearly establishes that Dresdner Bank loaned very large sums of money to various SS enterprises which employed large numbers of inmates of concentration camps and also to Reich enterprises and agencies engaged in the so-called resettlement program".[45] In this way, the Tribunal noted:

> The real question is, is it a crime to make a loan, knowing or having good reason to believe that the borrower will use the funds in financing enterprises which are employed in using labor in violation of either national or international law? Does he stand in any different position than one who sells supplies or raw materials to a builder building a house, knowing that the structure will be used for an unlawful purpose? A bank sells money or credit in the same manner as the merchandiser of any other commodity. It does not become a partner in enterprise and the interest charged is merely the gross profit which the bank realizes from the transaction, out of which it must deduct its business costs and from which it hopes to realize a net profit. Loans or sale of commodities to be used in an unlawful enterprise may well be condemned from a moral standpoint and reflect no credit on the part of the lender or seller in either case, but the transaction can hardly be said to be

41 The Krupp Trial, *Trial of War Criminals Before the Nuremberg Military Tribunals*, Vol. IX. 1388.

42 *United States v. Von Weizsaecker*, *Trials Under Control Council Law No. 10*, Washington, DC: United States Government Printing Office, 1949, Trial of War Criminals Before the Nuremberg Military Tribunals, vol. 12–14 (the Ministries Case). 1949. See for a detailed discussion, Kyle Rex Jacobson, 'Doing Business with the Devil: The Challenges of Prosecuting Corporate Officials Whose Business Transactions Facilitate War Crimes and Crimes Against Humanity', 56 *Air Force Law Review* 167 (2005).

43 *Trial of War Criminals Before the Nuremberg Military Tribunals*, Vol. 12, 13, 38, 43, 50, 56.

44 *Trial of War Criminals Before the Nuremberg Military Tribunals*, Vol .14, p. 621.

45 Ibid.

> a crime. Our duty is to try and punish those guilty of violating international law and we are not prepared to state that such loans constitute a violation of that law, nor has our attention been drawn to any ruling to the contrary.[46]

Rasche was thereafter convicted only of war crimes and crimes against humanity relating to looting. However, the tribunal acquitted Rasche of aiding crimes through his approval of Dresdner Bank loans, as it held that the financial transactions cannot be described as crime.[47] The Tribunals refrained from imposing criminal liability on a high-ranking official of Dresdner Bank who was alleged to have "made a loan, knowing or having good reason to believe that the borrower will use the funds in financing enterprises which are employed in using labour either in violation of either national or international law",[48] but was not proven to have made the loan with the purpose of facilitating the corporations' socio-economic rights violations. The USNMT noted that "we cannot go so far as to enunciate the proposition that the official of a loaning bank is chargeable with the illegal operations alleged to have resulted from the loans or which may have been contemplated by the borrower".[49] The USNMT here distinguished between providing capital and actively participating in Nazi looting efforts. In this way, it held that it was not proved that "Rasche knew any part of the fund to which the bank made contributions was intended to be or was ever used by Himmler for unlawful purposes".[50]

The USNMT considered in *Rasche* that knowledge was not enough for accessory liability. It must be noted that the International Criminal Tribunals have so far constantly held that knowingly assisting the commission of a crime was sufficient for establishing accessory liability.[51] This decision may reflect a general reluctance to hold bankers liable for their involvement in the Nazis' crimes.

By the end of the Second World War, the British and French military courts also started to prosecute corporate managers for complicity in crimes against humanity. The British military court in Hamburg, for example, indicted in the Zyklon B case the owner, Bruno Tesch, and two employees, Weinbacher and Drosihn, of the corporation for complicity in war crimes for knowingly selling to Zyklon B a poisonous gas for concentration camps.[52] This gas had been employed

46 Ibid., p. 622.
47 Ibid.
48 Ibid.
49 Ibid., p. 854.
50 Ibid., p. 622.
51 See, Larissa Van den Herik and Jernej Letnar Černič, 'Regulating Corporations Under International Law: From Human Rights to International Criminal Law and Back Again', 8(3) *Journal of International Criminal Justice* 725 (2010).
52 *The Zyklon B Case, I Law Reports of Trial of War Criminals 93, 94* (British Military Court, Hamburg, Germany, 1–8 March 1946). The accused were charged with 'supply of poison gas used for the extermination of allied nationals interned in concentration camps well knowing that the said gas was to be so used', p. 93. For the legal basis of the British Military Court in Hamburg see the Royal Warrant, 14 June 1945, Army Order 81/45. Ibid., p. 105.

to exterminate four and a half million prisoners in Auschwitz/Birkenau alone. The Court held that Tesch knew that the gas was used to exterminate prisoners in concentration camps. It noted that "it was also unbelievable that Tesch had no knowledge of the amounts of gas being supplied to the S.S. and to Auschwitz in particular, by a firm which was wholly his property"[53] and that "all that Tesch knew must, from the nature of the inner organisation of the business, have also been known by Weinbacher".[54] In other words, the prosecution was only required to prove that the supplied agent was to be used as such a weapon. Such reasoning rests on the inference that:

> Competent business person in a leadership position will know the context behind the major efforts of his business. Indeed, it is only logical that a person selling a product will try to assess the needs of his or her customer in order to increase sales. Thus, tribunals will impute knowledge to certain corporate officials if the officials ordinarily must have knowledge of that type to effectively carry out his or her duties.[55]

As to the substantive law, the Court concluded that

> the activities with which the accused in the present case were charged were commercial transactions conducted by civilians. The Military Court acted on the principle that any civilian who is an accessory to a violation of the laws and customs of war is himself also liable as a war criminal.[56]

Similarly, the Superior Military Court of the French Occupation Zone in Germany convicted in the *Commissioner v. Röchling* case the directors of Röchling Company for war crimes.[57] Herman Röchling was convicted on the basis of command responsibility for participating in the deportation of over two hundred thousand persons from the occupied territories to his Iron and Steel Corporation, where they were forced to work under dreadful conditions.[58] The Court noted that he

53 *The Zyklon B Case, I Law Reports of Trial of War Criminals 93, 94* (British Military Court, Hamburg, Germany, 1–8 March 1946), pp. 101–102.

54 Ibid., pp. 101–102.

55 Kyle Rex Jacobson, 'Doing Business with the Devil: The Challenges of Prosecuting Corporate Officials Whose Business Transactions Facilitate War Crimes and Crimes Against humanity', 56 *Air Force Law Review* 167, 195 (2005).

56 *The Zyklon B Case, I Law Reports of Trial of War Criminals 93, 94* (British Military Court, Hamburg, Germany, 1–8 March 1946), p. 103.

57 *French Government Commissioner v. Röchling*, Superior Military Government Court of French Occupation zone in Germany (1949), Trials of War Criminal Before Nuremberg Tribunal Judgment of the General Tribunal of Military Government for the French Zone of Occupation in Germany, 30 June, 1948. Trials of War Criminals before the Nuremberg Military Tribunals Under Control Council Law No. 10, Vol. 14, p. 1119.

58 Ibid., p. 1127, p. 1134, pp. 1137–1139, pp. 1135–1136.

> was connected with the war crime of deportation for the purpose of forced labor and he was co-responsible for the deportation of all those workers who had been assigned to the iron and steel industry as of 29 May 1942, the day on which he assumed his supreme command of this industry.[59]

In this way, he was convicted of participation in a forced labour programme.[60] The Court concluded that it was Röchling's "duty to keep himself informed about the treatment of the deportees; the fact that he did no longer concern himself about their fate, could only increase his responsibility".[61] However, it also noted that *Röchling* "had repeated opportunities during the inspection of his concerns to ascertain the fate meted out to his personnel, since he could not fail to notice the prisoner's uniform on those occasions".[62] The USNMT rightly observed in Farben that "it is plain . . . that Hermann Röchling . . . were not moved by the lack of moral choice but, on the contrary, embraced the opportunity to take full advantage of the slave-labour programme".[63] In this light, the Court held that Röchling:

> Actually agreed that the industry of which he was the leading administrator should employ prisoners of war who were placed at his disposal by the Reich government in contravention to the international agreement. He did this not only without raising the slightest protest, but he even demanded that such labor should be made available and submitted plans to his superior authorities for the better utilization of the prisoners of war.[64]

It appears that he had an obligation to know what was happening in parts of his corporate business. In other words, Röchling was held responsible because he did nothing to prevent such violations taking place. Read together, criminal prosecutions by the British and French military courts played a seminal role in preparing a legal basis and precedent for trials of war crimes before the Nuremburg Military Tribunals.

Even before the International Military Tribunal for the Far East, which was created by a Special Proclamation of the Supreme Allied Commander "to try and punish Far Eastern war criminals", some Japanese economic and financial leaders were prosecuted. Two corporate managers were defendants before

59 Ibid., p. 1130.

60 Law Reports of Trials of War Criminals, Selected and Prepared by the United Nations War Crimes Commission, vol. X, The I.G. Farben and Krupp Trials, London, 1949, 56.

61 *Trials of War Criminals before the Nuremberg Military Tribunals under Control Council Law No. 10*, 1951, Vol. XIV, Appendix B, p. 1136.

62 Ibid., p. 1136.

63 Law Reports of Trials of War Criminals, Selected and Prepared by the United Nations War Crimes Commission, vol. X, The I.G. Farben and Krupp Trials, London, 1949, p. 57.

64 *Trials of War Criminals Before the Nuremberg Military Tribunals Under Control Council Law No. 10*, 1951, Vol XIV, 1139.

the International Military Tribunal for the Far East: Hoshino Naoki and Kaya Okinori.[65] Both were convicted of the same five counts, although each had been charged with other crimes. They were both convicted of conspiring to wage and indeed of aiding in the waging of various wars of aggression.[66] Hoshino Naoki operated in Japanese occupied Manchuria and the Tribunal held that "in these positions he was able to exercise a profound influence upon the economy of Manchukuo and did exert that influence towards Japanese domination of the commercial and industrial development of that country".[67]

More importantly perhaps, there were a number of domestic trials against corporate managers. In the Kinkaseki Mine Trial before the Hong Kong British War Crime Court a case was brought against nine civilian employees of the Nippon Mining Company "for the mistreatment prisoners of war who were forced to labour in the Kinkaseki Mine, on the then island of Formosa".[68] Fafo website notes that "the mining company manager and supervisor were found guilty even though they did not directly participate in the beatings or mistreatment of the prisoners".[69] Similarly, the Netherlands Temporary Court Martial at Batavia held that Washio Awochi,[70] a Japanese hotel worker in Batavia, was responsible for war crime of "enforced prostitution" of Dutch women during the Japanese occupation of Batavia and the Court sentenced him to ten years' imprisonment.[71]

Interim conclusion

The regulatory framework after the Second World War did not allow for prosecution of corporations. In this light, the post–Second World War military courts employed the concept of individual criminal responsibility to prosecute corporate managers.[72] Even more so, German corporations refused to apologize and denied victims any substantial compensation, arguing that they were

65 See, *United States v. Araki*, R. International Military Tribunal for the Far East (1948), 48414. See, United reprinted in 101 Tokyo Major War Crimes Trial: The Judgment, Separate Opinions, Proceedings in Chambers, Appeals and Reviews of the International Military Tribunal for the far East (R. John Pritchard ed., 1998).

66 These were Counts 1, 27, 29, 31 and 32. Tokyo Major War Crimes Trial (reprint) 49793-95 (Hoshino) and 49801-02 (Kaya).

67 *United States v. Araki*, International Military Tribunal for the Far East (1958) reprinted in 101 Tokyo Major War Crimes Trial (reprint), 49793.

68 Fafo Institute, Business and International Crime, www.fafo.no/liabilities/part_II-2forc-lab.htm.

69 Ibid.

70 *In re Awochi*, Nent. Temporary Court Martial Batvia, in 'United Nations War Crimes Commission', 13 *Law Reports of Trials of War Criminals* 122–125 (1949).

71 Ibid., p. 123.

72 Also the ICTY invoked these post–Second Word War cases in *Prosecutor v. Duško Tadić*, Opinion and Judgment, 7 May 1997, No. IT-94–1-T, § 674–92; *Prosecutor v. Furundžija*, Judgment, 10 December 1998, ICTY Case No. IT-95–17/1-T, § 193–226.

forced to employ forced labour. As mentioned, the Flick corporation refused reparations, while Friedrich Flick died in 1972 with personal assets of over one billion dollars.[73] The survivors of the Farben-Auschwitz plant received merely 1,700 dollars; and each of Krupp's Jewish workers was provided with less than 825 dollars.[74] In this regard, the gradual development of individual criminal responsibility in the post–Second World War period creates a precedent for corporate accountability for international crimes and socio-economic rights for at least two reasons. For one, even though international criminal law is not addressed to legal persons, it refers to individuals, which collectively form corporations. Second, managers, directors and employees can be prosecuted for international crimes. For both reasons, individual criminal responsibility may serve as a precedent for corporate accountability. The next part of this chapter turns to development in the context of corporate accountability after the Second World War.

Corporate accountability and the post–Second World War period

By the end of the Vietnam War, hundreds of individual claims and class actions were brought in front of US courts on behalf of the 2.5 million veterans who served in Vietnam and their families against the corporations that manufactured Agent Orange. Agent Orange is a cancerous herbicide and defoliant that was employed by the US military during the Vietnam War. The plaintiffs claimed that "exposure to Agent Orange had caused a number of veterans to suffer a wide variety of illnesses" and deteriorated their socio-economic livelihood.[75] The plaintiffs were, however, "unable to prove that Agent Orange was likely to cause any disease and they were unable to establish the level of any individual's exposure to Agent Orange".[76] Defendants settled the claims in 1984 to the tune of $180 million in order to end years of "potential litigation and globally resolve the issue for less the cost of the defence".[77] It must be noted that "the settlement included all potential future Agent Orange claims".[78] Nonetheless, in 2003 in the case of *Dow Chemical Company v. Stephenson* in a 4–4 split decision, the US Supreme Court confirmed the decision of the 2nd Circuit Court of Appeals holding that settlement involving the corporations of the US military asked to produce Agent Orange during the Vietnam War did not preclude Vietnam veterans

73 See, Benjamin B. Ferencz, *Less Than Slaves: Jewish Forced Labor and the Question for Compensation*, Cambridge, MA: Hardvard University Press (1979), pp. 170, 188.

74 Ibid.

75 Background on Agent Orange, http://veteransinfo.tripod.com/Background_on_Agent_Orange.pdf (last accessed 19 January 2018).

76 Ibid.

77 Ibid.

78 Ibid. "The district court then held a number of settlement hearings throughout the U.S. and approved the settlement as fair, reasonable and adequate."

and was not adequately represented in the original settlement from pursuing claims against those corporations.[79]

Similarly, the South African Truth and Reconciliation Commission noted that "during the Apartheid regime business was central to the economy that sustained the South-African state during the apartheid years".[80] Further, it noted in its Final Report that the business plans of mining corporations included "influencing legislation that forced black workers in the wage system; state-endorsed monopolistic recruiting practices; the capping of African wages; divisive labour practices in managing compounds".[81] It observed that corporations that played a instrumental role in helping to devise them engaged in first order involvement with the abusive regime and so "must be held responsible and accountable for the suffering that resulted".[82] In this regard, the final conclusion was that corporations benefited financially and materially from Apartheid policies. The Truth and Reconciliation Commission noted that Swiss banks (Credit Suisse, UBS, etc.) benefited over several decades from the exploitation of majority non-white populations, whose socio-economic rights were violated.[83] Further, it was claimed that the banks ignored the request for sanctions and continue to benefit from the regime. Similarly, it was held that mining corporations (Anglo American Corporation) are to provide reparation to the victims. *Khulumani v. Barclay National Bank* and *Ntsebeza v. Daimler Chrysler Corp.*, under the Alien Torts Claim Acts before US courts, involved class actions filed on behalf of all persons who lived under the Apartheid system in South Africa. The defendants were approximately fifty international corporations and banks and the damages sought were estimated at approximately USD 400 billion.[84] In sum, the South African Truth and Reconciliation Commission distinguished between three orders of involvement of corporations in Apartheid: "playing a central role in helping to design and implement apartheid"; "engaging directly in activities that promoted state repression"; and "benefiting indirectly

79 *Dow Chemical Company v. Stephenson*, 539 U.S. 111 (2003), www.oyez.org/cases/2000-2009/2002/2002_02_271/ (last accessed 19 January 2018).

80 Final Report of the Truth and Reconciliation Commission (South-Africa), vol. 4, chapter 2, Business and Labour, p. 58. See for general overview, Penelope E. Andrews, 'Reparation for Apartheid's victims: The Path to Reconciliation', 53 *DePaul Law Review* 1155 (2004).

81 Ibid., p. 7.

82 Ibid., p. 3.

83 Ibid., Vol. 4, Section 2, Chapter 5, p. 23.

84 See also, similar cases *Lungisile Ntsbeza et al v. Daimler AG et al.*, 134 S. Ct. 746 (2014) and *Khulumani et al. v. Barclays National Bank et al.*, 02 MDL 1499 (SAS), US District Court, Southern District of New York, United States. This case and the following were after the decision of the US Supreme Court in *Kiobel v. Royal Dutch Petroleum* Co, 569 U.S. 108 (2013) (US) dismissed: *Balintulo v. Ford*, IBM, 14-4104 (L), US Court of Appeals for the Second Circuit, 27 Jul 2015; *In re South African Apartheid Litigation*, 1:02-md-01499-SAS US District Court for the Southern District of New York, 29 August 2014. *In re South African Apartheid Litigation*, US District Court for the Southern District of New York, 26 December 2013.

by . . . operating within apartheid society".[85] Unfortunately, it appears that the Truth and Reconciliation Commission did not have the institutional framework to address socio-economic rights violations by or involving corporations.

Conclusion

The role of corporations in the perpetration of human rights, including indirectly socio-economic rights violations during the slave trade, the colonial and Apartheid periods were significant. The concerns regarding past socio-economic rights violations remain cogent today. Notwithstanding the fact that normative frameworks have been unsatisfactory in the past, it is hard to construe a possible remedy even under the current normative framework for past human rights violations. As noted, an historical analysis illustrates that courts have employed a variety of means to indirectly address socio-economic rights violations by and involving corporations during past centuries. The Military Tribunals after the Second World War employed the concept of individual criminal responsibility to prosecute German industrialists, whereas the South African Truth and Reconciliation Commission concentrated on corporate accountability. A holistic approach to responsibility appears to be the best course to enforce responsibility for socio-economic rights by or involving corporations. As elucidated later, the regulatory framework is present; however, it also remains convoluted. Nevertheless, one must be mindful of the fact that an uneasy relationship of corporations with socio-economic rights is not a new phenomenon. What is new is a growing significance of the further developments of a normative framework for corporate accountability. The most obvious solution may be for corporations to provide compensation or project funding on a voluntary basis. Yet, as enticing as voluntarism may seem, it would fail any normative test of justice.

Bibliography

Books

Bernaz, Nadia, *Business and Human Rights: History, Law and Policy – Bridging the Accountability Gap*, Oxford: Routledge (2017).
Bowen, Huw V., *The Business of Empire: The East India Company and imperial Britain*, Cambridge: Cambridge University Press (2006).
Davies, Paul Lyndon and Gower, Laurence Cecil Bartlett, *Gower and Davies Principles of Modern Company Law*, London: Sweet & Maxwell (2003).
Emmer, Pieter, *The Dutch in the Atlantic Economy 1580–1880*, London: Ashgate (1998).
Ferencz, Benjamin B., *Less than Slaves: Jewish Forced Labor and the Question for Compensation*, Cambridge, MA: Harvard University Press (1979).
French, Derek, Mason, Stephen W. and Ryan, Christopher L., *Company Law*, Oxford: Oxford University Press (2007).

85 Final Report of the Truth and Reconciliation Commission (South-Africa), vol. 4, chapter 2 'Business and Labour' (1998), paras 23, 26 and 33.

Hochschild, Adam, *King Leopold's Ghost*, Buena vista: Mariner Books (1998).
Meltzer, Milton, *Slavery: A World History*, Boston: Da Capo Press (1993).
Pakenham, Thomas, *The Scramble for Africa*, New York: Harper Collins (1992).
Thomas, Hugh, *The Slave Trade: The History of the Atlantic Slave Trade 1440–1879*, London: Picador (1997).

Journal articles

Andrews, Penelope E., 'Reparation for Apartheid's Victims: The Path to Reconciliation', 53 *DePaul Law Review* 1155 (2004).
Heller, Kevin Jon, 'Retreat from Nuremberg: The Leadership Requirement in the Crime of Aggression', 18(3) *European Journal of International Law* (2007).
Jacobson, Kyle Rex, 'Doing Business with the Devil: The Challenges of Prosecuting Corporate Officials Whose Business Transactions Facilitate War Crimes and Crimes Against Humanity', 56 *The Air Force Law Review* 167 (2005).
Lippman, Matthew, 'War Crimes of German Industrialists: The "other Schindlers" ', 9 *Temple International Law & Comparative Law Journal* 173 (1995).
Ramasastry, Anita, 'Secrets and Lies? Swiss Banks and International Human Rights', 31 *Vanderbilt Transnational Law Journal* 325 (1998).
Ramasastry, Anita, 'Corporate Complicity: From Nuremberg to Rangoon: An Examination of Forced Labor Cases and Their Impact on the Liability of Multinational Corporations', 20 *Berkeley Journal International Law* 91 (2002).
Sarkin, Jeremy, 'The Coming of Age of Claims for Reparations for Human Rights Abuses Committed in the South', 1(1) *Sur Journal of Human Rights* (2004).
Van den Herik, Larissa and Letnar Černič, Jernej, 'Regulating Corporations Under International Law: From Human Rights to International Criminal Law and Back Again', 8(3) *Journal of International Criminal Justice* 725 (2010).

Treaties

Agreement for the Prosecution and Punishment of the Major War Criminals of the European Axis, London Charter of the International Military Tribunal, 8 August 1945.

Official documents

Control Council Law No. 10, 'Punishment of Persons Guilty of War Crimes, Crimes Against Peace and Against Humanity', 20 December 1945.

Cases

Balintulo v. Ford, IBM, 14-4104 (L), US Court of Appeals for the Second Circuit, 27 July 2015.
British Military Courts for the Trial of War Criminal Was Based on the Royal Warrant, 14 June 1945, Army Order 81/45.
Dow Chemical Company v. *Stephenson*, 539 US 111. 2003, www.oyez.org/cases/2000-2009/2002/2002_02_271/ (last accessed 19 January 2018).
French Government Commissioner v. Röchling, Superior Military Government Court of French Occupation zone in Germany, 1949.

Herero People's Reparations Corp. v. Deutsche Bank, A.G., 370 F.3d 1192 (D.C. Cir. 2004).
Khulumani et al. v. Barclays National Bank et al., 02 MDL 1499 (SAS), US District Court, Southern District of New York.
Kiobel v. Royal Dutch Petroleum Co, 569 U.S. 108, 2013.
In re Awochi, Nent. Temporary Court Martial Batvia, in 'United Nations War Crimes Commission', 13 *Law Reports of Trials of War Criminals* (1949).
In re South African Apartheid Litigation, US District Court for the Southern District of New York, 26 December 2013.
In re South African Apartheid Litigation, 1:02-md-01499-SAS US District Court for the Southern District of New York, 29 August 2014.
Law Reports of Trials of War Criminals, Selected and Prepared by the United Nations War Crimes Commission, vol. IX and X, 'The Flick Trial', London, 1949.
Trials of War Criminals Before the Nuremberg Military Tribunals Under Control Council Law No. 10, vol. VI 'The Flick Case', 1951.
Lungisile Ntsbeza et al v. Daimler AG et al., 134 S. Ct. 746, 2014.
Prosecutor v. Duško Tadić, Opinion and Judgment, ICTY, 7 May 1997, No. IT-94-1-T.
Prosecutor v. Furundžija, Judgment, 10 December 1998, ICTY Case No. IT-95-17/1-T.
The Zyklon B Case, I Law Reports of Trial of War Criminals, British Military Court, Hamburg, Germany, 1–8 March 1946.
Tokyo Major War Crimes Trial (reprint) 49793-95 (Hoshino) and 49801-02 (Kaya). *United States v. Araki*, International Military Tribunal for the Far East (1958) *reprinted in* 101 Tokyo Major War Crimes Trial (reprint), 49793.
Trial of Alfried Felix Alwyn Krupp von Bohlen und Halbach and eleven others, United States Military Tribunal, Nuremberg, 17 November 1947–1930 June 1948.
The Krupp Trial, Trial of War Criminals Before the Nuremberg Military Tribunals, Vol. IX.
Trials of War Criminals Before the Nuremberg Military Tribunals Under Control Council Law No. 10, vol. XIV, 1951.
Trials of War Criminal Before Nuremberg Tribunal Judgment of the General Tribunal of Military Government for the French Zone of Occupation in Germany, 30 June 1948.
Trial of War Criminals Before the Nuremberg Military Tribunals, vol. XII–XIX, 1949.
Trials of the Major War Criminals Nuremberg Military Tribunal, vol. VII, 19.
Trial of War Criminals Before the Nuremberg Military Tribunals, vol. VIII, 1189.
Trial of War Criminals Before the Nuremberg Military Tribunals, vol. VIII. 1190.
United Reprinted in 101 The Tokyo Major War Crimes Trial: The Judgment, Separate Opinions, Proceedings in Chambers, Appeals and Reviews of the International Military Tribunal for the far East, (R. John Pritchard ed., 1998).
United States v. Araki, R. International Military Tribunal for the Far East, 1948, 48414.
U.S. v. Krauch et. al, The I.G. Farben Case, Allied Control Council Law No. 10, 20 December 1945, Preamble, 15 Trials of War Criminals Before the Nuremberg Military Tribunals under Control Council Law No. 10, 1951.
U.S. v Krauch, et al., The I.G. Farben case, 14 August–29 July 1948.
United States v. Von Weizsaecker, Trials under Control Council Law No. 10 (Washington, DC: United States Government Printing Office, 1949).

Reports and miscellaneous

Boddy-Evans, Alistair, 'How Many Slaves Were Taken from Africa?' ThoughtCo., https://www.thoughtco.com/the-trans-atlantic-slave-trade-44544 (last accessed 19 January 2018).

Background on Agent Orange, http://veteransinfo.tripod.com/Background_on_Agent_Orange.pdf (last accessed 19 January 2018).

Final Report of the Truth and Reconciliation Commission (South-Africa), vol. 4, chapter 2 'Business and Labour', 1998.

Kenniscentrum, www.voc-kenniscentrum.nl/themas.html#Jan (last accessed 19 January 2018).

3 Globalization, investment and the socio-economic environment

Introduction 40
Globalization 41
Investment 46
Human dignity, equality and the socio-economic environment 50
Conclusion 59

Introduction

This chapter introduces and analyzes the seminal concepts of this book by describing, dissecting and analyzing them. The main topic addressed by the book does not exist in isolation, as business obligations concerning socio-economic rights are directly connected to the wider subjects of globalization, investment, human dignity and the socio-economic environment. It is thus essential to theoretically examine their primary conceptual notions in order to build a robust conceptual framework for the main argument concerning corporate accountability for socio-economic rights. Corporations as businesses and social actors affect the day-to-day workings of local and international societies. They form a seminal part of the everyday lives of any human society and state. They generate workplaces and tax revenues, and are instrumental in advancing economic growth and living standards.[1] They contribute to the socio-economic livelihoods of millions, yet in certain instances over short periods of time they may affect the human dignity of those people.

For many decades, investment has been regarded as a harbinger of economic success and development.[2] However, such success is not unconditional and without any limitations.[3] Salmon, Tostensen and Vandenhole argued that

1 Magnus Blomström and Ari Kokko, 'Multinational Corporations and Spillovers', 12(3) *Journal of Economic Surveys* 247 (1998).

2 Nicholas Turner, Obijiofor Aginam and Vesselin Popovski, 'Post-Conflict Countries and Foreign Investment', United Nations University -Policy Brief No. 8 (2008), p. 2.

3 John H. Dunning, 'Re-Evaluating the Benefits of Foreign Direct Investment', 3 *Transnational Corporations* 23 (1994), p. 32.

> the existence and perseverance of poverty cannot be disassociated from the global structural environment that produces and reproduces it and from the political economy that sustains it and that provides some but not others with a disproportionate opportunity for access to wealth.[4]

Even the correlation between socio-economic development and improving living standards is becoming less and less clear. States hold the primary responsibilities to uphold socio-economic rights in their territory and beyond, but corporate obligations should not be disregarded as they are obliged to comply with human dignity. The rest of this chapter is devoted to exploring these three main foundational issues concerning corporate obligations and socio-economic rights. The second part dissects the notion of globalization by describing and analyzing its constituent parts. The third section examines the notion of investment while stressing the role of foreign direct investment. Foreign direct investment contributes on one hand to a nation's socio-economic development, yet it can also negatively affect ordinary individuals' enjoyment of their human rights, particularly when the regular environment is under the control of powerful and influential corporations. The fourth section analyzes how globalization and investment impact the role of the socio-economic environment and how they can be reconciled with the human dignity and equality.[5] All in all, this introductory chapter lays the foundations for analyzing corporate obligations concerning socio-economic rights and how they apply to corporate conduct.

Globalization

In the past few decades globalization has become the norm of business environments at local, regional and national levels. National environments have merged into the global economy. In recent decades, state borders have become increasingly marginal due to globalization, with even developed countries losing out to other players in international society. Globalization is thus a process of doing away with national borders in economic, educational, cultural and other fields, allowing the more or less free exchange of goods and services and in particular facilitating connections between different parts of the world economy.[6] It is "linked to the growth of social interconnectedness across existing geographical

4 Margot E. Salomon, Arne Tostensen and Wouter Vandenhole, 'Human Rights, Development and new Duty-bearers', *in* Margot E. Salomon, Arne Tostensen and Wouter Vandenhole (eds.), *Casting the Net Wider, Human Rights, Development and New Duty-Bearers*, Antwerp and Oxford: Intersentia (2007), pp. 10–11.

5 Surya Deva, 'Bhopal: The Saga Continues 31 Years On', *in* Dorothée Baumann-Pauly and Justine Nolan (eds.), *Business and Human Rights: From Principles to Practice*, London: Routledge (2016) pp. 22–26. See also, Surya Deva, *Regulating Corporate Human Rights Violations: Humanizing Business*, London: Routledge (2012), p. 202.

6 Philipp Strobl and Manfred Kohler (eds.), *The Phenomenon of Globalization: A Collection of Interdisciplinary Globalization Research Essays*, Frankfurt am Main: Peter Lang (2013).

and political boundaries. In this view, deterritorialization is a crucial facet of globalization".[7] Globalization is a positive development, particularly for the Global South where extreme poverty is now at historical lows. In contrast, the Global North has taken the lion's share of the benefits. However, Stiglitz argues

> that globalization – the removal of barriers to free trade and closer integration of national economies – can be a force for good and that it has the potential to enrich everyone in the world, particularly the poor . . . the way globalization has been managed . . . needs to be radically rethought.[8]

This phenomenon has transformed national and international environments, with Scheuerman arguing that

> globalization refers to fundamental changes in the spatial and temporal contours of social existence, according to which the significance of space or territory undergoes shifts in the face of a no less dramatic acceleration in the temporal structure of crucial forms of human activity.[9]

Yet globalization can be employed as a stimulus for good, but only if managed properly. Much thus depends on corporations, which have become one of the principal generators of globalization.

The contribution of globalization to socio-economic development has been at least twofold. On one hand, it facilitates the proper functioning of the business environment. On the other, it has helped millions climb their way out of poverty. Palmisiano observes that "the rise in global living standards has been a remarkable achievement. From 1990 to 2010, for example, 1.2 billion people moved into the middle class throughout the world and 1.8 billion more are projected to do so by 2025".[10] The reduction of poverty is one of the great selling points of globalization, yet its proponents often overlook the fact that globalization also means greater social inequality at the expense of global communities and to the benefit of the global financial elite. The 2016 World Wealth Report shows that "the bottom half collectively own less than 1 percent of total wealth, the wealthiest top 10 percent own 89 percent of all global assets".[11] Bourguignon, accordingly, argues that "practical steps such as these should remind policymakers that even though global inequality and domestic inequality have moved in opposite

7 'Stanford Encyclopedia of Philosophy', *Globalization*, 10 June 2014.

8 Joseph E. Stiglitz, *Globalization and Its Discontents*, London: Allen Lane (2002), p. IX. See also, John Sweeny, 'There Is a Growing Consensus That Globalization Must Now Be Reshaped to Reflect Values Broader Than Simply the Freedom of Capital', *The Globalist*, 15 November 2000.

9 William Scheuerman, 'Globalization', *Stanford Encyclopedia of Philosophy* (Summer 2014 Edition).

10 Sam Palmisano, 'The Global Enterprise', *Foreign Affairs*, 14 October 2016.

11 Credit Suisse, 'The Global Wealth Report 2016', 22 November 2016.

directions for the past few decades, they need not do so forever".[12] Nonetheless, prosperity is therefore expanding around the world, as shown by statistical indicators. Fewer people today are living in extreme poverty than twenty years ago, which is impressive given the high growth of the world population during the same period. Yet some indicators have seen any considerable change in the long term. Most developed countries are still largely found in Europe and North America. The highest share of the population living in destitution remains in the Global South, but still a step forward has been taken. An individual born in any Asia or Africa today has greater chances of survival and education than someone born in the same country twenty years ago. But such a person still enjoys fewer benefits than someone born yesterday in Norway or in the United States. The balance of power in the world is changing, allowing the neglected to take advantage of opportunities once offered only to their peers who had the good fortune to be born in Western Europe or North America. One of striking features of globalization is the shrinking role of the state and the rise of other powerful actors, particularly in the financial and corporate sectors. The rise and reaffirmation of transnational corporations is a feature of globalization.[13]

Globalization also calls for changes both within and outside corporations. The interplay of human resources and business operations can work to the mutual benefit of both American, Asian, European and other corporations. Globalization facilitates access to information and information technology. Never before has the world been so interconnected and intertwined. Access to at least basic information technology systems provides more equal starting positions than any tech product has ever done before. This enables the more effective exercise of the right to education for all. Globalization in essence strives for a certain balance among the various world economies that could previously only be dreamed of. Today is witness to changes in both the national and international community that vary only in their type and intensity. The march of globalization places, for example, many corporations in a completely new role, forcing them to adapt to the changes in business and industry. The old role of states in the international community is withdrawing into a new, collaborative role with other participants in the national and international community at large.

In recent decades developed economies and businesses have become much stronger by efficiently exploiting globalization's advantages. In so doing, they have not paid much attention to the protection of human rights and sustainable development in the areas in which they operate.[14] If the benefits of globalization have so far been enjoyed especially by high-tech companies, the wheel of fortune has turned against those countries in which people live on just a few dollars a day.

12 François Bourguignon, 'Inequality and Globalization: How the Rich Get Richer as the Poor Catch Up', *Foreign Affairs*, January/February 2016, p. 15.

13 Surya Deva, *Regulating Corporate Human Rights Violations: Humanizing Business*, London: Routledge (2012).

14 Juan Pablo Bohoslavsky and Jernej Letnar Černič (eds.), *Making Sovereign Financing and Human Rights Work*, Oxford: Hart Publishing (2014).

Narula argues that "the liberalization of trade and the privatization and deregulation of economies and have substantially reduced the state's influence on the daily economic lives of its citizens".[15] Yet states remain the chief actor that is responsible for observing human rights and ensuring that human rights are observed by all individuals. Shelton hence states that

> the legal relationship between globalization and human rights can be analyzed from the perspective of economic regulation as well as that of human rights law . . . In respect to both inquiries, the fundamental question is whether a human rights system premised on state responsibility to respect and ensure human rights can be effective in a globalized world.[16]

Globalization has thus necessitated new carriers of human rights obligations and expanded them to cover other actors such as transnational corporations not traditionally linked with human rights. The traditional mechanisms for protecting human rights can no longer respond to the threats posed by such other actors. Deva goes even further, asserting that the response has been "inadequate and has been unable to ensure effective accountability of companies for human rights violations".[17] The systems in place hardly provide individuals with recourse to justice regarding the activities of transnational corporations.[18] Vandenhole argues that

> when it comes to issues of poverty and the lack of realisation of economic, social and cultural rights, the territorial State sits not always in the driving seat: decisions of other, equally powerful actors, such as the international economic institutions, transnational corporations and/or other States may have a much larger and profound impact on the realisation of socio-economic human rights than the territorial State has.[19]

Globalization foregrounds the need for corporations to play a role ensuring that socio-economic rights are fully adhered to. It requires a shift in focus from the state as the sole carrier of related duties to alternative carriers. Vandenhole says that "business enterprises themselves have a complementary obligation, albeit

15 Smita Narula, 'The Right to Food: Holding Global Actors Accountable Under International Law', 44 *Columbia Journal of Transnational Law* 691 (2006), p. 750.

16 Dinah Shelton, 'Protecting Human Rights in a Globalized World', 25(2) *Boston College International and Comparative Law Review* 273 (2002), p. 274.

17 Surya Deva, *Regulating Corporate Human Rights Violationss*, London: Routledge (2012), p. 188.

18 Ronen Shamir, 'Corporate Social Responsibility: A Case of Hegemony and Counter-Hegemony', *in* Boaventura de Sousa Santos and César A. Rodríguez-Garavito (eds.), *Law and Globalization from Below*, Cambridge: Cambridge University Press (2005), pp. 92–117.

19 Wouter Vandenhole, 'Emerging Normative Frameworks on Transnational Human Rights Obligations', EUI Working Papers, RSCAS 2012/17 (2012), p. 1.

simultaneously with States".[20] However, as this book argues such obligations are not only complementary, but also self-standing.[21] Globalization has had some unexpected outcomes. Ruggie therefore rightly observes that:

> the core challenge is that globally operating firms are not regulated globally. Instead, each of their component entities is subject to the individual jurisdiction in which it operates. Yet even where national laws exist prohibiting abusive conduct, which cannot always be taken for granted, states in many cases fail to implement them – because they lack the capacity, fear the competitive consequences of doing so, or because their leaders subordinate the public good for private gain.[22]

Globalization thus also requires that corporate conduct be regulated and made subject to human rights obligations. The economic boom enjoyed by the Asian countries does not of course go without consequences in the highly developed countries. The creation of new jobs, for example, in India and China at least indirectly also implies certain job losses in European countries.[23] For some time, globalization has been associated in European countries with shrinking employment opportunities and a decrease in personal income.[24] Some European governments have thus for pragmatic political reasons advocated an increasingly strong protectionist policy and are not fully insistent on their corporations respecting human rights when doing business abroad.[25] Overall, the effect is not so much fewer jobs in total around the world, but a restructuring of the economy bringing about a redistribution of jobs from one geographical area to another. However, it also creates new opportunities that would not have been available without integration with companies and countries on the other side of the planet.[26] In essence, globalization strives for a certain balance among various economies that even today might seem unattainable. Today, changes are taking place in the national and international community that vary only in their type and intensity. The march of globalization is putting companies in a completely new role, obliging them to adapt their business policies in line with environmental and human

20 Ibid., p. 15.

21 Ruggie's 2008 report, para 9.

22 John Ruggie, 'Just Business: Multinational Corporations and Human Rights', Roundtable Report: Implementing the UN Guiding Principles on Business and Human Rights (Thomas J. Dodd Research Center, University of Connecticut), 28 February 2013, p. 2.

23 Maria-Gabriela Manea, 'Human Rights and the Interregional Dialogue Between Asia and Europe: ASEAN-EU Relations and ASEM', 21(3) *The Pacific Review* 369 (2008).

24 Josef Blahož, 'The Welfare Social State, European Union and Globalization', 3 *The Lawyer Quarterly* 178 (2014).

25 Upendra D. Acharya, 'Globalization and Hegemony Shift: Are States Merely Agents of Corporate Capitalism?', 36(2) *Boston College International and Comparative Law Review* 937 (2013).

26 Jeffrey F. Addicott, Jahid Hossain Bhuiyan and Tareq M.R. Chowdhury (eds.), *Globalization, International Law, and Human Rights*, Oxford: Oxford University Press (2012).

rights considerations. This may lead to the old practices in developed countries being replaced by more collaborative roles with other participants in the wider international community.

Investment

Foreign investment is one tool any state can use to embark on large infrastructure projects, increase economic growth and development and provide more generous welfare to its population. Such investment has therefore been steadily rising over the last decade, affecting the socio-economic environment in the recipient countries. It contributes to the stronger protection of socio-economic rights.[27] The 2016 World Investment Report notes that

> the geographic pattern tilted in favour of developed economies in 2015, although developing Asia remained the largest recipient of FDI flows. Flows to developed economies nearly doubled (up 84 per cent) rising from $522 billion in 2014 to $962 billion. FDI to developing economies – excluding Caribbean financial centres – increased to $765 billion, a rise of 9 per cent, while those to transition economies fell by 38 per cent to $35 billion.[28]

The Report also highlights that

> the top 100 MNEs in UNCTAD's Transnationality Index have on average more than 500 affiliates each, across more than 50 countries. They have 7 hierarchical levels in their ownership structure . . ., they have about 20 holding companies owning affiliates across multiple jurisdictions and they have almost 70 entities in offshore investment hubs.[29]

Foreign investment is crucial for advancing the global economy and the socio-economic environment of individual states and also for developing democracy and the rule of law. For it to thrive, the recipient states are expected to ensure the stability and protection of the investments made, particularly the investors' assets. It is not uncommon for government to decide to nationalize after only a few years into a foreign investment in the name of often undefined public or national interests. Investors therefore require that states put measures in place to protect them from such governmental decisions. These measures in particular insist that national judicial institutions uphold the rule of law and that judicial proceedings proceed fairly, independently and impartially. Such

27 Jernej Letnar Černič, 'Corporate Human Rights Obligations under Stabilization Clauses', 11 *German Law Journal* 210 (2010).
28 UNCTAD, 'World Investment Report 2017', p. 4.
29 Ibid., p. Xiii.

principles and measures are necessary to uphold the rights and especially the assets of investors and curtail any arbitrary use of power by national governments concerning the investment.

Despite certain justified concerns of investors, a foreign investment cannot just go ahead without any regulations. Just like it is necessary to limit the arbitrary use of power by states, it is also essential to keep a lid on the often-powerful interests of corporate investors. States are accordingly obliged to regulate the tendency of corporations to exceed their authorities and trample on human rights and to protect individuals from the impacts of their activities.[30] Amadeo contends that

> by adopting these practices, they enhance their employees' lifestyles. That raises the standard of living for more people in the recipient country. FDI rewards the best companies in any country. It reduces the influence of local governments over them, making them less able to pursue poor economic policies.[31]

However, the adoption of foreign investment polices has not proceeded without setbacks as its impacts must be revaluated in certain domestic contexts.[32] More specifically, recent decades have witnessed the rise of the rights of investors whereas their obligations often seem to have been forgotten, particularly in the workings of international investment bodies.[33] The gist of the problem is that investment law only bestows rights but does not impose obligations.[34]

The relationship between foreign direct investment and an increase in the socio-economic standards of individuals in fact remains unclear. Nussbaum notes that

> in general, the benefits of increased wealth resulting from foreign investment go in the first instance to elites . . . The benefits of this increased wealth do not reach the poor, unless those local elites are committed policies of redistribution of wealth.[35]

30 Wesley Scholz, 'International Regulation of Foreign Direct Investment', 31(3) *Cornell International Law Journal* 485 (1998).

31 Kimberly Amadeo, 'Foreign Direct Investment: Pros, Cons and Importance', *The Balance*, 14 September 2016 (updated 24 June 2017).

32 Kojo Yelpaala, 'Costs and Benefits from Foreign Direct Investment: A Study of Ghana', 2 *New York Law School Journal of International & Comparative Law* 72 (1980).

33 Doak Bishop, James Crawford and Michael Reisman, *Foreign Investment Disputes: Cases, Materials and Commentary*, The Hague: Wolters Kluwer (2005).

34 Abdullah Al Faruque, 'Mapping the Relationship Between Investment Protection and Human Rights', 11 *Journal of World Investment & Trade* 539 (2010), pp. 542 and 548; Gabisa Henok, 'The Fate of International Human Rights Norms in the Realm of Bilateral Investment Treaties (BITs): Has Humanity Become a Collateral Damage?', 48(2) *The International Lawyer* 153 (2014).

35 Martha C. Nussbaum, *Creating Capabilities*, Cambridge, MA and London: The Belknap Press of Harvard University Press (2011), p. 13.

Further, foreign direct investment can negatively impact the observance of individuals' socio-economic rights particularly through unfavourable clauses and provisions in bilateral investment treaties and investment contracts.[36] Such contracts can affect the ability of states to ensure even the minimum socio-economic environment for their people. That is particularly in a situation where they depend on corporate investments for the country's socio-economic development, for example in a post-conflict and transitional context.[37]

The World Economic Report on "Responsible Investment in Fragile Contexts" observes that

> International and local businesses have a critical role to play in finding ways to minimize fragility and build resilience. A key reason, among others, is because fragility – including conflict and crime – is bad for business. It generates direct and indirect opportunity costs all along the value chain.[38]

However, problems arise when business take advantage of fragile situations in order to reap benefits without considering the local population's socio-economic concerns. Such developments in the Global South are not new, as in for most of them the law has for decades played second fiddle to the arbitrary power of influential stakeholders. The rule of law, which would otherwise restrict this power, is only declaratory, with much remaining to be done. The law has not managed to limit the arbitrary power of either government or corporations, but this is completely impossible to achieve given the imbalances in favour of corporate structures.[39]

However, corporate investors acknowledge their obligations to uphold human rights, albeit their extent remains unclear. These obligations should be understood as the means to achieve the objectives of corporate accountability. Moreover, corporations are themselves recognizing that respecting socio-economic human rights is one of primary objectives of their operations. For instance, the African Union (AU) Commissioner for Political Affairs, Aisha Abdullahi, stated: "all too often have human rights concerns fallen by the wayside in the race to attract foreign investment. We have to fundamentally break with this logic and ensure that business and respect for human rights go hand-in-hand".[40] According

36 See for more, Jernej Letnar Černič, 'Corporate Human Rights Obligations Under Stabilization Clauses', 11 *German Law Journal* 210 (2010).

37 Kojo Yelpaala, 'Rethinking Foreign Direct Investment Processes and Incentives in Post-Conflict Transition Countries', 30 *Northwestern Journal of International Law & Business* 23 (2010).

38 World Economic Report, Report on 'Responsible Investment in Fragile Contexts', Global Agenda Council on Fragility, Violence & Conflict, May 2016, p. 8.

39 Benjamin J. Appel and Cyanne E. Loyle, 'The Economic Benefits of Justice: Post-Conflict Justice and Foreign Direct Investment', 49(5) *Journal of Peace Research* 685 (2012).

40 UNHCHR, 'UN and AU Commit to Advance Business and Human Rights Agenda in Africa', 18 September 2014.

to Abdalla Hamdok, Deputy Executive Secretary of the United Nations (UN) Economic Commission for Africa, "not only is this the only way to ensure the interest and welfare of the people of Africa, it is also good business and critical for the sustainability of investments".[41]

Many corporations explicitly recognize and assume responsibility for their operations under the fundamental human rights enshrined in the Universal Declaration of Human Rights. Ruggie argued in his 2016 UN Business and Human Rights Forum address that "for business to fully realize its contribution to sustainable development, it must put efforts to advance respect for human rights at the heart of the people part of sustainable development".[42] Yet the latter is easier said than done. For the case of Zambia, Muyoyeta argues that

> since the 1990s, Foreign Direct Investment (FDI) has played an increasingly important role in the country's economy, rehabilitating the copper industry and boosting production and exports of non-traditional products and services. However, this investment has not been used effectively to promote development and reduce poverty. Instead, it is contributing to an erosion of people's rights, including development rights, the right to food, education, a clean environment and women's participation in political decision-making.[43]

Recently, investment bodies have attempted to regulate the negative effects of globalization. The NAFTA Tribunal noted in *Methanex Corp v The United States*:

> But as a matter of general international law, a non-discriminatory regulation for a public purpose, which is enacted in accordance with due process and, which affects, inter alios, a foreign investor or investment is not deemed expropriatory and compensable unless specific commitments had been given by the regulating government to the then putative foreign investor contemplating investment that the government would refrain from such regulation.[44]

Klein argues that it is time for

> understanding investment protection as one right among others that first needs to be understood as minimum standard and second, needs to be balanced with other human rights may serve investment tribunals in the future

41 Ibid.

42 John Ruggie, 'Making Globalization Work for All: Achieving the Sustainable Development Goals Through Business Respect for Human Rights', Shift, November 2016.

43 Lucy Muyoyeta, 'Foreign Direct Investment and the Fulfilment of Key Rights', Social Watch 2010.

44 *Methanex Corp. v United States*, Jurisdiction and Merits (NAFTA Ch. 11 Arb. Trib. August 3, 2005), Part IV, chapter D, p. 4, para 7.

as conceptual tool to effectively balance investment protection with other human rights.[45]

Yet investment treaties usually do not refer to human rights, only in exceptional cases.[46] A reference to human rights is more often made in investment arbitral decisions.[47] In this context, the Office of the High Commissioner has drafted ten principles for responsible investment contracts. More specifically, principle 8 notes that a "State should be able to monitor the project's compliance with relevant standards to protect human rights, while providing the necessary assurances to business investors against arbitrary interference in the project".[48] Responsible investment that is consistent with socio-economic rights is therefore good for business. Of course, even an investment of this nature does not absolve businesses of being accountable for their observance of socio-economic rights.[49]

Human dignity, equality and the socio-economic environment

The socio-economic environment refers to all components of individuals' social livelihoods. It basically refers to food, water, housing, education, health and social services. The socio-economic environment also refers to a specific dimension of business operations of a certain company. It includes the framework for regulatory settings, tax policies, anti-corruption, the rule of law and investment incentives in the environment where a corporation operates. It also includes the living conditions of the local population. Often the nature of such conditions and also government subsidies will determine whether a corporation decides to invest in a particular state. As they are just so many investing and many struggling states of the Global South and North, the power and affluence possessed by corporations also means that they can take advantage of those countries' desperate desire for investment. Corporate actors can pressure them to lower regulatory standards even by disregarding the national constitutional framework, not to mention human rights and environmental standards. In spite of this, corporations are obliged to adapt to the local socio-economic standards, which fall within the concept of human dignity.

45 Nicolas Klein, 'Human Rights and International Investment Law: Investment Protection as Human Right?', 4 *Goettingen Journal of International Law* 199 (2012), p. 215.

46 Kathryn Gordon, Joachim Pohl and Marie Bouchard, 'Investors Rights and Human Rights – Interactions Under Investment Treaty Law', LSE – Laboratory for Advanced Research on the Global Economy – Investment & Human Rights Project, 22 September 2014.

47 Ibid.

48 Office of the High Commissioner for Human Rights, *The Corporate Responsibility to Respect Human Rights: An Interpretative Guide*, New York: United Nations (2012), pp. 38–39.

49 Abdullah Al Faruque, 'Mapping the Relationship Between Investment Protection and Human Rights', 11 *Journal World Investment & Trade* 539 (2010), p. 544; Jernej Letnar Černič, 'Corporate Human Rights Obligations Under Stabilization Clauses', 11 *German Law Journal* 210 (2010).

Human dignity has been difficult to identify in specific cases as it differs from society to society. However, its legal nature is no longer controversial. Human dignity is an individual and collective value that belongs to all people living in a respective society. It represents the lowest common denominator of values of a society that must be exercised by all individuals in that society. It is the set of minimum civilizational assumptions that apply there. Corporations have a negative and positive obligation to ensure the respect, protection and realization of human dignity. At the same time, the obligation to implement human dignity is shared by all entities in that society. Human dignity is also not an imaginary philosophical value since it can be adhered to in each concrete case. When one intervenes with an individual's human dignity, it thus intervenes in the collective value of the entire society. Human dignity is not an individual value that cannot be denied by anyone. It belongs to all individuals who live in a given society. Human dignity must therefore be distinguished from the wider concept of personal dignity. Personal dignity thus forms the narrowest part of human dignity. They also differ in that they one can decide on one's own to waive the protection of personal dignity but not the protection of human dignity.

Human dignity is made up of physical and intellectual integrity. Further, McCruden notes that

> a basic minimum content of the meaning of human dignity can be discerned: that each human being possesses an intrinsic worth that should be respected, that some forms of conduct are inconsistent with respect for this intrinsic worth and that the state exists for the individual not vice versa.[50]

Additionally, Clapham observes that human dignity derives from four elements:

> (1) the prohibition of all types of inhuman treatment, humiliation, or degradation by one person over another; (2) the assurance of the possibility for individual choice and the conditions for "each individual's self-fulfilment", autonomy, or self-realization; (3) the recognition that the protection of group identity and culture may be essential for the protection of personal dignity; (4) the creation of the necessary conditions for each individual to have their essential needs satisfied.[51]

Human dignity has been central to the concept of corporate accountability for socio-economic rights. On top of human dignity, equality is essential for the concept of corporate accountability for socio-economic rights.

One of the most convincing interpretations of equality in recent decades was developed by the Indian economist Amartya Sen. In his 1979 lecture "Equality

50 Christopher McCruden, 'Human Dignity and Judicial Interpretation of Human Rights', 19 *European Journal of International Law* 655 (2008), pp. 655–724, 723.

51 Andrew Clapham, *Human Rights Obligations of Non-State Actors*, Oxford: Oxford University Press (2006), pp. 545–46.

of What?", Sen criticized the existing concepts of equality and offered an explanation of equality, writing that a person must be able to do certain basic things: "the ability to meet one's nutritional requirements, the wherewithal to be clothed and sheltered, the power to participate in the social life of the community".[52] The latter summarized the basic needs in a concept he called "basic capability equality".[53] Abilities chiefly relate to the basic needs and desires of the individual in life and the ability to fulfil their desires. In this sense, Sen's concept is close to the doctrine of equal opportunities. If an individual is unable to realize his/her basic needs and desires, he/she is directly pushed to the outskirts of society. Consequently, the concept of equal abilities is very important as it enables individuals to meet their needs along with the needs of their family members. Sen argues that the "equality of basic capabilities" approach may be "general" and is primarily "conditional on the nature of the society".[54] In order for an individual to enjoy equality in a particular field, he must have at least access basic necessities such as water, food and a decent residence. Without these basics, an individual cannot act on an equal footing. However, income inequality does not tell us anything. Sen argues that "the disadvantage of ability . . . is more important than a measure of neglect, such as low income, because it is only instrumental in significance, with its implementation value conditioned by a number of social and economic circumstances".[55] If an individual and his/her children are not provided with primary goods, their capabilities for basic human development are limited, if not completely eliminated. The capabilities of an individual and his/her family not only relate to income but also to the possibility of accessing health services and education. Such dilemmas are also found in cities and villages across the Global South and North. It is only when an individual is provided with decent living conditions, when his/her basic goods are guaranteed and he/she also acquires personal freedom that he can decide for himself what he will dedicate his life to and that he will also invest in raising his/her own living standard and that of his/her children. Only then can a person have various options available from which to choose. Such changes cannot occur overnight since even in the best cases whole generations are needed.

Sen has included his "capabilities" concept in the Human Development Index published every year by the UN and not solely based on income comparisons of countries, but also includes interdisciplinary criteria and indicators that assess different levels of individual capacity in a given country. His concept of equality of basic abilities has also found its way into human rights doctrine since the Committee on Economic, Social and Cultural Rights (CESCR) formulated the "core" of any socio-economic right that each state must protect regardless of its financial

52 Amartya Sen, 'Equality of What?' *in The Tanner Lecture on Human Values*, Stanford: Stanford University, 22 May 1979, p. 218.

53 Ibid.

54 Ibid., p. 219.

55 Amartya Sen, *Commodities and Capabilities*, New York: Oxford University Press (1999), p. 131.

capability.[56] The "capabilities" concept was later transformed into the minimum obligations of states to provide minimum socio-economic opportunities and was complemented by the philosopher Martha Nussbaum who asks "what activities characteristically performed by human beings are so central that they seem definitive of a life that is truly human?".[57] She has thus argued that each individual must be provided with the basic goods to allow him to later use his freedom for self-realization.[58]

In 2000, UN member states at the Durban Conference formulated and adopted eight Millennium Development Goals (MDGs) for the socio-economic development of humankind to be reached by states and fulfilled by 2015.[59] The goals were simply drafted and placed in the field of combating poverty, improving education, gender, prevention of infant and maternal mortality, reduction of the prevalence of certain diseases (such as HIV and malaria), an increase in environmental sustainability, and an improvement of mutual and global development cooperation.[60] In short, they all referred to improving different dimensions as part of developing the socio-economic environment. More specifically, states committed themselves by 2015 "to halve the number of people living on less than one dollar a day and who suffer from hunger. Up to this date must halve the number of people without access to clean water, or cannot afford it"[61]; "to ensure that . . . all children throughout the world, both boys and girls can complete their primary education and have equal access to all levels of education";[62] to the "promotion of equal treatment of women and men and women's rights";[63] "to reduce by three quarters the maternal mortality ratio"[64] and "the mortality rate of children under five by two thirds";[65] "to retain and begin to reverse the spread of HIV, malaria and other major diseases that attack mankind";[66] "to protect the natural environment";[67] and "to create global partnership for development".[68] Both the Declaration and the targets themselves were not binding and merely represented guidelines for the conduct of states, international organizations,

56 UN, CESCR, 'General comment No. 3: The Nature of States Parties', Obligations (1991), para 10.

57 Martha C. Nussbaum, *Sex and Social Justice*, Oxford: Oxford University Press (1999), p. 39.

58 Martha C. Nussbaum, Creating capabilities.

59 United Nations Millennium Declaration, A/RES/55/2, 18 September 2000.

60 See more specifically, Guido Schmidt-Traub, 'The Millennium Development Goals and Human Rights-Based Approaches: Moving Towards a Shared Approach', 13 *The International Journal of Human Rights* 72 (2009).

61 UN, General Assembly, 'United Nations Millennium Declaration Goals [MDG]', UN Doc. A/RES/55/2, 18 September 2000, para. 19.

62 MDG no. 2, para 19.

63 Ibid., para 20.

64 MDG no. 4.

65 MDG no. 5, para 19.

66 MDG no. 6, para 19.

67 MDG no. 7, paras 21–23.

68 MDG no. 8, paras 11–18.

non-governmental organizations and other participants in the global arena. Therefore, the Millennium Development Goals have been heavily criticized for their lack of enforceability.[69] Despite this, the majority of the Millennium Development Goals was achieved by the deadline.

Sustainable development is one of the fundamental goals of the United Nations, its members and all participants within local and international communities. In 2012, the UN member states agreed at the Rio de Janeiro summit to replace MDGs by 2015 with Sustainable Development Goals (SDGs), which include seventeen ambitious goals as part of the "The 2030 Agenda for Sustainable Development", which includes most aspects of human development, not just financial and economic.[70] The Sustainable Development Goals include the following goals:

Goal 1: End poverty in all its forms everywhere
Goal 2: End hunger, achieve food security and improved nutrition and promote sustainable agriculture
Goal 3: Ensure healthy lives and promote well-being for all at all ages
Goal 4: Ensure inclusive and equitable quality education and promote lifelong learning opportunities for all
Goal 5: Achieve gender equality and empower all women and girls
Goal 6: Ensure availability and sustainable management of water and sanitation for all
Goal 7: Ensure access to affordable, reliable, sustainable and modern energy for all
Goal 8: Promote sustained, inclusive and sustainable economic growth, full and productive employment and decent work for all
Goal 9: Build resilient infrastructure, promote inclusive and sustainable industrialisation and foster innovation
Goal 10: Reduce inequality within and among countries
Goal 11: Make cities and human settlements inclusive, safe, resilient and sustainable
Goal 12: Ensure sustainable consumption and production patterns
Goal 13: Take urgent action to combat climate change and its impacts
Goal 14: Conserve and sustainably use the oceans, seas and marine resources for sustainable development
Goal 15: Protect, restore and promote sustainable use of terrestrial ecosystems, sustainably manage forests, combat desertification and halt and reverse land degradation and halt biodiversity loss

69 Ellen Dorsey, 'Falling Short of our Goals: Transforming the Millennium Development Goals into Millennium Development Rights', 28 *Netherlands Quarterly of Human Rights* 516 (2010).

70 Jeffrey D. Sachs, 'From Millennium Development Goals to Sustainable Development Goals', 379 *The Lancet* 2206 (2012).

Goal 16: Promote peaceful and inclusive societies for sustainable development, provide access to justice for all and build effective, accountable and inclusive institutions at all levels

Goal 17: Strengthen the means of implementation and revitalise the global partnership for sustainable development

Goals 1–4, 6 and 10 particularly relate to socio-economic environments and the livelihoods of individuals. The SDGs differ from the MDGs in the number and content of the proposed objectives.[71] The SDGs state in Goal 11 that it is necessary to make cities and human settlements "inclusive, secure, flexible and sustainable". The new areas include the need to ensure "sustainable guidelines for consumption and production",[72] "measures to monitor climate change and resolving their consequences"[73] and "conserve and sustainably use oceans, seas and marine resources sustainable development".[74] It seems the current Sustainable Development Goals are too opaque since the large number of goals has become lost in the multitude of sub-goals. The number of objectives should be reduced since quite a few are of a soft nature, as they were drafted by officials and diplomats at various United Nations conferences. It seems necessary to draw precise measurable indicators to be independently and impartially verified by the United Nations in order to formulate adequate responses and measures.

Although income poverty has been reduced over the last decade, hundreds of millions of people are still living in extreme poverty.[75] Greater success has been achieved in some areas, such as reducing extreme poverty and hunger, while in others it has not. The SDGs have been a subject of constant criticism since being adopted as they do not primarily focus on protecting human rights, the rule of law and democracy and good governance policy, and, instead, often get lost in vague objectives. They mention the protection of selected human rights only indirectly.[76] This approach was likely decided on in order to facilitate a consensus, but that would be easier to achieve if the draft did not mention requirements that are unacceptable in most countries around the world. Therefore, the SDGs chiefly focus on the economic/social context with an emphasis on environmental protection and sustainable development. It is clear that the sustainable development of each area, in addition to realizing the socio-economic and environmental

71 Ved P. Nanda. 'The Journey from the Millennium Development Goals to the Sustainable Development Goals', 44 *Denver Journal of International Law and Policy* 389 (2016).

72 SDG 12.

73 SDG 13.

74 SDG 14.

75 Oliver Cann, 'How Can the Development Goals Be Achieved?' *World Economic Forum*, 23 September 2015.

76 For example, in sub-objective 4.7 regarding education in sub-objective 16.2 on the abuse and exploitation of children and in 16.3 with regard to the rule of law and the right to judicial protection.

objectives, also need to ensure that the state and other entities do not interfere in their individual political and civil freedoms and socio-economic livelihoods. However, it is unclear who is largely accountable for their realization.[77] Autocratic governance might not hinder a state's economic development, but it certainly does not contribute to a holistic perception of development, including the protection of human dignity as an individual and collective good of all human communities. They must be consistent with socio-economic objectives such as those relating to political and civil freedoms. It is true it is more difficult to establish indicators in the fields of the rule of law and protection of human rights, but otherwise it is impossible to provide for comprehensive sustainable development. The latter facilitates the exercise of fundamental socio-economic rights while permitting the individual to manifest their potential by participating in social life and exercising their freedom.

The living standards of individuals in different parts of the world vary dramatically. The global economic and financial environment exacerbates these differences due to the absence of any regulation. How to ensure comprehensive sustainable development in all parts of the world so that everyone can live a dignified life? More importantly, who is responsible for achieving these Sustainable Development Goals? Is it really only up to states? The United Nations noted its declaration on "*Transforming Our World: The 2030 Agenda for Sustainable Development*" that

> eradicating poverty in all its forms and dimensions, including extreme poverty, is the greatest global challenge and an indispensable requirement for sustainable development. We are committed to achieving sustainable development in its three dimensions – economic, social and environmental – in a balanced and integrated manner.[78]

To achieve socio-economic development, one is obliged to address the equality of opportunities or, as Sen argues, the "equality of basic capabilities" – it is necessary to ensure the realization of some of the basic, truly fundamental living conditions.[79] The question is who should bear the prime responsibility for achieving the above objectives. Are states mainly responsible for their implementation or is the responsibility to be borne by wealthier countries and the entire international community? The fact is that some states will never be able to achieve their own goals, which makes the cooperation of the international community

77 Siobhán McInerney-Lankford and Hans-Otto Sano, 'Human Rights and the Post-2015 Sustainable Development Goals: Reflections on Challenges and Opportunities', 7 *The World Bank Legal Review* 167 (2016).

78 UN General Assembly, 'Resolution Transforming our World: The 2030 Agenda for Sustainable Development', UN Doc. A/RES/70/1, 21 October 2015, para 2.

79 Amartya Sen, *Development as Freedom*, New York: Alfred Knopf (1999). See also, Todd Landman and Marco Larizza, 'Inequality and Human Rights: Who Controls What, When, and How', 53 *International Studies Quarterly* 715 (2009).

necessary. The Millennium Declaration referred in section 6 to "shared responsibility" "for managing worldwide economic and social development, as well as threats to international peace and security". What about other possible duty-bearers such as corporations? Although referring to states, shared responsibility should be also divided between non-state actors. Corporations are not only required to be aware of the socio-economic environment, but to include it their business operations. In order not to endanger the socio-economic livelihoods of the local population, they have to conduct a socio-economic impact assessment to determine how can they improve or at a minimum not interfere with the local people's living standards. However, one cannot expect a corporation to entirely fill the shoes of states when, for example, seeking to combat child mortality. On the other hand, before they begin to invest one can at least require corporations not to worsen the level of standards.

What will be the role of private actors in achieving the Sustainable Development Goals since states in both the Global North and Global South have become increasingly marginalized?[80] Their role has been taken over by transnational corporations, financial corporations, and pension funds and other actors in the global economy. Unfortunately, the documents supporting the realization of the United Nations' responsibilities continue to focus only on the state as the main bearer ensuring the obligations and development objectives are met. Financial centres in today's global cities are too powerful to allow the smallest details to be left to chance; in other words, financial market actors require a minimum of regulation. Do corporations truly hold binding commitments to contribute financially to the realization of the right to food, water or decent living? The new original approaches are likely to benefit both ordinary people and societies. Such approaches should be adapted to the needs of the local environment and population.

Many would agree that it is only countries which are responsible for achieving the Sustainable Development Goals since several aims relate to the realization of social and economic rights, which should traditionally fall within the realm of the state. Yet the exercise of socio-economic rights largely depends on a state's financial possibilities. In human rights law, these commitments only oblige the pursuit of socio-economic rights and not the actual result, as more developed countries can provide a broader range of socio-economic rights than less developed ones. But even states in the Global South should provide at least a reasonable core of socio-economic rights, alone or with international assistance. However, it is more difficult to require private actors to implement them since they do not have the primary task of providing socio-economic rights, but at the very least are obliged to not directly interfere with them.[81] But this traditional understanding has been out of date for at least a decade. Private entities, mainly corporations

80 Kate Donald, 'Sally-Anne Way, Accountability for the Sustainable Development Goals: A Lost Opportunity?' 30 *Ethics and International Affairs* 201 (2016).

81 See, Chapter 6.

of different sizes, must also strive to ensure the realization of socio-economic rights. Sustainable Development Goal 17 thus stipulates the need to "Strengthen the means of implementation and revitalize the Global Partnership for Sustainable Development".[82] The Global Partnership focuses on helping countries in the Global South. The Sustainable Development Agenda does not explicitly describe the notion of "global partnership", but paragraph 60 states that

> the revitalized Global Partnership will facilitate an intensive global engagement in support of implementation of all the Goals and targets, bringing together Governments, civil society, the private sector, the United Nations system and other actors and mobilizing all available resources.[83]

The Global Partnership is therefore understood as cooperation or as the emerging obligations on all actors in the global community to pursue sustainable development and socio-economic rights in all parts of the world. It is difficult to derive from the Partnership any already binding requirement on the private sector to help implement these obligations.

Differences in living standards will continue to exist, but modern society cannot leave all activities up to the free market, liberalization and deregulation, without setting any minimum conditions. There is no doubt that some kind of socio-political and civic minimum must be provided. If all actors contribute to the Sustainable Development Goals it will become much easier to eradicate extreme poverty and socio-economic rights violations while there is no shortage of natural resources and only a question of disproportionate distribution. The current Sustainable Development Goals are too broad and therefore it is utopian to expect that in the next few years they will all be achieved. Therefore, certain priority goals must be selected with a view to achieving them by 2030.

SDG 17 contains nineteen ambitious sub-goals ranging from financing and technology through economic and systemic issues. The most difficult task will be to achieve individual commitments in the area of financing. Sub-item 17.1 thus states that

> developed countries to implement fully their official development assistance commitments, including the commitment by many developed countries to achieve the target of 0.7 per cent of gross national income for official development assistance (ODA/GNI) to developing countries and 0.15 to 0.20 per cent of ODA/GNI to least developed countries; ODA providers are encouraged to consider setting a target to provide at least 0.20 per cent of ODA/GNI to least developed countries.[84]

82 SDG 17.

83 UN, General Assembly, Resolution, 'Transforming our World: The 2030 Agenda for Sustainable Development', para 60.

84 Ibid., SDG 17.1, p. 26.

The question is whether this can be achieved before 2030. A number of international organizations recently emphasized the primacy of private sector contributions in achieving the Sustainable Development Goals. For example, the Organisation for Economic Cooperation and Development (OECD) organized a forum devoted entirely to the private sector's role in pursuing the sustainable development objectives. But their role is not as simple and self-evident as it might seem at the general level. More specifically, SDG 2 states the global community must work to "end hunger, achieve food security and improved nutrition and promote sustainable agriculture";[85] SDG 6 points out the need to "Ensure availability and sustainable management of water and sanitation for all" and SDG 11 calls to make "cities and human settlements inclusive, safe, resilient and sustainable". Corporations working in the food and water industry must thus strive to combat hunger, although it is difficult to say they have binding obligations concerning exercise of the right to food. Their obligation only complements that of the state. Likewise, corporations that manage water supply systems must aim to meet the same level of commitment as the state.[86] SDG 11 is more difficult to achieve for the private sector since it seems that is a state's primary obligation to carefully manage cities and settlements. Of course, the private sector must ensure it does not act directly or indirectly against sustainable settlements and cities and does not violate the associated human rights and freedoms. All in all, negative obligations of the private sector are accompanied by its positive commitments to bring added value to both the local population and wider community.

Conclusion

This chapter examined the fundamental conceptual notions of globalization, investment and the socio-economic environment for building the theoretical pillars of the corporate accountability for socio-economic rights concept. Globalization has brought to the fore the power of corporate actors and their obligations and accountability for the socio-economic rights of individuals. On the other hand, the need to remove individuals from poverty has given an almost free hand in attracting investment nearly without any constitutional limits. States play the dominant role in achieving the Sustainable Development Goals, but the private sector also plays an equally important role in guaranteeing socio-economic livelihoods, especially where they carry out traditional state tasks. Corporations not only have negative but also positive commitments to help achieve the sustainable development objectives by consistently and carefully implementing socio-economic rights. However, at the moment one can only talk about the emerging obligations of the private sector. In the end, however, it all depends on the quality of the institutions in each country, as pointed out in SDG 16, which states it is necessary to "encourage peaceful and inclusive societies for sustainable

85 Ibid., SDG 2.
86 See, Chapter 6.

development, provide everyone with access to justice and create effective, responsible and open institutions at all levels". Different stakeholders therefore agree that, without the rule of law, substantive and procedural justice, and strong institutions, the sustainable development objectives will remain unrealized or underrealized. Therefore, corporations should also strive to not violate the goals of sustainable development while simultaneously creating the conditions to ensure the least reasonable core of socio-economic rights is ensured.

Bibliography

Books

Addicott, Jeffrey F., Hossain Bhuiyan, Jahid and Chowdhury, Tareq M.R. (eds.), *Globalization, International Law and Human Rights*, Oxford: Oxford University Press (2012).
Bishop, Doak, Crawford, James and Reisman, Michael, *Foreign Investment Disputes: Cases, Materials and Commentary*, The Hague: Kluwer Law International (2005).
Bohoslavsky, Juan Pablo and Letnar Černič, Jernej (eds.), *Making Sovereign Financing and Human Rights Work*, Oxford: Hart Publishing (2014).
Clapham, Andrew, *Human Rights Obligations of Non-State Actors*, Oxford: Oxford University Press (2006).
Deva, Surya, *Regulating Corporate Human Rights Violations: Humanizing Business*, London: Routledge (2012).
Nussbaum, Martha C., *Sex and Social Justice*, Oxford: Oxford University Press (1999).
Nussbaum, Martha C., *Creating capabilities*, Cambridge, MA and London: The Belknap Press of Harvard University Press (2011).
Office of the High Commissioner for Human Rights, *The Corporate Responsibility to Respect Human Rights: An Interpretative Guide*, New York: United Nations (2012).
Sen, Amartya, *Commodities and Capabilities*, New York: Oxford University Press (1999).
Sen, Amartya, *Development as Freedom*, New York: Alfred Knopf (1999).
Stiglitz, Joseph E., *Globalization and Its Discontents*, London: Allen Lane (2002).
Strobl, Philipp and Kohler, Manfred (eds.), *The Phenomenon of Globalization: A Collection of Interdisciplinary Globalization Research Essays*, Frankfurt am Main: Peter Lang (2013).

Journal articles

Acharya, Upendra D., 'Globalization and Hegemony Shift: Are States Merely Agents of Corporate Capitalism?', 36(2) *Boston College International and Comparative Law Review* 937 (2013).
Al Faruque, Abdullah, 'Mapping the Relationship Between Investment Protection and Human Rights', 11 *Journal of World Investment & Trade* 539 (2010).
Allen, William T., 'Our Schizophrenic Conception of the Business Corporation', 14 *Cardozo Law Review* 271 (1992).
Appel, Benjamin J. and Loyle, Cyanne E., 'The Economic Benefits of Justice: Post-Conflict Justice and Foreign Direct Investment', 49(5) *Journal of Peace Research* 685 (2012).

Blahož, Josef, 'The Welfare Social State, European Union and Globalization', 3 *The Lawyer Quarterly* 178 (2014).

Blomström, Magnus and Kokko, Ari, 'Multinational Corporations and Spillovers', 12(3) *Journal of Economic Surveys* 247 (1998).

Donald, Kate, 'Sally-Anne Way, Accountability for the Sustainable Development Goals: A Lost Opportunity?' 30 *Ethics and International Affairs* 201 (2016).

Dorsey, Ellen, 'Falling Short of our Goals: Transforming the Millennium Development Goals into Millennium Development Rights', 28 *Netherlands Quarterly of Human Rights* 516 (2010).

Dunning, John H., 'Re-Evaluating the Benefits of Foreign Direct Investment', 3 *Transnational Corporations* 23 (1994).

Henok, Gabisa, 'The Fate of International Human Rights Norms in the Realm of Bilateral Investment Treaties (BITs): Has Humanity Become a Collateral Damage?', 48(2) *The International Lawyer* 153 (2014).

Klein, Nicolas, 'Human Rights and International Investment Law: Investment Protection as Human Right?', 4 *Goettingen Journal of International Law* 199 (2012).

Landman, Todd and Larizza, Marco, 'Inequality and Human Rights: Who Controls What, When and How', 53 *International Studies Quarterly* 715 (2009).

Letnar Černič, Jernej, 'Corporate Human Rights Obligations under Stabilization Clauses', 11 *German Law Journal* 210 (2010).

Manea, Maria-Gabriela, 'Human Rights and the Interregional Dialogue Between Asia and Europe: ASEAN-EU Relations and ASEM', 21(3) *The Pacific Review* 369 (2008).

McCruden, Christopher, 'Human Dignity and Judicial Interpretation of Human Rights', 19 *European Journal of International Law* 655 (2008).

McInerney-Lankford, Siobhán and Sano, Hans-Otto, 'Human Rights and the Post-2015 Sustainable Development Goals: Reflections on Challenges and Opportunities', 7 *The World Bank Legal Review* 167 (2016).

Nanda, Ved P., 'The Journey from the Millennium Development Goals to the Sustainable Development Goals', 44 *Denver Journal of International Law and Policy* 389 (2016).

Narula, Smita, 'The Right to Food: Holding Global Actors Accountable Under International Law', 44 *Columbia Journal of Transnational Law* 691 (2006).

Sachs, Jeffrey D., 'From Millennium Development Goals to Sustainable Development Goals', 379 *The Lancet* 2206 (2012).

Schmidt-Traub, Guido, 'The Millennium Development Goals and Human Rights-Based Approaches: Moving Towards a Shared Approach', 13 *The International Journal of Human Rights* 72 (2009).

Scholz, Wesley, 'International Regulation of Foreign Direct Investment', 31(3) *Cornell International Law Journal* 485 (1998).

Shelton, Dinah, 'Protecting Human Rights in a Globalized World', 25(2) *Boston College International and Comparative Law Review* 273 (2002).

Yelpaala, Kojo, 'Costs and Benefits from Foreign Direct Investment: A Study of Ghana', 2 *New York Law School Journal of International & Comparative Law* 72 (1980).

Yelpaala, Kojo, 'Rethinking Foreign Direct Investment Processes and Incentives in Post-Conflict Transition Countries', 30 *Northwestern Journal of International Law & Business* 23 (2010).

Book chapters

Deva, Surya, 'Bhopal: The Saga Continues 31 Years On', *in* Dorothée Baumann-Pauly and Justine Nolan (eds.), *Business and Human Rights: From Principles to Practice*, London: Routledge (2016), pp. 22–26.

Salomon, Margot E., Tostensen, Arne and Vandenhole, Wouter, 'Human Rights, Development and New Duty-Bearers', *in* Margot E. Salomon, Arne Tostensen and Wouter Vandenhole (eds.), *Casting the Net Wider, Human Rights, Development and New Duty-Bearers*, Antwerp and Oxford: Intersentia (2007), pp. 3–24.

Shamir, Ronen, 'Corporate Social Responsibility: A Case of Hegemony and Counter-Hegemony', *in* Boaventura de Sousa Santos and César A. Rodríguez-Garavito (eds.), *Law and Globalization from Below*, Cambridge: Cambridge University Press (2005), pp. 92–117.

Magazine articles

Bourguignon, François, 'Inequality and Globalization, How the Rich Get Richer as the Poor Catch Up', *Foreign Affairs*, January/February 2016.

Palmisano, Sam, 'The Global Enterprise', *Foreign Affairs*, 14 October 2016.

Sweeny, John, 'There Is a Growing Consensus That Globalization Must Now Be Reshaped to Reflect Values Broader Than Simply the Freedom of Capital', *The Globalist*, 15 November 2000.

Official documents

UN, CESCR, 'General Comment No. 3: The Nature of States Parties', Obligations, 1991.

UNCTAD, 'World Investment Report 2017'.

UN, General Assembly, 'Transforming Our World: The 2030 Agenda for Sustainable Development', UN Doc. A/RES/70/1, 21 October 2015.

UN, General Assembly, 'United Nations Millennium Declaration', UN Doc. A/RES/55/2, 18 September 2000.

Cases

Methanex Corp. v United States, Jurisdiction and Merits (NAFTA Ch. 11 Arb. Trib. August 3, 2005).

Reports and miscellaneous

Amadeo, Kimberly, 'Foreign Direct Investment: Pros, Cons and Importance', *The Balance*, 14 September 2016 (updated 24 June 2017).

Cann, Oliver, 'How Can the Development Goals Be Achieved?' *World Economic Forum*, 23 September 2015.

Credit Suisse, 'The Global Wealth Report 2016', 22 November 2016.

Gordon, Kathryn, Pohl, Joachim and Bouchard, Marie, 'Investors Rights and Human Rights – Interactions Under Investment Treaty Law', LSE – Laboratory for Advanced Research on the Global Economy – Investment & Human Rights Project, 22 September 2014.

Muyoyeta, Lucy, 'Foreign Direct Investment and the Fulfilment of Key Rights', Social Watch 2010.

Ruggie, John, 'Just Business: Multinational Corporations and Human Rights', Roundtable Report: Implementing the UN Guiding Principles on Business and Human Rights (Thomas J. Dodd Research Center, University of Connecticut), 28 February 2013.

Ruggie, John, 'Making Globalization Work for All: Achieving the Sustainable Development Goals Through Business Respect for Human Rights', Shift, November 2016.

Scheuerman, William, 'Globalization', Stanford Encyclopedia of Philosophy (Summer 2014 Edition).

Sen, Amartya, 'Equality of What?' The Tanner Lecture on Human Values, Stanford University, 22 May 1979.

'Stanford Encyclopedia of Philosophy', *Globalization*, 10 June 2014.

Turner, Nicholas, Aginam, Obijiofor and Popovski, Vesselin, 'Post-Conflict Countries and Foreign Investment', United Nations University -Policy Brief No. 8, 2008.

UNHCHR, 'UN and AU Commit to Advance Business and Human Rights Agenda in Africa', 18 September 2014.

Vandenhole, Wouter, 'Emerging Normative Frameworks on Transnational Human Rights Obligations', EUI Working Papers, RSCAS 2012/17 (2012).

World Economic Report, Report on 'Responsible Investment in Fragile Contexts', Global Agenda Council on Fragility, Violence & Conflict, May 2016.

4 Business, socio-economic rights and good practices

Introduction 64
The nature of business provision of socio-economic rights 67
Good practices concerning individual socio-economic rights 69
Good business practices concerning the right to education 69
Good business practices concerning the right to food 71
Good business practices concerning the right to health 72
Good business practices concerning the right to adequate housing 74
Good business practices concerning the right to water 76
The contribution of the corporate good practices to the provision of socio-economic rights 78
Conclusion 79

Introduction

States traditionally carry primary obligations to respect, protect and fulfil socio-economic rights. Home state bears the primary obligation to protect human rights in its territory in order to realize human dignity of its residents. When the host state does not meet its obligations, secondary or complementary obligations emerge for transnational corporations that operate in the specific local environments.[1] Corporations can also fulfil their obligations concerning socio-economic

1 UN, CESCR, 'General Comment No. 24 (2017) on State Obligations Under the International Covenant on Economic, Social and Cultural Rights in the Context of Business Activities', UN Doc. E/C.12/GC/24, 10 August 2017. UN, Committee on the Rights of the Child, General comment No. 16 on State Obligations Regarding the Impact of the Business Sector on Children's Rights, UN Doc. CRC/C/GC/16, 17 April 2013. See also, Olivier De Schutter, 'Corporations and Economic, Social, and Cultural Rights', *in* Eibe Riedel, Gilles Giacca and Christophe Golay (eds.), *Economic, Social, and Cultural Rights in International Law: Contemporary Issues and Challenges*, Oxford: Oxford University Press (2014), pp. 193–226; Ben Saul, David Kinley and Jacqueline Mowbray, *The International Covenant on Economic, Social and Cultural Rights: Commentary, Cases, and Materials*, Oxford: Oxford University Press (2016), pp. 133–172.

rights by adopting good practices aimed at employees and members of local communities. Do corporations have an ethical or legal obligation to guarantee the minimum standard level of socio-economic rights? What are good practices relating to socio-economic rights? As often the focus has been concentrated only on alleged or real corporate abuses of socio-economic rights, this chapter describes and analyzes selected good practices of businesses guaranteeing a decent level of socio-economic rights to their employees and wider communities. It examines existing businesses' good practices relating to right to education, food, health, housing and water. It thereafter outlines and examines some of the philosophical challenges as good practices may provide evidence of the emerging corporate obligations to protect and fulfil human rights. The request for private efforts derives also from corporate commitments to Sustainable Development Goals. The former UN Secretary-General Ban Ki-Moon has argued that

> now is the time to mobilize the global business community as never before. The case is clear. Realizing the Sustainable Development Goals will improve the environment for doing business and building markets. Trillions of dollars in public and private funds are to be redirected towards the SDGs, creating huge opportunities for responsible companies to deliver solutions.[2]

Objectives of SDGs are also in the line with the corporate obligations concerning socio-economic rights.[3] The World Council for Business argues that "pursuing sustainable development makes firms more competitive, more resilient and nimble in a fast changing world and more likely to win and retain customers".[4] United Nations and businesses themselves therefore agree that corporations have a seminal role in providing for SDGs.[5]

Good practices include activities on the part of corporations that contribute to the maintenance and increase in the level of the socio-economic rights protections. They complement governmental and civil society activities in the provision of socio-economic rights; however one cannot argue that they substitute them or that corporations should take over the role of the state. For instance, Oxfam argues that corporations "should look at how core commercial practices around issues such as wages and taxation either detract from or enable a world without poverty. They should change their core business functions to align them with the

2 Cited in Business Fights Poverty, http://businessfightspoverty.org (last accessed 19 January 2018). SDG Fund, Harvard Kennedy School CSR Initiative and Inspiris Limited, 'Business and the United Nations: Working Together Towards the Sustainable Development Goals: A Framework for Action', (2015).

3 See, Chapter 3.

4 World Business Council for Sustainable Development, 'WBCSD FAQ', http://wbcsdpublications.org/faq/ (last accessed 19 January 2018).

5 Caroline Rees, 'Business, Human Rights, and the Sustainable Development Goals: Forging a Coherent Vision and Strategy', Shift, November 2016.

SDGs".[6] However, another question has been how this will be financed.[7] Oxfam argues that

> a recent report on 52 institutional investors, based in every region of the world and with over £4 trillion of assets under management, showed that 95 percent of respondents planned to engage with investee companies on issues covered by the SDGs; 84 percent intended to allocate capital to investments supporting the SDGs; while 89 percent claimed that they would support regulatory reforms that promote the SDGs. Much of this change has come as a result of increased regulatory pressure, improved awareness of ESG risks and increasing demands from civil society groups. (footnote omitted)[8]

Such substantial numbers illustrate that businesses agree that they have obligations beyond rhetorical commitments.

Good practices of corporations also fall within their positive obligations of protect and fulfil to attempt to guarantee the minimum of socio-economic rights of their employees and environment where they operate. As Anisa Kamadoli Costa, Chief Sustainability Officer at Tiffany & Co., puts it, "we believe there is increasing demand for companies to address human rights in their operations in order to have a social license to operate, whether consumer facing or not".[9] However, transnational and local corporations have often in public highlighted their effort to maintain and/or increase socio-economic livelihood of individuals in the environments where they have conducted their business activities. Therefore, it is often difficult to assess the real impact of their activities on the ground through fair, independent and impartial monitoring based on indicators. Most often, good practices can only be developed after a corporation has conducted human rights impact assessment. Oxfam has observed that "people should be at the centre of the due diligence process, which means hearing their perspectives, experiences and ideas . . . Of course, companies need to be aware of the power imbalances that can make such engagement challenging in practice".[10] Moreover, UN Guiding Principles have argued that "business enterprises should track the effectiveness of their response" and "tracking should . . . be based on appropriate qualitative and quantitative indicators".[11]

6 Oxfam, 'Raising the Bar: Rethinking the Role of Business in the Sustainable Development Goals', February 2017, p. 23.

7 Horni Kharas, 'Financing for Development: International Financial Flows After 2015', Brookings Institution, 8 July 2014.

8 Share Action, 'Investors Can Play a Central Role in Achieving the Sustainable Development Goals', 21 March 2016.

9 Ana Zbona, 'Interview with Anisa Kamadoli Costa, Chief Sustainability Officer at Tiffany & Co.', Business and Human Rights Resource Centre, April 2017.

10 Shift, Oxfam and Global Compact Network Netherlands, 'Doing Business with Respect for Human Rights: A Guidance Tool for Companies', (2nd Edition, 2016), p. 95.

11 UN, Human Rights Council, 'Guiding Principles for Business and Human Rights: Implementing the United Nations "Protect, Respect and Remedy" Framework, UN Doc. A/HRC/17/31, 21 March 2011, principle 20 (a).

The UN Working Group has argued that "States and business enterprises should scale up and sustain efforts to implement the Guiding Principles, including . . . by establishing measurable and transparent indicators to assess their effective implementation"[12] and that

> the development of performance indicators that can be used by stakeholders to encourage proper functioning of grievance mechanisms is important and can be used by stakeholders to understand how operational-level grievance mechanisms are working and to hold business enterprises accountable.[13]

All in all, this chapter describes and analyzes good practices of corporations concerning individual socio-economic rights.

The nature of business provision of socio-economic rights

Good practices are a concept that goes beyond legal and contractual obligations of corporations. It is possible to define good practices as a corporation's ongoing commitment to observe human rights; combat corruption; protect the environment; engage in ethical behaviour; promote economic development; and improve the quality of life and socio-economic conditions of its employees, local communities and society as a whole.[14] Social responsibility through good practices also means that the objectives and results of corporations cannot be determined and evaluated only on the basis of the traditional criteria of success of the company, which includes profitability, but is also based on the involvement of corporations in the wider society and in relation to employees, based on the respect and promotion of human rights and environmental protection.[15]

Good practices in short include that corporations must not only comply with legal obligations in all areas of common interest to work for the socio-economic welfare of employees and the wider community in general. The main part of good practices lies in the fact that the company doing the real work must do something more than what constitutional obligations impose. Corporations may also seek to improve working conditions and support employees in balancing work commitments and their socio-economic self-realizations. Research shows that the profits of socially responsible companies have been higher in comparison

12 UN, 'Report of the Working Group on the Issue of Human Rights and Transnational Corporations and other Business Enterprises: Developments in the Embedding of the Guiding Principles into Global Governance Frameworks', UN Doc. A/67/285, 10 August 2012, para 79.

13 UN, 'Report of the Working Group on the Issue of Human Rights and Transnational Corporations and other Business Enterprises', UN Doc. A/68/279, 7 August 2013, para 41.

14 Catherine J. Morrison-Paul and Donald S. Siegel, 'Corporate Social Responsibility and Economic Performance', Rensselaer Working Papers in Economics, No. 0605, March 2006.

15 Lois A. Mohr, Deborah J. Webb and Katherine E. Harris, 'Do Consumers Expect Companies to be Socially Responsible? The Impact of Corporate Social Responsibility on Buying Behaviour', 35(1) *The Journal of Consumer Affairs* 45 (2001).

to competing corporations and that they operate better than their competitors.[16] The main advantages of good practice have been working towards better society, a healthier environment and sustainable development.[17] Although the concept of good practices has been often carried out by mainly large and multinational corporations, it applies to all corporations, regardless of size.[18] Good practices do not imply that corporations themselves have fulfilled their contractual and legal obligations, but also it means they actively contribute to their respecting and guaranteeing socio-economic rights, also through good and best practices.[19]

Good practices also encompass a corporation's attitude to the local and wider community and its social responsibility to consumers.[20] Corporate responsibility to the local and broader community refers to a company's attitude to its nearby and wider surroundings, which may include support and sponsorship for communities, infrastructure and education projects.[21] A corporation can provide assistance in the form of employees' voluntary work, contributions in kind and charitable contributions to the provision of socio-economic rights. Social responsibility to the community is also reflected in the provision of socio-economic rights and job creation, regular settlement of tax liabilities and social security contributions, organizing annual leave for employees and their families, and care for the environment (including the introduction of environmental measures and reducing the amount of wastewater and emissions).[22] The external dimension includes a corporation's commitments to the local and wider community and its social responsibility to the consumer, which means that busineses should operate in favour of consumers.[23]

Corporations can promote the development and use of environmentally friendly technologies. In doing so, they must provide and promote respect for

16 Karin Buhmann, 'Integrating Human Rights in Emerging Regulation of Corporate Social Responsibility: The EU Case', 7(2) *International Journal of Law in Context* 139 (2011).

17 See, Surya Deva, 'Sustainable Good Governance and Corporations: An Analysis of Asymmetries', 18 *The Georgetown International Environmental Law Review* 707 (2006).

18 Ibid.

19 Atle Midttun and Germán Granada, 'Innovación y responsabilidad social empresarial', 10 *Cuadernos Forética* (2007).

20 Jeb Brugmann and Coimbatore Krishnarao Prahalad, 'Cocreating Business's New Social Compact', 85(2) *Harvard Business Review* 80 (2007).

21 Karin Buhmann, 'Balancing Power Interests in Reflexive Law Public-Private CSR Schemes: The Global Compact and the EU's Multi-Stakeholder Forum on CSR', *in* Karin Buhmann, Lynn Roseberry and Mette Morsing (eds.), *Corporate Social and Human Rights Responsibilities: Global Legal and Management Perspectives*, London: Palgrave MacMillan (2011), pp. 77–107.

22 Jacob D. Rendtorff, 'Institutionalization of Corporate Ethics and Corporate Social Responsibility Programmes in Firm', *in* K. Buhmann, L. Roseberry and L. Morsing (eds.), *Corporate Social and Human Rights Responsibilities: Global Legal and Management Perspectives*, London: Palgrave MacMillan, (2011), pp. 244–265.

23 European Parliament, Resolution on Corporate Social Responsibility: New Partnership, 2006/2133(INI), para 34.

socio-economic rights obligations, at least in their field of operation. In the area of socio-economic rights, they must specify their obligations to the local and wider community by drafting voluntary ethical codes of conduct and policies, as well as voluntary social and environmental reports, which set out their commitment to the protection and promotion of these values.[24] At the same time, corporations must ensure that associated and subsidiary corporations, business partners and suppliers also undertake to respect and promote socio-economic rights to prevent corruption.[25] Providing the same level of respect and promotion of socio-economic rights may entail a subsidiary helping to independently monitor and verify the entire internal structure and supply chain. Only a handful of corporations control the entire supply chain. In developing countries, corporations can contribute with new investments to the fight against poverty and support the principles of fair trade and good governance by taking measures to promote respect for human rights and environmental protection, particularly in the areas where regulatory regimes are weak or non-existent.

Good practices concerning individual socio-economic rights

Good business practices concerning the right to education

Businesses have long contributed to the individual enjoyment of right to education through various ways such as for example funding and scholarships. However, as one commentator notes, "companies have a vested interest in promoting the right to education for the development of skilled workforce".[26] Nonetheless, they present themselves as providers of education in the form of primary and secondary schools, universities or other non-formal educational level. Could corporations contribute to the availability, accessibility, acceptability, quality and adaptability of education? The UN special rapporteur on the right to education observed that "Regulations should prescribe full financial and performance reporting requirements for all private schools. It should be obligatory for all private providers to report regularly to designated public authorities on their financial operations".[27] The CESCR considered in its General Comment no. 13 that "the failure to ensure private educational institutions conform to the 'minimum

24 Joel Bakan, *The Corporation: The Pathological Pursuit of Profit and Power*, London: Constable (2005).

25 Lois A. Mohr, Deborah J. Webb and Katherine E. Harris, 'Do Consumers Expect Companies to be Socially Responsible? The Impact of Corporate Social Responsibility on Buying Behaviour', 35(1) *The Journal of Consumer Affairs* 45 (2001).

26 James Featherby (ed.), *Global Business and Human Rights: Jurisdictional Comparisons*, London: European Lawyer/Future Lex (2011), p. 62.

27 UN, Human Rights Council, 'Report of the Special Rapporteur on the Right to Education, Kishore Singh, Protecting the Right to Education Against Commercialization', UN Doc. A/HRC/29/30, 10 June 2015, para 125.

educational standards' required by article 13 (3) and (4) of the International Covenant on Economic, Social and Cultural Rights constituted a violation of the right to education".[28] In the absence of the effective and efficient state regulations, businesses have to exercise diligent and careful supervision in order to achieve minimum educational standards.

Several corporations have been involved in building schools in the area where they operate. For instance, Nestlé boasts that it built forty schools in 2015 and another forty in 2016.[29] Azim Premji Foundation, founded by one of the wealthiest Indian businessmen, aims to provide education to vulnerable groups.[30] Azim Premji University therefore boasts "to make significant contributions towards a just, equitable, humane and sustainable society".[31] Similarly, the Newmont Ahafo Development Foundation provides various incentives concerning the exercise of the right to education in Ghana.[32] The Melinda and Bill Gates Foundation through its "K-12 Education program aims to ensure that all students graduate from high school prepared to succeed in college".[33] Several leading global universities have in recent years joined or set up massive open online courses (MOOC) in order to democratize access to university education. For instance, Harvard University and MIT established in 2012 courses through EDX, an MOOC provider, which is an online platform for enhancing "teaching and learning on campus and online" and advancing "teaching and learning through research".[34] Such platforms have really grown in recent years.[35] Further, the Lego Corporation supports "charitable organisations which promote children's play, learning and creativity" and "marginalised and vulnerable children".[36]

Moreover, the Siemens Foundation has contributed "more than $90 million in the United States to advance workforce development and education initiatives in science, technology, engineering and math".[37] Technology corporations such

28 UN, CESCR, 'General comment No. 13: The Right to Education', UN Doc. E/C.12/1999/10, 8 December 1999, para 65.

29 Nestlé, 'Our Commitment: Roll Out the Nestlé Cocoa Plan with Cocoa Farmers', www.nestle.com/csv/communities/nestle-cocoa-plan (last accessed 19 January 2018).

30 Azim Premji Foundation, www.azimpremjifoundation.org/schoolteachers (last accessed 19 January 2018).

31 Azim Premji University, www.azimpremjifoundation.org/APU (last accessed 19 January 2018).

32 Newmont Ahafo Development Foundation, 'Education Beneficiaries'.

33 Bill and Melinda Gates Foundation, What We Do: K 12 Education Programme: Strategy Overview, www.gatesfoundation.org/What-We-Do/US-Program/K-12-Education (last accessed 19 January 2018).

34 EdX, www.edx.org/about-us (last accessed 19 January 2018).

35 See for example, Coursera, https://www.coursera.org (last accessed 19 January 2018); Udemy, https://www.udemy.com (last accessed 19 January 2018); and Khan Academy, https://www.khanacademy.org (last accessed 19 January 2018).

36 Lego, Charity and Donations, www.lego.com/en-us/aboutus/contact/charity-donations (last accessed 19 January 2018).

37 Siemens Foundation, www.usa.siemens.com/en/about_us/corporate_responsibility/foundation.htm (last accessed 19 January 2018).

as Qualcomm have been bringing wireless technology to vulnerable communities in order to "foster entrepreneurship, aid in public safety, enhance the delivery of health care, enrich teaching and learning".[38] Microsoft supports Microsoft Youth Spark, a global initiative, to enhance access of young people to education opportunities in computer science.[39] However, corporate initiatives have not been always successful.[40] They often pursue certain ideological agendas; however this is also true of state education in many countries. Nonetheless, several corporations accept that they have obligations to adopt good practices relating to the right to education.

Good business practices concerning the right to food

The food industry has been one of the largest in the world and many corporations have developed sophisticated good practices in the terms of food provision. Corporations can be active in the food industry as food producers and consumers. For instance, Walmart praises itself as one of the leaders in good practices.[41] Corporations should aim to achieve good practices in direct productions and in supply chains.[42] Citigroup notes its statement that "Citi encourages suppliers to follow best practices in the areas of freely chosen employment; child labour avoidance; working hours; respect in the workplace; wages and benefits; and health and safety".[43] Nestlé has developed the so-called Nestlé Cocoa Plan in Ivory Coast, Ghana, Brazil, Ecuador, Venezuela, Mexico and Indonesia, which aims at "Better farming, addressing issues such as agricultural practices and rejuvenation of plantations; Better lives, which seeks to empower women and eliminate child labour; and Better cocoa, which covers certification and building long-term relationships in our supply chain".[44] Such practices and commitments are indeed impressive; however without independently and impartially verifiable supervisory mechanisms they do not bring much added value. Moreover, Flamingo Horticulture Ltd has been engaged in several sustainability projects from energy conservation, water management to environmental projects.[45] Further, "since 2011,

38 Qualcomm, www.qualcomm.com/company/wireless-reach (last accessed 19 January 2018).
39 Microsoft, Youthspark, www.microsoft.com/en-us/philanthropies/youthspark (last accessed 19 January 2018).
40 The Global Initiative for Economic, Social and Cultural Rights, 'Kenyan Court Upholds the Closure of Bridge International Academies Over Failure to Respect Standards', 17 April 2017.
41 Walmart, 'About Us', http://corporate.walmart.com/our-story (last accessed 19 January 2018).
42 Felicity Lawrence, 'Costco and CP Foods Face Lawsuit Over Alleged Slavery in Prawn Supply Chain', *The Guardian*, 19 August 2015.
43 Citigroup, 'Statement on Human Rights', April 2004.
44 Nestlé, 'Our commitment: Roll Out the Nestlé Cocoa Plan with Cocoa Farmers', www.nestle.com/csv/communities/nestle-cocoa-plan (last accessed 19 January 2018).
45 Flamingo Horticulture Ltd, http://flamingo.net/sustainability/ (last accessed 19 January 2018).

Outnumber Hunger (General Mills, Big Machine Label Group and Feeding) has helped Feeding America secure more than 45 million meals for local food banks".[46] Several corporations have been involved in Malawi Tea 2020 Programme, which "brings together the organisations who can deliver the changes required to achieve a competitive and profitable Malawian tea industry where workers earn a living wage and smallholders earn a living income".[47] All in all, such practices show that some corporations active in the food industry are prepared to take part in the provision of socio-economic rights, at least in the proximity of their operations.

Good business practices concerning the right to health

The right to health has been of the most prominent socio-economic rights. Several corporations active in the health industry have been contributing to enhancing the right to health in recent decades by developing several good practices either to boast its public reputation or to enhance protection in the limited sphere. As developed in Chapter 6, corporations can be active as private hospitals and clinics, private health insurance providers and pharmaceutical corporations.[48] However, this groups together almost all corporations asked to ensure the health and safety standards in their operations.

Following the Rana Plaza disaster when over one thousand people died after the collapse of a garment factory building, the parties signed the so-called Rana Plaza arrangement.[49] The arrangement stipulates in section 1 (2) that its objective is "to provide payments to the victims of the Rana Plaza accident and their families and dependents (RP victims) in a transparent and equitable manner according to their losses, as well as access to medical care for victims in need".[50] It appears that payments concerning improving the right to health have been

46 Feeding America, www.feedingamerica.org/about-us/about-feeding-america/partners/current-promotions/general-mills-outnumber.html?referrer=http://sdgfunders.org/blog/how-17-companies-are-tackling-sustainable-development-goals-and-your-company-can-too/ (last accessed 19 January 2018).

47 Malawi 2020 Tea Revitalisation Programme, www.malawitea2020.com/ (last accessed 19 January 2018).

48 See, Antenor Hallo De Wolf and Brigit Toebes, 'Assessing Private Sector Involvement in Health Care and Universal Health Coverage in Light of the Right to Health', 18 *Health and Human Rights Journal* 79 (2016), p. 83.

49 Rana Plaza Arrangement, 'Understanding for a Practical Arrangement on Payments to the Victims of the Rana Plaza Accident and their Families and Dependents for their Losses', Ranaplaza-arrangement.org, 20 November 2013 (last accessed 19 January 2018). The signatories include: Government: The Ministry of Labour and Employment, Bangladesh; Bangladesh Garment Manufacturers' Association (BGMEA), Bangladesh Employers Federation (BEF), Industrial Bangladesh Council (IBC), National Coordination Committee for Workers' Education (NCCWE), Industrial Global Union, Bonmarché, El Corte Ingles, Loblaw and Primark; Bangladesh Institute of Labour Studies (BILS) and Clean Clothes Campaign (CCC).

50 Ibid., section 1 (a).

completed.[51] It seems businesses do not systematically engage business and human rights, whereby they only do so *ad hoc* in light of immense public pressure.[52] Further, the parties immediately after the disaster signed the Accord on Fire and Building Safety in Bangladesh's garment industry.[53] The accord aims to achieve "a safe and sustainable Bangladeshi Ready Made Garment ('RMG') industry in which no worker needs to fear fires, building collapses, or other accidents that could be prevented with reasonable health and safety measures". It provides for inspections, training, complaints processes, transparency and reporting and supplier incentives.[54] As for complaints, it provides that "the Safety Inspector shall establish a worker complaint process and mechanism".[55] However, the overreaching causes for such disasters in the Bangladeshi garment industry and elsewhere have so far not been removed, as they are connected with the general rule-of-law challenges.[56] Further, Anglo American has supported health-related projects through a variety of their operations. More specifically, it has funded "new R8.8 million ($750,000) Postmasburg District Clinic" which "is the result of a partnership between Kumba, the Northern Cape Department of Health and the Tsantsabane Municipality".[57]

Businesses' commitment to the right to health has also been necessary regarding access to medicines. For instance, the Access to Medicine Index measures the conduct of the twenty largest pharmaceutical corporations as to their commitment to improving access to medicines around the world.[58] The 2016 Access to Medicine Index Report identifies several good practices.[59] Transnational pharmaceutical corporations such as AstraZeneca, Merck KGaA and Merck & Co., Inc., have in the past year improved quality controlling of their supply chains and have been involved in health education programmes.[60] Moreover, Novartis boasts that it has improved its strategy as to equitable commercial models for the access to medicines, family health plans and zero-profit plans in low-income groups.[61] Further, it boasts of the Novartis Malaria Initiative, which is said to have delivered more than "800 million treatments without profit – including

51 Rana Plaza Arrangement, http://ranaplaza-arrangement.org/ (last accessed 19 January 2018).

52 Dorothée Baumann-Pauly, Justine Nolan, Auret van Heerden and Michael Samway, 'Industry-Specific Multi-Stakeholder Initiatives That Govern Corporate Human Rights Standards: Legitimacy Assessments of the Fair Labor Association and the Global Network Initiative', 143(4) *Journal of Business Ethics* 771 (2015).

53 Accord on Fire and Building Safety in Bangladesh, 13 May 2013.

54 Ibid.

55 Ibid., section 18.

56 Jana Kasperkevic, 'Rana Plaza Collapse: Workplace Dangers Persist Three Years Later, Reports Find', New York: *The Guardian*, 31 May 2016.

57 Anglo American, 'Keeping Communities Healthy: Launch of the Postmasburg District Clinic', 13 April 2015.

58 Access to Medicines Foundation, 'What Is the Access to Medicine Index?' http://accessto medicineindex.org/about-the-index/#what-we-measure (last accessed 19 January 2018).

59 Access to Medicines Foundation, 'Access to Medicines Index Report 2016', November 2016.

60 Ibid., pp. 16–17.

61 Novartis, 2016 Corporate Responsibility Performance Report, pp. 11 and 12.

more than 300 million dispersible paediatric treatments – mostly to the public sector of malaria-endemic countries since 2001".[62] Moreover, AstraZeneca has developed an innovative compliance assessment of their suppliers and argues that only works "with third parties that embrace standards of ethical behaviour that are consistent with our own".[63] In 2008, the former special rapporteur on the right to health highlighted the Positive Action Programme, which is "GSK's long-term, international HIV/AIDS community investment programme, facilitating access to treatment by supporting HIV education, care and other related community initiatives".[64] In 2017, Positive Action Programme is still running.[65] The rapporteur commended "the work done by GSK and some other companies, as well as philanthropic institutions and civil society organisations, to promote research into these diseases".[66] Nonetheless, De Felice argues that "the success of new business models depends on both the willingness and the ability of pharmaceutical companies to fully integrate access to medicine into their business strategies".[67] Nonetheless, several corporations operating in the health industry appear through their good practice to recognize their obligations concerning the right to health.

Good business practices concerning the right to adequate housing

Businesses have wide-raging impact on the right to adequate housing, both positive and negative. The Office of the High Commissioner for Human Rights notes negative influences are particularly prevailing

> in the context of the construction of large dams and other development projects, especially those involving resource extraction such as gas and oil, which may force residents to move or cause environmental degradation. Landlords, private owners, housing agencies or estate agencies can also affect the enjoyment of the right to adequate housing, notably if they carry out forced evictions or discriminate against particular groups, for instance by charging prohibitive rents.[68]

62 Ibid., p. 12.

63 AstraZeneca, 'Ethical Business Practices', www.astrazeneca.com/content/dam/az/our-company/Sustainability/Ethical-Business-Practices.pdf, p. 2.

64 UN, Human Rights Council, 'Report of the Special Rapporteur on the Right of Everyone to the Enjoyment of the Highest Attainable Standard of Health: Paul Hunt, Mission to GlaxoSmithKline', UN Doc. A/HRC/11/12/Add.2, 5 May 2009, para 49.

65 Viiv Healthcare, 'Positive Action: Working to Support Vulnerable Communities', www.viivhealthcare.com/ch/positive-action.aspx (last accessed 19 January 2018).

66 UN, Human Rights Council, 'Report of the Special Rapporteur on the Right of Everyone to the Enjoyment of the Highest Attainable Standard of Health: Paul Hunt, Mission to GlaxoSmithKline', para 90.

67 Damiano De Felice, 'How Pharma Can Fix Its Reputation and Its Business at the Same Time', *Harvard Business Review*, 3 February 2017.

68 UN, OHCHR, 'The Right to Adequate Housing', Fact Sheet No. 21/Rev.1, p. 36.

On the other hand, despite several allegations there are several examples that businesses can positively contribute to the enjoyment of the right to adequate housing. They range from financing and constructing housing projects, paying housing subsistence to cooperating with the state authorities in ensuring the minimum level of the right to adequate housing. Another wave has been in recent decades for states, cities and corporations to focus on green building, sustainable design and green urbanism.[69]

For instance, the South African extractive industry corporation Anglo American boasts of investing "in improving the housing and living conditions of employees and making it possible for them to buy their own homes in sustainable areas near our mining operations".[70] More specifically, they argue that "across our business units in South Africa, we have invested more than $391 million . . . on improving the housing and living conditions of our employees".[71] Further, Anglo American argues that it "has built 718 houses for employees as part of an integrated approach that allows the houses to form part of the current community without creating a separate mining town".[72]

Further, the International Council on Mining and Minerals, an organization of twenty-three extractive industry corporations, argued in its 2015 report on land acquisition and resettlement that "any resettlement solution should be considered in the local context and offer choices to those being resettled, with the informed participation of affected people and statutory authorities".[73] Newmont Ahafo Development Foundation (established by the extractive industry corporation), Newmont Ghana Gold Limited and the Ahafo Social Responsibility Forum have funded various infrastructure and social projects aimed at improving socio-economic livelihoods of local communities.[74] More specifically, it has been able to meet the commitment of Newmont Ghana Gold Limited to provide annually "US$1 per ounce of gold produced and 1% of net profit from the Ahafo Mine".[75]

Equally, the Equatorial Palm Oil's Palm Bay Plantation, which is under control of the Malaysian corporation Kuala Lumpur Kepong Berhad, has changed its approach in Grand Bassa Country, Liberia after civil society pressure and committed itself to a consultations process with local communities. It notes that "in 2015 it went through a process of determining which communities contested its occupation and use of parts of the concession property" and therefore

69 See, Jeremy L. Caradonna, *Sustainability: A History*, Oxford: Oxford University Press (2014), pp. 195–205.

70 Anglo American, 'Improving Housing in South Africa', 14 March 2013.

71 Anglo American, 'Our People', www.angloamerican.com/sustainability/our-people (last accessed 19 January 2018).

72 Anglo American, 'Keeping Communities Healthy: Launch of the Postmasburg District Clinic'.

73 International Council on Mining and Minerals, 'Land Acquisition and Resettlement: Lessons Learned', (2015), p. 30.

74 Newmont Ahafo Development Foundation, 'Projects'.

75 Newmont Ahafo Development Foundation, 'Who We Are?'

"launched an effort to reach agreement with those communities and arrive at formal agreements".[76] What is more, a recent initiative of CEOs of German corporations "encourages companies to share efforts in getting migrants jobs and apprenticeships, language training, housing".[77] In 2013, Goldmann Sachs launched "a $250m 'social impact' fund whose returns are linked to the success of projects such as affordable housing, pre-school education".[78] Further, the Mahindra Rural Housing Finance in India in 2013 expressed its "commitment to extend housing finance to customers in rural India as it joined a global initiative that encourages private sector efforts to fight poverty".[79] Moreover, several real estate corporations worldwide are contributing to the access to affordable housing. For instance, CEMEX boasts that it "contributed to the construction of 2,400 affordable and/or energy-efficient buildings in 13 countries".[80] Total, an extractive industry transnational corporation, has also developed good practices concerning adequate housing.[81] Moreover, there are some examples from rural Brazil that both states and corporations have been addressing housing crises.[82]

Good business practices concerning the right to water

Several transnational corporations active in the water industry have over recent years developed best strategies and good practices to uphold the right to water in order to comply with their normative obligations and commitments. Some of them have joined the CEO Water Mandate established by the UN Global Compact.[83] Its mission stipulates that corporations "recognize that through individual and collective action they can identify and reduce critical short-term water risks to their businesses and contribute to the realization of Sustainable Development Goals".[84] The mandate argues under the section on "Community Engagement" its members should "be active members of the local community and encourage or provide support to local government, groups and initiatives

76 Nomogaia, 'Human Right Risk Assessment: Equatorial Palm Oil's Palm Bay Plantation: Grand Bassa Country, Liberia', p. 17.
77 Patrick McGee, 'German Billionaire Rallies Business to Migrant Cause', *Montabaur: Financial Times*, 8 January 2017.
78 Tom Braithwaite, 'Goldman Plans $250m "Social Impact" Fund', *Financial Times*, 3 November 2013.
79 United Nations Development Programme, 'Business Call to Action: Member Commits to Extend Housing Finance Access to Rural India', 20 March 2013.
80 CEMEX, 'Sustainable Development In Action: Delivering Solutions for Affordable Housing and Efficient Buildings', 31 August 2016.
81 Total, Human Rights Guide, www.total.com/sites/default/files/atoms/files/human_rights_internal_guide_va.pdf (last accessed 19 January 2017).
82 Business and Human Rights Centre, 'Confronting Asymmetrical Power: Empowering Brazil's Rural Communities to Assert Their Legal Rights & Challenge Corporate Impunity. Interview with Danilo Chammas – Lawyer and Activist for Justiça nos Trilhos (Justice on the Rails, Brazil)'.
83 UN, 'CEO Water Mandate', http://ceowatermandate.org/what-we-do/mission-governance/ (last accessed 19 January 2018).
84 Ibid.

seeking to advance the water and sanitation agendas", "undertake water-resource education and awareness campaigns in partnership with local stakeholders" and "work with public authorities and their agents to support – when appropriate – the development of adequate water infrastructure, including water and sanitation delivery systems".[85] So far over 130 corporations have endorsed CEO Water Mandate and have followed its right to water policies.[86] However, one of its shortcomings has been that it has not established a diligent and effective supervisory mechanism based on verifiable indicators.

Coca Cola has been working since 2007 with UN-HABITAT to improve water access and sustainability. The cooperation started in India, but has since several years expended also to another eleven countries in Asia and India.[87] Further, Nestlé argues that it will "work with expert partners to improve access to water and sanitation across our value chain. . . [and] support education initiatives to help our employees, communities, suppliers and consumers make better-informed decisions on how to protect water".[88] Those are ambitious goals; however it is not clear how they will be verifiable and what will be the consequences when these goals are not met. Therefore, they have to be joined with independent supervisory mechanisms.

Similarly, Suez Environment notes that it provides "management solutions for the entire water cycle – from the production and distribution of drinking water to treating wastewater".[89] Suez Environment in 2008 established the Water for All Foundation, which in 2011 became Fonds Suez Environment Initiative.[90] The Initiative has funded "concrete actions to sustainably develop access to essential services (water, sanitation and waste) for underprivileged populations in developing countries".[91] In this way, it has supported over 600 projects all over the Global South, such as in Bangladesh, Burkina Faso, Lebanon, Niger, and Congo, as well as in France and elsewhere.[92] More specifically, it has assisted project of CARE, a non-governmental organisation, in Lebanon concerning "rehabilitation and improvement of water and sanitation service infrastructures and awareness campaigns for Syrian refugees and host populations".[93] In Bangladesh, it has financed GK Savar's project concerning "supply of water which has been treated

85 UN Global Compact, 'CEO Water Mandate, Report 2011', p. 11.

86 UN Global Compact, 'CEO Water Mandate', Endorsing corporations.

87 Coca Cola, 'Water Stewardship and Replenish Report', Our Partners: UN-HABITAT, www.coca-colacompany.com/stories/our-partners-un-habitat (last accessed 19 January 2018).

88 Nestlé, 'Access and Conservation', www.nestle.com/csv/water/access-conservation (last accessed 19 January 2018).

89 Suez Environment, www.mysuezwater.com/about-us/suez-environnement (last accessed 19 January 2018).

90 Suez Environment – ParisTech "Water for All" Chair, or how to transfer your know-how, 4 July 2012.

91 Suez, The Founds SUEZ initiatives, www.suez.com/en/Who-we-are/A-commited-group/The-Fonds-SUEZ-initiatives (last accessed 19 January 2018).

92 Ibid.

93 Suez, 'Achievements 2011-2016, Lebanon: Care', www.fsi-realisations.fr/map.html?lang=en&country=liban&project=care (last accessed 19 January 2018).

to ensure that it is fit for human consumption".[94] Further, it has funded a project concerning "emergency aid for displaced populations living in the state of Borno, in north-east Nigeria".[95] All in all, it seems that independent assessment of the proposed projects is not available.

Moreover, Procter & Gamble has provided water purification technology in powder form to ensure clear and drinkable water in areas where access is not provided.[96] The corporation boasts that, since the start of the programme in 2014, it has ensured "clean water in no more than 75 countries and helped to raise awareness of the clean water through a diverse network of 150 partners".[97] Further, PepsiCo has in recent years demonstrated strong commitment to upholding different dimensions of the right to water by "establishing strategic public-private partnerships with innovative organizations to make an impact on water scarcity", including

> the Columbia University Earth Institute's Global Water Centre, Water.org, the Safe Water Network, The Energy Resources Institute (TERI), the China Women's Development Foundation (CWDF) and many others to launch a host of projects which are helping to install village water and irrigation systems; establish water health centres; construct rainwater harvesting cisterns; improve sanitation programs; and recharge aquifers in developing communities.[98]

In contrast to several other corporations, PepsiCo has developed a strong sustainability reporting and established a corporate governance structure (the so-called Sustainability Task Force) that reports directly to the CEO.[99] All in all, it seems that several corporations recognized not only their negative, but also their positive, obligations concerning the right to water. However, it is not clear how developed the outside reporting and reporting mechanisms are.

The contribution of the corporate good practices to the provision of socio-economic rights

Good practices of business in the exercise and implementation of socio-economic rights contribute to the contestations that businesses not only have a role to play in providing for socio-economic livelihoods of individuals, but also some of them

94 Suez, 'Achievements 2011-2016, Bangladesh: GK Savar', www.fsi-realisations.fr/map.html?lang=en&country=bangladesh&project=gk-savar (last accessed 19 January 2018).

95 Suez, 'Achievements 2011-2016, Nigeria: GK Médecins Sans Frontiéres', www.fsi-realisations.fr/map.html?lang=en&country=nigeria&project=medecins-sans-frontieres (last accessed 19 January 2018).

96 Procter & Gamble, 'A Simple Way to Clean Water', www.csdw.org/csdw/pur-packet-technology.shtml (last accessed 19 January 2018).

97 Ibid.

98 PepsiCo, 'Water Stewardship Report', p. 5.

99 PepsiCo, '2016 Sustainability Report'.

understand that they are obliged to do so. Corporations possess either negative obligations of non-interference or positive obligations of taking reasonable active steps. They offer benchmarks for other corporations; competitors in the sector can look over in order to improve their performance. They are illustrations of internal commitment to negative and positive corporate obligations concerning socio-economic rights. They provide evidence that businesses can have and do have self-standing and complementary obligations to provide socio-economic rights. In other words, they illustrate emerging proofs that corporations have obligations towards rights-holders. Such provisions can be and have been as effective as those of the state. It is understandable that businesses cannot substitute full national social welfare systems, which depend on tax-payers' contributions; however, they are other financial means of contributions. Nonetheless, good practices can complement existing state provision of socio-economic rights.

As for their legal nature, they are voluntary and dependent on financial resources and the good will of corporations concerned. They cannot be described as legal or quasi-legal. Good practices can also be described as a test case for the enforcement responsibilities of corporations for the realization of socio-economic rights. The point of this investigation is primarily to conclusively argue that corporations have obligations concerning socio-economic rights. Before entering into a particular state, corporations must conduct a diligent assessment of the reasonableness of such steps with aspects of human rights protection and operational, commercial, financial and environmental risks. In today's highly interconnected global economy, it would be unrealistic to say that the corporations are also asked to do more outside their legal obligations and they are to strive to gather financial resources for the provision of socio-economic rights. One thing that is essential is to improve supervisory and auditing mechanisms that would control voluntary commitments and good practices of the corporations, as good practices without proper supervision do not contribute to corporate obligations concerning socio-economic rights.

Conclusion

This chapter has illustrated that some businesses are committed to providing socio-economic rights of individuals through a variety of initiatives, foundations and actions. However, some of them have to be taken with a pinch of salt, as it is doubtful what their added value is. Corporations will be always interested in improving their public image in order to enhance their position in their markets and generate more revenue and profits for their shareholders. This is acceptable, but what is new is that corporations can do so hand in hand with protecting socio-economic rights. They can reconcile both goals without undermining their primary objectives of generating revenues and making profits. However, some of them may be generously interested in contributing to the common good and the protection of human dignity. There are differences between corporations and industries concerning particular rights. For these reasons, good practices vary and are diverse, and it is difficult to draw uniform conclusions. Nonetheless, one should not expect that corporations will take over the role of the state as the primary duty-bearer of socio-economic rights. They are also duty-bearers; however, the leading role falls with the state and state-related actors. Their good practices contribute to individuals' enjoyment of socio-economic rights. What is clear is that corporations can never undermine socio-economic rights, which the state is primarily obliged to guarantee. Corporations contribute to achieving such objectives through their good practices.

Bibliography

Books

Bakan, Joel, *The Corporation: The Pathological Pursuit of Profit and Power*, London: Constable (2005).

Caradonna, Jeremy L., *Sustainability: A History*, Oxford: Oxford University Press (2014).

Featherby, James (ed.), *Global Business and Human Rights: Jurisdictional Comparisons*, London: European Lawyer/Future Lex (2011).

Saul, Ben, Kinley, David and Mowbray, Jacqueline, *The International Covenant on Economic, Social and Cultural Rights: Commentary, Cases and Materials*, Oxford: Oxford University Press (2016).

Journal articles

Baumann-Pauly, Dorothée, Nolan, Justine, van Heerden, Auret and Samway, Michael, 'Industry-Specific Multi-Stakeholder Initiatives That Govern Corporate Human Rights Standards: Legitimacy Assessments of the Fair Labor Association and the Global Network Initiative', 143(4) *Journal of Business Ethics* 771 (2017).

Buhmann, Karin, 'Integrating Human Rights in Emerging Regulation of Corporate Social Responsibility: The EU Case', 7(2) *International Journal of Law in Context* 139 (2011).

Brugmann, Jeb and Prahalad, Coimbatore Krishnarao, 'Cocreating Business's New Social Compact', 85(2) *Harvard Business Review* 80 (2007).

Deva, Surya, 'Sustainable Good Governance and Corporations: An Analysis of Asymmetries', 18 *The Georgetown International Environmental Law Review* 707 (2006).

De Wolf, Antenor Hallo and Toebes, Brigit, 'Assessing Private Sector Involvement in Health Care and Universal Health Coverage in Light of the Right to Health', 18 *Health and Human Rights Journal* 79 (2016).

Mohr, Lois A., Webb, Deborah J. and Harris, Katherine E., 'Do Consumers Expect Companies to Be Socially Responsible? The Impact of Corporate Social Responsibility on Buying Behaviour', 35(1) *The Journal of Consumer Affairs* 45 (2001).

Book chapters

Buhmann, Karin, 'Balancing Power Interests in Reflexive Law Public-Private CSR Schemes: The Global Compact and the EU's Multi-Stakeholder Forum on CSR', *in* Karin Buhmann, Lynn Roseberry and Mette Morsing (eds.), *Corporate Social and Human Rights Responsibilities: Global Legal and Management Perspectives*, London: Palgrave MacMillan (2011), pp. 77–107.

De Schutter, Olivier, 'Corporations and Economic, Social and Cultural Rights', *in* Eibe Riedel, Gilles Giacca and Christophe Golay (eds.), *Economic, Social and Cultural Rights in International Law: Contemporary Issues and Challenges*, Oxford: Oxford University Press (2014), pp. 193–226.

Rendtorff, Jacob D., 'Institutionalization of Corporate Ethics and Corporate Social Responsibility Programmes in Firm', *in* K. Buhmann, L. Roseberry and L. Morsing (eds.), *Corporate Social and Human Rights Responsibilities: Global Legal and Management Perspectives*, London: Palgrave MacMillan, (2011), pp. 244–265.

Newspaper articles

Braithwaite, Tom, 'Goldman Plans $250m "Social Impact" Fund', *Financial Times (UK)*, 3 November 2013.

Kasperkevic, Jana, 'Rana Plaza Collapse: Workplace Dangers Persist Three Years Later, Reports Find', New York: *The Guardian*, 31 May 2016.

Lawrence, Felicity, 'Costco and CP Foods Face Lawsuit Over Alleged Slavery in Prawn Supply Chain', *The Guardian*, 19 August 2015.

McGee, Patrick, 'German Billionaire Rallies Business to Migrant Cause', Montabaur: *Financial Times*, 8 January 2017.

Official documents

European Parliament, Resolution on Corporate Social Responsibility: New Partnership, 2006/2133(INI).

UN, CESCR, 'General Comment No. 13: The Right to Education', UN Doc. E/C.12/1999/10, 8 December 1999.

UN, CESCR, 'General Comment No. 24 (2017) on State Obligations Under the International Covenant on Economic, Social and Cultural Rights in the Context of Business Activities', UN Doc. E/C.12/GC/24, 10 August 2017.

UN, Committee on the Rights of the Child, 'General Comment No. 16 on State Obligations Regarding the Impact of the Business Sector on Children's Rights', UN Doc. CRC/C/GC/16, 17 April 2013.

UN, Human Rights Council, 'Guiding Principles for Business and Human Rights: Implementing the United Nations "Protect, Respect and Remedy" Framework', UN Doc. A/HRC/17/31, 21 March 2011.

UN, Human Rights Council, 'Report of the Special Rapporteur on the Right of Everyone to the Enjoyment of the Highest Attainable Standard of Health: Paul Hunt, Mission to GlaxoSmithKline', UN Doc. A/HRC/11/12/Add.2, 5 May 2009.

UN, Human Rights Council, 'Report of the Special Rapporteur on the Right to Education, Kishore Singh, Protecting the Right to Education Against Commercialization', UN Doc. A/HRC/29/30, 10 June 2015.

UN, OHCHR, 'The Right to Adequate Housing', Fact Sheet No. 21/Rev.1.

UN, 'Report of the Working Group on the Issue of Human Rights and Transnational Corporations and other Business Enterprises: Developments in the Embedding of the Guiding Principles into Global Governance Frameworks', UN Doc. A/67/285, 10 August 2012.

UN, 'Report of the Working Group on the Issue of Human Rights and Transnational Corporations and other Business Enterprises', UN Doc. A/68/279, 7 August 2013.

Websites

Access to Medicines Foundation, 'What Is the Access to Medicine Index?' http://accesstomedicineindex.org/about-the-index/#what-we-measure (last accessed 19 January 2018).

'Accord on Fire and Building Safety in Bangladesh', 13 May 2013, http://bangladeshaccord.org (last accessed 19 January 2018).

Anglo American, 'Our People', www.angloamerican.com/sustainability/our-people (last accessed 19 January 2018).

Azim Premji Foundation, www.azimpremjifoundation.org/schoolteachers (last accessed 19 January 2018).

Azim Premji University, www.azimpremjifoundation.org/APU (last accessed 19 January 2018).

Bill and Melinda Gates Foundation, 'What We Do: K 12 Education Programme: Strategy Overview', www.gatesfoundation.org/What-We-Do/US-Program/K-12-Education (last accessed 19 January 2018).

Business Fights Poverty, http://businessfightspoverty.org (last accessed 19 January 2018).

Coca Cola, 'Water Stewardship and Replenish Report', Our Partners: UN-HABITAT, www.coca-colacompany.com/stories/our-partners-un-habitat (last accessed 19 January 2018).

Coursera, https://www.coursera.org (last accessed 19 January 2018).

EdX, www.edx.org/about-us (last accessed 19 January 2018).

Flamingo Horticulture Ltd, http://flamingo.net/sustainability/ (last accessed 19 January 2018).

Feeding America, www.feedingamerica.org/about-us/about-feeding-america/partners/current-promotions/general-mills-outnumber.html?referrer=http://sdgfunders.org/blog/how-17-companies-are-tackling-sustainable-development-goals-and-your-company-can-too/ (last accessed 19 January 2018).

Khan Academy, https://www.khanacademy.org (last accessed 19 January 2018).

Lego, Charity and Donations, www.lego.com/en-us/aboutus/contact/charity-donations (last accessed 19 January 2018).

Malawi 2020 Tea Revitalisation Programme, www.malawitea2020.com/ (last accessed 19 January 2018).

Microsoft, Youthspark, www.microsoft.com/en-us/philanthropies/youthspark (last accessed 19 January 2018).

Nestlé, 'Access and Conservation', www.nestle.com/csv/water/access-conservation (last accessed 19 January 2018).

Nestlé, 'Our Commitment: Roll Out the Nestlé Cocoa Plan with Cocoa Farmers', www.nestle.com/csv/communities/nestle-cocoa-plan (last accessed 19 January 2018).

Procter & Gamble, 'A Simple Way to Clean Water', www.csdw.org/csdw/pur-packet-technology.shtml (last accessed 19 January 2018).

Qualcomm, www.qualcomm.com/company/wireless-reach (last accessed 19 January 2018).

Siemens Foundations, www.usa.siemens.com/en/about_us/corporate_responsibility/foundation.htm (last accessed 19 January 2018).

Suez, 'Achievements 2011-2016, Bangladesh: GK Savar', www.fsi-realisations.fr/map.html?lang=en&country=bangladesh&project=gk-savar (last accessed 19 January 2018).

Suez, 'Achievements 2011-2016, Lebanon: Care', www.fsi-realisations.fr/map.html?lang=en&country=liban&project=care (last accessed 19 January 2018).
Suez, 'Achievements 2011-2016, Nigeria: GK Médecins Sans Frontiéres', www.fsi-realisations.fr/map.html?lang=en&country=nigeria&project=medecins-sans-frontieres (last accessed 19 January 2018).
Suez Environment, www.mysuezwater.com/about-us/suez-environnement (last accessed 19 January 2018).
Suez, 'The Founds SUEZ Initiatives', www.suez.com/en/Who-we-are/A-committed-group/The-Fonds-SUEZ-initiatives (last accessed 19 January 2018).
Udemy, https://www.udemy.com (last accessed 19 January 2018).
Walmart, 'About Us', http://corporate.walmart.com/our-story (last accessed 19 January 2018).
World Business Council for Sustainable Development, 'WBCSD FAQ', http://wbcsdpublications.org/faq/ (last accessed 19 January 2018).

Reports and miscellaneous

Access to Medicines Foundation, 'Access to Medicines Index 2016', November 2016.
Anglo American, 'Improving Housing in South Africa', 14 March 2013.
Anglo American, 'Keeping Communities Healthy: Launch of the Postmasburg District Clinic', 13 April 2015.
AstraZeneca, 'Ethical Business Practices'.
Business and Human Rights Centre, 'Confronting Asymmetrical Power: Empowering Brazil's Rural Communities to Assert Their Legal Rights & Challenge Corporate Impunity. Interview with Danilo Chammas – Lawyer and Activist for Justiça nos Trilhos (Justice on the Rails, Brazil)'.
CEMEX, 'Sustainable Development in Action: Delivering Solutions for Affordable Housing and Efficient Buildings', 31 August 2016.
Citigroup, 'Statement on Human Rights', April 2004.
De Felice, Damiano, 'How Pharma Can Fix Its Reputation and Its Business at the Same Time', *Harvard Business Review Blog*, 3 February 2017.
International Council on Mining and Minerals, 'Land Acquisition and Resettlement: Lessons Learned', 2015.
Kharas, Horni, 'Financing for Development: International Financial Flows After 2015', Brookings Institution, 8 July 2014.
Midttun, Atle and Granada, Germán, 'Innovación y Responsabilidad Social Empresarial', 10 Cuadernos Forética, 2007.
Morrison-Paul, Catherine J. and Siegel, Donald S., 'Corporate Social Responsibility and Economic Performance', Rensselaer Working Papers in Economics, No. 0605, March 2006.
Newmont Ahafo Development Foundation, 'Education Beneficiaries'.
Newmont Ahafo Development Foundation, 'Projects'.
Newmont Ahafo Development Foundation, 'Who We Are?'
Nomogaia, 'Human Right Risk Assessment: Equatorial Palm Oil's Palm Bay Plantation: Grand Bassa Country, Liberia'.
Novartis, '2016 Corporate Responsibility Performance Report'.
Oxfam, 'Raising the Bar: Rethinking the Role of Business in the Sustainable Development Goals', February 2017.
PepsiCo, '2016 Sustainability Report'.

PepsiCo, 'Water Stewardship Report'.

Rana Plaza Arrangement, http://ranaplaza-arrangement.org/ (last accessed 19 January 2018).

Rana Plaza Arrangement, 'Understanding for a Practical Arrangement on Payments to the Victims of the Rana Plaza Accident and Their Families and Dependents for Their Losses', *Ranaplaza-arragenent.org*, 20 November 2013.

Rees, Caroline, 'Business, Human Rights and the Sustainable Development Goals: Forging a Coherent Vision and Strategy', Shift, November 2016.

SDG Fund, Harvard Kennedy School CSR Initiative and Inspiris Limited, 'Business and the United Nations: Working Together Towards the Sustainable Development Goals: A Framework for Action', 2015.

Share Action, 'Investors Can Play a Central Role in Achieving the Sustainable Development Goals', 21 March 2016.

Shift, Oxfam and Global Compact Network Netherlands, 'Doing Business with Respect for Human Rights: A Guidance Tool for Companies', 2nd Edition 2016.

Suez Environment – ParisTech, '"Water for All" Chair, or How to Transfer Your Know-How', 4 July 2012.

The Global Initiative for Economic, Social and Cultural Rights, 'Kenyan Court Upholds the Closure of Bridge International Academies Over Failure to Respect Standards', 17 April 2017.

Total, Human Rights Guide, www.total.com/sites/default/files/atoms/files/human_rights_internal_guide_va.pdf (last accessed 19 January 2017).

UN Global Compact, 'CEO Water Mandate', Endorsing corporations.

UN Global Compact, 'CEO Water Mandate', http://ceowatermandate.org/what-we-do/mission-governance/ (last accessed 19 January 2018).

UN Global Compact, 'CEO Water Mandate', Report 2011.

United Nations Development Programme, 'Business Call to Action: Member Commits to Extend Housing Finance Access to Rural India', 20 March 2013.

Viiv Healthcare, 'Positive Action: Working to Support Vulnerable Communities', www.viivhealthcare.com/ch/positive-action.aspx (last accessed 19 January 2018).

Zbona, Ana, 'Interview with Anisa Kamadoli Costa, Chief Sustainability Officer at Tiffany & Co.' Business and Human Rights Resource Centre, April 2017.

Part II

Corporate accountability for socio-economic rights

5 Corporate human rights obligations under socio-economic rights

Introduction 87
The origins of corporate socio-economic rights obligations 89
Domestic legal systems 91
International layer 96
Voluntary commitments 100
Interim conclusion 101
The legal characteristics, nature and scope of corporate socio-economic rights obligations 102
The nature and scope of corporate socio-economic rights obligations 102
Corporate obligation to respect socio-economic rights 105
Corporate obligation to protect socio-economic rights 106
Corporate obligation to fulfil socio-economic rights 113
Conclusion 116

Introduction

This chapter studies corporate human rights obligations concerning socio-economic rights. Socio-economic rights are, as noted earlier, human rights which are essential for sustaining individual livelihoods and creating human capabilities. They are foundational for the exercise of civil and political rights. Without food, water, adequate housing, health and education, it is difficult to imagine that individuals would be able to fully and freely exercise, for instance, their freedom of expression or right to a fair trial. As socio-economic rights are greatly connected to the provision of basic services, they are linked to budgetary financial resources. They are mostly dependent on state resources, but also require financial resources from private actors, particularly when governments are absent. International documents, such as ICESCR, provide that socio-economic rights generally create only states' obligations of conduct, not of result.[1] In this way, these documents imply that states have to realize those

1 See also, Godefridus J.H. van Hoof, 'The Legal Nature of Economic, Social and Cultural Rights: A Rebuttal of Some Traditional Views', *in* Philip Alston and Katarina Tomaševski (eds.), *The Right to Food, From Soft to Hard Law*, Utrecht: SIM (1984), pp. 97–111.

obligations over a certain period of time, which falls under the discretion of respective states. Alston argues that "free markets and private enterprise hold the key to economic and social rights in the wake of clear governmental failures in this domain".[2] Nolan notes that "even if one accepts that socio-economic rights are not, in fact, realizable in a specific society at a given time, this does not mean that they are merely aspirational goals".[3]

Socio-economic rights are generally not as enforceable as civil and political rights. Their enforcement differs from one to another domestic system.[4] However, in recent decades, Langford argues, "ESC rights have gained increased acceptance in international law and comparative jurisprudence. This is evident in an array of new treaties and resolutions and the adoption of international complaint mechanisms that cover ESC rights".[5] However, socio-economic rights have still, despite recognition, been treated as inferior, particularly to civil and political rights.[6] Alston argues that

> despite the rhetoric of indivisibility, both national and international endeavours to promote and protect economic and social rights are overshadowed by the assumption that while economic and social rights are desirable long-term social goals, they should not be treated as full-fledged human rights.[7]

However, at least in some jurisdictions socio-economic rights have been accepted as proper human rights protected by national courts. Riedel, Giacca and Golay have argued that "the broad normative framework of ESC rights has attained a high degree of specificity in terms of content as well as efficacy of implementation mechanisms, most importantly at the national level".[8]

2 UN, Human Rights Council, 'Report of the Special Rapporteur on Extreme Poverty and Human Rights: Philip Alston', UN Doc. A/HRC/32/31, 28 April 2016, para 18.
3 Aoife Nolan, *Children's Socio-Economic Rights, Democracy and the Courts*, Oxford: Hart Publishing (2011), p. 29.
4 Paul O'Connell, *Vindicating Socio-Economic Rights: International Standards and Comparative Experiences*, Abingdon: Routledge (2012).
5 Malcolm Langford, Wouter Vandenhole, Martin Scheinin and Willem Van Genugten, 'Introduction: An Emerging Field', *in* Malcolm Langford, Wouter Vandenhole, Martin Scheinin and Willem Van Genugten (eds.), *Global Justice, State Duties: The Extraterritorial Scope of Economic, Social and Cultural Rights in International Law*, Cambridge: Cambridge University Press (2013), pp. 3–31, 7.
6 Paul O'Connell, 'Vindicating Socio-Economic Rights'.
7 UN, Human Rights Council, 'Report of the Special Rapporteur on Extreme Poverty and Human Rights: Philip Alston', para 65.
8 Eibe Riedel, Gilles Giacca and Christophe Golay, 'Introduction: The Development of Economic, Social and Cultural Rights in International Law', *in* Eibe Riedel, Gilles Giacca and Christophe Golay (eds.), *Economic, Social and Cultural Rights in International Law: Contemporary Issues and Challenges*, Oxford: Oxford University Press (2014), pp. 3–50, p. 4. See also, Sandra Fredman, 'Human Rights Transformed: Positive Duties and Positive Rights', Oxford Legal Studies Research Paper No 38 (2006).

A question frequently arises: Who are the duty-bearers of socio-economic rights obligations? Previous chapters have illustrated that corporations can negatively or positively affect socio-economic rights.[9] If corporations can affect the enjoyment of socio-economic rights, are they also obliged to follow them? Do corporations have socio-economic obligations?[10] This chapter argues that corporations, not only states, carry some obligations under socio-economic rights. Human rights obligations are most commonly connected with the concept of jurisdiction.[11] Understandably, corporations do not possess sovereign territory and therefore their obligations are not of the same nature and scope as those of states. However, one can argue, as this chapter does, that corporations have both preventive as well as some remedial obligations concerning socio-economic rights, particularly where they exercise control and influence or in the proximity of their operations.[12]

This chapter follows a simple structure. The second section deals with the sources of law of corporate socio-economic rights obligations by examining national, international and corporate internal levels. The third section deals with the nature of corporate obligations concerning socio-economic rights. It examines their potential corporate negative and positive obligations and obligations to respect, protect and fulfil. It is often submitted that, despite obvious hurdles, corporations have obligations to respect, protect and fulfil socio-economic rights. Whereas the obligation to respect is a negative obligation, the obligations to protect and fulfil are positive obligations. One can argue that corporations have immediate obligations, at least regarding the negative obligation to respect socio-economic rights.[13] Such negative obligations ensure that corporations do not actively violate socio-economic rights and are not complicit in their violations.

The origins of corporate socio-economic rights obligations

Much about corporations and business and human rights has to do with the question: Who are the duty-bearers in the context of business and socio-economic

9 See, Chapter 1.

10 Jernej Letnar Černič, 'Corporate Responsibility for Human Rights: Towards a Pluralist Approach', *in* Wouter Vandenhole (ed.), *Challenging Territoriality in Human Rights Law: Building Blocks for a Plural and Diverse Duty-Bearer Regime*, Abingdon: Routledge (2015), pp. 69–89.

11 Wouter Vandenhole, 'Obligations and Responsibility in a Plural and Diverse Duty – Bearer Human Rights Regime', *in* Wouter Vandenhole (ed.), *Challenging Terroriality in Human Rights Law: Building Blocks for a Plural and Diverse Duty-Bearer Regime*, Abingdon: Routledge (2015), pp. 119–121.

12 Ibid.

13 Jernej Letnar Černič, 'Sovereign Financing and Corporate Responsibility for Economic and Social Rights', *in* Juan Pablo Bohoslavsky and Jernej Letnar Černič (eds.), *Making Sovereign Financing and Human Rights Work*, Oxford and Portland: Hart Publishing (2014), pp. 139–160.

rights? States, individuals and/or corporations? States have been traditionally not only primary, but also the only holder of obligations in the context of business and socio-economic rights. However, recent decades have identified several other actors that can also assume human rights obligations and complement state obligations. Human rights law still too often rests on the vertical relationship between state authorities and individuals, whereas national and international fora have been slow to recognize that human rights obligations also exist in horizontal relationships between private actors.[14] Developments in recent years have illustrated that this paradigm has been slowly disappearing and the plurality actors can contribute to the observance of human rights. Therefore, other actors can only complement the state as a duty-holder.[15] Seiderman and Khalfan have submitted that "business are obliged to respect rights first and foremost because states must, as a legal obligation as part of the duty to protect, make them respect human rights and hold them accountable for any dereliction".[16] Vandenhole and others have previously, perhaps somewhat over-optimistically, argued that "human rights law . . . becomes applicable to all actors that hold power or exercise power, regardless of the identity of the power holder".[17]

However, it is not only the power but also legal obligations that directly and indirectly bind corporations to comply with observing socio-economic rights. The UN Working Group on Business and Human Rights also notes that

> while business enterprises generally do not have legal obligations directly relating to human rights emanating from international instruments, they will often have legal obligations resulting from State laws that incorporate international standards, or contractual obligations with regard to respecting international standards.[18]

14 Jennifer Corrin, 'From Horizontal and Vertical to Lateral: Extending the Effect of Human Rights in Post Colonial Legal Systems of the South Pacific', 58(1) *International and Comparative Law Quarterly* 31 (2009), pp. 33, 34 and 67–70.

15 Surya Deva and David Bilchitz, 'The Human Rights Obligations of Business: A Critical Framework for the Future', *in* Surya Deva and David Bilchitz (eds.), *Human Rights Obligations of Business*, Cambridge: Cambridge University Press (2013), pp. 1–26. See also, Jernej Letnar Černič, *Human Rights Law and Business: Corporate Responsibility for Fundamental Human Rights*, Groningen: Europa Law Publishing (2010).

16 Ashfaq Khalfan and Ian Seiderman, 'Extraterritorial Human Rights Obligations: Wider Implications of the Maastricht Principles and the Continuing Accountability Challenge', *in* Wouter Vandenhole (ed.), *Challenging Territoriality in Human Rights Law: Building Blocks for a Plural and Diversive Duty-Bearer Regime*, Abingdon: Routledge (2015), pp. 15–43, p. 26.

17 Wouter Vandenhole, Gamze Erdem Türkelli and Rachel Hammonds, 'Reconceptualizing Human Rights Duty-Bearers', *in* Anja Mihr and Mark Gibney (eds.), *The Sage Handbook of Human Rights*, London: Sage (2014), pp. 1031–1044, 1036.

18 UN, General Assembly, 'Report of the Working Group on the Issue of Human Rights and Transnational Corporations and Other Business Enterprises', UN Doc. A68/279, 7 August 2013, para 19.

However, as will later be illustrated, international law can indirectly provide sources of corporate socio-economic rights obligations. In this context, Backer observes that "in the context of emerging complex non-State governance orders, a recognition of anarchy in governance might liberate norm production from State control and permit more active engagement directly by civil society elements".[19] However, corporations are also individual human rights duty-holders. That means that not only states but also corporations have direct and indirect obligations under socio-economic rights. In fact, corporate obligations depend on the plurality of duty-bearer settings, where there exists a variety of holders that complement each other. Corporate obligations under socio-economic rights here refer to substantive and procedural human rights obligations of corporations deriving from national, international and unilateral commitments by corporations themselves. The next sections therefore examine the existing and potential sources of corporate socio-economic rights obligations deriving from national legal systems, international law and corporate voluntary commitments.

Domestic legal systems

Socio-economic rights obligations of corporations can be primary found directly in domestic systems of human rights protections. They are located in constitutions, statutes and elsewhere. Most domestic constitutions now directly bind legal persons, including corporations, to uphold constitutional human rights obligations, including socio-economic rights.[20] Macklem argues, in this context that

> although international human rights instruments may have provided a common lexicon for their domestic entrenchment, the presence of social and economic rights in any given domestic constitutional order is more likely the function of its unique constitutional past and projected future than a lofty development in international human rights law.[21]

Several constitutions around the world refer to binding socio-economic obligations of corporations.[22] More specifically, they can be found at every continent. The International Commission of Jurists

> has found that in a number of countries domestic constitutional or human rights provisions do in fact provide for a direct cause of action against a

19 Larry Catá Backer, 'At the Second UN Forum on Business and Human Rights: Reflections on Bilchitz and Deva (eds.), "Human Rights Obligations of Business: Beyond the Corporate Responsibility to Respect?"' *Law at the End of the Day (Blog)*, 1 December 2013.

20 For further discussion see Jernej Letnar Černič, 'Corporate Responsibility for Human Rights: Towards a Pluralist Approach', pp. 79–82.

21 Patrick Macklem, *The Sovereignty of Human Rights*, Oxford: Oxford University Press (2015), p. 68.

22 See, Chapter 6.

> non-state actor, including companies or company officials, alleging that their conduct infringed a protected right.[23]

Alston observes on the basis of a study that

> over 90 per cent of the Constitutions recognized at least one economic and social right. In around 70 per cent of the Constitutions, at least one economic and social right was explicitly justiciable and around 25 per cent of them recognized 10 or more justiciable economic and social rights.[24]

The constitutional protections traditionally apply to natural and legal persons. Altogether, they provide perhaps the strongest basis for corporate obligations under the socio-economic rights.[25]

Corporate obligations derive their legitimacy and basis from the horizontal application of domestic and international human rights law. Traditionally, only states were obliged to observe them in their relationship with private actors. States have positive obligations to control the conduct of private actors.[26] However, it has now been accepted that human rights apply not only in vertical, but also in horizontal relationships between various non-state actors.[27] Further, one can concur here with Nolan, who argues that "horizontality is not necessarily incompatible with the presumptions underlying liberal constitutional theory".[28] Liberal democracies derive their legitimacy from the rule of law, which *inter alia* requires respect for human rights, not only from state authorities, or actors with a state nexus, but also from private actors. The horizontal application of human rights law is therefore based in the components of the rule of law deriving its legitimacy from the people. However, even though human rights law has a horizontal nature, it is enforced through state apparatuses (see Figure 5.1).

23 International Commission of Jurists (ICJ), 'Corporate Complicity and Legal Accountability, Volume 3: Civil Remedies', Expert Legal Panel on Corporate Complicity in International Crimes, Geneva, September 2008, p. 7.

24 UN, Human Rights Council, 'Report of the Special Rapporteur on Extreme Poverty and Human Rights: Philip Alston', para 33.

25 Jernej Letnar Černič, *Human Rights Law and Business: Corporate Responsibility for Fundamental Human Rights*, Groningen: Europa Law Publishing (2010). See also, Sandra Liebenberg, 'The Protection of Economic and Social Rights in Domestic Legal Systems', *in* Asbjørn Eide, Catarina Krause and Allan Rosas (eds.), *Economic, Social and Cultural Rights: A Textbook*, Dordrecht, Boston and London: Martinus Nijhoff Publishers (2001), pp. 55–84.

26 Angus Campbell, 'Positive Obligations Under the ECHR: Deprivation of Liberty by Private Actors', 10(3) *Edinburgh Law Review* 399 (2006).

27 András Sajó and Renáta Uitz, *Constitutional Topography: Values and Constitutions*, Utrecht: Eleven International Publishing (2005), pp. 33–53.

28 Aoife Nolan, 'Holding Non-State Actors to Account for Constitutional Economic and Social Rights Violations: Experiences and Lessons from South Africa and Ireland', 12(1) *International Journal of Constitutional Law* 61, 65 (2014).

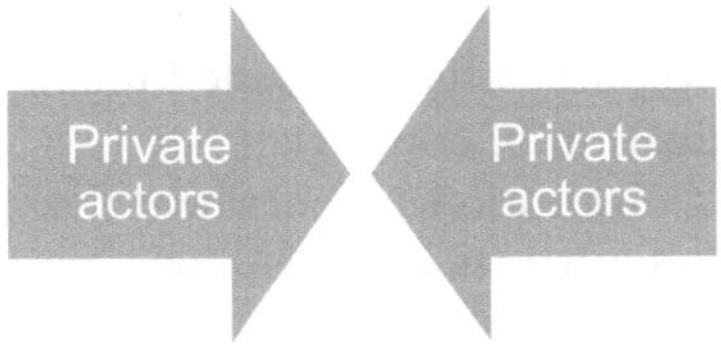

Figure 5.1 Horizontal human rights application between private actors
(Source: author's own work)

Several domestic constitutions provide for horizontal application of human rights. For instance, the Constitution of Slovenia, which applies to both natural and legal persons, provides in Article 70a that "Everyone has the right to drinking water".[29] The Constitution of the Republic of South Africa provides that "provision of the Bill of Rights binds a natural or a juristic person if and to the extent that, it is applicable, taking into account the nature of the right and the nature of any duty imposed by the right".[30] Further, Section 9(4) places an obligation on private actors not to discriminate against others.[31] This provision has been the subject of judicial interpretation which has recognized a number of (in)direct obligations upon corporations. In this way, the Constitutional Court of South Africa has interpreted such provisions as to impose several socio-economic obligations on corporations, including obligations under the right to access to water,[32] right to health[33] and social security.[34] In such cases, it indirectly confirmed this horizontal application of human rights in relationships between private actors. Similarly, the Kenyan Constitution of 2010 confirms that "the Bill of Rights applies to all and binds all State organs and all persons",[35] which includes juridical persons. Even jurisdictions such as the United Kingdom that do not expressly recognize legal human rights responsibilities of corporate entities place a fiduciary duty on directors

29 Constitution of the Republic of Slovenia, Official Gazette RS Nos. 33/91-I, 42/97, 66/00, 24/03, 69/04, 68/06, and 47/13.
30 Constitution of South Africa (1996), Section 8(2).
31 Ibid., chapter 2, section 9(4).
32 *Mazibuko and Others v City of Johannesburg and Others*, CCT 39/09 (Constitutional Court of South Africa), 8 October 2009. Peter Danchin, 'A Human Right to Water? The South African Constitutional Court's Decision in the Mazibuko Case', *EJIL: Talk!* 13 January 2010.
33 *Soobramoney v Minister of Health*, CCT 32/97 (Constitutional Court of South Africa), 27 November 1997. *Minister of Health v Treatment Action Campaign*, CCT 8/02 (Constitutional Court of South Africa), 5 July 2002.
34 *Fose v Minister of Safety and Security*, CCT14/96 (Constitutional Court of South Africa), 5 June 1997.
35 The Constitution of Kenya, 27 August 2010, Section 20(1), http://www.refworld.org/docid/4c8508822.html (last accessed 28 May 2018).

to consider the impact of their decisions on the community and the environment[36] and to produce reports which include human rights questions, which can be described as obligation of conduct.[37]

Equally, the German Constitutional Court held that basic rights apply also in private relationships. It held that the constitutional

> system of values, centering on the freedom of the human being to develop in society, must apply as a constitutional axiom throughout the whole legal system: it must direct and inform legislation, administration and judicial decision. It naturally influences private law as well; no rule of private law may conflict with it.[38]

Further, international human rights bodies have clearly expressed that socio-economic rights also apply in horizontal relationships between private actors.[39] Similarly, De Schutter observes that "national institutions, including national courts, routinely apply international human rights norms directly to the acts of private parties: there should be no obstacle in principle to allow this to develop at the international level".[40] All actors that operate in a given society are obliged to respect human rights, including socio-economic human rights. Private relationships are governed by private law, but they are constrained by the constitutional and administrative rules of public law.[41] However, as rightly observed by Aharon Barak, former judge of the Supreme Court of Israel, "where constitutional provisions do not contain limitations clauses regarding the restriction of one person's right arising from the right of another, the obvious result is that judges will

36 United Kingdom Companies Act 2006 (c. 46), section 172.

37 Ibid., see section 414C concerning obligatory strategic reports concerning environmental, social, community and human rights issues.

38 Lüth case, BVerfGE 7, 198 (1 BvR 400/51), 15 January 1958: German Case: Foreign Law Translations, University of Texas, Translated by Tony Weir, https://law.utexas.edu/transnational/foreign-law-translations/german/case.php?id=1369 (last accessed 19 January 2018). See also, Matej Avbelj, 'Is There Drittwirkung in EU Law?' *in* András Sajó and Renáta Uitz (eds.), *The Constitution in Private Relations: Expanding Constitutionalism*, Utrecht: Eleven International Publishing (2005), pp. 145–163.

39 UN, Human Rights Committee (HRC), 'General Comment 31, The Nature of the General Legal Obligation on States Parties to the Covenant', UN Doc. CCPR/C/21/Rev.1/Add.13, 26 May 2004, para 8.

40 Olivier De Schutter, *International Human Rights Law*, Cambridge: Cambridge University Press (2010), p. 395. See also, UN, OHCHR, 'Business and Human Rights: A Survey of NHRI Practices', 23 May 2008, www.reports-and-materials.org/OHCHR-National-Human-Rights-Institutions-practices-Apr-2008.doc (last accessed 19 January 2018). OECD Watch, Remedy Remains Rare (2015), www.oecdwatch.org/publications-en/Publication_4201 (last accessed 19 January 2018), highlighting the inadequacies of the OECD National Contact Point system.

41 Brice Dickson, 'The Horizontal Application of Human Rights Law', *in* Angela Hegarty and Siobhan Leonard (eds.), *Human Rights: An Agenda for the 21st Century*, London and Sydney: Cavendish Publishing Limited, 1999, pp. 59–78.

have to create judicial limitations clauses".[42] However, one can hardly object to corporate obligations under socio-economic rights, as they are part of "objective system of values" enshrined in domestic law. Therefore, corporations have both negative and positive obligations to comply with socio-economic rights.

Constitutional obligations are usually concurred on by specialized statutes, which in some instances and in some states bind corporations to comply with socio-economic rights. For instance, several domestic legislations provide evidence of corporate socio-economic rights obligations, which indirectly derive from administrative, criminal and civil levels. CESCR noted in General Comment no. 24 that

> there are . . . a large number of domestic laws designed to protect specific economic, social and cultural rights, that apply directly to business entities, such as in the areas of non-discrimination, health-care provision, education, the environment, employment relations and consumer safety.[43]

In France, the statute on the duty of care of parent and subcontracting companies entered into force on 24 March 2017.[44] It obliges corporations to report and ensure reasonable care measures to conduct due diligence throughout their supply chains. Further illustrations of binding obligations of corporations that also relate to socio-economic rights can be also found in the US Foreign Corrupt Practices Act[45] and the UK Bribery Act,[46] which aim to eliminate corrupt practices of businesses when doing business abroad and which may result in socio-economic rights violations. Further, the Dodd-Frank Wall Street Reform and Consumer Protection Act (2010) states that corporations in the United States are under Section 1502 obliged to submit annual disclosures to the Securities and Exchange Commission concerning whether any minerals they source originated in the Democratic Republic of Congo or an adjoining country. More specifically, Section 1504 requires extractive companies to annually make public "any payment made by the issuer, a subsidiary, or an entity under its control to a foreign government or the federal government for the purpose of the commercial development of oil, natural gas, or minerals".[47] Further, the Transparency in Supply Chains Act (2015) in California requires medium and large companies to disclose their initiatives to eradicate slavery and human trafficking from their

42 Aharon Barak, 'Constitutional Human Rights and Private Law', *in* Dan Friedmann and Daphne Barak-Erez (eds.), *Human Rights in Private Law*, Oxford: Hart Publishing (2002), pp. 1–42, p. 17.

43 UN, CESCR, 'General Comment No. 24 (2017) on State Obligations Under the International Covenant on Economic, Social and Cultural Rights in the Context of Business Activities', UN Doc. E/C.12/GC/24, 10 August 2017, para 4.

44 Law no. 2017-399, National Assembly (France), Relating to the Duty of Vigilance of the Parent Companies and the Companies Giving Orders, 27 March 2017.

45 Foreign Corrupt Practices Act (1977), amended 15 U.S. Code § 78dd-1.

46 Bribery Act (UK, 2010), section 23.

47 Dodd-Frank Wall Street Reform and Consumer Protection Act (2010), H.R. 4173.

supply chains.[48] The United Kingdom has also passed the Modern Slavery Act (2015) which, among other things, requires corporations to produce a statement on slavery and human trafficking in their annual report.[49] All these statutes impose reporting requirements and indirectly provide evidence of emerging socio-economic obligations despite valid criticisms of how effective reporting mechanisms are. Indirect corporate socio-economic obligations can be also found in domestic civil law.[50] Several domestic systems include corporate criminal responsibility for crimes against humanity and war crimes.[51] For instance, the French Criminal Code states that "legal persons may incur criminal liability for crimes against humanity pursuant to the conditions set out under Article 121–2".[52] All in all, domestic systems directly and indirectly provide sources for corporate obligations under socio-economic rights.

International layer

International law sources grant a secondary level for indirect corporate obligations concerning socio-economic rights. International law already imposes in different areas indirect human rights obligations on corporations, although it is certainly correct that it suffers due to the lack of binding enforcement fora.[53] Corporations are already now obliged to observe international protections of socio-economic rights, including the ICESCR.[54] Moreover, one should certainly not underestimate the international landscape on business and human rights, for example the importance of the initiatives for the binding UN Treaty on Business and Human Rights for development on national levels.[55] Carrillo-Santarelli

48 See for further information, Kamala D. Harris, 'The California Transparency in Supply Chains Act: A Resource Guide', 2015.

49 Modern Slavery Act UK, 26 March 2015 (c. 30), http://www.legislation.gov.uk/ukpga/2015/30/pdfs/ukpga_20150030_en.pdf (last accessed 19 January 2018). See also, Business and Human Rights Resource Centre, 'UK Modern Slavery Act', https://business-humanrights.org/en/uk-modern-slavery-act (last accessed 19 January 2018).

50 See for example, *Association France-Palestine Solidarité v. Société Alstom Transport SA*, Judgment, Court of Appeal Versailles, 22 March 2013.

51 Amnesty International & International Corporate Accountability Roundtable, The Corporate Crimes Principles: Advancing Investigations and Prosecutions in Human Rights Cases, 6 Oct 2016.

52 Criminal Code of the French Republic, Act no. 2000-647, 10 July, Art. 8, Official Journal, 11 July 2000, Article 213 (3).

53 See for a detailed discussion, Jernej Letnar Černič, 'An Elephant in a Room of Porcelain: Establishing Corporate Responsibility for Human Rights', *in* Jernej Letnar Černič and Tara van Ho (eds.), *Human Rights and Business: Direct Corporate Accountability for Human Rights*, Oisterwijk: Wolf Legal Publishers (2015), pp. 131–158, pp. 144–149. Jernej Letnar Černič, 'Corporate Responsibility for Human Rights: Towards a Pluralist Approach', pp. 75–79.

54 UN, CESCR, General comment No. 24, para 5.

55 Olivier De Schutter, 'Towards a New Treaty on Business and Human Rights', 1(1) *Business and Human Rights Journal* 41 (2016). David Bilchitz, 'The Necessity for a Business and Human Rights Treaty', 1(2) *Business and Human Rights Journal* 203 (2016).

rightly argues that "since corporations have the factual capacity to violate human rights, an individual- and victim-centred international law (as it ought to be) must permit and require the full protection of all victims".[56] An actor in the international arena does not need to become a state party of human rights treaties in order for them to bind it.[57] Several non-state actors can be indirectly, through states, bound by obligations. In this respect, Clapham observes that it "makes sense to talk about the parties to a human rights treaty rather than use the expression States parties, which indicates that states are exclusive members of every human rights regime".[58] Moreover, several international treaties already impose obligations on corporations.[59] The UN Working Group on Business and Human Rights mentioned in its 2013 report that corporations have "duties and responsibilities".[60] It added "that companies have a responsibility to respect human rights".[61]

Moreover, the UN Human Rights Council adopted the UN Guiding Principles on Business and Human Rights in June 2011 by "consensuses".[62] The UN Guiding Principles are structured in three parts: state responsibility to protect, corporate responsibility for human rights and access to remedy.[63] They can be described as a soft law international document, which nonetheless provides evidence of international legal obligations of corporations as to all human

56 Nicolás Carrillo-Santarelli, 'Corporate Human Rights Obligations: Controversial but Necessary', Business and Human Rights Resource Center, November 2016, https://business-humanrights.org/en/corporate-human-rights-obligations-controversial-but-necessary (last accessed 19 January 2018).

57 See, Jernej Letnar Černič, 'Corporate Responsibility for Human Rights: Towards a Pluralist Approach', pp. 76–77.

58 Andrew Clapham, *Human Rights Obligations of Non-State Actors*, Oxford: Oxford University Press (2006), p. 91.

59 Convention on Civil Liability for Damage Resulting from Activities Dangerous to the Environment, Treaty No. 150, Council of Europe, 21 June 1993, art. 6(1); International Convention on Civil Liability for Oil Pollution Damage, 973 UNTS 3, 29 November 1969, art. 3(1); Convention on the Third Party Liability in the Field of Nuclear Energy, 956 UNTS 251, Paris 29 July 1960; Convention Relating to Civil Liability in the field of Maritime Carriage of Nuclear Material, 974 UNTS 255, Brussels 17 December 1971; OECD Convention on Combating Bribery of Foreign Public Officials in International Business Transactions, S. Treaty Doc. 105-43, 37 ILM 1, 18 December 1997.

60 UN, Human Rights Council, 'Report of the Working Group on the Issue of Human Rights and Transnational Corporations and other Business Enterprises', A/HRC/23/32, 14 March 2013, para 69.

61 Ibid., para 14.

62 Surya Deva, 'Treating Human Rights Lightly: A Critique of the Consensus Rhetoric and the Language Employed by the Guiding Principles', *in* Surya Deva and David Bilchitz (eds.), *Human Rights Obligations of Business: Beyond the Corporate Responsibility to Respect?* Cambridge: Cambridge University Press (2013), pp. 78–104.

63 UN, Human Rights Council, 'Report of the Special Representative of the Secretary General on the Issue of Human Rights and Transnational Corporations and Other Business Enterprises', John Ruggie, 'Guiding Principles on Business and Human Rights: Implementing the United Nations "Protect, Respect and Remedy" Framework' ['The Guiding Principles'], UN Doc. A/HRC/17/31, 21 March 2011, principles 1–2.

rights. Despite such consensus, only 19 states have so far adopted National Action Plans to implement the UN Guiding Principles.[64] Several more quasi-legal international instruments such as the OECD Guidelines for Multinational Enterprises,[65] the UN Global Compact[66] and the ILO Tripartite Declaration[67] illustrate the corporations may have human rights, including socio-economic obligations at international stage. The OECD Guidelines for Multinational Enterprises advise multinational enterprises to "respect the human rights of those affected by their activities consistent with the host government's international obligations and commitments".[68] The Commentary to the Guidelines appears to suggest that enterprises have an obligation to respect human rights because "respect for human rights is the global standard of expected conduct for enterprises".[69]

Additionally, for some years discussion have been proceeding on the proposed UN Treaty on Business and Human Rights, which could provide direct binding obligations for corporations[70] and clarify already existing obligations. The UN Working Group has so far held three session and recently also published elements of the treaty; however it remains to be seen if the consensus will be formed in the next years to adopt the treaty.[71] Moreover, several developments in the European and Inter-American regional human system suggest that corporations have some (in)direct obligations.[72]

Moreover, several international human rights bodies have in recent years recognized the horizontal application of human rights in private relationships and corresponding obligations of states to protect individuals in such relationships.

64 Business and Human Rights Resource Centre, National Action Plans, www.business-humanrights.org/en/un-guiding-principles/implementation-tools-examples/implementation-by-governments/by-type-of-initiative/national-action-plans (last accessed 19 January 2018).

65 OECD Guidelines for Multinational Enterprises (2011 Edition).

66 UN Global Compact, www.unglobalcompact.org/ (last accessed 19 January 2018).

67 ILO, 'Tripartite Declaration of Principles Concerning Multinational Enterprises and Social Policy', 83 *ILO Official Bulletin* (2000). See also, UN, Commission on Human Rights, 'Norms on the Responsibilities of Transnational Corporations and Other Business Enterprises with Regard to Human Rights', UN Doc. E/CN.4/Sub.2/2003/12/Rev.2, 26 August 2003.

68 OECD Guidelines for Multinational Enterprises (2000), p. 14.

69 OECD Guidelines for Multinational Enterprises (2011 Edition), p. 32.

70 See in details, Jernej Letnar Černič and Nicolas Carrillo-Santarelli (eds.), *The Future of Business and Human Rights*, Cambridge: Intersentia (2018).

71 UN, Human Rights Council, 'Elaboration of an International Legally Binding Instrument on Transnational Corporations and Other Business Enterprises with Respect to Human Rights', A/HRC/26/L.22/Rev.1, 25 June 2014. See for example, Humberto Cant Cantú Rivera, 'Negotiating a Treaty on Business and Human Rights: The Early Stages', 40(3) *UNSW Law Journal Volume* 1200 (2017).

72 Jernej Letnar Černič, 'Towards a Holistic Approach to Business and Human Rights in the European Union', 10(1) *Human Rights and International Legal Discourse* 160 (2016). Humberto Cantú Rivera, *Derechos Humanos y Empresas: Reflexiones desde América Latina*, San José: Instituto Interamericano de Derechos Humanos (2017).

For instance, CESCR observed in "Concluding Observations on Canada" (2016) that

> it recommends that the State party strengthen its legislation governing the conduct of corporations registered or domiciled in the State party in their activities abroad . . . It also recommends that the State party introduce effective mechanisms to investigate complaints filed against these corporations and adopt the necessary legislative measures so as to facilitate access to justice before domestic courts by victims of these corporations' conduct.[73]

Similarly, CESCR recommended in "Concluding Observations on Netherlands" (2017) that states should

> (a) Include a formal monitoring mechanism in the national action plan on business and human rights; . . . (b) Take measures to ensure compliance with human rights obligations for companies operating on the territory of the State party; . . . (e) Remove the legal and practical obstacles to holding companies domiciled under the State party's jurisdiction accountable for violations of economic, social and cultural rights, resulting from their operations on the national territory or abroad.[74]

In 2016, CESCR urged the United Kingdom to "establish a clear regulatory framework for companies operating in the State party to ensure that their activities do not negatively affect the enjoyment of economic, social and cultural human rights".[75]

The Committee on the Rights of the Child (CRC) has noted in General Comment no. 16 that "home States have (human rights) obligations . . . in the context of businesses' extraterritorial activities and operations, provided that there is a reasonable link between the State and the conduct concerned".[76] Further, CERD noted in 2012 in its concluding observations on Australia that

> with concern the absence of a legal framework regulating the obligation of Australian corporations at home and overseas whose activities, notably in

73 UN, CESCR, 'Concluding Observations: Canada', UN Doc. E/C.12/CAN/CO/6, 23 March 2016, para 16.

74 UN, CESCR, 'Concluding Observations: Netherlands', UN Doc. E/C.12/NLD/CO/6, 6 July 2017, para 16. See also, UN, 'Human Rights Committee, Concluding Observations: Canada', UN Doc. CCPR/C/CAN/CO6, 13 August 2015, para 6; UN, 'Human Rights Committee, Concluding Observations: Germany', UN Doc. CCPR/C/DEU/CO/6, 12 November 2012, para 16.

75 UN, CESCR, 'Concluding Observations: United Kingdom of Great Britain and Northern Ireland', UN Doc. E/C.12/GBR/CO/6, 14 July 2016, para 12 (a).

76 UN, Committee on Rights of the Child, 'General Comment No. 16 on State Obligations Regarding the Impact of the Business Sector on Children's Rights', U.N. Doc. CRC/C/GC/16, 17 April 2013, para 43.

> the extractive sector, when carried out on the traditional territories of Indigenous peoples, have had a negative impact on Indigenous peoples' rights to land, health, living environment and livelihoods.[77]

and urged it to "regulate the extraterritorial activities of Australian corporations abroad".[78] All in all, international human rights bodies agree that socio-economic rights apply also in horizontal relationships between private actors. Therefore, several international sources provide for indirect imposition of socio-economic rights obligations on corporations through state obligations. Corporations already now have obligations to respect socio-economic rights deriving from domestic law and indirectly from international law. Moreover, quasi-legal documents offer further evidence of socio-economic rights obligations of corporations.

Voluntary commitments

Voluntary commitments, either by individual corporations and or in sectors, may also contribute to corporate obligations concerning socio-economic rights. They can be found in internal corporate human rights policies or in codes of conduct. The United Nations defines human rights policy as

> a public statement adopted by the company's highest governing authority committing the company to respect international human rights standards and to do so by having policies and processes in place to identify, prevent or mitigate human rights risks, and remediate any adverse impact it has caused or contributed to.[79]

Further, the ILO describes it as "a written policy, or statement of principles, intended to serve as the basis for a commitment to particular enterprise conduct".[80] Several corporations affirm in their human rights policies that they respect socio-economic rights. For instance, PepsiCo notes that

77 UN, Committee on the Elimination of Racial discrimination, 'Concluding Observations: Australia', CERD/C/AUS/CO/15-17, 13 September 2010, para 13. See also, UN, Committee on the Elimination of Racial discrimination, 'Concluding Observations: United Kingdom of Great Britain and Northern Ireland', CERD/C/GBR/CO/18-20, 14 September 2011, para 29.

78 Ibid.

79 Lucy Amis, 'A Guide for Business: How to Develop a Human Rights Policy', 2011, p. 4. See also, Jernej Letnar Černič, *Human Rights Law and Business: Corporate Responsibility for Fundamental Human Rights*, Groningen: Europa Law Publishing (2010), pp. 43–46.

80 ILO, Working Party on the Social Dimensions of the Liberalization of International Trade, 'Overview of Global Developments and Office Activities Concerning Codes of Conduct, Social Labeling and Other Private Sector Initiatives Addressing Labour Issues: Executive Summary', GB.273/WP/SDL/1, November 1998, para 26.

> In 2009, we publicly committed to respecting water as a basic human right. Our understanding what it means to respect the human right to water in practice continues to evolve, as we aim to improve our water use without compromising the ability of others to enjoy their human right to water.[81]

Unilever states that "we base our human rights policy commitment on the International Bill of Human Rights (consisting of the Universal Declaration of Human Rights, the International Covenant on Civil and Political Rights and the International Covenant on Economic, Social and Cultural Rights)".[82] Further, Kellogg Corporation provides that

> social accountability and responsible sourcing are fundamental parts of our daily activities and enable Kellogg to deliver sustainable and dependable growth year after year. Kellogg Company is committed to respecting human rights in accordance with international standards like the International Labour Organization, U.N. Guiding Principles and the Universal Declaration of Human Rights.[83]

The text of such human policy statements is quite promising, but the legal nature is questionable and they can be best described as *lex imperfecta*,[84] as they do not provide sanctions for violations. Therefore, their value for victims enforcing their socio-economic rights is low, as they mostly do not provide legal basis for claims. Victims can in the best-case scenario count on the internal grievance mechanisms of corporations.

Interim conclusion

All in all, one can conclude that corporate socio-economic rights obligations derive from national, regional and international levels. Socio-economic rights obligations of corporations derive from different levels, mostly indirectly, but also directly in some cases. Additionally, voluntary commitments of corporations themselves appear to provide another illustration of corporate commitments to socio-economic rights. Such analysis contributes to the understanding that state socio-economic rights obligations are not unique, but are complemented by those of several non-state actors and corporations, which differ from them in extent and nature. All in all, the plurality of normative structures illustrates that corporations, as one of the most influential actors in local and global societies, carry their part of obligations to ensure the provision of socio-economic rights.

81 PepsiCo, 'Global Human Rights Statement', June 2017.

82 Unilever's Human Rights Policy Statement, 2017, https://www.unilever.com/Images/unilever-human-rights-policy-statement_tcm244-422954_en.pdf (last accessed 19 Janaury 2018) p. 1.

83 Kellogg Company, 'Human Rights Position Statement', 1 December 2016.

84 Imperfect legal norm, which does not provide sanctions.

The legal characteristics, nature and scope of corporate socio-economic rights obligations

What is the nature and scope of corporate obligations under socio-economic human rights? Are they of the same nature and scope as state obligations? Where do they apply? On the territory where corporations operate or beyond? They differ, particularly as far positive obligations go, from state obligations under socio-economic rights in their extent and nature.[85] Whereas states have obligations to respect, protect and fulfil socio-economic rights, the nature of corporate socio-economic obligations is not that clear cut, definitive and full fledged.

The nature and scope of corporate socio-economic rights obligations

Corporations have negative and positive obligations concerning socio-economic rights. They are obliged not to directly infringe on socio-economic rights, but also to adopt active measures to guarantee their provision. However, the nature and scope of corporate socio-economic rights obligations differs from state obligations. States are primarily obliged to guarantee at the least the minimum core of socio-economic rights given their territorial sovereignty, as well as their monopoly to collect tax revenues and to decide how to allocate budgetary resources, which provide financial sources for the provision of socio-economic rights.[86] Certainly, state-owned corporations or those private corporations with licenses and concessions to deliver public services have wider obligations to uphold socio-economic rights, which can be almost compared with state obligations.

Therefore, corporations are first asked to observe them within their corporate groups and in the local communities where they operate.[87] It is submitted that this substantive standard of proximity or closeness should be employed when determining the scope of the corporate socio-economic rights obligations (see Figure 5.2). Second, corporations are obliged to follow procedural standards when conducting due diligence throughout their supply chains. De Schutter argues in this context that

> imposing on corporations certain obligations in the area of economic and social rights is thus justified theoretically, where they exercise a command

85 Brigit C. A. Toebes and Jernej Letnar Černič, 'Corporate Human Rights Obligations Under Economic, Social, and Cultural Rights', *in* Jeffrey F. Addicott, Md Jahid Hossain Bhuiyan, Tareq M.R. Chowdhury (eds.), *Globalization, International Law and Human Rights*, Oxford: Oxford University Press (2012), pp. 1–33.

86 CESCR, General Comment 3, The nature of States parties' obligations (Fifth session, 1990), U.N. Doc. E/1991/23, annex III at 86 (1991).

87 Allan Rosas and Martin Scheinin, 'Categories and Beneficiaries of Human Rights', *in* Raija Hanski and Markku Suksi (eds.), *An Introduction to the International Protection of Human Rights: A Textbook*, Turku: Åbo Akademi University, Institute for Human Rights (2nd Revised Edition, 2004), pp. 49–62; Jernej Letnar Černič, 'State Obligations Concerning Indigenous Peoples' Rights to Their Ancestral Lands: Lex Imperfecta?', 28 *American University International Law Review* 1129 (2013).

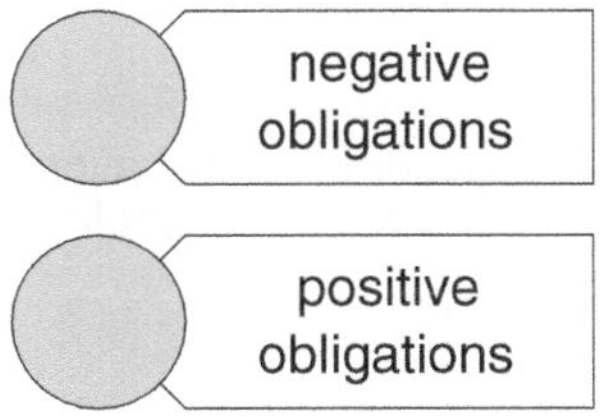

Figure 5.2 Positive and negative socio-economic rights obligations of corporations
(Source: author's own work)

> over goods or resources that are essential to the enjoyment of those rights (whether as a result of the position they acquired in the market or whether by decree).[88]

States are obliged to ensure that state-owned corporations and those private corporations with concessions respect, protect and fulfil socio-economic rights.

Corporate obligations in the area of socio-economic rights can be first described within a negative and positive dichotomy. Thereafter, they are often also explained with the tripartite approach of obligations to respect, protect and respect socio-economic rights (see Figure 5.3).[89] Negative obligations of corporations oblige them to respect socio-economic rights and avoid directly interfering with them, whereas positive obligations include obligations to protect and fulfil the reasonable minimum core of socio-economic rights.[90] The tripartite approach appears to be the most appropriate to describe and analyze the nature and scope of corporate obligations concerning socio-economic rights, as it covers all dimensions of corporate conduct and operations from its own business operations, including employee relations to their relationships with suppliers, contractors, distributors and the wider community. It covers both positive and negative obligations and the obligations of result and conduct.

88 Olivier De Schutter, 'Corporations and Economic, Social and Cultural Rights', *in* Eibe Riedel, Gilles Giacca and Christophe Golay (eds.), *Economic, Social, and Cultural Rights in International Law: Contemporary Issues and Challenges*, Oxford: Oxford University Press (2014), pp. 193–224, p. 217.

89 Asbjørn Eide, 'Realization of Social and Economic Rights and the Minimum Threshold Approach', 10 *Human Rights Law Journal* 35 (1989). See, UN, Commission on Human Rights, 'The Right to Adequate Food and to Be Free from Hunger – Updated Study on the Right to Food, submitted by Asbjørn Eide', UN Doc. E/CN.4/Sub.2/1999/12, 28 June 1999. Oliver de Schutter, International Human Rights, pp. 241–257. Allan Rosas and Martin Scheinin, 'Categories and Beneficiaries of Human Rights', *in* Raija Hanski and Markku Suksi (eds.), *An Introduction to the International Protection of Human Rights: A Textbook*, Turku: Åbo Akademi University, Institute for Human Rights (2nd Revised Edition, 2004).

90 Jernej Letnar Černič, *Human Rights Law and Business: Corporate Responsibility for Fundamental Human Rights*, Groningen: Europa Law Publishing (2010).

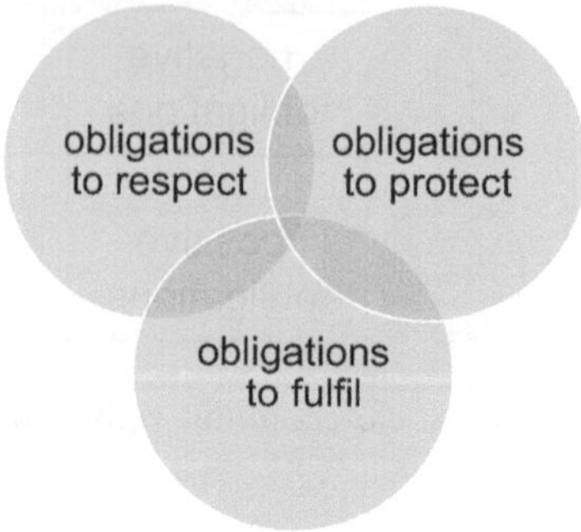

Figure 5.3 Tripartite obligations of corporations concerning socio-economic rights (Source: author's own work)

Which is the most appropriate way to measure socio-economic rights? The former special rapporteur for the right to education, Katarina Tomaševski, has developed criteria to measure the implementation of socio-economic rights through a 4As model (first in relation to the right to education, but later, *mutatis mutandis*, translated to most socio-economic rights, with some changes). The model includes availability, accessibility, acceptability and adaptability of socio-economic rights. The CESCR has explained the model on the right to education in the following way: availability – "functioning educational institutions and programmes have to be available in sufficient quantity"; accessibility – "educational institutions and programmes have to be accessible to everyone, without discrimination"; acceptability – "the form and substance of education, including curricula and teaching methods, have to be acceptable (e.g. relevant, culturally appropriate and of good quality) to students and, in appropriate cases, parents"; and adaptability – "education has to be flexible so it can adapt to the needs of changing societies and communities and respond to the needs of students within their diverse social and cultural settings".[91] It explains that an individual rights-holder has several entitlements as to socio-economic rights. For instance, De Schutter argues that "4A's' describe the characteristics of the good of service that the individual right-holder has a right to".[92] Importantly, it appears that there is not a consistent approach to indicators, as some international human rights bodies prefer the "AAAQ" framework, which includes availability, accessibility, acceptability and quality.[93] Nonetheless, 3As of the AAAQ model serve as a counterpart to the obligations to respect, protect and

91 UN, CESCR, 'General Comment No. 13: The Right to Education', UN Doc. E/C.12/1999/10, 8 December 1999, para 6(d).

92 Olivier De Schutter, *International Human Rights Law*, Cambridge: Cambridge University Press (2010), p. 256.

93 The Danish Institute for Human Rights, 'The AAAQ Framework and the Right to Water: International indicators', 2014.

fulfil socio-economic rights since it measures their realization. Such models could be instrumental in measuring how states and corporations comply with their obligations to respect, protect and fulfil socio-economic rights, which are described in the next section.

Corporate obligation to respect socio-economic rights

The corporate obligation to respect is in essence a negative obligation which requires corporations not to interfere with individuals' socio-economic rights with their direct or indirect actions.[94] The UN Guiding Principles on Business and Human Rights are based on the three pillars of the "protect, respect and remedy" framework.[95] The UN Guiding Principles on business and human rights cautiously provide in Principle 11 that corporations "should respect human rights", which "means that they should avoid infringing on the human rights of others and should address adverse human rights impacts with which they are involved".[96] Its Commentary nonetheless observes that such corporate obligation "exists independently of States' abilities and/or willingness to fulfil their own human rights obligations and does not diminish those obligations. And it exists over and above compliance with national laws and regulations protecting human rights".[97] It adds that "because business enterprises can have an impact on virtually the entire spectrum of internationally recognized human rights, their responsibility to respect applies to all such rights".[98] Vandenhole critically observes that "the Guiding Principles evoke a weak corporate responsibility to respect human rights",[99] As it does not derive from legal sources, but on societal expectations,[100] which thereby "is not an obligation under international human rights law imposed

94 Jernej Letnar Černič, 'Sovereign Financing and Corporate Responsibility for Economic and Social Rights', *in* Juan Pablo Bohoslavsky and Jernej Letnar Černič (eds.), *Making Sovereign Financing and Human Rights Work*, Oxford and Portland: Hart Publishing (2014), pp. 152–154.

95 The Guiding Principles; Nicola Jägers, 'UN Guiding Principles on Business and Human Rights: Making Headway Towards Real Corporate Accountability?', 29(2) *Netherlands Quarterly of Human Rights* 159 (2011). See also, Claire Methven O'Brien, Amol Mehra, Sara Blackwell and Cathrine Bloch Poulsen-Hansen, 'National Action Plans: Current Status and Future Prospects for a New Business and Human Rights Governance Tool', 1(1) *Business and Human Rights Journal* 117 (2015). Damiano de Felice and Andreas Graf, 'The Potential of National Action Plans to Implement Human Rights Norms: An Early Assessment with Respect to the UN Guiding Principles on Business and Human Rights', 7(1) *Journal of Human Rights Practice* 40 (2015).

96 Ibid., p. 11.

97 The Guiding Principles, Principle 11, commentary.

98 The Guiding Principles, Principle 12, commentary.

99 Wouter Vandenhole, 'Emerging Normative Frameworks on Transnational Human Rights Obligations', EUI Working Paper RSCAS 2012/17, p. 12.

100 The Guiding Principles, principle 12; John Gerard Ruggie, 'Regulating Multinationals: The UN Guiding Principles, Civil Society, and International Legalization', 2015 Regulatory Policy Program Working Paper RPP-2015-04, p. 3.

directly upon companies".[101] Further, several other international documents state that corporations already have human rights obligations.[102]

The corporate obligation to respect requires corporations not to interfere with the socio-economic rights of individuals. In short, corporations are obliged not to violate individuals' socio-economic rights and cause any harm to individuals. Corporations are therefore prohibited from interfering with availability, accessibility, acceptability, quality and adaptability of right to education, food, health, housing, water and other socio-economic rights of individuals. It is a negative obligation, which is divided into preventive and remedial parts. The former part does not impose any obligations on corporations to take up any active measures. It only requires corporations not to violate or be involved in human rights violations in complicity with state or other private actors.

The preventive part of the obligation to respect would require corporate actors to adopt comprehensive human rights policies and conduct human rights impact assessments and due diligence before taking on a new investment and production projects.[103] They have to make sure that the project will not deteriorate socio-economic livelihoods and people's capabilities to ensure decent livelihoods for themselves and their families. In this context, it would require them to realize the right to prior, free and informed consent of local communities, Indigenous peoples and other vulnerable communities to obtain their opinions on the potential positive, but also adverse, implications of the proposed project. If the investment project will interfere with people's socio-economic livelihoods, corporations would have to offer them similar living conditions somewhere else. Their activities would have to also be externally supervised either by state authorities or independent bodies. To this end, corporations would be obliged to periodically monitor their activities. Necessary measures to be taken depend on the size, investment and industry where the corporation operates. The remedial part of the obligation to respect would include obligations upon corporations to support and not interfere with fair, independent and impartial judicial proceedings; submit themselves to periodic, fair, independent and impartial supervisions; and provide compensation to victims (see Table 5.1).

Corporate obligation to protect socio-economic rights

Corporations are not only obliged to respect socio-economic human rights, but they are also obliged to protect socio-economic rights; that is, to adopt preventive

101 Cindy S. Woods, '"It Isn't a State Problem": The Minas Conga Mine Controversy and the Need For Binding International Obligations on Corporate Actors', 46(2) *Georgetown Journal of International Law* 629, 649 (2015).

102 UN, Human Rights Council, 'The Guiding Principles on Extreme Poverty and Human Rights, submitted by the Special Rapporteur on Extreme Poverty and Human Rights, Magdalena Sepúlveda Carmona', UN Doc. A/HRC/21/39, 18 July 2012, para 100.

103 International Commission of Jurists (ICJ), 'Proposals for Elements of a Legally Binding Instrument on Transnational Corporations and Other Business Enterprises', October 2016.

Table 5.1 Categorization of corporate obligations: obligation to respect

Preventive corporate obligation to respect	*Remedial corporate obligation to respect*
Not cause harm to individuals' enjoyment of socio-economic rights. Not interfere with state provision of socio-economic rights.	Undertake human rights assessment prior to the start of the project. Submit themselves to periodic fair, independent and impartial supervisions.
Adopt full-fledged human rights policy, which has to be disseminated internally and externally to all relevant stakeholders and business partners, and be included into all its policies.	Submit themselves to fair, independent, and impartial reporting and auditing.
Draft and implement detailed due diligence processes, which have to be disseminated internally and externally to all relevant stakeholders and business partners, and include all its policies.	Establish transparent supervisory mechanisms monitoring compliance with socio-economic rights.
Set up an internal department tasked with designing preventive and remedial measures.	Establish internal complaints mechanisms aimed to hear allegations of their socio-economic rights violations.
Not interfere with the judicial rule-of-law processes examining their alleged involvement in socio-economic rights violations.	Support and do not interfere with the administration of justice.
Contribute to the rule-of-law environment in areas where they operate that will be conducive to the observance of rights.	Support the rule-of-law environment and do not interfere with fair, independent and impartial judicial proceedings, including the award of compensation.

measures so that their connected corporations in groups of corporations, business partners, suppliers and distributers do not violate socio-economic rights or at minimum their reasonable minimum cores in their global supply chains.[104] This would mean that they have to have and exercise control over their subsidiaries and their business partners in order to comply with availability, accessibility, acceptability, quality and adaptability of the rights to education, food, health, housing, water and other socio-economic rights. However, such obligations to

104 For a detailed discussion of minimum core see Audrey R. Chapman, 'A Violations Approach' for Monitoring the International Covenant on Economic, Social and Cultural Rights', 18 *Human Rights Quaterly* 23, 32 (1996). Yeshanew argues that the minimum core model, "more or less concentrates on the content of the rights to identify minimum obligation", whereas reasonabless approach "focuses on the obligations of states or measures to realize rights." Sisay Alemahu Yeshanew, *The Justiciability of Economic, Social and Cultural Rights in the African Regional Human Rights System*, Cambridge: Intersentia (2013), p. 294. See also Katharine Young, 'The Minimum Core of Economic and Social Rights: A Concept in Search of Content', 33(1) *Yale Journal of International Law* (2008).

protect are not obligations of result, but mostly of conduct, particularly in complex environments.[105] What is the scope of the corporate obligation to protect socio-economic rights?

The international level provides only limited guidance.[106] The ILO Resolution concerning decent work in global supply chains provides that "business has a responsibility to respect labour rights in their operations as laid out in the UN Guiding Principles on Business and Human Rights . . . and governments have the duty to implement and enforce national laws and regulations".[107] It further advises states to

> (i) set out clearly the expectation that all business enterprises domiciled in their territory and/ or jurisdiction respect human rights throughout their operations and the fundamental principles and rights at work for all workers, including migrant workers, homeworkers, workers in non-standard forms of employment and workers in EPZs.[108]

It is difficult to advance here with arguments of obligations as the Resolution refers to "expectation", without explaining the term. Therefore, it is more appropriate to talk about recommendations.

Further, OECD has developed some sectorial guides on protecting human rights protections in global supply chains. First, the OECD "Due Diligence Guidance for Responsible Supply Chains of Minerals from Conflict-Affected and High-Risk Areas" states that

> a company assesses risk by identifying the factual circumstances of its activities and relationships and evaluating those facts against relevant standards provided under national and international law, recommendations on responsible business conduct by international organisations, government-backed tools, private sector voluntary initiatives and a company's internal policies and systems.[109]

105 Justine Nolan, 'The Corporate Responsibility to Respect Human Rights: Soft Law or Not Law?' *in* Surya Deva and David Bilchitz (eds.), *Human Rights Obligations of Business: Beyond the Corporate Responsibility to Respect?* Cambridge: Cambridge University Press (2013), pp. 138–161. Justine Nolan, 'Human Rights and Global Supply Chains: Is Effective Supply Chain Accountability Possible?' *in* Surya Deva and David Bilchitz (eds.), *Building a Treaty on Business and Human Rights: Context and Contours*, Cambridge: Cambridge University Press (2017), pp. 238–265.

106 The Guiding Principles, principle 17. See also, Jernej Letnar Černič, 'Moving Towards Protecting Human Rights in Global Business Supply Chains', 35 *Boston University International Law Journal* 101 (2018).

107 ILO, 'Resolution Concerning Decent Work in Global Supply Chains', 10 June 2016, section 10.

108 Ibid., section 16.

109 OECD, 'Due Diligence Guidance for Responsible Supply Chains of Minerals from Conflict-Affected and High-Risk Areas', (3rd Edition, 2016), p. 13. See for example, Holly Cullen, 'The Irresistible Rise of Human Rights Due Diligence: Conflict Minerals and Beyond', 48(4) *The George Washington International Law Review* 743 (2016).

However its practical relevance has yet to be shown. The OECD has designed even a supervisory mechanism to enforce the Guidelines.[110] Second, the OECD in 2017 published "Due Diligence Guidance for Responsible Supply Chains in the Garment and Footwear Sector".[111] It recommends corporations to take preventive measures to "strengthen management systems in order to conduct due diligence on risks of harm in the enterprise's own operations and in its supply chain"[112] and remedial steps "to take active measure to prevent risk, supervise supply chains and to provide remedy".[113] Both OECD documents on due diligence complement the OECD Guidelines for Multinational Enterprises by bolstering their preventive dimensions. However, the non-binding legal nature of both documents casts doubt on their added value for guaranteeing socio-economic rights in the corporate supply chains.

One could argue that in complicated and wide corporate structures, the "mother" corporation would have obligations to ensure that its subordinated companies, even if in other jurisdictions, comply with socio-economic rights. Skinner, McCorquodale and De Schutter observe that "the duty of the parent company to exercise due diligence by controlling the subsidiary to ensure it does not engage in human rights violations".[114] In short, they would have an obligation of conduct. Whereas in open business relationships outside the same corporate structures, the obligation to protect would only amount to an obligation to conduct due diligence that socio-economic rights will be not be infringed. Such an obligation is not only wishful thinking, but derives from several domestic legal sources. California's Transparency in Supply Chains Act (2015) and the UK Modern Slavery Act (2015) require corporations to report their supply chains.[115] Moreover, Section 1502 of the Dodd-Frank Wall Street Reform Act contributes with disclosure requirements to the same aim.[116] The French statute on the duty of care of parent and subcontracting companies imposes a similar reporting duty.[117] Further, the English Court of Appeal noted in *Chandler* that:

110 OECD, 'Implementing the OECD Due Diligence Guidance', www.oecd.org/corporate/mne/implementingtheguidance.htm (last accessed 19 January 2018).

111 OECD, 'OECD Due Diligence Guidance for Responsible Supply Chains in the Garment and Footwear Sector', 2017.

112 Ibid., 1.1.

113 Ibid.

114 Gwynne Skinner, Robert McCorquodale, Olivier De Schutter and Andie Lamb, 'The Third Pillar: Access to Judicial Remedies for Human Rights Violations by Transnational Business', *ICAR, CORE and ECCJ* 65 (2013).

115 California Transparency in Supply Chains Act 2010; Modern Slavery Act 2015 (UK), section 54.

116 Dodd-Frank Wall Street Reform and Consumer Protection Act (2010), H.R. 4173, section 1502(b)(1)(A) and (E), 124 Stat. 2213-18. See also, Benjamin Thomas Greer and Jeffrey Purvis, 'Corporate Supply Chain Transparency: California's Seminal Attempt to Discourage Forced Labour', 20(1) *The International Journal of Human Rights* 55 (2016).

117 Law no. 2017-399, National Assembly (France).

> in appropriate circumstances the law may impose on a parent company responsibility for the health and safety of its subsidiary's employees. Those circumstances include a situation where, as in the present case, (1) the businesses of the parent and subsidiary are in a relevant respect the same; (2) the parent has, or ought to have, superior knowledge on some relevant aspect of health and safety in the particular industry; (3) the subsidiary's system of work is unsafe as the parent company knew, or ought to have known; and (4) the parent knew or ought to have foreseen that the subsidiary or its employees would rely on its using that superior knowledge for the employees' protection.[118]

Such wording implies that a parent company has responsibilities in supervising subsidiaries' conduct as to health and safety. *Mutatis mutandis*, this could be translated to business obligations under socio-economic rights. The obligation to protect requires corporations to conduct transparent, speedy, fair, independent, impartial and efficient investigations of their supply chains with the view of ensuring socio-economic rights throughout their business networks.[119] Such an obligation will often require corporations to exercise extraterritorial control outside the primary territory of registration since, due to the global character of current business relationships, it does not suffice that corporations only exercise control over business partners, suppliers and distributers in their national territory. They have to ensure that their business partners throughout the supply chain do not infringe upon or deprive individuals of their basic socio-economic livelihoods.[120] In other words, businesses are obliged to conduct human rights due diligence, which is defined as "an ongoing management process that a reasonable and prudent enterprise needs to undertake, in light of its circumstances (including sector, operating context, size and similar factors) to meet its responsibility to respect human rights".[121]

The minimum common denominator of such obligations lies therefore in corporations ensuring at least respect for the reasonable minimum core of socio-economic rights throughout their supply chains. They are obliged to do all that is

118 *Chandler v Cape plc*, EWCA Civ 525 (Court of Appeal), 25 April 2012, para 80. See also, *Lungowe & Ors v Vedanta Resources Plc & Anor*, EWCA Civ 1528 (Court of Appeal), 13 October 2017. Detailed discussion, Gabrielle Holly, 'Access to Remedy Under the UNGPs: Vedanta and the Expansion of Parent Company Liability', EJIL Talk! 31 October 2017, www.ejiltalk.org/if-the-pleading-represents-the-actuality-vedanta-access-remedy-and-the-prospect-of-a-duty-of-care-owed-by-a-parent-company-to-those-affected-by-acts-of-subsidiaries/ (last accessed 19 January 2018).

119 See, Justice Nolan, Submission to UN Open Ended Inter-Governmental Working Group on Transnational Corporations & Other Business Enterprises with Respect to Human Rights, 30 August 2016.

120 Bassina Farbenblum and Justine Nolan, 'The Business of Migrant Worker Recruitment: Who has the Responsibility and Leverage to Protect Rights?', 52(1) *Texas International Law Journal* (2017).

121 UN, OHCHR, The Corporate Responsibility to Respect Human Rights: An Interpretive Guide (2012), p. 4.

possible to ensure the minimum core of the rights to education, food, adequate housing, water and other socio-economic rights in order not to infringe on individuals' rights aspirations. This core includes at least compliance with minimum levels of human dignity, which are directed both towards its employees and towards individuals in immediate proximity to where the corporations operate. Corporate obligation to protect therefore works both towards employees, but also externally towards communities where corporations operate. The obligation to protect requires businesses to do whatever is possible to ensure the minimum levels of socio-economic rights for both their employees and communities. However, the Guiding Principles provide that

> the responsibility of business enterprises to respect human rights applies to all enterprises regardless of their size, sector, operational context, ownership and structure. Nevertheless, the scale and complexity of the means through which enterprises meet that responsibility may vary according to these factors and with the severity of the enterprise's adverse human rights impacts.[122]

The obligation to protect would insist that corporations periodically (for example, at least once a month) check and supervise the activity of their suppliers and other business partners. Such periodic supervision should be considered essential for minimum and diligent exercise of the obligation to protect socio-economic rights.

How far are corporations obliged to ensure human rights compliance in their supply chains? There do not exist binding obligations at the moment to control any tier of supply chains. Such a task is very difficult in practice, but not impossible, as regulatory attempts of the European Union in the supply chain of the European pharmaceutical industry illustrate.[123] For example, there are practices of corporations, such as Daimler Mercedes, of exercising control only in the first tier of the supply chain, where they have direct relationships with their partners. Ford Corporation exercises control over the first tier of the supply chain.[124] Nonetheless, they have to strive to the minimum level of compliance with socio-economic rights. Further, the international community has attempted to establish some supervisory mechanisms following horrific human rights violations involving businesses.[125] The Bangladesh Accord, agreed after the Rana Plaza disaster, obliges all stakeholders to ensure "a safe and sustainable Bangladeshi Ready-Made Garment ('RMG') industry in which no worker needs to fear fires, building collapses, or other accidents that could be prevented with

122 The Guiding Principles, para 14.

123 European Commission's Guidelines of 19 March 2015 on principles of Good Distribution Practice of active substances for medicinal products for human use, 2015/C 95/01.

124 Ford Corporation, Sustainability Report 2016/17.

125 Baskut Tuncak, 'Lessons from the Samarco Disaster', 2 *Business and Human Rights Journal* 157 (2017).

Table 5.2 Categorization of corporate obligations: obligation to protect

Preventive corporate obligation to protect	*Remedial corporate obligation to protect*
Make sure that their subsidiaries, suppliers and other business partners do not directly cause or contribute harm to individuals' enjoyment of socio-economic rights.	Establish strict internal and external corporate policies which assist to mitigate the potential of violations of socio-economic rights.
Apply international human rights law and socio-economic rights protections internally in corporate policies and externally in contracts and other dealings with contractors, subcontractors and any other business partners.	Develop full-fledged socio-economic impact assessments across their global supply chains.
Undertake due diligence across their supply chain.	Establish external periodic independent verification of these procedures, and generate reports to address specific abuses and devise ways of promoting respect for human rights.
Strive to control all tiers of their supply chains.	Establish internal grievances procedures where victims could bring recourse to complaints mechanisms.
Develop systematic supervisory mechanisms within and outside their corporate group.	Provide internal remedies and compensation in times of violations
Conduct internal, effective, transparent and diligent investigations in the case of violations.	Establish a special task force in charge of investigations.
Support and not interfere with domestic judicial systems.	Submit themselves to fair, independent and impartial judicial proceedings, and provide compensation.

reasonable health and safety measures".[126] However, the obligation to protect socio-economic rights through due diligence is an obligation of conduct which obliges corporations to take both preventive and remedial procedural measures to control their supply chains (see Table 5.2). First, this means that corporations should also adopt general and systematic measures to establish strict supervision, and second, that it should strengthen the system of supervision in concrete cases by conducting swift, fair, transparent, efficient, independent and impartial investigations, as well as provide victims with access to justice. In short, corporations have to illustrate concerted efforts to control their supply chains. For instance, IKEA informs that

> we ask our tier 1 suppliers to communicate IWAY Must requirements with their own suppliers and to register them on our sub-supplier tracking system.

126 Accord on Fire and Building Safety in Bangladesh, 13 March 2013, http://bangladeshaccord.org/wp-content/uploads/the_accord.pdf (last accessed 19 January 2018).

> It is the responsibility of our tier 1 suppliers to audit their critical sub-suppliers and ensure IWAY Must compliance.[127]

It seems that the most appropriate approach would be to follow the recent OECD Guidance, which proposes the following six steps for corporations to take in order observe human rights in their supply chains:[128] "Embed responsible business conduct in enterprise policy and management systems"; "Identify actual and potential harms in the enterprise's own operations and in its supply chain"; "Cease, prevent or mitigate harm in the enterprise's own operations and in its supply chain"; "Track"; "Communicate"; and "Provide for or co-operate in remediation when appropriate".[129] By complying with those steps corporations would be closer to protecting the minimum level of socio-economic rights through their global supply chains. Corporate obligations to protect are therefore procedural obligations in the sense that they concentrate on processes, but they are also substantive in that they require corporations to provide for the minimum level of socio-economic rights.

Corporate obligation to fulfil socio-economic rights

The obligation to fulfil is of a positive character, as it requires corporations to take active measures to ensure compliance with all five dimensions of socio-economic rights to the maximum of their available financial resources in order to eliminate deprivation of individuals.[130] This obligation is " 'central to the realisation of economic and social rights".[131] However, it is almost impossible to construct these obligations as strictly legal, as they belong more to the spheres of philosophical aspirations. Further, corporate obligation to fulfil socio-economic rights differs from state obligations in nature and scope. For instance, the South Gauteng High Court in Johannesburg, South Africa, observed in this regard that

> It is correct that the positive obligation to enforce Constitutional rights horizontally between private entities is not analogous to the positive duty owed by organs of State . . . As such, the full extent of the positive obligation imposed upon the State . . . to "respect, protect, promote or fulfill"

127 IKEA Group, '2016 Sustainability Report', https://www.ikea.com/ms/en_US/pdf/sustainability_report/IKEA_Group_Sustainability_Report_2016.pdf, (last accessed 19 Janauary 2018) p. 73.

128 OECD, 'Due Diligence Guidance For Responsible Supply Chains in The Garment and Footwear Sector', 2017.

129 Ibid., p. 5.

130 Jernej Letnar Černič, 'Sovereign Financing and Corporate Responsibility for Economic and Social Rights', *in* Juan Pablo Bohoslavsky and Jernej Letnar Černič (eds.), *Making Sovereign Financing and Human Rights Work*, Oxford and Portland: Hart Publishing (2014).

131 Matthew Craven, *The International Covenant on Economic, Social and Cultural Rights: A Perspective on its Development*, Oxford: Clarendon Press (1995), p. 109.

constitutional rights cannot always be extended to private entities such as Continental.[132]

Corporations generally do not possess an internal apparatus such as states do to provide different socio-economic rights. Nonetheless, corporations may have an emerging obligation to ensure the accessibility, acceptability, availability, adaptability and quality of the minimum core of the right to education, food, health, housing, water and other socio-economic rights in the geographical proximity of their operations and, particularly where they are no public resources. As many corporations now operate within corporate groups, it is first necessary to insist on the compliance of the obligation to fulfil within corporate groups to ensure that all the corporations within such groups, including those registered under different national jurisdictions, comply with the core of socio-economic rights. Second, outside corporate groups in relationship with wider communities, corporations are obliged to ensure some minimum level of socio-economic rights to their maximum of available resources, particularly where government services are absent. Elsewhere, they have to endeavour, possibly in cooperation with governments, to ensure provisions of the minimum reasonable core of the right to education, food, health, housing, water and other socio-economic rights as applied in the proximity of the geographical areas where they operate.

Such is the role particularly in the countries and regions where the state is absent and cannot provide even the bare minimum of socio-economic rights. The obligation to fulfil is traditionally an obligation of conduct, not of result.[133] States and corporations have to strive to achieve realizations of socio-economic rights to the highest possible extent. Two categories of corporate obligations to fulfil have to be distinguished: preventive and remedial. The preventive dimension of the corporate obligation to fulfil would mean that corporations should create conditions for maintenance and improvements of socio-economic livelihoods of individuals and groups. This can be described as an obligation of conduct. However, with the first category of corporate obligations to fulfil with large corporate groups, one could argue that its obligations are an obligation of result. Such obligations are particularly present within the location where corporations operate and also in wider local communities. Corporations "can be required in contracts to meet certain human rights-priorities: to achieve particular targets".[134] Corporations should implement a coherent human rights policy throughout the

132 *Boycott, Divestment And Sanctions South Africa and Another v Continental Outdoor Media (Pty) Ltd and Others*, 2013/19700 (South Africa: South Gauteng High Court, Johannesburg), 11 September 2014, para 79.

133 Magdalena Sepúlveda, *The Nature of the Obligations under the International Covenant on Economic, Social and Cultural Rights*, Antwerp, Oxford and New York: Intersentia (2003).

134 Nicholas McMurry, 'Privatisation and the Obligation to Fulfill Rights', *in* Jernej Letnar Černič and Tara van Ho (eds.), *Human Rights and Business: Direct Corporate Accountability for Human Rights*, Oisterwijk: Wolf Legal Publishers (2015), pp. 251–262, p. 256.

corporate structure to promote an environment where socio-economic rights may be fully realized.

Corporations should provide financial resources in order to fulfil the reasonable minimum core of socio-economic rights. SDGs also mention these financial partnerships in SDG 17, which calls to "strengthen the means of implementation and revitalize the global partnership for sustainable development". Sub-goal 17.16 further urges to

> enhance the global partnership for sustainable development, complemented by multi-stakeholder partnerships that mobilize and share knowledge, expertise, technology and financial resources, to support the achievement of the sustainable development goals in all countries, in particular developing countries.

Such financial resources and partnerships are necessary where individuals are in particularly severe socio-economic positions and where they cannot develop their capabilities to self-realize themselves. Corporations are not asked to replace local and state authorities, but to assist them financially with the provision of socio-economic rights.[135]

Remedial dimension of the corporate obligation to fulfil concerns the question: How can one measure if corporations fulfil their task under the obligation to fulfil? As noted earlier, the UN Committee on Economic, Social and Cultural Rights has developed human rights indicators for monitoring states' compliance with those rights.[136] They aim to supervise the implementation of socio-economic rights in domestic systems and explain the obstacles encountered. Thus they are an essential tool in improving the methodology of socio-economic rights supervision.[137] Such indicators, with some modifications, could be also employed in the business context, particularly when assessing the implementation of human rights impact assessments. They can be divided into structural, process and outcome indicators.[138] Such indicators offer promising advantage in comparison to traditional supervision bodies in terms of measuring human rights. They can also offer some advice in ensuring equal provision of all socio-economic rights. Such indicators can be, *mutatis mutandis*, translated to the corporate context, as corporations should contribute to meeting the obligation to fulfil (see Table 5.3).

135 See, Surya Deva, *Regulating Corporate Human Rights Violations: Humanizing Business*, Adington: Routledge (2012).

136 UN, CESCR, 'General Comment No.14 (2000): The Right to the Highest Attainable Standard of Health', UN Doc. E/C.12/2000/4, 11 August 2000, para 57–58.

137 Eitan Felner, 'A New Frontier in Economic and social Rights Advocacy? Turning Quantitative Data into a Tool for Human Rights Accountability', 9 *Sur International Journal on Human Rights* 109 (2008), p. 126.

138 Oliver De Schutter, *International Human Rights Law*, Cambridge: Cambridge University Press (2010), pp. 480–481.

Table 5.3 Categorization of corporate obligations: obligation to fulfil

Preventive corporate obligation to fulfil	*Remedial corporate obligation to fulfil*
Create conditions for individuals' enjoyment of socio-economic rights.	Help local communities in providing individuals with socio-economic rights.
Strive to assist states in providing at least the reasonable minimum core of socio-economic rights, particularly in the local communities where they operate.	Work with the governments and other actors in providing the reasonable minimum core of socio-economic rights.
Participate in partnerships and make financial commitments to contribute to individuals' enjoyment of socio-economic rights.	Create internal funds and contribute to external funds to be used to provide for rights to education, food, health, adequate housing and water.
Provide for rights to education, food, health, housing, water for their employees, and strive to provide the core of those rights for members of local community.	Work with employees, organizations and local communities in order to improve provision of socio-economic rights.
Commit themselves to contribute to infrastructure projects, particularly where state or local community is absent.	Provide financial resources to contribute to the construction of infrastructure projects in fragile environments.

Conclusion

Corporate obligations under socio-economic rights derive primarily from domestic systems, international law and voluntary commitments of corporations. They are of a horizontal nature, as they apply between corporations and individuals and/or groups. Corporations have negative and potentially positive human rights obligations in global business environments to observe socio-economic rights, which result in three forms. First, negative corporate obligations to respect socio-economic rights are now no longer controversial. They require corporations not to do harm or violate socio-economic rights. Corporations are to ensure respect of socio-economic rights within their corporate groups and generally not to interfere with individual enjoyment of socio-economic rights. Second, positive obligations of corporations to protect refer to safeguarding socio-economic rights in their global supply chains. Such obligations of due diligence within and outside corporate groups have been framed as an obligation of conduct not as an obligation of result. However, such corporate human rights obligations are progressive, not immediate obligations, and are binding only relating to minimum levels of socio-economic rights. Further, an emerging obligation to fulfil requires corporations to contribute financial resources to the provision of socio-economic rights, particularly in the fragile environment where state government is largely absent and where corporations provide socio-economic rights through the exercise of public functions on the basis of public licenses or state ownership. All in all, obligations require corporations to be more transparent in communications with individuals and communities as to the effects of corporate operations.

Both negative and positive obligations require that corporations cooperate with state authorities in ensuring the right to the effective remedy.

Bibliography

Books

Cantú Rivera, Humberto, *Derechos Humanos y Empresas: Reflexiones desde América Latina*, San José: Instituto Interamericano de Derechos Humanos (2017).

Clapham, Andrew, *Human Rights Obligations of Non-State Actors*, Oxford: Oxford University Press (2006).

Craven, Matthew, *The International Covenant on Economic, Social and Cultural Rights: A Perspective on Its Development*, Oxford: Clarendon Press (1995).

De Schutter, Olivier, *International Human Rights Law*, Cambridge: Cambridge University Press (1st Edition 2010).

Deva, Surya, *Regulating Corporate Human Rights Violations: Humanizing Business*, Adington: Routledge (2012).

Letnar Černič, Jernej, *Human Rights Law and Business: Corporate Responsibility for Fundamental Human Rights*, Groningen: Europa Law Publishing (2010).

Letnar Černič, Jernej and Carrillo-Santarelli, Nicolas (eds.), *The Future of Business and Human Rights*, Cambridge: Intersentia (2018).

Letnar Černič, Jernej and Van Ho, Tara (eds.), *Human Rights and Business: Direct Corporate Accountability for Human Rights*, Oisterwijk: Wolf Legal Publishers (2015).

Macklem, Patrick, *The Sovereignty of Human Rights*, Oxford: Oxford University Press (2015).

Nolan, Aoife, *Children's Socio-economic Rights, Democracy and the Courts*, Oxford: Hart Publishing (2011).

O'Connell, Paul, *Vindicating Socio-Economic Rights: International Standards and Comparative Experiences*, Abingdon: Routledge (2012).

Sajó, andrás and Uitz, Renáta, *Constitutional Topography: Values and Constitutions*, Utrecht: Eleven International Publishing (2005).

Sepúlveda, Magdalena, *The Nature of the Obligations Under the International Covenant on Economic, Social and Cultural Rights*, Antwerp, Oxford and New York: Intersentia (2003).

Yeshanew, Sisay Alemahu, *The Justiciability of Economic, Social and Cultural Rights in the African Regional Human Rights System*, Cambridge: Intersentia (2013), p. 294.

Journal articles

Bilchitz, David, 'Corporate Law and the Constitution: Towards Binding Human Rights Responsibilities for Corporations', 125(4) *South African Law Journal* 754 (2008).

Bilchitz, David, 'The Necessity for a Business and Human Rights Treaty', 1(2) *Business and Human Rights Journal* 203 (2016).

Campbell, Angus, 'Positive Obligations Under the ECHR: Deprivation of Liberty by Private Actors', 10(3) *Edinburgh Law Review* 399 (2006).

Cantu Riviera, Humberto, 'Negotiating a Treaty on Business and Human Rights: The Early Stages', 40(3) *UNSW Law Journal Volume* 1200 (2017).

Chapman, Audrey R., 'A Violations Approach' for Monitoring the International Covenant on Economic, Social and Cultural Rights', 18 *Human Rights Quaterly* 23, 32 (1996).

Corrin, Jennifer, 'From Horizontal and Vertical to Lateral: Extending the Effect of Human Rights in Post Colonial Legal Systems of the South Pacific', 58(1) *International and Comparative Law Quarterly* 31 (2009).

Cullen, Holly, 'The Irresistible Rise of Human Rights Due Diligence: Conflict Minerals and Beyond', 48(4) *The George Washington International Law Review* 743 (2016).

de Felice, Damiano and Graf, Andreas, 'The Potential of National Action Plans to Implement Human Rights Norms: An Early Assessment with Respect to the UN Guiding Principles on Business and Human Rights', 7(1) *Journal of Human Rights Practice* 40 (2015).

De Schutter, Olivier, 'Towards a New Treaty on Business and Human Rights', 1(1) *Business and Human Rights Journal* 41 (2016).

Eide, Asbjørn, 'Realization of Social and Economic Rights and the Minimum Threshold Approach', 10 *Human Rights Law Journal* 35 (1989).

Farbenblum, Bassina and Nolan, Justine, 'The Business of Migrant Worker Recruitment: Who Has the Responsibility and Leverage to Protect Rights?', 52(1) *Texas International Law Journal* (2017).

Felner, Eitan, 'A New Frontier in Economic and social Rights Advocacy? Turning Quantitative Data into a Tool for Human Rights Accountability', 9 *Sur International Journal on Human Rights* 109 (2008).

Greer, Benjamin Thomas and Purvis, Jeffrey, 'Corporate Supply Chain Transparency: California's Seminal Attempt to Discourage Forced Labour', 20(1) *The International Journal of Human Rights* 55 (2016).

Jägers, Nicola, 'UN Guiding Principles on Business and Human Rights: Making Headway Towards Real Corporate Accountability?', 29(2) *Netherlands Quarterly of Human Rights* 159 (2011).

Letnar Černič, Jernej, 'State Obligations Concerning Indigenous Peoples' Rights to Their Ancestral Lands: Lex Imperfecta?', 28 *American University International Law Review* 1129 (2013).

Letnar Černič, Jernej, 'Moving Towards Protecting Human Rights in Global Business Supply Chains', 35 *Boston University International Law Journal* 101 (2018).

Methven O'Brien, Claire, Mehra, Amol, Blackwell, Sara and Poulsen-Hansen, Cathrine Bloch, 'National Action Plans: Current Status and Future Prospects for a New Business and Human Rights Governance Tool', 1(1) *Business and Human Rights Journal* 117 (2015).

Nolan, Aoife, 'Holding Non-State Actors to Account for Constitutional Economic and Social Rights Violations: Experiences and Lessons from South Africa and Ireland', 12(1) *International Journal of Constitutional Law* 61 (2014).

Tuncak, Baskut, 'Lessons from the Samarco Disaster', 2 *Business and Human Rights Journal* 157 (2017).

Woods, Cindy S., '"It Isn't a State Problem": The Minas Conga Mine Controversy and the Need for Binding International Obligations on Corporate Actors', 46(2) *Georgetown Journal of International Law* 649 (2015).

Young, Katharine, 'The Minimum Core of Economic and Social Rights: A Concept in Search of Content', 33(1) *Yale Journal of International Law* (2008).

Book chapters

Avbelj, Matej, 'Is There Drittwirkung in EU Law?' *in* András Sajó and Renáta Uitz (eds.), *The Constitution in Private Relations: Expanding Constitutionalism*, Utrecht: Eleven International Publishing (2005), pp. 145–163.

Barak, Aharon, 'Constitutional Human Rights and Private Law', *in* Dan Friedmann and Daphne Barak-Erez (eds.), *Human Rights in Private Law*, Oxford: Hart Publishing (2002), pp. 1–42.

De Schutter, Olivier, 'Corporations and Economic, Social and Cultural Rights', *in* Eibe Riedel, Gilles Giacca and Christophe Golay (eds.), *Economic, Social and Cultural Rights in International Law: Contemporary Issues and Challenges*, Oxford: Oxford University Press (2014), pp. 193–224.

Deva, Surya, 'Treating Human Rights Lightly: A Critique of the Consensus Rhetoric and the Language Employed by the Guiding Principles', *in* Surya Deva and David Bilchitz (eds.), *Human Rights Obligations of Business: Beyond the Corporate Responsibility to Respect?* Cambridge: Cambridge University Press (2013), pp. 78–104.

Deva, Surya and Bilchitz, David, 'The Human Rights Obligations of Business: A Critical Framework for the Future', *in* Surya Deva and David Bilchitz (eds.), *Human Rights Obligations of Business*, Cambridge: Cambridge University Press (2013), pp. 1–26.

Dickson, Brice, 'The Horizontal Application of Human Rights Law', *in* Angela Hegarty and Siobhan Leonard (eds.), *Human Rights: An Agenda for the 21st Century*, London and Sydney: Cavendish Publishing Limited, 1999, pp. 59–78.

Hoof, Godefridus J.H. van, 'The Legal Nature of Economic, Social and Cultural Rights: A Rebuttal of Some Traditional Views', *in* Philip Alston and Katarina Tomaševski (eds.), *The Right to Food, From Soft to Hard Law*, Utrecht: SIM (1984), pp. 97–111.

Khalfan, Ashfaq and Seiderman, Ian, 'Extraterritorial Human Rights Obligations: Wider Implications of the Maastricht Principles and the Continuing Accountability Challenge', *in* Wouter Vandenhole (ed.), *Challenging Territoriality in Human Rights Law: Building Blocks for a Plural and Diversive Duty-Bearer Regime*, Abingdon: Routledge (2015), pp. 15–43.

Langford, Malcolm, Vandenhole, Wouter, Scheinin, Martin and Van Genugten, Willem, 'Introduction: An Emerging Field', *in* Malcolm Langford, Wouter Vandenhole, Martin Scheinin and Willem Van Genugten (eds.), *Global Justice, State Duties: The Extraterritorial Scope of Economic, Social and Cultural Rights in International Law*, Cambridge: Cambridge University Press (2013), pp. 3–31.

Letnar Černič, Jernej, 'Sovereign Financing and Corporate Responsibility for Economic and Social Rights', *in* Juan Pablo Bohoslavsky and Jernej Letnar Černič (eds.), *Making Sovereign Financing and Human Rights Work*, Oxford and Portland: Hart Publishing (2014), pp. 139–160.

Letnar Černič, Jernej, 'An Elephant in a Room of Porcelain: Establishing Corporate Responsibility for Human Rights', *in* Jernej Letnar Černič and Tara van Ho (eds.), *Human Rights and Business: Direct Corporate Accountability for Human Rights*, Oisterwijk: Wolf Legal Publishers (2015), pp. 131–158.

Letnar Černič, Jernej, 'Corporate Responsibility for Human Rights: Towards a Pluralist Approach', *in* Wouter Vandenhole (ed.), *Challenging Territoriality in Human Rights Law: Building Blocks for a Plural and Diverse Duty-Bearer Regime*, Abingdon: Routledge (2015), pp. 69–89.

Liebenberg, Sandra, 'The Protection of Economic and Social Rights in Domestic Legal Systems', *in* Asbjørn Eide, Catarina Krause and Allan Rosas (eds.), *Economic, Social and Cultural Rights: A Textbook*, Dordrecht, Boston and London: Martinus Nijhoff Publishers (2001), pp. 55–84.

McMurry, Nicholas, 'Privatisation and the Obligation to Fulfill Rights', *in* Jernej Letnar Černič and Tara van Ho (eds.), *Human Rights and Business: Direct Corporate Accountability for Human Rights*, Oisterwijk: Wolf Legal Publishers (2015), pp. 251–262.

Nolan, Justine, 'The Corporate Responsibility to Respect Human Rights: Soft Law or Not Law?', *in* Surya Deva and David Bilchitz (eds.), *Human Rights Obligations of Business: Beyond the Corporate Responsibility to Respect?* Cambridge: Cambridge University Press (2013), pp. 138–161.

Nolan, Justine, 'Human Rights and Global Supply Chains: Is Effective Supply Chain Accountability Possible?' *in* Surya Deva and David Bilchitz (eds.), *Building a Treaty on Business and Human Rights: Context and Contours*, Cambridge: Cambridge University Press (2017), pp. 238–265.

Riedel, Eibe, Giacca, Gilles and Golay, Christophe, 'Introduction: The Development of Economic, Social and Cultural Rights in International Law', *in* Eibe Riedel, Gilles Giacca and Christophe Golay (eds.), *Economic, Social and Cultural Rights in International Law: Contemporary Issues and Challenges*, Oxford: Oxford University Press (2014), pp. 3–50.

Rosas, Allan and Scheinin, Martin, 'Categories and Beneficiaries of Human Rights', *in* Raija Hanski and Markku Suksi (eds.), *An Introduction to the International Protection of Human Rights: A Textbook*, Turku: Åbo Akademi University, Institute for Human Rights (2nd revised Edition, 2004), pp. 49–62.

Toebes, Brigit C.A. and Letnar Černič, Jernej, 'Corporate Human Rights Obligations Under Economic, Social and Cultural Rights', *in* Jeffrey F. Addicott, Md Jahid Hossain Bhuiyan, Tareq M.R. Chowdhury (eds.), *Globalization, International Law and Human Rights*, Oxford: Oxford University Press (2012), pp. 1–33.

Vandenhole, Wouter, 'Obligations and Responsibility in a Plural and Diverse Duty – Bearer Human Rights Regime', *in* Wouter Vandenole (ed.), *Challenging Terroriality in Human Rights Law: Building Blocks for a Plural and Diverse Duty-Bearer Regime*, Abingdon: Routledge (2015), pp. 119–121.

Vandenhole, Wouter, Türkelli, Gamze Erdem and Hammonds, Rachel, 'Reconceptualizing Human Rights Duty-Bearers', *in* Anja Mihr and Mark Gibney (eds.), *The Sage Handbook of Human Rights*, London: Sage (2014), pp. 1031–1044.

Newspaper articles

Agence France Press, 'Belgium Reopens Myanmar Humanity Crimes Probe Against Oil Giant Total', 2 October 2007.

Ceaux, Pascal and Follorou, Jacques, 'Total va indemniser ses accusateurs', *Le Monde*, 30 Novembre 2005.

Le Monde.fr with Reuters, 'Total: la Belgique rouvre une enquête pour crimes contre l'humanité', *Le Monde*, 1 October 2007.

Legislation and official documents

Bribery Act 2010, c. 23, UK, http://www.legislation.gov.uk/ukpga/2010/23/contents (last accessed 19 January 2018).

California Transparency in Supply Chains Act, 2010, Civil Code Section 1714.43.
Constitution of Kenya, 27 August 2010, http://www.refworld.org/docid/4c8508822.html (last accessed 28 May 2018).
Constitution of the Republic of Slovenia, Official Gazette RS Nos. 33/91-I, 42/97, 66/00, 24/03, 69/04, 68/06 and 47/13.
Constitution of South Africa, No. 108 of 1996, National Gazette No. 17678, 18 December 1996.
Convention on Civil Liability for Damage Resulting from Activities Dangerous to the Environment, Treaty No. 150, Council of Europe, 21 June 1993.
Convention on the Third Party Liability in the Field of Nuclear Energy, 956 UNTS 251, Paris 29 July 1960.
Convention Relating to Civil Liability in the field of Maritime Carriage of Nuclear Material, 974 UNTS 255, Brussels, 17 December 1971.
Dodd-Frank Wall Street Reform and Consumer Protection Act, 2010, H.R. 4173.
European Commission's Guidelines of 19 March 2015 on principles of Good Distribution Practice of active substances for medicinal products for human use, 2015/C 95/01.
Criminal Code of the French Republic, Act no. 2000-647, 10 July, Art. 8, Official Journal, 11 July 2000, Article 213 (3).
Foreign Corrupt Practices Act, 1977, amended 15 U.S. Code § 78dd-1.
ILO, 'Tripartite Declaration of Principles Concerning Multinational Enterprises and Social Policy', 83 *ILO Official Bulletin* (2000).
ILO, 'Resolution Concerning Decent Work in Global Supply Chains', 10 June 2016.
ILO, Working Party on the Social Dimensions of the Liberalization of International Trade, 'Overview of Global Developments and Office Activities Concerning Codes of Conduct, Social Labeling and Other Private Sector Iaddressing Labour Issues: Executive Summary', GB.273/WP/SDL/1, November 1998.
International Convention on Civil Liability for Oil Pollution Damage, 973 UNTS 3, 29 November 1969, art. 3(1).
Law no. 2017-399, National Assembly (France), Relating to the Duty of Vigilance of the Parent Companies and the Companies Giving Orders, 27 March 2017.
Modern Slavery Act, UK, 26 March 2015 (c. 30), http://www.legislation.gov.uk/ukpga/2015/30/pdfs/ukpga_20150030_en.pdf (last accessed 19 January 2018).
OECD Convention on Combating Bribery of Foreign Public Officials in International Business Transactions, S. Treaty Doc. 105-43, 37 ILM 1, 18 December 1997.
United Kingdom Companies Act, 2006 (c. 46).
UN, Commission on Human Rights, 'The Right to Adequate Food and to Be Free from Hunger – Updated Study on the Right to Food, submitted by Asbjørn Eide', UN Doc. E/CN.4/Sub.2/1999/12, 28 June 1999.
UN, Commission on Human Rights, 'Norms on the Responsibilities of Transnational Corporations and Other Business Enterprises with Regard to Human Rights', UN Doc. E/CN.4/Sub.2/2003/12/Rev.2, 26 August 2003.
UN, Committee on Rights of the Child, 'General Comment No. 16 on State Obligations Regarding the Impact of the Business Sector on Children's Rights', U.N. Doc. CRC/C/GC/16, 17 April 2013.
UN, Committee on the Elimination of Racial discrimination, 'Concluding Observations: Australia', CERD/C/AUS/CO/15-17, 13 September 2010.

UN, Committee on the Elimination of Racial discrimination, 'Concluding Observations: United Kingdom of Great Britain and Northern Ireland', CERD/C/GBR/CO/18-20, 14 September 2011.
UN, CESCR, 'General Comment No. 13: The Right to Education', UN Doc. E/C.12/1999/10, 8 December 1999.
UN, CESCR, 'General Comment No.14 (2000): The Right to the Highest Attainable Standard of Health', UN Doc. E/C.12/2000/4, 11 August 2000.
UN, CESCR, 'Concluding Observations: Canada', UN Doc. E/C.12/CAN/CO/6, 23 March 2016.
UN, CESCR, 'Concluding Observations: United Kingdom of Great Britain and Northern Ireland', UN Doc. E/C.12/GBR/CO/6, 14 July 2016.
UN, CESCR, 'Concluding Observations: Netherlands', UN Doc. E/C.12/NLD/CO/6, 6 July 2017.
UN, CESCR, 'General Comment No. 24 (2017) on State Obligations Under the International Covenant on Economic, Social and Cultural Rights in the Context of Business Activities', UN Doc. E/C.12/GC/24, 10 August 2017.
UN, General Assembly, 'Report of the Working Group on the Issue of Human Rights and Transnational Corporations and Other Business Enterprises', UN Doc. A68/279, 7 August 2013.
UN, Human Rights Committee (HRC), 'General Comment 31 [80], The Nature of the General Legal Obligation on States Parties to the Covenant', UN Doc. CCPR/C/21/Rev.1/Add.13, 26 May 2004.
UN, Human Rights Committee, 'Concluding Observations: Canada', UN Doc. CCPR/C/CAN/CO6, 13 August 2015.
UN, Human Rights Committee, 'Concluding Observations: Germany', UN Doc. CCPR/C/DEU/CO/6, 12 November 2012.
UN, Human Rights Council, Report of the Special Representative of the Secretary General on the Issue of Human Rights and Transnational Corporations and Other Business Enterprises, John Ruggie, 'Guiding Principles on Business and Human Rights: Implementing the United Nations "Protect, Respect and Remedy" Framework', UN Doc. A/HRC/17/31, 21 March 2011.
UN, Human Rights Council, 'The Guiding Principles on Extreme Poverty and Human Rights', submitted by the Special Rapporteur on Extreme Poverty and Human Rights, Magdalena Sepúlveda Carmona, UN Doc. A/HRC/21/39, 18 July 2012.
UN, Human Rights Council, 'Report of the Working Group on the Issue of Human Rights and Transnational Corporations and other Business Enterprises', UN Doc. UN Doc. A/HRC/23/32, 14 March 2013.
UN, Human Rights Council, 'Elaboration of an International Legally Binding Instrument on Transnational Corporations and Other Business Enterprises with Respect to Human Rights', A/HRC/26/L.22/Rev.1, 25 June 2014.
UN, Human Rights Council, 'Report of the Special Rapporteur on Extreme Poverty and Human Rights: Philip Alston', UN Doc. A/HRC/32/31, 28 April 2016.
UN, OHCHR, 'The Corporate Responsibility to Respect Human Rights: An Interpretive Guide', 2012.
UN, OHCHR, 'Business and Human Rights: A Survey of NHRI Practices', 23 May 2008, www.reports-and-materials.org/OHCHR-National-Human-Rights-Institutions-practices-Apr-2008.doc (last accessed 20 December 2017).

Cases and opinions

Association France-Palestine Solidarité v. *Société Alstom Transport SA*, Judgment, Court of Appeal Versailles, 22 March 2013.

Boycott, Divestment And Sanctions South Africa and Another v Continental Outdoor Media (Pty) Ltd and Others, 2013/19700 (South Africa: South Gauteng High Court, Johannesburg), 11 September 2014.

Chandler v Cape plc, EWCA Civ 525 (Court of Appeal), 25 April 2012.

Danchin, Peter, 'A Human Right to Water? The South African Constitutional Court's Decision in the Mazibuko Case', *EJIL: Talk!* 13 January 2010.

Fose v Minister of Safety and Security, CCT14/96 (Constitutional Court of South Africa), 5 June 1997.

Government of the Republic of South Africa and Others v Grootboom and Others, CCT 11/00 (Constitutional Court of South Africa), 4 October 2000.

Lungowe & Ors v Vedanta Resources Plc & Anor, EWCA Civ 1528 (Court of Appeal), 13 October 2017.

Lüth case, BVerfGE 7, 198 (1 BvR 400/51), 15 January 1958: German Case: Foreign Law Translations, University of Texas, Translated by Tony Weir, https://law.utexas.edu/transnational/foreign-law-translations/german/case.php?id=1369 (last accessed 19 January 2018).

Mazibuko and Others v City of Johannesburg and Others, CCT 39/09 (Constitutional Court of South Africa), 8 October 2009.

Minister of Health v *Treatment Action Campaign*, CCT 8/02 (Constitutional Court of South Africa), 5 July 2002.

Soobramoney v Minister of Health, CCT 32/97 (Constitutional Court of South Africa), 27 November 1997.

Reports and miscellaneous

Accord on Fire and Building Safety in Bangladesh, 13 March 2013, http://bangladeshaccord.org/wp-content/uploads/the_accord.pdf (last accessed 19 January 2018).

Amis, Lucy, 'A Guide for Business: How to Develop a Human Rights Policy', 2011.

Business and Human Rights Resource Centre, National Action Plans, www.business-humanrights.org/en/un-guiding-principles/implementation-tools-examples/implementation-by-governments/by-type-of-initiative/national-action-plans (last accessed 19 January 2018).

Business and Human Rights Resource Centre, 'UK Modern Slavery Act', https://business-humanrights.org/en/uk-modern-slavery-act (last accessed 19 January 2018).

Carrillo-Santarelli, Nicolás, 'Corporate Human Rights Obligations: Controversial but Necessary', Business and Human Rights Resource Center, November 2016, https://business-humanrights.org/en/corporate-human-rights-obligations-controversial-but-necessary (last accessed 19 January 2018).

Larry Catá Backer, 'At the Second UN Forum on Business and Human Rights: Reflections on Bilchitz and Deva (eds.), "Human Rights Obligations of Business: Beyond the Corporate Responsibility to Respect?"' Law at the End of the Day (Blog), 1 December 2013.

Fredman, Sandra, 'Human Rights Transformed: Positive Duties and Positive Rights', Oxford Legal Studies Research Paper No. 38 (2006).

Ford Corporation, 'Sustainability Report 2016/17'.
Harris, Kamala D., 'The California Transparency in Supply Chains Act: A Resource Guide', 2015.
Holly, Gabrielle, 'Access to Remedy Under the UNGPs: Vedanta and the Expansion of Parent Company Liability', *EJIL Talk!* 31 October 31, 2017,
IKEA Group, '2016 Sustainability Report', https://www.ikea.com/ms/en_US/pdf/sustainability_report/IKEA_Group_Sustainability_Report_2016.pdf (last accessed 19 Janauary 2018).
International Commission of Jurists (ICJ), 'Corporate Complicity and Legal Accountability, Volume 3: Civil Remedies', Expert Legal Panel on Corporate Complicity in International Crimes, Geneva, September 2008.
International Commission of Jurists (ICJ), 'Proposals for Elements of a Legally Binding Instrument on Transnational Corporations and Other Business Enterprises', October 2016.
Kellogg Company, 'Human Rights Position Statement', 1 December 2016.
Nolan, Justice, 'Submission to UN Open Ended Inter-Governmental Working Group on Transnational Corporations & Other Business Enterprises with Respect to Human Rights', 30 August 2016.
OECD, 'Implementing the OECD Due Diligence Guidance', www.oecd.org/corporate/mne/implementingtheguidance.htm (last accessed 19 January 2018).
OECD, 'Draft Due Diligence Guidelines for Responsible Business Conduct (Draft 2.1)', 2016.
OECD, 'Due Diligence Guidance for Responsible Supply Chains in the Garment and Footwear Sector', 2017.
OECD, 'Due Diligence Guidance for Responsible Supply Chains of Minerals from Conflict-Affected and High-Risk Areas', (3rd Edition, 2016).
OECD, 'Watch, Remedy Remains Rare, 2015, www.oecdwatch.org/publications-en/Publication_4201 (last accessed 19 January 2018).
OECD, 'Guidelines for Multinational Enterprises', 2000.
OECD, 'Guidelines for Multinational Enterprises', 2011 Edition.
PepsiCo, 'Global Human Rights Statement', June 2017.
Ramasastry, Anita and Thompson, Robert C., 'Commerce, Crime and Conflict: A Comparative Survey of Legal Remedies for Private Sector Liability for Grave Breaches of International Law', Fafo-report 536, 2006.
Ruggie, John Gerard, 'Regulating Multinationals: The UN Guiding Principles, Civil'.
Skinner, Gwynne, McCorquodale, Robert, De Schutter, Olivier and Lamb andie, 'The Third Pillar: Access to Judicial Remedies for Human Rights Violations by Transnational Business', ICAR, CORE and ECCJ, 2013.
'Society and International Legalization', 2015, Regulatory Policy Program Working Paper RPP-2015-04.
The Danish Institute for Human Rights, 'The AAAQ Framework and the Right to Water: International indicators', 2014.
Unilever'sHumanRightsPolicyStatement,2017,https://www.unilever.com/Images/unilever-human-rights-policy-statement_tcm244-422954_en.pdf (last accessed 19 Janaury 2018).
UN Global Compact, www.unglobalcompact.org/ (last accessed 19 January 2018).
Vandenhole, Wouter, 'Emerging Normative Frameworks on Transnational Human Rights Obligations', EUI Working Paper RSCAS 2012/17.

6 Corporate human rights obligations under specific socio-economic rights

Introduction	125
Corporate socio-economic obligations relative to specific rights	127
Corporate obligations in relation to the human right to education	127
Corporate obligations in relation to the human right to food	128
Corporate obligations in relation to the human right to health	134
Corporate obligations in relation to the human right to adequate housing	139
Corporate obligations in relation to the human right to water	143
Conclusion	146

Introduction

Whereas the previous chapter addressed the general theoretical underpinnings of corporate obligations concerning socio-economic rights, this chapter focuses on corporate human rights obligations with regard to specific socio-economic rights. Socio-economic rights are a *condition sine qua non* for the development of any individual. They form part of the collective value of human dignity that underpins all dimensions of human rights. This chapter focuses on these five key socio-economic rights by examining corporate obligations concerning the human rights to education, food, health, adequate housing and water. In this way, compliance with those rights contributes to the specific and general well-being of the individual and their human dignity. For instance, the African Commission on Human and Peoples' Rights stated that

> the right to food is inseparably linked to the dignity of human beings and is therefore essential for the enjoyment and fulfilment of such other rights as health, education, work and political participation . . . the Nigerian Government should not destroy or contaminate food sources. It should not allow private parties to destroy or contaminate food sources and prevent peoples' efforts to feed themselves.[1]

1 African Commission on Human and Peoples' Rights, '155/96: Social and Economic Rights Action Center (SERAC) and Center for Economic and Social Rights (CESR) / Nigeria', 27 October 2001, para 65.

Socio-economic rights also contribute to the advancement of an individual's socio-economic livelihood and those rights are selected for closer examination given their value in individuals' socio-economic livelihood as they help an individual in self-realization. Nussbaum observes that "the purpose of global development . . . is to enable people to live full and creative lives, developing their potential and fashioning a meaningful existence commensurate with their equal human dignity".[2] Observance of such rights therefore adds to human dignity and the ability to actuate oneself.

As seen in the previous chapter, corporations are required to respect socio-economic rights and observe them particularly their minimum core when complying with obligations to protect and fulfil. Section 12 of the former UN Norms stated that "corporations shall respect and contribute to the realization of economic, social and cultural rights, which is in fact a less onerous obligation than that required of States in the ICESCR".[3] This chapter argues that corporations are obliged to ensure a reasonable minimum core with respect to socio-economic rights.[4] They not only have negative[5] but also positive obligations[6] stemming from national, international and internal levels. All of the examined rights are closely interlinked and interdependent, as they add to the individual's sustainable livelihood and dignity. Corporate obligations concerning socio-economic rights are part of the "the 2030 Agenda for Sustainable Development".[7]

The rest of this chapter examines corporate obligations regarding individual socio-economic rights, namely the right to education, the right to food, the right to health, the right to decent housing and the right to water. The second section of this chapter deals with corporate obligations concerning the right to education, whereas the third section addresses such obligations with the right to food. The fourth section then deals with corporate obligations with the right to health, the fifth section with the right to decent housing and the sixth section

2 Martha C Nussbaum, Creating Capabilities, *The Human Development Approach*, Cambridge, MA: The Belknap Press of Harvard University Press (2011), p. 185.

3 UN 'Norms on the Responsibilities of Transnational Corporations and Other Business Enterprises with Regard to Human Rights', U.N. Doc. E/CN.4/Sub.2/2003/38/Rev.2 (2003), Section 12.

4 See for instance, Olivier De Schutter, 'Corporations and Economic, Social, and Cultural Rights', *in* Eibe Riedel, Gilles Giacca and Christophe Golay (eds.), *Economic, Social, and Cultural Rights in International Law: Contemporary Issues and Challenges*, Oxford: Oxford University Press (2014), pp. 193–224.

5 UN, Human Rights Council, Report of Special Representative of the Secretary-General on the Issue of Human Rights and Transnational Corporations and Other Business Enterprises, John Ruggie, 'Guiding Principles on Business and Human Rights: Implementing the United Nations "Protect, Respect and Remedy" Framework' ['The Guiding Principles'], UN Doc. A/HRC/17/31, 21 March 2011, principle 13 (Commentary to Principle 11).

6 See for instance, UN, OHCHR, 'Key Messages on Human Rights and Climate Change', 27 November 2015, para 8.

7 UN, 'Transforming Our World: The 2030 Agenda for Sustainable Development, Outcome Document of the United Nations Summit to Adopt the Post-2015 Development Agenda', UN Doc. A/69/L.85, 12 August 2015. See Chapter 3 of this book.

with the right to water. The conclusion contends that corporations have negative and emerging positive obligations with respect to the human rights to education, food, health, housing and water.

Corporate socio-economic obligations relative to specific rights

This following section analyzes individual corporate obligations concerning individual socio-economic rights by examining the source and nature of individual socio-economic rights.

Corporate obligations in relation to the human right to education

The business sector has been heavily involved at all levels in the provision of the right to education, particularly in areas where states are unable to provide it publicly. The right to education is internal to the development of an individual's capabilities and their self-realization generally. ILO observes that "the international community's efforts and the obligations . . . towards ending child labour and ensuring inclusive and equitable quality education for all . . . are inextricably linked".[8]

This derives from domestic constitutional protections, international level commitments and corporate internal commitments. Over 80% of domestic constitutions protect the right to education.[9] Constitutional protections typically also bind legal entities, including corporations.[10] Further, the international level provides for mainly indirect corporate obligations. Paragraph 1 of Article 13 of the International Covenant on Economic, Social and Cultural Rights provides that "States Parties . . . recognize everyone the right to education. They agree that education must have the full development of human personality and dignity and that it must strengthen respect for human rights and fundamental freedoms".[11] Protocol no. 1 of the European Convention for the Protection of Human Rights and Fundamental Freedoms stipulates in Article 2 that "no one shall be deprived of the right to education".[12] Those obligations thereby also apply indirectly to corporations and other non-state actors. Additionally, CESCR has on several occasions emphasized the need to establish a regulatory framework to control

8 ILO, 'Ending Child Labour by 2025: A Review of Policies and Programmes', Geneva, 2017, p. 41.

9 See, Jody Heymann, Amy Raub and Adèle Cassola, 'Constitutional Rights to Education and Their Relationship to National Policy and School Enrolment', 39 *International Journal of Educational Development* 121 (2014), p. 135.

10 See, chapter 5.

11 UN, 'International Covenant on Economic, Social and Cultural Rights', GA res. 2200A (XXI), 21 UN GAOR Supp. (No. 16) at 49, UN Doc. A/6316, Treaty Series, vol. 993, 16 December 1966.

12 Council of Europe, Protocol no. 1 of the European Convention for the Protection of Human Rights and Fundamental Freedoms, 20 March 1952, Article 2.

private actors when providing the right to education.[13] Further, the business sector itself accepts that it has responsibilities concerning the provision of the right to education.[14]

States and corporations must actively create the conditions for the exercise of the right to education. States have the obligation to respect, protect and exercise the right to education. States have a primary obligation to protect human rights and fundamental freedoms within their territory and are also positively obliged to protect human rights in private relationships. This not only constitutes an obligation of effort but also an emerging obligation of results. The right to education is particularly protected in relation to the institutions of all three branches of state authority and individuals who exercise public functions. Constitutional provisions on the right to education impose on corporations a negative obligation to not interfere with the enjoyment of an individual's right to education and a positive obligation to prevent their business partners from interfering with it. Corporations are therefore obliged to respect the right to education by first not causing harm. Further, they are obliged to comply with their positive obligations by attempting to ensure that, for instance, their suppliers do not infringe the right to education. They carry positive obligations of protecting and fulfilling the provision of at least the minimum level of right to education when they perform public functions as either state-owned corporations or via licenses or concessions.

Whereas the corporate negative obligation to respect the right to education is an obligation of result, their positive obligations to protect and fulfil are obligations of conduct (see Table 6.1). Corporations have a positive obligation to not only respect the right to education, but also to protect at least its minimum core and create the conditions for its realization, particularly in the proximity of their operations. If there is a violation of the right to education, corporations must take appropriate measures to prevent further violations of the right to education and provide compensation. Corporations need to choose the most appropriate measure in a given situation, carefully and tactfully, in order to safeguard the best interests of a student and wider community, and realize at least the minimum of the right to education.

Corporate obligations in relation to the human right to food

Food is an essential component that facilitates individuals in their efforts to achieve sustainable livelihoods. SGD 2 states the objective to "end hunger, achieve food security and improved nutrition and promote sustainable agriculture". CESRC observed in its General Comment no. 12 that "violations of the right to food can occur through the direct action of States or other entities insufficiently regulated by States".[15]

13 UN, CESCR, 'Concluding Observations: Uganda', UN Doc. E/C.12/UGA/CO/1, 8 July 2015, para 36, c.

14 See, chapter 4.

15 UN, CESCR, 'General Comment No. 12: The Right to Adequate Food (Art.11)', UN Doc. E/C.12/1999/5, 12 May 1999, para 19.

Table 6.1 Corporate obligations to respect, protect and fulfil concerning the right to education

Right to education	*Preventive dimension*	*Remedial dimension*
Corporate obligation to respect	Not cause harm to individuals' enjoyment of the right to education.	Undertake a human rights assessment prior to starting a project and submit themselves to fair, independent and impartial judicial proceedings.
	Not interfere with a judicial rule-of-law process examining their alleged involvement in right-to-education violations.	Support and do not interfere with fair, independent, and impartial reporting and auditing.
	Draft and implement a detailed human rights policy, which must be disseminated internally and externally to all relevant stakeholders and business partners, and incorporated into all its policies.	Submit themselves to fair, independent and impartial judicial proceedings in case of violations of human rights policy, and provide the right to effective remedies to victims and their families.
Corporate obligation to protect	Undertake due diligence across their global supply chains to ensure that their business partners do not violate the minimum levels of right to education.	Establish external periodic independent verification of these procedures, and the reports they generate must address specific abuses and devise ways of promoting respect for socio-economic rights.
	Develop a systematic supervisory mechanism within and outside their corporate group.	Establish internal grievance procedures where victims can seek recourse in a complaints mechanism, and submit themselves to fair, independent and impartial judicial proceedings, including compensation.
	Conduct an internal, effective, transparent and diligent investigation into the alleged violations in the case of violations.	Establish a special task force in charge of investigating the alleged violations.
Corporate obligation to fulfil	Create conditions for individuals' enjoyment of the right to education.	Help local communities with providing individuals with the right to education.
	Participate in partnerships and make financial commitments to contribute to individuals' enjoyment of the right to education.	Create internal funds and contribute to external funds for use in providing for the right to education.
	Strive to assist states in providing at least the reasonable minimum core of the right to education, particularly in the local communities in which they operate.	Work with governments to provide the reasonable minimum core of the right to education.

Corporate obligations regarding the human right to food arise from three levels of legal sources: national legal systems, the international level and unilateral voluntary commitments made by corporations themselves. Several domestic constitutions protect the right to food through national constitutions either directly or indirectly through the right to life or other human rights. Over twenty-four states recognize and protect the right to food in their national constitutions.[16] For instance, Article 27 of the Constitution of South Africa provides that "1. Everyone has the right to have access to [. . .] b. sufficient food and water". The Constitution of Bolivia states that "every person has the right to water and food".[17] Further, the Constitution of Ecuador states that "persons and community groups have the right to safe and permanent access to healthy, sufficient and nutritional food, preferably produced locally and in keeping with their various identities and cultural traditions".[18] In addition, national statutes in several states provide for protections of the right to food.[19] Article 1 of the Law on Food Sovereignty and Food Security and Nutrition No. 693 of 2009 of the Republic of Nicaragua[20] includes these objectives:

> to guarantee the right of all Nicaraguans to rely on sufficient, innocuous and nutritious foods, in harmony with their vital need, that these be physically, economically, socially and culturally available in a timely and permanent manner. Food should be available in a stable and sufficient manner by means of State development and governance with public policies for the implementation of food sovereignty and nutrition.[21]

16 Food and Agriculture Organization of the United Nations (FAO), 'The Right to Food: Past Commitment, Current Obligation, Further Action for the Future: A Ten-Year Retrospective on the Right to Food Guidelines', 2014, www.fao.org/3/a-i4145e.pdf (last accessed 20 December 2017), para 20. See also, Lidija Knuth and Margret Vidar, 'Constitutional and Legal Protection of the Right to Food around the World', Food and Agriculture Organization of the United Nations (FAO), Rome 2011, p. 16. See also, Sven Söllner, 'The "Breakthrough" of the Right to Food: The Meaning of General Comment No. 12 and the Voluntary Guidelines for the Interpretation of the Human Right to Food', 11(1) *Max Planck Yearbook of United Nations Law Online* 391 (2007), 395.

17 Constitution of 2009 of the Plurinational State of Bolivia, 7 February 2009, http://pdba.georgetown.edu/Constitutions/Bolivia/bolivia.html (last accessed 19 January 2018), art. 16.

18 Constitution of Ecuador, Official Journal 448, 20 October 2008, http://www.refworld.org/docid/3dbd62fd2.html (last accessed 19 January 2018), art. 13.

19 Food and Agriculture Organization of the United Nations (FAO), 'The Right to Food: Past Commitment, Current Obligation, Further Action for the Future: A Ten-Year Retrospective on the Right to Food Guidelines', 2014, para 20 (Legal framework). See for an examination of particular regional developments, The Domestic Implementation of the Olivier De Schutter, 'Right to Food in Latin America and the Caribbean', *in* Humberto Cantú Rivera (ed.), *The Special Procedures of the Human Rights Council: A Brief Look from the Inside and Perspectives from Outside*, Cambridge, Antwerp and Portland: Intersentia (2015), pp. 25–52.

20 National Assembly of the Republic of Nicaragua, 'Law of Food and Nutrition Sovereignty and Security', Act No. 693, published in La Gaceta, Official Bulletin No. 133, 16 July 2009.

21 Ibid.

On top of this, the highest national courts have either directly or indirectly (mostly via the right to life) protected this right.[22] The national level therefore provides the strongest evidence that corporations are also obliged to observe the right to food. However, this level is thereafter supplemented by emerging international regulation and voluntary commitments made by various food industry sectors and corporations themselves.

At the international level, the ICESCR protects the right to food in Article 11. Even though it primarily only binds states, one can argue is also indirectly binds corporations. The Committee articulated its understanding of the core of the right to food as "the availability of food . . . sufficient to satisfy the dietary needs of individuals . . .".[23] It continues that a state "in which any significant number of individuals is deprived of essential foodstuffs . . . is, prima facie, failing to discharge its obligations under the Covenant".[24] De Schutter argued that:

> The human right to food would be violated if people depending on land for their livelihoods, including pastoralists, were cut off from access to land, without suitable alternatives; if local incomes were insufficient to compensate for the price effects resulting from the shift towards the production of food for exports; or if the revenues of local smallholders were to fall following the arrival on domestic markets of cheaply priced food, produced on the more competitive large-scale plantations developed thanks to the arrival of the investor.[25]

Article 11(1) of the ICESCR notes that

> the States Parties to the present Covenant recognize the right of everyone to an adequate standard of living for himself and his family, including adequate food, clothing and housing and to the continuous improvement of living conditions. The States Parties will take appropriate steps to ensure the realization of this right, recognizing to this effect the essential importance of international co-operation based on free consent.[26]

22 See for example, *Kishen Pattnayak & Another v. State of Orissa,* A.I.R. 1989 S.C. 677 (Supreme Court of India); *People's Union for Civil Liberties v. Union of India & Ors. S.C.* 2001, Writ Petition (Civil) No. 196/2001 (Supreme Court of India), reprinted in Colin Gonsalves, Right to Food, New Delhi (2004). See also, *G v. An Bord Uchtála*, 1980, IR 32.

23 UN, CESCR, General Comment 12, paras 1–20.

24 Ibid., General Comment 3, para 10. See for more detail, Asbjørn Eide, 'The International Human Rights System', *in* Asbjørn Eide, Wenche Barthe Eide, Susantha Goonatilake, Joan Gussow and Omawale (eds.), *Food as a Human Right*, Tokyo: United Nations University Press (1984), pp. 152–161; Asbjørn Eide, 'The Right to Adequate Food and to Be Free from Hunger: Updated Study on the Right to Food', submitted in accordance with Sub-Commission decision 1998/106, E/CN.4/Sub.2/1999, 28 June 1999.

25 UN, Human Rights Council, 'Report of the Special Rapporteur on the Right to Food: Olivier De Schutter', UN Doc. A/HRC/13/33/Add.2, 22 December 2009, Annex: Minimum human rights principles applicable to large-scale land acquisitions or leases, para 4.

26 UN, International Covenant on Economic, 'Social and Cultural Rights, GA res. 2200A (XXI), 21 UN GAOR Supp. (No. 16) at 49', UN Doc. A/6316, Treaty Series, vol. 993, 16 December 1966.

Further, the Committee on the Rights of the Child observed that

> the activities and operations of business enterprises can impact on the realization of Article 6 in different ways. For example, environmental degradation and contamination arising from business activities can compromise children's rights to health, food security and access to safe drinking water and sanitation.[27]

Traditionally, CESCR has believed that "the right to adequate food, like any other human right, imposes three types or levels of obligations on States parties: the obligations to respect, to protect and to fulfil".[28] This includes a state obligation to control, supervise and prevent violations by businesses.[29] Those obligations therefore indirectly also apply to corporations.

The emerging corporate obligations also arise from codes of conduct of corporations operating in the food industry. For instance, the Global Social Compliance Programme "brings together key actors of the consumer goods industry to collaborate on a common goal: driving positive change and business efficiency in the areas of social and environmental sustainability along the supply chain".[30] Moreover, GLOBALG.A.P has established "voluntary standards for the certification of agricultural products around the globe – and more and more producers, suppliers and buyers are harmonizing their certification standards to match".[31] At a national level, the Australian Competition and Consumer Commission drafted the Food and Grocery Code of Conduct which guides corporations in the food sector.[32] Further, several corporations have internal sustainability polices. For example, the McDonald's Corporation notes that "at McDonald's, we conduct our activities in a manner that respects human rights as set out in The United Nations Universal Declaration of Human Rights" and "each of our employees throughout the world deserves to be treated with fairness, respect and dignity".[33] The company code of ethics of Kellogg's provides that "our position on human

27 UN, Committee on the Rights of the Child, 'General comment No. 16 on State Obligations Regarding the Impact of the Business Sector on Children's Rights', UN Doc. CRC/C/GC/16, 17 April 2013.

28 UN, CESCR, 'General Comment 12', para 15.

29 UN, CESCR, 'General Comment 15: The Right to Water (Art. 11 and 12)', UN Doc E/C.12/2002/11, 20 January 2003. paras 23–24.

30 Global Social Compliance Programme, 'Mission', www.theconsumergoodsforum.com/initiatives/social-sustainability/key-projects/global-social-compliance-programme-gscp (last accessed 19 January 2018).

31 GLOBALG.A.P, 'About Us', www.globalgap.org/uk_en/who-we-are/about-us/ (last accessed 19 January 2018).

32 Australian Competition and Consumer Commission, 'Food and Grocery Code of Conduct', www.accc.gov.au/business/industry-codes/food-and-grocery-code-of-conduct#the-code (last accessed 19 January 2018).

33 McDonald's corporation, 'Standards of Business Conduct. The Promise of the Golden Arches', March 2017, p. 20.

rights is compatible with the United Nations Universal Declaration of Human Rights and the core conventions of the International Labour Organization" and "we are committed to maintaining an ethical and transparent supply chain free of forced labor, including slavery and human trafficking".[34]

Corporations operating in the food industry must thus strive to combat hunger, although it is difficult to say they hold binding obligations in the exercise of the right to food. One could easily argue their sole obligation is to not to limit access to food in the country in question. However, the corporate obligation to respect, that is, to avoid causing any harm to individuals' enjoyment of food is straightforward and cannot be questioned. Further, they are obliged to comply with their positive obligations by attempting to ensure that their business partners do not infringe the right to food. They have positive protect and fulfil obligations to provide at least the minimum level of the right to food when they perform public functions as either state-owned corporations or via licenses or concessions. Whereas the corporate negative obligation to respect the right to food is an obligation of result, their positive obligations to protect and fulfil are obligations of conduct. The corporate obligation to protect means corporations must strive to guarantee protections of the right to food across their supply chains and business relationships.

Corporations should control their supply chains in order to avoid direct infringement of the right to food. As noted above, the corporate obligations to protect as well as fulfil are obligations of conduct, not of result. Corporations have to, by employing due diligence processes and ensuring respect of human rights, control and supervise their supply chains. In the case of the agriculture sector, this means transnational food corporations must ensure that their subsidiaries comply with both the right to food and other socio-economic rights as well. The former special rapporteur for the right to food drafted minimum guidelines for large-scale land acquisitions and leases intended for both states and corporations.[35] More specifically, Principle 4 of those guidelines provides that

> the local population should benefit from the revenues generated by the investment agreement. Investment contracts should prioritize the development needs of the local population and seek to achieve solutions which represent an adequate balance between the interests of all parties.[36]

Yeshanew and Windfuhr argued that "the main challenge is to maximize the benefits of FDI in agriculture while minimizing the risks, possibly through inclusive business models with the participation of smallholders (FAO, 2012c)".[37]

34 Kellogg Company, 'Kellogg Company's Global Code of Ethics', September 2013, p. 39.

35 UN, Human Rights Council, 'Report of the Special Rapporteur on the Right to Food: Olivier De Schutter'.

36 Ibid., principle 4, p. 16.

37 Sisay Alemahu Yeshanew and Michael Windfuhr, 'International Dimensions of the Right to Adequate Food', Food and Agriculture Organization of the United Nations (FAO), Rome 2014, p. 7.

The corporate obligation to fulfil depends on the available measures and financial resources of particular business actors. In the business context, this means agricultural businesses would have to invest more in food supply of local environment. For instance, the Institute for Business and Human Rights proposed business-specific SDG 2 as one of two proposed Implementation Indicators for Business concerning SDG 17.[38] It reads as follows: "Businesses contribute directly to the Goals according to capacity and expertise".[39] Those targets would be framed around two pillars "(i) alignment of social investment strategies with SDG targets (ii) SDG Development partnerships".[40] Moreover, Farming First, an NGO, claimed that "reaching the SDG targets simply will not be possible without a strong and sustainable agricultural sector".[41] Therefore, businesses should not only comply with their obligations to respect, protect and fulfil, but should seriously consider their existing and potential financial contribution to sustainable development (see Table 6.2). Moreover, such obligations are reinforced in a fragile context where action by the state is often missing.

Corporate obligations in relation to the human right to health

The right to health is another right that facilitates the individual's socio-economic welfare and livelihood. It is divided into two parts: the right to access health services and the right to access the fundamental components of the right to health. States are traditionally obliged to ensure the availability, accessibility, acceptability and quality of both sets of components that make up the right to health. Domestic constitutional systems offer wide protections of the right to health or the right to a healthy environment. Jeffords observes that

> 142 out of 198 national constitutions . . . include at least one reference to the environment as of 2010. Out of these 142 constitutions, 125 contain provisions that are explicitly related to environmental human rights and ten include a direct human right to water.[42]

Several domestic courts have confirmed and protected the right against corporate conduct. In the notorious Bhopal case, the Supreme Court of India confirmed

38 Institute for Human Rights and Business (IHRB), 'State of Play. Business and the Sustainable Development Goals: Mind the Gap – Challenges for Implementation', September 2015, p. 20.

39 Ibid.

40 Ibid.

41 Farming First, 'The Story of Agriculture and the Sustainable Development Goals', 2015, www.farmingfirst.org/sdg-toolkit#home (last accessed 19 January 2018).

42 Christopher Jeffords, 'Constitutional Environmental Human Rights: A Descriptive Analysis of 142 National Constitutions', Economic Rights Working Paper Series No. 16, University of Connecticut, 2011, p. 2.

Table 6.2 Corporate obligations to respect, protect and fulfil concerning the right to food

Right to food	*Preventive dimension*	*Remedial dimension*
Corporate obligation to respect	Not cause harm to individuals' enjoyment of the right to food.	Undertake a human rights assessment prior to starting a project and submit themselves to fair, independent and impartial judicial proceedings.
	Not interfere with a judicial rule-of-law process examining their alleged involvement in right-to-food violations.	Support and do not interfere with fair, independent, and impartial reporting and auditing.
	Draft and implement a detailed human rights policy, which must be disseminated internally and externally to all relevant stakeholders and business partners and be incorporated into all its policies.	Submit themselves to fair, independent and impartial judicial proceedings in case of violations of human rights policy, and provide the right to effective remedies to victims and their families.
Corporate obligation to protect	Undertake due diligence across their global supply chains to ensure that their business partners do not violate the minimum levels of right to food.	Establish external periodic independent verification of these procedures, and the reports they generate must address specific abuses and devise ways of promoting respect for socio-economic rights.
	Develop a systematic supervisory mechanism within and outside their corporate group.	Establish internal grievance procedures where victims can seek recourse in a complaints mechanism, and submit themselves to fair, independent and impartial judicial proceedings.
	Conduct an internal, effective, transparent and diligent investigation into the alleged violations in the case of violations.	Establish a special task force in charge of investigating the alleged violations.
Corporate obligation to fulfil	Create conditions for individuals' enjoyment of the right to food.	Help local communities with providing individuals with the right to food.
	Participate in partnerships and make a financial commitment to contribute to individuals' enjoyment of the right to food.	Create internal funds and contribute to external funds for use in providing for the right to food.
	Strive to assist states in providing at least the reasonable minimum core of right to food, particularly in the local communities in which they operate.	Work with governments to provide the reasonable minimum core of the right to food.

that the right to health applies to corporations.[43] International human rights have broadly recognized the right to health. More specifically, CESCR notes in its General Comment no. 14 that also in the private sector in general corporations carry obligations concerning the right to health. More specifically, it observes that:

> all members of society – individuals, including health professionals, families, local communities, intergovernmental and non-governmental organizations, civil society organizations, as well as the private business sector – have responsibilities regarding the realization of the right to health. State parties should therefore provide an environment which facilitates the discharge of these responsibilities.[44]

The Committee also noted that

> payment for health-care services, as well as services related to the underlying determinants of health, has to be based on the principle of equity, ensuring that these services, whether privately or publicly provided, are affordable for all, including socially disadvantaged groups.[45]

Further, General Comment no. 14 notes that states are obliged

> to ensure that privatization of the health sector does not constitute a threat to the availability, accessibility, acceptability and quality of health facilities, goods and services; to control the marketing of medical equipment and medicines by third parties; and to ensure that medical practitioners and other health professionals meet appropriate standards of education, skill and ethical codes of conduct.[46]

Moreover, several other regional bodies have stressed the obligation with respect to the right to health. The Inter-American Court of Human Rights noted in the case of *Ximenes-Lopes v. Brazil* concerning the functioning of a private mental care body in Brazil that "the States must regulate and supervise all activities related to the health care given to the individuals under the jurisdiction".[47]

Corporations hold both negative and positive obligations to ensure the individual's enjoyment of the right to health (see Table 6.3). The negative obligation of respect of the right to health is the most straightforward, requiring businesses to

43 *Charan Lal Sahu v. Union of India*, 1990 (1) SCC, 613 (Bhopal Gas Disaster Case) (Supreme Court of India).

44 UN, CESCR, 'General Comment 14: The Right to the Highest Attainable Standard of Health (Art.12)', UN Doc. E/C.12/2000/4, 11 August 2000, para 42.

45 Ibid., para 12(b)(iii).

46 Ibid., para 35.

47 *Ximenes-Lopes v. Brazil*, Judgment of 4 July 2006, Series C No. 149 (Inter-American Court of Human Rights – IACHR), para 85.

Table 6.3 Corporate obligations to respect, protect and fulfil concerning the right to health

Right to health	*Preventive dimension*	*Remedial dimension*
Corporate obligation to respect	Not cause harm to individuals' enjoyment of the right to health.	Undertake a human rights assessment prior to starting a project and submit themselves to fair, independent and impartial judicial proceedings.
	Not interfere with a judicial rule-of-law process examining their alleged involvement in right to health violations.	Support and do not interfere with fair, independent, and impartial reporting and auditing.
	Draft and implement a human rights policy which must be disseminated internally and externally to all relevant stakeholders and business partners, and be incorporated into all its policies.	Submit themselves to fair, independent and impartial judicial proceedings in the case of violations of human rights policy, and provide the right effective remedies to victims and their families.
Corporate obligation to protect	Undertake due diligence across their global supply chains to ensure that their business partners do not violate the minimum levels of right to health.	Establish external periodic independent verification of these procedures, and the reports they generate must address specific abuses and devise ways of promoting respect for socio-economic rights.
	Develop a systematic supervisory mechanism within and outside their corporate group.	Establish internal grievance procedures where victims can seek recourse in a complaints mechanism, and submit themselves to fair, independent and impartial judicial proceedings, including compensation.
	Conduct an internal, effective, transparent and diligent investigation into the alleged violations in the case of violations.	Establish a special task force in charge of investigating the alleged violations.
Corporate obligation to fulfil	Create the conditions for individuals' enjoyment of the right to health.	Help local communities with providing individuals with the right to health
	Participate in partnerships and make financial commitments to contribute to individuals' enjoyment of the right to health.	Create internal funds and contribute to external funds for use in providing for the right to health.
	Strive to assist states in providing at least the reasonable minimum core of right to health, particularly in the local communities in which they operate.	Work with governments in a reasonable minimum core of the right to health.

not interfere with the individual's enjoyment of the right to health. Their obligation in relation to the internal sphere is particularly strong, namely in relation to employees and in the context of local communities. Further, they are obliged to comply with their positive obligations by attempting to ensure that their business partners do not infringe the reasonable core of the right to health. They carry positive obligations to protect and fulfil to provide at least the minimum level of the right to food when they perform public functions as either state-owned corporations or via licenses or concessions. In contrast, the other two obligations are more controversial. Whereas the corporate negative obligation to respect the right to food is an obligation of result, their positive obligations to protect and fulfil are obligations of conduct. The obligation to protect comes into play for corporations in the context where they act as service providers or suppliers.[48] In this setting, they are obliged to control their whole network of connected companies and business partners. As for obligations to protect, Jägers argues that:

> For corporations the duty to protect the right to health will come into play especially with the regard to the 'underlying determinants' of the right to health, such as food and nutrition, housing, access to safe and potable water and adequate sanitation, safe and healthy working conditions and a healthy environment. The duty to protect may require a corporation to adopt guidelines in order to ensure that the activities of business partners will not lead to violations of other individuals' right to health[49] (footnotes omitted).

As for the other part of positive obligations, businesses are required to fulfil at least in relation to their employees, which could be extended to wider local communities where the state is absent or does not have the financial means to provide for at least the minimum level of health services. However, as Clapham and Rubio note, "articulating the legal regime for the relevant rights and responsibilities in the context of corporate health care is not simple".[50] All in all, different levels of sources illustrate that corporations are obliged to respect the right to health and at a minimum to protect the reasonable minimum core of the right to health in their global supply chains and in the proximity of their operations.[51]

48 See for example, William Savedoff and Karen Hussmann, 'Why Are Health Systems So Prone to Corruption?' *in* Transparency International (ed.), *Global Corruption Report 2006: Special Focus – Corruption and Health*, London and Ann Arbor: Pluto Press (2006), pp. 4–16.

49 Nicola Jägers, *Corporate Human Rights Obligations: In Search of Accountability*, Antwerp: Intersentia (2002), p. 87.

50 Andrew Clapham and Mariano Garcia Rubio, 'The Obligations of States with Regard to Non-State Actors in the Context of the Right to Health', Health and Human Rights Working Paper Series No 3 (2002), p. 4.

51 Brigit Toebes, 'Direct Corporate Human Rights Obligations Under the Right to Health: From Mere "respecting" Towards Protecting and Fulfilling', *in* Jernej Letnar Černič and Tara van Ho (eds.), *Human Rights and Business: Direct Corporate Accountability for Human Rights*, Oisterwijk: Wolf Legal Publisher (2015), pp. 263–278.

Corporate obligations in relation to the human right to adequate housing

The right to adequate housing is an essential socio-economic right that contributes to decent socio-economic standards. It was not developed as a fully fledged right, but as part of the right to an adequate standard of living. Corporations can be involved in the housing context as landlords, investors, developers, construction corporations, even as a body that evicts people. Millions worldwide now do not have access to adequate housing due to rising inequality caused by governments, but also private investors. Leilani Farha, the UN special rapporteur on adequate housing as a component of the right to an adequate standard of living and on the right to non-discrimination in this context, rightly observes that "housing and real estate markets have been transformed by corporate finance, including banks, insurance and pension funds, hedge funds, private equity firms and other kinds of financial intermediaries with massive amounts of capital and excess liquidity".[52] She adds that "housing and commercial real estate have become the 'commodity of choice' for corporate finance and the pace at which financial corporations and funds are taking over housing and real estate in many cities is staggering".[53] In recognition of their power, those corporations must take responsibility to follow the negative obligation to respect the right to housing and positively at least to ensure a minimum level of adequate housing.

Traditionally, it does not create a state obligation of result, but of conduct. In international human rights law, states are asked to strive for a "maximum of available resources" to guarantee such rights. In practice, this means that states are obliged to create minimum conditions for each individual to establish adequate housing for the individual and their family. As part of their obligations, states but also businesses are not to infringe the right to adequate housing of vulnerable groups and are to strive to create the conditions for the enjoyment of those rights.

Corporate obligations with respect to the right to adequate housing derive from national, international and internal corporate levels. Like always, the strongest legal source for corporate obligations have been the domestic legal systems, especially constitutional protections that theoretically apply to both natural and legal persons, including corporations and other business forms. Therefore, several national constitutions provide for constitutional protections of the right to adequate housing. Article 4 of the Constitution of Mexico provides that "every family has the right to enjoy decent and proper housing. The law shall establish the instruments and necessary supports to reach the said goal".[54]

52 UN, Human Rights Council, 'Report of the Special Rapporteur on Adequate Housing as a Component of the Right to an Adequate Standard of Living, and on the Right to Non-Discrimination in This Context: Leilani Farha', UN Doc. A/HRC/34/51, 18 January 2017.

53 Ibid.

54 Constitution of the United Mexican States, 1917 (as amended). Washington: Pan American Union, art. 4.

The Constitution of Portugal provides in paragraph 1 of Article 65 that "all have the right, both personally and for their family, to a dwelling of adequate size that meets satisfactory standards of hygiene and comfort and preserves personal and family privacy".[55] The Constitution of the Russian Federation provides in Article 40 (1) that "everyone has the right to a home. No one may be arbitrarily deprived of a home".[56] Article 26 of the Constitution of South Africa states that "(1) Everyone has the right to have access to adequate housing".[57] Further, the domestic legislation from different areas of law also conveys the obligation to ensure adequate housing at least to vulnerable groups.

The primacy of the domestic level also follows from decisions made by the highest national courts. Their decisions provide additional evidence of the emergence of corporate obligations concerning the right to adequate housing.[58] At the international level, several sources of law confirm that corporations are at least indirectly, through the state, obliged to ensure adequate housing. Article 11 (1) of the ICESCR says that state parties "recognize the right of everyone to an adequate standard of living for himself and his family, including adequate food, clothing and housing and to the continuous improvement of living conditions".[59] The Committee has noted in its General Comment no. 4 that the right to adequate housing "is to be realized and maintained by all groups in society".[60] ILO Recommendation No. 115 provides that

> national housing programmes should aim at ensuring, consistently with other national goals and within limits set by housing and related needs, that all private and public resources which can be made available for the purpose are co-ordinated and utilized for the construction of workers' housing and related community facilities.[61]

Those authorities at the international level also indirectly bind corporations.

The private sector must ensure it does not act directly and indirectly against adequate housing sustainable settlements and cities and that it does not violate related human rights. The right to adequate housing includes six key elements corporations must observe: "Legal security of tenure"; "Affordability"; "Habitability"; "Availability of services, materials, facilities and infrastructure";

55 Constitution of Portugal (1976, fourth revision based on Constitutional Law No. 1/97 of 20 September 1997), art. 65.
56 The Constitution of the Russian Federation (December 1993), art. 40 (1).
57 Constitution of South Africa (1996), art. 26.
58 *Absa Bank Limited v. Moore and another*, CCT 03/16 (Constitutional Court of South Africa).
59 ICESCR, art. 11 (1).
60 UN, CESCR, General Comment 14, para 9.
61 International Labour Organization (ILO), 'R115 – Workers' Housing Recommendation, 1961 (No. 115)', Geneva: 45th ILC session, 28 June 1961, para 9.

"Accessibility"; "Location"; and "Cultural Adequacy".[62] The corporate obligation to respect the right to adequate housing means that corporations are obliged to not interfere with the individual's enjoyment of such housing. Corporations are obliged to not involve themselves in forced evictions, violations of the right to private and family life, and violations of the freedom of movement.[63] This negative obligation on the private sector is accompanied by its positive commitments to bring added value to both the local population and the wider community. Such positive obligations include corporate obligations to protect and fulfil the right to adequate housing; for instance, by striving to ensure adequate housing at least for vulnerable groups. Obligations to protect include positive steps that corporations need to take in order to ensure their business partners do not infringe on the adequate housing of individuals, particularly of vulnerable groups. For instance, a corporation has an obligation to construct and provide adequate housing for its employees in underdeveloped areas where housing infrastructure is lacking.[64] Such an obligation is reinforced in areas where "where the government has a reduced capacity to realise the right, certainly in the time scale of the business operations".[65]

Farha argues that

> business and human rights guidelines in the housing sector must recognize the responsibility of private investors and the obligations of regulators of capital markets to ensure that the needs of vulnerable and marginalized groups are adequately addressed through inclusive investment strategies and to contribute to the realization of the right to housing.[66]

Her statement reads as a call for the businesses obligation to fulfil. However, it is not quite straightforward that business would have an obligation to fulfil. These obligations depend on the businesses' available financial resources. Do corporations then have to allocate sufficient resources to provide for the right to adequate housing, and, if so, to whom? Corporate obligations to fulfil would include considerations of adequate housing policies in the investment and business strategy of businesses (see Table 6.4). In contrast, it does not require a business to alter its overall business strategy in order to integrate housing concerns that may jeopardize the future existence of the business. One may argue that the corporate obligation to protect under the right to housing is strongest with regard to their employees and the local community in which it operates. It is unrealistic that a

62 UN Office of the High Commissioner for Human Rights (OHCHR), 'The Right to Adequate Housing', fact sheet No. 21/Rev.1.

63 Human Rights and Business Dilemmas Forum, 'Access to Adequate Housing', http://hrbdf.org/dilemmas/housing/#.WYNbaYh942w (last accessed 19 January 2018).

64 Ibid.

65 Ibid.

66 UN, Human Rights Council, 'Report of the Special Rapporteur on Adequate Housing', para 66.

Table 6.4 Corporate obligations to respect, protect and fulfil concerning the right to adequate housing

Right to housing	*Preventive dimension*	*Remedial dimension*
Corporate obligation to respect	Not cause harm to individuals' enjoyment of the right to adequate housing.	Undertake a human rights assessment prior to starting a project, and submit themselves to fair, independent and impartial judicial proceedings.
	Not interfere with a judicial rule-of-law process examining their alleged involvement in right-to-housing violations.	Support and do not interfere with fair, independent, and impartial reporting and auditing.
	Draft and implement a detailed human rights policy, which must be disseminated internally and externally to all relevant stakeholders and business partners, and be incorporated into all its policies.	Submit themselves to fair, independent and impartial judicial proceedings in the case of violations of human rights policy, and provide the right to effective remedies to victims and their families.
Corporate obligation to protect	Undertake due diligence across their global supply chains to ensure that their business partners do not violate the minimum levels of right to adequate housing.	Establish external periodic independent verification of these procedures, and the reports they generate must address specific abuses and devise ways of promoting respect for socio-economic rights.
	Develop a systematic supervisory mechanism within and outside their corporate group.	Establish internal grievance procedures where victims can seek recourse in a complaints mechanism, and submit themselves to fair, independent and impartial judicial proceedings, including compensation.
	Conduct an internal, effective, transparent and diligent investigation into the alleged violations in the case of violations.	Establish a special task force in charge of investigating the alleged violations.
Corporate obligation to fulfil	Create the conditions for individuals' enjoyment of the right to adequate housing.	Help local communities with providing individuals with the right to adequate housing.
	Participate in partnerships and make financial commitments to contribute to individuals' enjoyment of the right to adequate housing.	Create internal funds and contribute to external funds for use in providing for the right to adequate housing.
	Strive to assist states in providing at least the reasonable minimum core of the right to adequate housing, particularly in the local communities in which they operate.	Work with governments in providing the reasonable minimum core of the right to housing.

corporation would be obliged to ensure adequate housing across the whole state territory or even that such obligations would be global in character. However, in a limited context the corporate obligation to fulfil the right to adequate housing might be realistic within a narrow scope.

Corporate obligations in relation to the human right to water

SDG 6 requires states and other actors to "ensure access to water and sanitation for all". Past and present examples from everyday life around the world show corporations can directly and indirectly affect individuals' enjoyment of the human right to water. Some positive efforts in business and human rights, on the other hand, also show that corporations can positively contribute to the enjoyment of water, thereby adding to the evidence that corporations can also positively contribute to efforts to comply with the obligation to fulfil that require financial resources. UN CESCR's General Comment no. 15 notes that "the human right to water entitles everyone to sufficient, safe, acceptable, physically accessible and affordable water for personal and domestic uses".[67] It further observes that "any persons or groups who have been denied their right to water should have access to effective judicial or other appropriate remedies at both national and international levels".[68]

Who are the duty-bearers of the human right to water? States, but also corporations, can carry the duty enshrined in the human right to water, particularly where they perform public functions. This section argues that corporate obligations in relation to the human right to water stem from three levels of legal sources: national legal systems, the international level and unilateral voluntary commitments made by corporations themselves.[69] First, a number of national constitutional systems indirectly protect for the right to water, thereby imposing obligations on natural and legal persons, including corporations. For instance, Article 27 of the Constitution of South Africa provides that "everyone has the right to have access to . . . sufficient . . . water".[70] Further, the Constitution of the Lao People's Democratic Republic states that "all organizations and citizens must protect . . . water sources",[71] thereby implying that this provision also intends to address corporate actors. Similarly, several other states provide for the human right to water in their

67 UN, CESCR, General Comment 15, para 2.

68 Ibid., para 55.

69 Jernej Letnar Černič, 'Corporate Obligations Under the Human Right to Water', 39(2) *Denver Journal of International Law and Policy* 303 (2011). See also, Chiara Macchi, 'Right to Water and the Threat of Business: Corporate Accountability and the State's Duty to Protect', 35(3) *Nordic Journal of Human Rights* 186 (2017).

70 Constitution of South Africa, No. 108 of 1996, National Gazette No. 17678, 18 December 1996, chapter II, art. 8 (2).

71 Constitution of the Lao People's Democratic Republic, 6 May 2003, http://www.refworld.org/docid/3ae6b5221a.html (accessed 19 January 2018), art. 17.

national constitutions.[72] Another layer of obligations can be found in domestic statutes in the field of administrative law.[73] Moreover, decisions of the highest domestic tribunals also demonstrate that corporations are obliged with respect to the human right to water. For example, the Constitutional Court of Colombia noted in *Hernán Galeano Díaz c/ Empresas Públicas de Medellín ESP* that the state-owned water company of Medellín has an obligation to provide access to a daily minimum amount of water.[74] In another development, the Supreme Court of India interpreted the right to water through the constitutional right to life, which applies to all actors in the Indian legal system.[75] Other high courts in other jurisdictions also have confirmed that state and corporations are obliged to ensure a reasonable minimum amount of water.[76]

Further, the international level provides more evidence of at least indirect corporate obligations concerning the right to water. CESCR emphasizes that "Steps should be taken by State parties to prevent their own citizens and companies from violating the right to water of individuals and communities in other countries".[77] The CESCR has thereafter expanded its understanding and interpretation of state obligations to control corporate actors when doing business at home[78] and abroad.[79] In this way, the CESCR has gone much further than the UN Guiding Principles on Business and Human Rights, which limits the obligation of the

72 Constitution of the Republic of Slovenia, Official Gazette RS Nos. 33/91-I, 42/97, 66/00, 24/03, 69/04, 68/06, and 47/13., art. 70; Constitution of Uruguay (1967), https://www.constituteproject.org/constitution/Uruguay_2004.pdf?lang=en, (last accessed 19 January 2018), section 47; Constitution of the Republic of The Gambia, 1997, 16 January 1997, http://www.refworld.org/docid/4811c33f2.html (last accessed 19 January 2018], art. 216 (4); Constitution of the Federal Democratic Republic of Ethiopia, 21 August 1995, http://www.refworld.org/docid/3ae6b5a84.html (last accessed 19 January 2018), art. 90 (1).

73 See for instance, Public Utility Code of California, section 739.8(a), which provides that: 'access to an adequate supply of healthful water is a basic necessity of human life, and shall be made available to all residents of California, at the affordable cost'.

74 *Hernán Galeano Díaz c/ Empresas Públicas de Medellín ESP,y Marco Gómez Otero y Otros c/Hidropacífico SA ESP y Otros*, T-616/10, 5 August 2010 (Constitutional Court of Colombia).

75 Business and Human Rights Resource Centre, 'Vedanta Resources lawsuit (re Dongria Kondh in Orissa)', 2016. See, Jérémie Gilbert, 'Indigenous peoples, Consultation and Mining: Lessons from the Supreme Court of India', *Rights as Usual Blog*, 23 April 2013.

76 *Lindiwe Mazibuko & Others v City of Johannesburg & Others* (2009), Case CCT 39/09, ZACC 28 (Constitutional Court of South Africa); *Matsipane Mosetlhanyane & Ors v The Attorney General* (2011), CA CACLB-074-10 (Court of Appeal of the Republic of Botswana).

77 UN, CESCR, General Comment 15, para 33.

78 See for example, UN, CESCR, 'Concluding Observations: Argentina', UN Doc E/C.12/ARG/CO/3, 14 December 2011, para 9; Concluding Observations: Peru, UN Doc E/C.12/PER/CO/2-4, 30 May 2012, para 22; Concluding Observations: Tanzania, UN Doc E/C.12/TZA/CO/1-3, 30 November 2012, para 25.

79 UN, CESCR, 'Concluding Observations: Canada', E/C.12/CAN/CO/6, 23 March 2016, para 16.

state to protect its own national territory. It has allowed for the extraterritorial application of the state obligations to protect the right to water and other socio-economic rights by regulating and supervising corporations registered in a state party's territory.[80] In so doing, it indirectly recognizes that businesses have at a minimum indirect obligations to observe the right to water. Equally, corporations that manage water supply systems must strive to meet the same level of commitment as the state. Moreover, emerging case law of some quasi-judicial bodies at the international level confirms that corporations may hold obligations concerning the right to water. The UK National Contact Point in the case of *RAID v ENRC* examined specific instances under the OECD Guidelines for Multinational Enterprises concerning alleged violations of a clean water supply in the village of Kisankala in the Democratic Republic of Congo and concluded that "ENRC has failed the obligation to address human rights impacts with which it is involved: part of the general obligation to respect human rights".[81] In addition, the International Centre of Settlement of Investment Disputes (ICSID) recently in *Urbaser S.A. and Consorcio de Aguas Bilbao Bizkaia, Bilbao Biskaia Ur Partzuergoa v. Argentine Republic* noted that businesses are obliged to not negatively affect the right to water.[82] Further, the UN Human Rights Committee in *Poma Poma v. Peru* found several violations of the right to access water of the Aymara Indigenous community in Peru.[83] Earlier, the Supreme Court of Chile in the same case upheld the right to access water of the Aymara Indigenous community against Agua Mineral Chusmiza, a private corporation.[84]

There is also some evidence of voluntary commitments made by corporations themselves. The International Federation of Private Water Operators through its ethics policy

> encourages its members to carry out their business while promoting integrity in ethical practices in every aspects of water services: in particular supporting and respecting international human rights and labour right within their sphere of influence, banning any kind of corrupt trading practices.[85]

80 UN, CESCR, 'Concluding Observations: Germany', UN Doc E/C.12/DEU/CO/5, 20 May 2011, para 10.

81 UK National Contact Point final statement, *RAID v ENRC*, February 2016. See also, Business and Human Rights Resource Centre, 'Vedanta Resources lawsuit (re Dongria Kondh in Orissa)', 2016.

82 *Urbaser S.A. and Consorcio de Aguas Bilbao Bizkaia*, Bilbao Biskaia Ur Partzuergoa v. Argentine Republic, ICSID Case No. ARB/07/26, 8 December 2016.

83 *Ángela Poma Poma v. Peru*, UN Human Rights Committee, CCPR/C/95/D/1457/2006, 24 April 2009.

84 Jeremy Valeriote, 'Chile's Supreme Court Uphold Indigenous Water Use Rights', *The Santiago Times (Chile)*, 30 November 2009. See also, *Usuarios y Consumidores en Defensa de sus Derechos Asociación Civil c/ Aguas del Gran Buenos Aires* SA (2002), 44.453, Juez de paz (Moreno, Buenos Aires).

85 AquaFed – The International Federation of Private Water Operators, 'Code of Ethics', revision 12 September 2011, para 1.

In addition, CEO Water Mandate recognizes that business have a responsibility to respect the right to water. Therefore, the sources of corporate obligations concerning the right to water are plentiful and straightforward.

What are is the nature and scope of corporate obligations to respect, protect and fulfil the right to water? Corporations bear three potential responsibilities concerning the right to water: as a user or consumer, as an enabler of access to water, and as a provider or distributor of water. It is quite clear that corporations have negative obligations not to interfere with the individual's enjoyment of their socio-economic rights. However, what still needs to be clarified is the nature of their positive obligations, namely the obligation to protect and fulfil the reasonable minimum of the right to water (see Table 6.5). It seems that a corporate obligation is emerging to co-provide funds to fulfil the human right to water. Corporations are to make positive efforts involving active steps and efforts to control supply chains, while attempting to adopt business policies to internalize the right to water.

Conclusion

This chapter examined corporate human rights obligations concerning socio-economic rights. Some commentators believe that only states are responsible for achieving the goals of sustainable development since several objectives relate to the realization of social and economic rights, which traditionally fall within the domain of the state. Surely, states play a primary role in achieving the Sustainable Development Goals, but the private sector plays an equally important role, especially where it performs traditional public tasks. The exercise of economic and social rights, however, largely depends on states' financial capabilities. This chapter has shown that corporations hold obligations concerning socio-economic rights by analyzing their responsibilities with regard to five socio-economic rights: the rights to education, food, health, adequate housing and water. The analysis showed there are many examples of corporate obligations in relation to socio-economic rights, particularly in domestic settings. Yet it is more difficult to require private actors to be involved in their implementation since their primary task is not to provide social-economic rights, even though they are at a minimum obliged to not directly interfere with them. There is hardly any doubt that corporations carry a negative obligation to not interfere with socio-economic rights. However, corporations therefore hold not only negative, but also positive, commitments to contribute to the achievement of the sustainable development objectives through the consistent and careful implementation of socio-economic rights.

Under some domestic human rights systems, they are also potentially bound by the positive protect and fulfil obligations at least relative to the minimum core of socio-economic rights, particularly where they act as a state-owned corporation or exercise public functions via licenses or concessions. Such obligations are of conduct, not of result. Their positive obligation is clearly stronger towards their employees and the local community in the proximity of their obligations. Corporate

Table 6.5 Corporate obligations to respect, protect and fulfil concerning the right to water

Right to water	*Preventive dimension*	*Remedial dimension*
Corporate obligation to respect	Not cause harm to individuals' enjoyment of the right to water.	Undertake a human rights assessment prior to starting a project, and submit themselves to fair, independent and impartial judicial proceedings.
	Not interfere with a judicial rule-of-law process examining their alleged involvement in right to water violations.	Support and do not interfere with fair, independent, and impartial reporting and auditing.
	Draft and implement a detailed human rights policy, which must be disseminated internally and externally to all relevant stakeholders and business partners, and be incorporated into all its policies.	Submit themselves to fair, independent and impartial judicial proceedings in case of violations of human rights policy, and provide the right to effective remedies to victims and their families.
Corporate obligation to protect	Undertake due diligence across their global supply chains to ensure that their business partners do not violate the minimum levels of right to water.	Establish external periodic independent verification of these procedures, and the reports they generate must address specific abuses and devise ways of promoting respect for socio-economic rights.
	Develop a systematic supervisory mechanism within and outside their corporate group.	Establish internal grievance procedures where victims can seek recourse in a complaints mechanism, and submit themselves to fair, independent and impartial judicial proceedings, including compensation.
	Conduct an internal, effective, transparent and diligent investigation into the alleged violations in the case of violations.	Establish a special task force in charge of investigating the alleged violations.
Corporate obligation to fulfil	Create the conditions for individuals' enjoyment of the right to water.	Help local communities with providing individuals with the right to water.
	Participate in partnership and make financial commitments to contribute to individuals' enjoyment of the right to water.	Create internal funds and contribute to external funds for use in providing for the right to water.
	Strive to assist states in providing at least the reasonable minimum core of right to water, particularly in the local communities in which they operate.	Work with governments in providing the reasonable minimum core of the right to water

positive obligations are certainly smaller in scope and nature than those of states, which are able to provide for a wider range of the exercise of socio-economic rights given their monopoly over tax collection and the distribution of related public funds. But even in the regions of the Global South, corporations are more likely to have to provide at least a minimum reasonable core of economic and social rights. Corporations must also strive to not violate the goals of sustainable development, while simultaneously creating the conditions for the realization of socio-economic rights, also through the allocation of some of their revenues to funds used in the assurance of socio-economic rights. All in all, corporations have negative and positive obligations to observe socio-economic rights.

Bibliography

Books

Jägers, Nicola, *Corporate Human Rights Obligations: In Search of Accountability*, Antwerp: Intersentia (2002).

Nussbaum, Martha C., *Creating Capabilities: The Human Development Approach*, Cambridge, MA: The Belknap Press of Harvard University Press (2011).

Journal articles

Heymann, Jody, Raub, Amy and Cassola, Adèle, 'Constitutional Rights to Education and Their Relationship to National Policy and School Enrolment', 39 *International Journal of Educational Development* 121 (2014).

Letnar Černič, Jernej, 'Corporate Obligations Under the Human Right to Water', 39(2) *Denver Journal of International Law and Policy* 303 (2011).

Macchi, Chiara, 'Right to Water and the Threat of Business: Corporate Accountability and the State's Duty to Protect', 35(3) *Nordic Journal of Human Rights* 186 (2017).

Söllner, Sven, 'The "Breakthrough" of the Right to Food: The Meaning of General Comment No. 12 and the Voluntary Guidelines for the Interpretation of the Human Right to Food', 11(1) *Max Planck Yearbook of United Nations Law Online* 391 (2007).

Book chapters

De Schutter, Olivier, 'Corporations and Economic, Social and Cultural Rights', *in* Eibe Riedel, Gilles Giacca and Christophe Golay (eds.), *Economic, Social and Cultural Rights in International Law: Contemporary Issues and Challenges*, Oxford: Oxford University Press (2014), pp. 193–224.

De Schutter, Olivier, 'Right to Food in Latin America and the Caribbean', *in* Humberto Cantú Rivera (ed.), *The Special Procedures of the Human Rights Council: A Brief Look from the Inside and Perspectives from Outside*, Cambridge, Antwerp and Portland: Intersentia (2015), pp. 25–52.

Eide, Asbjørn, 'The International Human Rights System', *in* Asbjørn Eide, Wenche Barthe Eide, Susantha Goonatilake, Joan Gussow and Omawale (eds.), *Food as a Human Right*, Tokyo: United Nations University Press (1984), pp. 152–161.

Savedoff, William and Hussmann, Karen, 'Why Are Health Systems So Prone to Corruption?' *in* Transparency International (ed.), *Global Corruption Report 2006: Special Focus – Corruption and Health*, London and Ann Arbor: Pluto Press (2006), pp. 4–16.
Toebes, Brigit, 'Direct Corporate Human Rights Obligations Under the Right to Health: From Mere "respecting" Towards Protecting and Fulfilling', *in* Jernej Letnar Černič and Tara van Ho (eds.), *Human Rights and Business: Direct Corporate Accountability for Human Rights*, Oisterwijk: Wolf Legal Publisher (2015), pp. 263–278.

Treaties

Council of Europe, Protocol no. 1 of the European Convention for the Protection of Human Rights and Fundamental Freedoms, 20 March 1952.
UN, 'International Covenant on Economic, Social and Cultural Rights', GA res. 2200A (XXI), 21 UN GAOR Supp. (No. 16) at 49, UN Doc. A/6316, Treaty Series, vol. 993, 16 December 1966.

Newspaper article

Jeremy Valeriote, 'Chile's Supreme Court Uphold Indigenous Water Use Rights', *The Santiago Times* (Chile), 30 November 2009.

Official documents

Constitution of 2009 of the Plurinational State of Bolivia, 7 February 2009, http://pdba.georgetown.edu/Constitutions/Bolivia/bolivia.html (last accessed 19 January 2018).
Constitution of Ecuador, *Official Journal* 448, 20 October 2008, http://www.refworld.org/docid/3dbd62fd2.html (last accessed 19 January 2018).
Constitution of the Federal Democratic Republic of Ethiopia, 21 August 1995, http://www.refworld.org/docid/3ae6b5a84.html (last accessed 19 January 2018).
Constitution of the Republic of The Gambia, 1997, 16 January 1997, http://www.refworld.org/docid/4811c33f2.html (last accessed 30 January 2018).
Constitution of the United Mexican States, 1917 (as amended). Washington: Pan American Union.
Constitution of Portugal, 1976, fourth revision based on Constitutional Law No. 1/97 of 20 September 1997.
Constitution of the Republic of Slovenia, Official Gazette RS Nos. 33/91-I, 42/97, 66/00, 24/03, 69/04, 68/06 and 47/13.
Constitution of South Africa, No. 108 of 1996, National Gazette No. 17678, 18 December 1996.
Constitution of the Lao People's Democratic Republic, 6 May 2003, available at: http://www.refworld.org/docid/3ae6b5221a.html (accessed 19 January 2018).
The Constitution of the Russian Federation (December 1993).
Constitution of Uruguay (1967), https://www.constituteproject.org/constitution/Uruguay_2004.pdf?lang=en, (last accessed 19 January 2018).
National Assembly of the Republic of Nicaragua, 'Law of Food and Nutrition Sovereignty and Security', Act No. 693, published in La Gaceta, Official Bulletin No. 133, 16 July 2009.

Public Utility Code of California.

ILO, 'R115 – Workers' Housing Recommendation, 1961 (No. 115)', Geneva: 45th ILC session, 28 June 1961.

UN, CESCR, 'Concluding Observations: Germany, UN Doc. E/C.12/DEU/CO/5, 20 May 2011; Concluding Observations: Argentina, UN Doc. E/C.12/ARG/CO/3, 14 December 2011; Concluding Observations: Peru, UN Doc. E/C.12/PER/CO/2-4, 30 May 2012; Concluding Observations: Tanzania, UN Doc. E/C.12/TZA/CO/1-3, 30 November 2012; Concluding observations: Uganda, UN Doc. E/C.12/UGA/CO/1, 8 July 2015; Concluding Observations: Canada, UNE/C.12/CAN/CO/6, 23 March 2016.UN, CESCR, General Comment 12: The right to adequate food (Art. 11)', UN doc. E/C.12/1999/5, 12 May 1999.

UN, CESCR, 'General Comment 14: The Right to the Highest Attainable Standard of Health (Art.12)', UN Doc. E/C.12/2000/4, 11 August 2000.

UN, CESCR, 'General Comment 15: The Right to Water (Art. 11 and 12)', UN Doc E/C.12/2002/11, 20 January 2003.

UN, Committee on the Rights of the Child, 'General Comment No. 16 on State Obligations Regarding the Impact of the Business Sector on Children's Rights', UN Doc. CRC/C/GC/16, 17 April 2013.

UN, Human Rights Council, Report of Special Representative of the Secretary-General on the Issue of Human Rights and Transnational Corporations and Other Business Enterprises, John Ruggie, 'Guiding Principles on Business and Human Rights: Implementing the United Nations "Protect, Respect and Remedy" Framework' ['The Guiding Principles'], UN Doc. A/HRC/17/31, 21 March 2011.

UN, Human Rights Council, 'Report of the Special Rapporteur on the Right to Food: Olivier De Schutter', UN Doc. A/HRC/13/33/Add.2, 22 December 2009.

UN, Human Rights Council, 'Report of the Special Rapporteur on Adequate Housing as a Component of the Right to an Adequate Standard of Living and on the Right to Non-Discrimination in This Context: Leilani Farha', UN Doc. A/HRC/34/51, 18 January 2017.

UN, OHCHR, 'Key Messages on Human Rights and Climate Change', 27 November 2015.

UN, OHCHR, 'The Right to Adequate Housing', Fact Sheet No. 21/Rev.1.

UN, 'Transforming Our World: The 2030 Agenda for Sustainable Development, Outcome Document of the United Nations Summit to Adopt the Post-2015 Development Agenda', UN Doc. A/69/L.85, 12 August 2015.

UN, 'Norms on the Responsibilities of Transnational Corporations and Other Business Enterprises with Regard to Human Rights', U.N. Doc. E/CN.4/Sub.2/2003/38/Rev.2, 2003.

Cases and opinions

Absa Bank Limited v. Moore and another, CCT 03/16 (Constitutional Court of South Africa).

Ángela Poma Poma v. Peru, CCPR/C/95/D/1457/2006, UN Human Rights Committee, 24 April 2009.

Business and Human Rights Resource Centre, 'Vedanta Resources lawsuit (re Dongria Kondh in Orissa)', 2016.

Charan Lal Sahu v. Union of India, 1990 (1) SCC, 613 (Bhopal Gas Disaster Case) (Supreme Court of India).

Hernán Galeano Díaz c/ Empresas Públicas de Medellín ESP,y Marco Gómez Otero y Otros c/Hidropacífico SA ESP y Otros, T-616/10, 5 August 2010.*G v. An Bord Uchtála*, 1980, IR 32 (Constitutional Court of Colombia).

Kishen Pattnayak & Another v. State of Orissa, A.I.R. 1989 S.C. 677 (Supreme Court of India).

Lindiwe Mazibuko & Others v City of Johannesburg & Others (2009), Case CCT 39/09, ZACC 28 (Constitutional Court of South Africa).

Matsipane Mosetlhanyane & Ors v The Attorney General (2011), CA CACLB-074-10 (Court of Appeal of the Republic of Botswana).

People's Union for Civil Liberties v. Union of India & Ors. S.C. 2001, Writ Petition (Civil) No. 196/2001 (Supreme Court of India), reprinted in Colin Gonsalves, *Right to Food*, New Delhi, 2004.

UK National Contact Point final statement, *RAID v ENRC*, February 2016.

Urbaser S.A. and Consorcio de Aguas Bilbao Bizkaia, Bilbao Biskaia Ur Partzuergoa v. Argentine Republic, ICSID Case No. ARB/07/26, 8 December 2016.

Usuarios y Consumidores en Defensa de sus Derechos Asociación Civil c/ Aguas del Gran Buenos Aires SA (2002), 44.453, Juez de paz (Moreno, Buenos Aires).

Ximenes-Lopes v. Brazil, Judgment of 4 July 2006, Series C No. 149 (Inter-American Court of Human Rights – IACHR).

Reports and miscellaneous

African Commission on Human and Peoples' Rights, '155/96: Social and Economic Rights Action Center (SERAC) and Center for Economic and Social Rights (CESR)/Nigeria', 27 October 2001.

AquaFed – The International Federation of Private Water Operators, 'Code of Ethics', revision 12 September 2011.

Asbjørn, Eide, 'The Right to Adequate Food and to Be Free from Hunger: Updated Study on the Right to Food', submitted in accordance with Sub-Commission decision 1998/106, E/CN.4/Sub.2/1999, 28 June 1999.

Australian Competition and Consumer Commission, 'Food and Grocery Code of Conduct', www.accc.gov.au/business/industry-codes/food-and-grocery-code-of-conduct#the-code (last accessed 19 January 2018).

Clapham, Andrew and Garcia Rubio, Mariano, 'The Obligations of States with Regard to Non-State Actors in the Context of the Right to Health', Health and Human Rights Working Paper Series No 3, 2002.

Farming First, 'The Story of Agriculture and the Sustainable Development Goals', 2015, www.farmingfirst.org/sdg-toolkit#home (last accessed 19 January 2018).

Food and Agriculture Organization of the United Nations (FAO), 'The Right to Food: Past Commitment, Current Obligation, Further Action for the Future: A Ten-Year Retrospective on the Right to Food Guidelines', 2014.

Gilbert, Jérémie, 'Indigenous Peoples, Consultation and Mining: Lessons from the Supreme Court of India', *Rights as Usual Blog*, 23 April 2013.

Global Social Compliance Programme, 'Mission', www.theconsumergoodsforum.com/initiatives/social-sustainability/key-projects/global-social-compliance-programme-gscp (last accessed 19 January 2018).

GLOBALG.A.P, 'About Us', www.globalgap.org/uk_en/who-we-are/about-us/ (last accessed 19 January 2018).

Human Rights and Business Dilemmas Forum, 'Access to Adequate Housing', http://hrbdf.org/dilemmas/housing/#.WYNbaYh942w (last accessed 19 January 2018).

ILO, 'Ending Child Labour by 2025: A Review of Policies and Programmes', Geneva, 2017.

Institute for Human Rights and Business (IHRB), 'State of Play: Business and the Sustainable Development Goals: Mind the Gap – Challenges for Implementation', September 2015.

Jeffords, Christopher, 'Constitutional Environmental Human Rights: A Descriptive Analysis of 142 National Constitutions', Economic Rights Working Paper Series No. 16, University of Connecticut, 2011.

Kellogg Company, 'Kellogg Company's Global Code of Ethics', September 2013.

Knuth, Lidija and Vidar, Margret, 'Constitutional and Legal Protection of the Right to Food around the World', Food and Agriculture Organization of the United Nations (FAO), Rome 2011.

McDonald's Corporation, 'Standards of Business Conduct: The Promise of the Golden Arches', March 2017.

Yeshanew, Sisay Alemahu and Windfuhr, Michael, 'International Dimensions of the Right to Adequate Food', Food and Agriculture Organization of the United Nations (FAO), Rome 2014.

7 Access to justice for victims of socio-economic rights violations

Introduction 153
General thoughts on corporate accountability for socio-economic rights and access to justice 155
Levels of corporate accountability for socio-economic rights 158
Domestic level 159
Domestic judicial mechanisms 159
Domestic non-judicial mechanisms 165
International Law 165
OECD Guidelines for Multinational Enterprises 166
The Tripartite Declaration of Principles concerning Multinational Enterprises and Social Policy 167
Arbitration 169
Internal complaints mechanisms 172
A bottom-up approach to access to justice 175
Challenges 177
Forum non conveniens 177
Confronting separation of legal entities in corporate structures 179
Holistic approach to accountability for socio-economic violations 182
Conclusion 183

Introduction

Victims often face challenges in accessing justice where they could enforce corporate accountability for corporate human rights violations. However, they encounter even more challenges when enforcing socio-economic rights, as those rights already anecdotally suffer problems with their justiciability. It is known that there hardly exist binding mechanisms at the international level to enforce socio-economic rights against corporations. Several jurisdictions at the domestic level allow for socio-economic rights enforcement; however generally this depends on the status of socio-economic rights in national constitutional systems, particularly whether they are enforceable.[1] CESCR observed in its General Comment no. 9 on the Domestic Application of the ICESCR that

> adoption of a rigid classification of economic, social and cultural rights which puts them, by definition, beyond the reach of the courts would thus be arbitrary and incompatible with the principle that the two sets of human rights are indivisible and interdependent. It would also drastically curtail the capacity of the courts to protect the rights of the most vulnerable and disadvantaged groups in society.[2]

However, rights-holders can enforce socio-economic rights against corporations also through civil and political rights. Victims enforcing legal accountability of corporations for socio-economic rights face, nonetheless, at least two seminal challenges. First, justiciability of socio-economic rights against corporations at domestic and international levels has been deficient. Langford has observed that "the scope for formal judicial review of ESC rights is rather limited outside the use of civil rights or international mechanisms".[3] Accordingly, Langford argues that, for instance,

> courts in India, Pakistan, Bangladesh, Sri Lanka and Nepal as well as the Costa Rica and Colombia have developed public interest litigation procedures that more easily facilitate individual and collective claims; e.g., cases can be triggered with a simple application (even a postcard) and courts play a more active procedural role.[4]

1 Lanse Minkler (ed.), *The State of Economic and Social Human Rights*, Cambridge: Cambridge University Press (2013). See also, Asbjørn Eide, 'Realisation of Social and Economic Rights and the Minimum Threshold Approach' 10(2) *Human Rights Law Journal* 37 (1989); and Jonathan R. Siegel, 'A Theory of Justiciability', 86 *Texas Law Review* 73 (2007).

2 UN, CESCR, 'General Comment No. 9: The Domestic Application of the Covenant', UN Doc. E/C.12/1998/24, 3 December 1998, para 10.

3 Malcolm Langford, 'Judicial Review in National Courts: Recognition and Responsiveness', *in* Eibe Riedel, Gilles Giacca and Christophe Golay (eds.), *Economic, Social and Cultural Rights in International Law: Contemporary Issues and Challenges*, Oxford: Oxford University Press (2014), pp. 417–447, p. 423.

4 Malcolm Langford, 'Domestic Adjudication and Economic, Social and Cultural Rights: A Socio-Legal Review', 6(11) *Sur International Journal of Human Rights* 91 (2009), p. 95. See for example, Ebenezer Durojaye, 'Litigating the Right to Health in Nigeria: Challenges and Prospects', *in* Magnus Killander (ed.), *International Law and Domestic Human Rights Litigation in Africa*, Pretoria: Pretoria University Law Press (2010), pp. 149–171; Cheluchi Onyemelukwe, 'Access to Anti-Retroviral Drugs as a Component of the Right to Health in International Law: Examining the Application of the Right in Nigerian Jurisprudence', 7 *African Human Rights Law Journal* 446 (2007). Akinola E. Akintayo, 'A Good Thing from Nazareth? Stemming the Tide of Neo-Liberalism Against Socio-Economic Rights: Lessons from the Nigerian Case of Bamidele Aturu v Minister of Petroleum Resources and Others',

Second, such challenge is even more aggravated by the justiciability of socio-economic rights against corporations. However, corporations are aware that the regulatory environment is still weak in the field of business and socio-economic rights. Nonetheless, public interest litigations have been in recent decades developed also concerning business and socio-economic rights. Therefore, access to the right to remedy faces even more challenges concerning socio-economic rights than enforcement of civil and political rights.

This chapter is thereafter divided into five parts. The balance of this chapter is dedicated to exploring corporate accountability for socio-economic rights. The second section examines the general concept for corporate accountability for socio-economic rights. The third section analyzes levels of corporate accountability for socio-economic rights. In doing so, five levels are analyzed: victims' access to justice in international law, domestic systems, internal corporate level, arbitration and bottom-up approaches. The fourth section addresses some of the challenges in bringing claims against corporations in domestic fora. The fifth section offers critical analysis and assessment of concurrence of different forms, levels and actors of accountability by arguing for a holistic approach to corporate accountability for socio-economic rights.

General thoughts on corporate accountability for socio-economic rights and access to justice

Corporate accountability refers to individuals' access to justice for alleged corporate violations of socio-economic rights. Access to justice for the purposes of this study refers to wide-ranging routes an individual may have to access to remedies, through either judicial, quasi-judicial or non-judicial forums.[5] It asks the question: How do we achieve corporate accountability for socio-economic rights and who or which actor can be held accountable for violations committed by or involving corporations? Victims as rights-holders must have access to justice to enforce corporate accountability for socio-economic rights violations.[6] Corporate accountability for socio-economic rights can be defined in a broader and narrower meaning or scope. In a narrower understanding it refers to accountability of corporations for their interference or (lack thereof)

15(2) *ESR Review: Economic and Social Rights in South Africa* 5 (2014); Stanley Ibe, 'Implementing Economic, Social and Cultural Rights in Nigeria: Opportunities and Challenges', 10 *African Human Rights Law Journal* 197 (2010).

5 UN, Human Rights Council, 'Improving Accountability and Access to Remedy for Victims of Business-related Human Rights Abuse', UN Doc. A/HRC/32/19, 10 May 2016.

6 UN, Report of the Working Group on the Issue of Human Rights and Transnational Corporations and other Business Enterprises, 'Access to Effective Remedies Under the Guiding Principles on Business and Human Rights: Implementing the United Nations Protect, Respect and Remedy Framework', UN Doc. A/72/162, 18 July 2017, para 18–25.

with socio-economic rights and socio-economic livelihoods. On the other hand, it refers in a broader meaning to accountability for corporate violations of socio-economic rights, which includes corporate, but also individual and state, accountability for socio-economic violations, thereby employing a holistic approach to accountability for socio-economic violations caused by corporations. Deva argues that the current existing frameworks are "inadequate and has been unable to ensure effective accountability of companies for human rights violations".[7] This book subscribes to the definition of corporate accountability that includes all levels of accountability and in which concurrence is possible between different levels and types of accountability in order to enforce rights of victims (see Figure 7.1). Deva rightly observes that "rights holders should be central to the entire remedy process, including to the question of effectiveness".[8] Corporate accountability for socio-economic rights refers to legal responses to the alleged violations of socio-economic rights. Victims should have a plurality of options available for enforcing corporate accountability for socio-economic rights.[9]

Accordingly, the UN Guiding Principles on Business and Human Rights state in principle 25 that "States must take appropriate steps to ensure, through judicial, administrative, legislative or other appropriate means, that when such abuses occur within their territory and/or jurisdiction those affected have access to effective remedy".[10] Further, Principle 26 asserts that, "States should take appropriate steps to ensure the effectiveness of domestic judicial mechanisms when addressing business-related human rights abuses, including considering ways to reduce legal, practical and other relevant barriers that could lead to a denial of access to remedy".[11] Fair, impartial and independent functioning of the judicial branch of power is the basis for the effective functioning of the rule-of-law and democratic state. The protection of human rights is an unconditional civilization standard, under which a democratic and the rule-of-law state should not fall into the autocratic state. This, of course, means that the access to justice as the part of the effective rule of law cannot be subordinate to the political, financial, private,

7 Surya Deva, ***Regulating Corporate Human Rights Violations: Humanizing Business***, London: Routledge (2012), p. 188.

8 Surya Deva, 'Access to Effective Remedy: Taking Human Rights and Rights Holders Seriously', *Cambridge Core Blog*, 14 November 2017.

9 See also, CESCR noted that "Ensuring corporate accountability for violations of Covenant rights requires reliance on various tools." UN, CESCR, General comment No. 24 (2017) on State obligations under the International Covenant on Economic, Social and Cultural Rights in the context of business activities, UN Doc. E/C.12/GC/24, 10 August 2017, para 49.

10 UN, Human Rights Council, Report of Special Representative of the Secretary-General on the Issue of Human Rights and Transnational Corporations and Other Business Enterprises, John Ruggie, 'Guiding Principles on Business and Human Rights: Implementing the United Nations "Protect, Respect and Remedy" Framework' ['The Guiding Principles'], UN Doc. A/HRC/17/31, 21 March 2011, principle 25.

11 Ibid., principle 26.

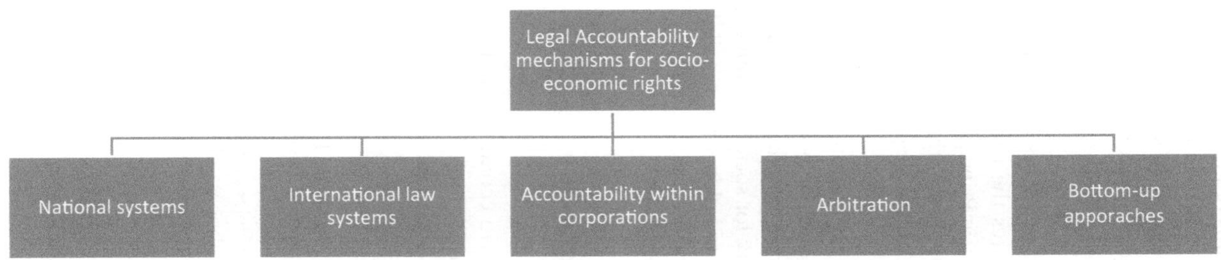

Figure 7.1 Five levels of legal accountability of corporations

(Source: author's own work)

family and other interests.[12] The latter is absolutely forbidden by the right to independent, impartial and fair decision-making and by the appearance of the absence of any conflict of interests.

The right to a remedy for victims of human rights violations is a pillar of every domestic judicial system. As only a few cases or claims have been so far brought to enforce corporate socio-economic obligations, this section addresses the potential avenues for protecting socio-economic rights. The effectiveness of all other rights rests on access to an effective legal remedy. The "Basic Principles and Guidelines on the Right to a Remedy and Reparation for Victims of Gross Violations of International Human Rights Law and Serious Violations of International Humanitarian Law" states the core steps that are required to address the suffering of victims.[13] The Basic Principles provide that states are required to "investigate violations effectively, promptly, thoroughly impartially and, where appropriate, take action against those allegedly responsible in accordance with domestic and international law";[14] "provide those who claim to be victims of a human rights or humanitarian law violation with equal and effective access to justice . . . irrespective of who may ultimately be the bearer of responsibility for the violation";[15] and "provide effective remedies to victims, including reparation".[16] All in all, corporate accountability for socio-economic rights functions on several different levels, which give rights-holders the possibility of pursuing the most appropriate avenue to protect socio-economic rights either at home, in the host state or before an international forum.[17]

Levels of corporate accountability for socio-economic rights

Corporate accountability for socio-economic rights operates at several levels. They all attempt to answer the question: Where can rights-holders enforce corporate accountability for socio-economic rights?[18] Where can individuals and

12 See, Martin Krygier, 'Rule of Law', *in* Michel Rosenfeld and András Sajó (eds.), *The Oxford Handbook of Comparative Constitutional Law*, Oxford: Oxford University Press (2012), pp. 233–249.

13 UN, General Assembly, 'Basic Principles and Guidelines on the Right to a Remedy and Reparation for Victims of Gross Violations of International Human Rights Law and Serious Violations of International Humanitarian Law' [Basic Principles and Guidelines], UN Doc. A/RES/60/147, 21 March 2006.

14 Ibid., para 3(b).

15 Ibid., para 3(c).

16 Ibid., para 3(d).

17 Christen Broecker, 'Better the Devil You Know: Home State Approaches to Transnational Corporate Accountability', 41(1) *New York University Journal of International Law and Politics* 159 (2008).

18 Jernej Letnar Černič and Tara Van Ho, 'Introduction', *in* Jernej Letnar Černič and Tara Van Ho (eds.), *Human Rights and Business: Direct Corporate Accountability for Human Rights*, Oisterwijk: Wolf Legal Publishers (2015), pp. 1–23; Pammela Q. Saunders, 'Rethinking Corporate Human Rights Accountability', 89 *Tulane Law Review* 603 (2014).

groups bring cases against corporations for violations of socio-economic rights? This section will in five steps illustrate that there exists evidence that there are some avenues to enforce socio-economic rights against corporations. First, it will argue that a plethora of domestic systems judicially protect socio-economic rights of individuals against corporations. Second, it will show that there exists some emerging international law fora to protect socio-economic rights against corporations. Third, it will present and dissect some proposals for enforcing business responsibilities for socio-economic rights through arbitration tribunals. Fourth, it will show that international norms derive indirectly from internal corporate complaints mechanisms of corporations. Last, it will analyze bottom-up approaches in bringing justice to rights-holders. This section in this way highlights some of the cases providing evidence for judicial, quasi-judicial and non-judicial enforcement of socio-economic rights. Further avenues and cases are described and analyzed in Part III of this book in individual case studies on Cambodia, China and Colombia.

Domestic level

In international law, there is no judicial forum which is competent to deal with complaints against transnational corporations for human rights violations. Rights-holders and non-governmental human rights organizations, therefore, put their hope in domestic legal systems. However, those have so far struggled to enforce socio-economic rights against corporations. Domestic legal systems are the level of enforcements where human rights are often best protected due to closeness to the rights-holders and the violations that occurred. Policy objective no. 1 of the "Guidance to improve corporate accountability and access to judicial remedy for business-related human rights abuses" provides that "domestic public law regimes that are relevant to the respect by business enterprises of human rights . . . are sufficiently detailed and robust to ensure that there is both effective deterrence from and effective remedy in the event of business-related human rights abuses".[19] However, access to remedies at the domestic level greatly depends on the general rule-of-law context, fairness, independence and impartiality of the judiciary. Generally, mechanisms at the domestic level are generally divided into judicial and non-judicial, whereas the former are prevailing (see Figure 7.2).

Domestic judicial mechanisms

Domestic judicial mechanisms are the first point of departure for victims enforcing corporate accountability for socio-economic rights. Several national legal orders provide directly or indirectly for judicial protections of socio-economic

19 UN, Human Rights Council, 'Improving Accountability and Access to Remedy for Victims of Business-Related Human Rights Abuse: Explanatory Notes for Guidance', UN Doc. A/HRC/32/19/Add.1, 12 May 2016, Section 1.

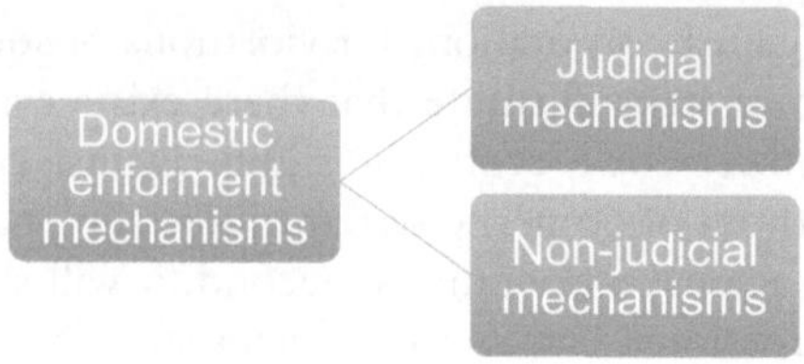

Figure 7.2 Domestic enforcement mechanisms
(Source: author's own work)

rights against corporations.[20] Cases have been brought on the plurality of legal bases, ranging from criminal law, administrative law through constitutional law to civil law. The Business and Human Rights Centre lists several cases of corporate legal accountability from around the world.[21] For instance, several criminal cases have so far resulted in convictions of corporations[22] or of responsible persons within corporations.[23] However, evidentiary matters have often posed insurmountable case in bringing criminal cases against corporations.[24] Some constitutional and supreme courts have also protected socio-economic rights against corporate conduct.[25]

For instance, Indian courts have been in the past very industrious in protecting socio-economic rights against corporations. The Supreme Court of India noted in *Olga Tellis v Bombay Municipal Corporation* concerning forced eviction of pavement dwellers by the state-owned corporations that the right to life includes also the right to socio-economic livelihood.[26] The Supreme Court of India further held in *Delhi Development Horticulture Employee's Union v Delhi*

20 See, Jernej Letnar Černič, 'Corporate Responsibility for Human Rights: Towards a Pluralist Approach', *in* Wouter Vandenhole (ed.), *Challenging Territoriality in Human Rights Law: Building Blocks for a Plural and Diverse Duty-Bearer Regime*, Abingdon: Routledge (2015), pp. 79–83.

21 Business and Human Rights Centre, 'Corporate Legal Accountability', https://business-humanrights.org/en/corporate-legal-accountability (last accessed 19 January 2018).

22 *Sa Majesté La Reine v Les Pétroles Global Inc*, Judgment 2013 QCCS 4262 (Superior Court of Quebec); *World Bank Group v Wallace* (Case No. 36315), Judgment [2016] SCC 15 (Supreme Court of Canada), paras 14–16; *State v Golfview Mining (Pty) Ltd* (Case No. 462/04/2009), Judgment ESH 82/11 (Ermelo Regional Court, South Africa).

23 *Prosecutor v Frans Van Anraat*, (2005) Case No. 09/751003-04, Judgment LJN: AU8685 (District Court of The Hague), 23 December 2005.

24 See for example, Valentina Azarov, 'Investigative or Political Barriers? Dutch Prosecutor Dismisses Criminal Complicity Case Against Riwal', *Rights as Usual Blog*, 29 May 2013.

25 *Mazibuko and Others v City of Johannesburg and Others*, CCT 39/09 (Constitutional Court of South Africa), 8 October 2009. See, Chapters 5 and 6.

26 *Olga Tellis v Bombay Municipal Corporation*, AIR 1986 SC 180 (Supreme Court of India), 10 July 1985.

Administration,[27] that "there is no doubt that broadly interpreted and as a necessary logical corollary, right to life would include the right to livelihood and therefore, right to work".[28] The courts have also on numerous occasions offered protections of the right to work.[29] In the years following the Bhopal gas disaster on 3 October 1984 several civil and criminal claims were brought against Union Carbide and Union Carbide India Limited before Indian and US courts. Apart from environmental disasters, more than 7000 people are believed to have died due to toxic gas leaks from a chemical plant in Bhopal, India. While claims in the United States were dismissed on jurisdictional grounds in relation to *forum non conveniens* grounds, the proceedings in India were settled five years after the human and environmental disaster. This case, *Union Carbide Corporation v Union of India*, was settled on 4 May 1989. The Supreme Court of India delivered on 15 February 1989 an order which specified that Union Carbide and Union Carbide India Limited were to pay USD 470 million in compensation "to the Union of India as claimant and for the benefit of all victims of the Bhopal Gas Disaster under the Bhopal Gas Leak Disaster (Registration and Processing of Claims) Scheme, 1985 and not as fines, penalties or punitive damages".[30] Additionally, the Supreme Court in May 1989 delivered an order stating that "no individual claimant shall be entitled to claim particular quantum of compensation even if his case is found to fall within any of the broad categories".[31] Consequently, some argue that "victims were denied their individual right to prove the extent of individual damages suffered and claim appropriate compensation, as the settlement was negotiated without participation of the victims".[32] Today it is still clear that not all victims have been compensated.

Moreover, several domestic systems provide judicial protections against corporations concerning civil damage. Fafo Report provides evidence for domestic legal bases for bringing civil cases against corporations for human rights violations.[33]

27 *Delhi Development Horticulture Employee's Union v Delhi Administration*, AIR 1992 SC 789 (Supreme Court of India), 4 February 1992.

28 Ibid.

29 See for example, *Air India Statutory Corporation v United Labour Union* (1997) 9 SCC 425 (Supreme Court of India), 6 November 1996.

30 *Union Carbide Corporation v Union of India Order 15-02-1989*, in Civil Appeal Nos. 3187-89 (Supreme Court of India), para 2c.

31 *Union Carbide Corporation v Union of India Order 05-04-1989*, in Civil Appeal Nos. 3187-89 (Supreme Court of India).

32 See, Amnesty International, 'Clouds of Injustice: Bhopal Disaster 20 Years on', 2004, p. 63. For a detailed discussion see Upendra Baxi, 'Human Rights Responsibility of Multinational Corporations, Political Ecology of Injustice: Learning from Bhopal Thirty Plus?', 1(1) *Business and Human Rights Journal* 21 (2016).

33 See, Anita Ramasastry and Robert C. Thompson, 'Business and International Crimes Project: Assessing the Liability of Business Entities for Grave Violations of International Law: A Survey of Sixteen Countries', Fafo-report 536 (2006).

More specifically, victims have successfully brought a number cases against corporations in Australia,[34] Belgium,[35] France,[36] Japan,[37] Netherlands,[38] Canada,[39] England[40] and elsewhere.[41] For instance, in Australia, tort claims were brought against Broken Hill Properties (BHP) for polluting the Fly River and endangering the livelihoods of 25,000 people in Papua New Guinea. BHP's subsidiary, the Ok Tedi Mining Ltd., dumped several tonnes of toxic waste in the Fly River.[42] The Supreme Court of Victoria denied a motion to dismiss and thereafter parties settled on 12 June 1996.[43] The settlement asked the corporation to repair the environmental damage caused and to award compensation to victims. In 2000 a case was brought before a Geneva court by Roma victims and families of victims of the Holocaust against IBM and one of IBM's German subsidiaries that allegedly facilitated the organization of the Holocaust.[44] Further, the Roma

34 *Dagi v BHP* (no. 2) [1997] 1 VR 428, (Supreme Court of Victoria – Australia), 12 June 1996. See Jernej Letnar Černič, 'Corporate Responsibility for Human Rights: Towards a Pluralist Approach', pp. 81 and 82.

35 Le Monde.fr with Reuters, 'Total: la Belgique rouvre une enquête pour crimes contre l'humanité', *Le Monde*, 1 October 2007.

36 See, Pascal Ceaux and Jacques Follorou, 'Total va indemniser ses accusateurs', *Le Monde*, 30 Novembre 2005. Agence France Press, 'Belgium Reopens Myanmar Humanity Crimes Probe Against Oil Giant Total', 2 October 2007. *Association France-Palestine Solidarité v Société Alstom Transport SA* (Case No. 11/05331), Versailles Court of Appeal, 22 March 2013.

37 Anita Ramasastry and Robert C. Thompson, 'Commerce, Crime, and Conflict: A Comparative Survey of Legal Remedies for Private Sector Liability for Grave Breaches of International Law', Fafo-report 536 (2006). See for a detailed discussion, Jernej Letnar Černič and Tara Van Ho (eds.), *Human Rights and Business: Direct Corporate Accountability for Human Rights*, Oisterwijk: Wolf Legal Publishers (2015), pp. 144–149.

38 *Akpan v Royal Dutch Shell*, C/09/337005/HA ZA 09-1580 (ECLI:NL:RBDHA:2013: BY9854), Plc (District Court of the Hague), 30 January 2014.

39 See, Business and Human Rights Resource Centre, 'Cambior lawsuit (re Guyana)', http://business-humanrights.org/en/cambior-lawsuit-re-guyana (last accessed 19 January 2018); *Recherches Internationales Québec v Cambior Inc., QJ No 2554*, (Québec Superior Court), 14 August 1998; Business and Human Rights Resource Centre, 'Anvil mining lawsuit (re Dem. Rep. of Congo)', http://business-humanrights.org/en/anvil-mining-lawsuit-re-dem-rep-of-congo (last accessed 19 January 2018); Anvil Mining Ltd v Association Canadienne contre l'Impunité, QCCA 117 (Québec Court of Appeal) Canada), 20 January 2012.

40 *Chandler v Cape plc*, EWCA Civ 525 (Court of Appeal), 25 April 2012, para 80. See also, *Lungowe & Ors v Vedanta Resources Plc & Anor*, EWCA Civ 1528 (Court of Appeal), 13 October 2017.

41 Business and Human Rights Centre, 'Corporate Legal Accountability', https://business-humanrights.org/en/corporate-legal-accountability (last accessed 19 January 2018).

42 *Dagi v BHP* (no. 2) [1997] 1 VR 428, (Supreme Court of Victoria – Australia), 12 June 1996.

43 Ibid.

44 See, Anita Ramasastry, 'A Swiss Court Allows Gypsies' Holocaust Lawsuit to Proceed: Case Questions Role of Corporate Giant IBM in World War II', *Find Law columnist – CNN.com*, 8 July 2004.

were granted leave by the Swiss Court of Appeal in June 2004 for the case to be heard in the Swiss courts.[45]

Moreover, several group litigations concerning Holocaust compensation cases succeeded against corporations before public bodies against corporations, for instance in Austria[46] and in the United States.[47] A number of civil claims have been successful under Japanese tort law in Japan for forced labour during the Second World War.[48] Further, several cases are pending before Canadian courts indirectly or directly relating to corporate involvement in abuses of socio-economic rights.[49]

The US Alien Tort Statute (ATS) establishes the right of an individual to bring an action for damages against corporations for alleged human rights violations by having knowledge of or directly assisting in such violations. It states that: "the district courts shall have original jurisdiction of any civil action by an alien for a tort only, committed in violation of the law of nations or a treaty of the United States".[50] It has also given opportunity to non-US victims of human rights violations to enforce the accountability of transnational corporations for violations committed outside US territory if the corporations are registered in the United States or do business there. US courts have to date examined more than 150 ATS cases brought against corporations.[51] Further, several claims are yet to

45 Ibid.

46 See cases, National Fund of Republic of Austria for Victims of National Socialism: www.nationalfonds.org/home.html, (last accessed 19 January 2018). See, in details Juan Pablo Bohoslavsky and Jernej Letnar Černič, 'Introduction', *in* Juan Pablo Bohoslavsky and Jernej Letnar Černič (eds.), *Making Sovereign Financing and Human Rights Work*, Oxford and Portland: Hart Publishing (2014), pp. 1–14.

47 *Bodner v Banque Paribas*, 114 F Supp. 2d 117 (United States District Court for the Eastern District of New York), 31 August 2000; *In re Holocaust Victim Assets Litigation*, 105 F. Supp. 2d 139 (United States District Court for the Eastern District of New York), 2 August 2000; See also, Michael Thad Allen, 'The Limits of Lex Americana: The Holocaust Restitution Litigation as a Cul-de-Sac of International Human-Rights Law', 17 *Widener Law Review* 1 (2011).

48 See, Judgment 50-12 SHOMU GEPPO 3444 (Niigata District Court, Japan), 26 March 2004. Judgment 50-12 SHOMU GEPPO 3646 (Fukuoka High Court, Japan), 24 May 2004. See, Judgment 51-12 SHOMU GEPPO (Hiroshima High Court, Japan), 19 January 2005. See, Jernej Letnar Černič, 'An Elephant in a Room of Porcelain: Establishing Corporate Responsibility for Human Rights', *in* Jernej Letnar Černič and Tara van Ho (eds.), *Human Rights and Business: Direct Corporate Accountability for Human Rights*, Oisterwijk: Wolf Legal Publishers (2015), pp. 131–158.

49 *Choc v Hudbay Minerals*, 2013 ONSC 1414 (Superior Court of Justice Ontario, Canada), 22 July 2003; *Araya v Nevsun Resources Ltd.*, 2016 BCSC 1856 (Superior Court of British Columbia, Canada), 6 October 2016; *Garcia v Tahoe Resources Inc.*, 2017 BCCA 39 (Superior Court of British Columbia, Canada), 26 January 2017; *Yaiguaje v Chevron Corporation*, 2015 SCC 42 (Supreme Court of Canada), 4 September 2015. See also, *Recherches Internationales Quebec v Cambior Inc.*

50 US Alien Torts Claims Act of 1789, 28 U.S.C. § 1350; See also, Judiciary Act of 1789, ch. 20, § 11, 1 Stat. 73.

51 US Chamber Institute for Legal Reform, Lawsuits Against Corporations Under the Alien Tort Statute, February 2016, p. 1.

be decided.[52] Victims were successful in some cases.[53] The US Supreme Court decided on 17 April 2013 in the case of *Kiobel et al. v Royal Dutch Petroleum Co* that "there is no indication that the ATS was passed to make the United States a uniquely hospitable forum for the enforcement of international norms"[54] and added that "even where the claims touch and concern the territory of the United States, they must do so with sufficient force to displace the presumption against extraterritorial application".[55] However, after the recent judgment of the US Supreme Court it remains doubtful if the US courts will continue to serve as potential forum for claims of victims for damages that occurred outside the US territory.[56]

However, examples of successful enforcement of corporate accountability for socio-economic rights are only a few. Socio-economic rights have been often protected against corporate actors only indirectly through statutes, which provide only their partial protection. Nonetheless, Langford notes that

> in a context of poverty and social inequality, the combination of rights awareness, the spread of litigation strategies and the increasing independence of the judiciary has led to ESC rights litigation in countries as diverse as China, Egypt, Namibia and the United States.[57]

It is clear that the domestic systems must reform to enhance corporate accountability for socio-economic rights. All in all, domestic systems are of essential importance in complying with victims' right to effective remedies and fair hearing. However, as there are only a few instances of effective judicial protection at the international level; domestic systems remain their best bet. Recent years illustrate that case law on corporate accountability for socio-economic rights has been growing at the domestic level. However, for domestic systems to become really viable options for victims in the next years, they have to move way from only "holding symbolic significance for victims" to efficient, effective, impartial and fair systems.

52 See, Michael D. Goldhaber, 'Corporate Human Rights Litigation in Non-US Courts: A Comparative Scorecard', 3(1) *UC Irvine Law Review* 127 (2013).

53 *Licea v Curacao Drydock Co.*, 584 F. Supp. 2d 1355 (Southern District of Florida), 31 October 2008; *Aguilar v Imperial Nurseries*, No. 3-07-cv-193 (JCH) (Connecticut District Court), 28 May 2008, cited in Michael D. Goldhaber, 'Corporate Human Rights Litigation in Non-US Courts: A Comparative Scorecard', 3(1) *UC Irvine Law Review* 127 (2013).

54 *Kiobel v Royal Dutch Petroleum Co.*, 569 U.S. 108 (2013) (Supreme Court of the United States), p. 12.

55 Ibid., p. 14.

56 *Jesner v Arab bank, PLC*, 584 U.S. ___ (2018).

57 Malcolm Langford, 'Domestic Adjudication and Economic, Social and Cultural Rights: A Socio-Legal Review', 6(11) *Sur International Journal of Human Rights* 91 (2009), p. 110.

Domestic non-judicial mechanisms

Non-judicial state mechanisms (NJMs) may provide additional possibilities for victims of socio-economic rights' violations to have their voice heard. OHCHR has collected information over forty-three jurisdictions, over 200 NJMs, including sixteen NHRIs and ten NCPs. NJMs may offer more efficient and quicker dispute resolution.[58] They are particularly efficient in labour, environmental, consumer and privacy law. They could provide another layer in the holistic ecosystem of enforcement mechanisms. However, NJMs are required to comply with due process. OHCHR stated that NHRI and NCPs are better suited to deal with more complex cases than other NJMs.[59] However, they can only provide to the efficiency of domestic system if they proceed on the basis of the principles of independence, accountability and impartiality. In this way, they can provide policy coherence between different mechanisms. All in all, few examples of existing remediation frameworks illustrate that there are several challenges in ensuring access to fair, independent and impartial remedy.[60]

International law

Rights-holders do not have access in international law to any judicial forum for the enforcement of corporate violations of socio-economic rights, or for any human rights violations.[61] Human rights treaty bodies have in recent decades developed quasi-judicial procedures to deal with complaints or communications under the international human rights treaties. For instance, the International Covenant for Economic, Social and Cultural Rights[62] had only their complaint procedures established when the Optional Protocol went into effect,[63] which at

58 OHCHR, Accountability and Remedy Project Part II: State-based non-judicial mechanisms, State-based non-judicial mechanisms for accountability and remedy for business-related human rights abuses: Supporting actors or lead players?, Discussion paper prepared for the 6th UN Annual Forum on Business and Human Rights, Geneva, 27–29 November 2017.

59 Ibid.

60 See for example, Barrick, 'The Porgera Joint Venture: Remedy Framework', 1 December 2014, http://s1.q4cdn.com/808035602/files/porgera/Porgera-Joint-Venture-Remedy-Framework-Dec1-2014.pdf (last accessed 19 January 2018); and Acacia Mining Remedial Programme at the North Mara Gold Mine, March 2015, https://business-humanrights.org/sites/default/files/documents/Acacia%20-%20Response%20to%20Raid%20-%20March%202015%20%282%29.pdf (last accessed 19 January 2018).

61 See, Jernej Letnar Černič, 'Corporate Responsibility for Human Rights: Towards a Pluralist Approach', *in* Wouter Vandenhole (ed.), *Challenging Territoriality in Human Rights Law: Building Blocks for a Plural and Diverse Duty-Bearer Regime*, Abingdon: Routledge (2015), pp. 75–79.

62 UN, International Covenant on Economic, 'Social and Cultural Rights', G.A. res. 2200A (XXI), 21 U.N.GAOR Supp. (No. 16) at 49, U.N. Doc. A/6316 Treaty Series, vol. 993, 16 December 1966.

63 UN, General Assembly, 'Optional Protocol to the International Covenant on Economic, Social and Cultural Rights', UN. Doc. A/RES/63/117, 5 March 2009.

the time of this writing has only twenty-two ratifications.[64] This is one of the few fully fledged international procedures to enforce socio-economic rights; however it does not deal directly with complaints against corporations. In fact, international human rights law currently does not have a forum whereby individuals can protect their socio-economic rights vis-à-vis corporate conduct.[65]

Further, there exists some quasi-judicial mechanisms developed in specialized international organizations such as OECD NCPs, Inspection Panel of the World Bank, the Compliance Advisor Ombudsman of the International Finance Corporation, among others. This chapter will therefore, due to the limitation of space, briefly introduce and analyze the OECD Guidelines for Multinational Enterprises and the Tripartite Declaration of Principles concerning Multinational Enterprises and Social Policy, as they have been so far the most relevant quasi-judicial mechanism for enforcing corporate accountability at the international level.[66] Some mechanisms such as the Compliance Advisor Ombudsman of the International Finance Corporation are considered in the chapters on individual case studies. However, as discussions illustrate, the international level lacks a binding forum where rights-holders can enforce corporate accountability for socio-economic rights and obtain compensation.

OECD Guidelines for Multinational Enterprises

The OECD Guidelines for Multinational Enterprises are "recommendations jointly addressed by governments to multinational enterprises".[67] They have so far been one of the most successful mechanisms for business and human rights at the international level. Corporations should "contribute to economic, environmental and social progress with a view to achieving sustainable development" and "respect the internationally recognized human rights of those affected by their activities".[68] Corporations are, more specifically, recommended to "respect human rights, which means they should avoid infringing on the human rights of others and should address adverse human rights impacts with which they are involved".[69] In this way, the OECD member states are obliged to establish National Contact Points (NCPs), which carry primary responsibility to ensure the implementation of the OECD Guidelines for Multinational Enterprises at the national level. The NCPs may provide an additional

64 Ibid., Status of Ratification, http://indicators.ohchr.org/ (last accessed 19 January 2018).

65 Larissa Van den Herik and Jernej Letnar Černič, 'Regulating Corporations Under International Law: From Human Rights to International Criminal Law and Back Again', 8 *Journal of International Criminal Justice* 725 (2010).

66 See for a discussion, SOMO, 'The Patchwork of Non-Judicial Grievance Mechanisms: Addressing the Limitations of the Current Landscape', Somo Paper, November 2014.

67 OECD Guidelines for Multinational Enterprises (2011 Edition), Part I, 'I. Concepts and Principles', para 1. See in detail: Jernej Letnar Černič, 'The 2011 Update of the OECD Guidelines for Multinational Enterprises', *ASIL Insights*, Vol. 4, Issue 4. 10 February 2012, https://www.asil.org/insights/volume/16/issue/4/2011-update-oecd-guidelines-multinational-enterprises (last accessed 19 January 2018).

68 Ibid., Part I, 'II. General Policies', paras A.1 and A.2.

69 Ibid., Part I, 'IV. Human Rights', para 1.

path for the enforcement of some socio-economic rights against corporations. The NCPs are "composed and organized such that they provide an effective basis for dealing with the broad range of issues covered by the Guidelines" and must "enable the NCP to operate in an impartial manner while maintaining an adequate level of accountability to the adhering government".[70] Several instances against corporations have so far been brought before respective NCPs.[71]

NCPs have in recent years delivered some decisions relating to the protections of socio-economic rights. For instance, in the *Final statement former employees of Bralima v. Bralima and Heineken*, Dutch NCP noted

> that operating in a conflict area enhances the need for enterprises to act according to the Guidelines. Enterprises should provide transparent and clear information to employees on their performance and on any changes that could have a major impact on their employees' livelihood.[72]

Additionally, UK NCP has in *Crude Accountability v KPO Consortium* found that "the KPO consortium did not meet its obligation under Chapter II, Paragraph 12 to seek to prevent or mitigate adverse impacts to which it was linked by a business relationship" concerning resettlement of two households.[73] Further, UK NCP has noted in *Raid v ENRC* that relating that "the impact on reliable access to safe water is a human rights impact . . . the UK NCP does not consider that ENRC has fully met its obligation to address this impact".[74] Nonetheless, the enforcement mechanism of OECD Guidelines' has been deficient mostly due to the quasi-judicial nature of the procedure before NCPs. Final statements of NCPs are generally non-binding recommendations. However, compliance with the Guidelines is progressively improving; in particular, the recent case law of the NCPs illustrates some progress.[75] Therefore, positive change has to spread across NCPs in all OECD member states to bolster the existing system of NCPs in order to provide efficient remedy for victims.

The Tripartite Declaration of Principles concerning Multinational Enterprises and Social Policy

The governing body of the International Labour Office adopted the Tripartite Declaration of Principles concerning Multinational Enterprises and Social Policy

70 Ibid.

71 European Center for Constitutional and Human Rights, 'A Comparison of National Contact Points: Best Practices in OECD Complaints Procedures', Berlin, November 2011.

72 Dutch National Contact Point OECD Guidelines, 'Final Statement Former Employees of Bralima vs. Bralima and Heineken', 18 August 2017, p. 6.

73 UK National Contact Point OECD Guidelines, 'Crude Accountability & KPO Consortium: Final Statement After Examination of Complaint', November 2017, para 74.

74 UK National Contact Point OECD Guidelines, 'Raid & ENRC: Final Statement After Examination of Complaint', February 2016, para 78.

75 Roel Nieuwenkamp, 'Outcomes from OECD National Contact Points cases: More remedy than you may think!', Cambridge Core blog, 10 November 2017.

on 16 November 1977,[76] and amended it in November 2000,[77] in March 2006[78] and again recently in March 2017.[79] The last update has adapted the wording of the Declaration to the developments in business and human rights field; in particular, it has included the reforms of the UN Guiding Principles on Business and Human Rights.[80] The Declaration and its enforcement mechanisms indirectly may provide additional mechanisms for enforcement of socio-economic rights. The preamble of the Declaration provides that corporations "can also make an important contribution to the promotion of economic and social welfare; to the improvement of living standards and the satisfaction of basic needs".[81] It "sets out principles in the fields of employment, training, conditions of work and life and industrial relations which governments, employers' and workers' organizations and multinational enterprises are recommended to observe on a voluntary basis".[82] It states that "all the parties concerned by this Declaration . . . should respect the Universal Declaration of Human Rights and the corresponding International Covenants adopted by the General Assembly of the United Nations".[83] As for socio-economic rights, the Declaration provides in Section 44 that

> multinational enterprises should maintain the highest standards of safety and health, in conformity with national requirements . . . They should also make available to the representatives of the workers and upon request, to the competent authorities and the workers' and employers' organizations in all countries in which they operate, information on the safety and health standards relevant to their local operations, which they observe in other countries.[84]

The enforcement of the Declaration has been unclear and vague. Annex 2 of the Guidelines entitled "Operational Tools" deals in Part III with the "Procedure for the examination of disputes concerning the application of the Tripartite Declaration of Principles concerning Multinational Enterprises and Social Policy by means of interpretation of its provisions".[85] Part III defines such procedure

76 ILO, 'Tripartite Declaration of Principles concerning Multinational Enterprises and Social Policy', adopted at its 204th Session (1st Edition, 1977).
77 ILO, 'Tripartite Declaration of Principles Concerning Multinational Enterprises and Social Policy', adopted at its 279th Session (3rd Edition, 2001).
78 ILO, 'Tripartite Declaration of Principles Concerning Multinational Enterprises and Social Policy', adopted at its 295th Session (4th Edition, 2006).
79 ILO, 'Tripartite Declaration of Principles Concerning Multinational Enterprises and Social Policy', adopted at its 329th Session (5th Edition, 2017). See Jernej, Letnar Černič, *Human Rights Law and Business: Corporate Responsibility for Fundamental Human Rights*, Groningen: Europa Law Publishing (2010), pp. 207–217.
80 Ibid., para 10.
81 Ibid., para 1.
82 Ibid., para 7.
83 Ibid., para 8.
84 Ibid., para 44.
85 Ibid., p. 24.

as "to interpret the provisions of the Declaration when needed to resolve a disagreement on their meaning, arising from an actual situation, between parties to whom the Declaration is commended".[86] However, it does not explain what is the added value of such a procedure. The enforcement of the Declaration has been supervised by the ILO Subcommittee on Multinational Enterprises and has been tasked: "to conduct periodic surveys on the effect given to the . . . Declaration" and "to consider requests for the interpretation of the provisions of the . . . Declaration".[87] The enforcement procedure has been non-transparent, as requests are not publicly published. As for enforcement, we have noted in 2010 that "the nature of this interpretation procedure is very limited since it cannot be invoked in respect of national law and practice or in respect of international labour conventions and recommendations".[88] However, since our observations were published in 2010, the information has been taken offline and neither this information nor how many requests have since been submitted can be found online now. It appears that the ILO does not diligently monitor the compliance with the Declaration. In other words, the ILO Declaration has been stripped of effectiveness, which certainly cannot be deemed useful and efficient for victims of socio-economic rights violations.

Arbitration

Lawyers for Better Business submitted in 2014 a proposal for the establishment of an international arbitration tribunal on business and human rights in order to address deficiencies in victims' access to justice. One of its proponents, Claes Cronstedt, has noted that "the proposed new expert arbitration tribunal would technically follow . . . existing civil international tribunals".[89] The Tribunal would hear "disputes arising out of business abuse of human rights".[90] As for the victims, Cronstedt argues that the Tribunal would hear "their alleged claims through mediation or to have them decided by a panel of arbitrators with expertise in the human rights responsibilities of business".[91] On the other hand, corporations would be attracted to such arbitration tribunals "to clear themselves from accusations of alleged human rights violations".[92] Cronstedt has further argued that "for victims, the Tribunal would, in many situations, likely be their only source of remedy. For businesses, more rapid time frames

86 Ibid.
87 ILO, 'Governing Body – Subcommittee on Multinational Enterprises', www.ilo.org/empent/Informationresources/WCMS_101252/lang—en/index.htm (last accessed 19 January 2018).
88 Jernej Letnar Černič, *Human Rights Law and Business: Corporate Responsibility for Fundamental Human Rights*, Groningen: Europa Law Publishing (2010), p. 213.
89 'International Arbitration Tribunal on Business and Human Rights: Reshaping Access to Remedy', Remarks by Claes Cronstedt, London, 29 September 2014.
90 Ibid.
91 Ibid.
92 Ibid.

for resolving human rights disputes may prove decisive".[93] The drafters suggest that human rights clauses should be inserted into arbitration agreements or bilateral investment contracts, which is an idea that has been around for several years.[94] They observe that "the contract gives enforcement rights to outside stakeholders who are not parties to the contract, as third-party beneficiaries".[95] Such beneficiaries may include victims or organizations representing them. Their proposal thereafter discusses issues such as: the nomination of arbitrators, mediators and experts;[96] procedural rules;[97] powers for the delivery of awards;[98] and avenues for the establishment of the tribunal.[99] The tribunal would also include mediators that "would handle human rights disputes that come before the Tribunal where the parties wish to seek an informal settlement"[100] and the draft proposal vaguely submits that "they would handle conflicts arising anywhere in the world".[101] The drafters have carefully identified four potential avenues for the establishment of such a tribunal, which include: the Permanent Court of Arbitration Model, the UNCITRAL Model, the ICSID Model and a proposal for a private institution.[102] They concluded in their draft proposal that "it is not acceptable for human suffering and environmental and property devastation to continue to plague the poor and vulnerable for decades to come".[103] All in all, such a proposal is based upon the efficiency with which a tribunal will function. Subsequently, the authors have modified the proposal, whereas several other organizations have joined in.[104]

Merits can certainly be found in the proposal on an arbitration tribunal on business and socio-economic rights, as it is centred upon the idea of improving victims' access to meaningful justice. An arbitration tribunal would certainly

93 Ibid., p. 4.
94 See also, Sheldon Leader, 'Risk Management, Project Finance and Rights-Based Development', *in* Sheldon Leader and David Ong (eds.), *Global Project Finance, Human Rights and Sustainable Development*, Cambridge: Cambridge University Press (2011), pp. 107–141; Sheldon Leader, 'Human Rights, Risks, and New Strategies for Global Investment', 9(3) *Journal of International Economic Law* 657 (2006); and Jernej Letnar Černič, 'Corporate Human Rights Obligations Under Stabilization Clauses', 11(2) *German Law Journal* 210 (2010).
95 Claes Cronstedt, Robert C. Thompson, Rachel Chambers, Adrienne Margolis, David Rönnegård and Katherine Tyler, 'An International Arbitration Tribunal on Business and Human Rights: Enhancing Access to Remedy' (International Arbitration Proposal) Version 4, 10 November 2014, p. 8.
96 Ibid., p. 11.
97 Ibid., pp. 11–13.
98 Ibid., pp. 13–14.
99 Ibid., pp. 14–15.
100 Ibid., p. 14.
101 Ibid., p. 14.
102 Ibid., pp. 14–15.
103 Ibid., p. 17.
104 Claes Cronstedt, Jan Eijsbouts and Robert C. Thompson, 'International Business and Human Rights Arbitration', (Proposal), 13 February 2017.

proceed with cases more expeditiously than an ordinary tribunal. Even though such an idea appears utopian at first glance, it fits well with the idea of a binding international treaty on business and human rights and the access to remedy pillars of the UN Guiding Principles. However, such an idea faces several obstacles that may prevent it from moving from proposal to fruition. Several of these obstacles are connected to those issues which often prevent human rights arguments in front of arbitration tribunals. Although arbitration tribunals have, in recent years, started to heed human rights arguments and considered them when resolving disputes, such references remain few and far between.[105]

First, few commercial contracts include reference to any human (socio-economic) rights considerations or third-party beneficiaries. The parties in commercial arbitration traditionally agree to abide by arbitration procedures according to their own wishes. Mostly, they prefer to exclude any potential surprises. It would take a huge turn in the practice of the conclusion of commercial contracts for the inclusion of human rights clauses to become things which are generally accepted and expected of contractual parties. Surely, as the proposal submits, that could be remedied by "post-dispute arbitrations agreements",[106] which are possible but not very likely in the practice of arbitration tribunals.[107]

Second, arbitration proceedings have never been very human rights savvy, as several dimensions of fair trial guarantees are not fully respected during arbitration proceedings.[108] Arbitration tribunals traditionally function differently from the ordinary courts as the arbitrators are nominated and chosen by the parties. Nonetheless, any legal representative of the victims would insist that arbitrators ensure the appearance of independence and impartiality in order to be able to sit on the panel. Another question that lingers is whether victims, by bringing their claims before arbitration tribunals, waive their right to bring their claims before ordinary national courts.

Third, as for the four proposed models, each offers a potential path by which to develop an arbitration tribunal. The Permanent Court of Arbitration Model could function as a starting point, particularly due to its Optional Rules for

105 See, Diane Desierto, *Public Policy in International Economic Law: The ICESCR in Trade, Finance, and Investment*, Oxford: Oxford University Press (2015); Pierre-Marie Dupuy, *Ernst-Ulrich Petersmann and Francesco Francioni, Human Rights in International Investment Law and Arbitration*, Oxford: Oxford University Press (2009). See also, European Centre for Constitutional and Human Rights, 'Human Rights Inapplicable in International Investment Arbitration?' Berlin, July 2012.

106 Claes Cronstedt, Robert C. Thompson, Rachel Chambers, Adrienne Margolis, David Rönnegård and Katherine Tyler, 'An International Arbitration Tribunal on Business and Human Rights: Enhancing Access to Remedy'(International Arbitration Proposal) Version 4, 10 November 2014, pp. 9 and 10.

107 See generally, Michael Z. Green, 'Measures to Encourage and Reward Post-Dispute Agreements to Arbitrate Employment Claims', 8 *Nevada Law Journal* 58 (2007).

108 *Hulki Güneş v Turkey*, Application no. 28490/95 (European Court of Human Rights), 19 June 2003, para 84.

Arbitration of Disputes Relating to the Environment and/or Natural Resources.[109] The ICSID Model could be brought into consideration in line with the discussion on the development of an international binding treaty on business and human rights. However, such initiative should include all stakeholders, including private corporations. The model based on UNCITRAL could work hand-in-hand with the proposal for the UN General Assembly Declaration on Business and Human Rights. The proposal for private institutions would have to be clarified further in order to be properly considered.

Fourth, as arbitrations function on the basis of the *pacta sunt servanda* principle as the overreaching principles of different private law fields, arbitration would not be the perfect forum for those victims who gave priority to the criminal prosecutions of those most responsible for alleged corporate human rights violations. Victims would be precluded from bringing such cases in any proceeding arbitration. For instance, in the seminal *Trafigura* case, victims decided to bring criminal claims, even though the civil claims were settled.[110] Nonetheless, this should not be a hurdle if the arbitration tribunal would be complemented by other avenues and existing judicial mechanisms.

All in all, the proposal for the creation of an international arbitration tribunal on business and human rights complements other existing and recent initiatives on business and human rights. Its strength lies in providing another efficient forum for access to justice for victims of corporate socio-economic human rights violations. On the other hand, it has several weaknesses and some may note that one should take it with a pinch of salt due to its "utopian" nature. Nonetheless, its contribution to the pluralistic debate on business and human rights and its role in proceeding with a holistic approach should not be underestimated.

Internal complaints mechanisms

Internal complaints mechanisms refer to company-based supervisory mechanisms where victims could turn in the first instance to resolve their complaints or grievances concerning socio-economic rights. They could be either found and established in an individual company, industry initiatives or under multi-stakeholder industry initiatives.[111] Those mechanisms differ in nature in terms of complexity and effectiveness between corporations and industries. Some are structured in various levels of accountability and potential outcomes; others are less complex in nature. Their advantages lie in the fact that they can provide swift resolution

109 Permanent Court of Arbitration, 'Optional Rules for Arbitration of Disputes Relating to the Environment and/or Natural Resources', 19 June 2001.

110 Amnesty International, 'UK:Threat of High Court Action Spurs Review of Corporate Conspiracy Claim', 20 November 2014.

111 See generally, Karin Lukas, Barbara Linder, Astrid Kutrzeba and Claudia Sprenger, *Corporate Accountability: The Role and Impact of Non-Judicial Mechanisms*, Cheltenham and Northampton: Edward Elgar Publishing (2016).

of the dispute close to the victim, particularly where domestic judicial or quasi-judicial mechanisms are absent. One can agree that "companies need to have a channel through which complaints can be recorded and dealt with, but what is more important is the discipline to learn from those issues and avoid them in the future".[112] Their disadvantages are that they have difficulties in generating the level of trust necessary to ensure a high level of legitimacy. Such trust and confidence in the mechanism is difficult to achieve within corporations that might be directly or indirectly responsible for violations. Lukas argues that

> the lack of trust in a mechanism prevents people from resorting to it and may result in complete boycott. One company mechanism very well conceived and human rights-compatible on paper, ultimately failed to be accepted by its potential users due to a massive lack of confidence in the company, resulting from corporate misbehaviour in the past (i.e. Anglo).[113]

Distrust is connected to expectations that such internal mechanisms are independent, impartial and fair, expectatiôn that corporations often fail to meet. Therefore, they can increase trust and confidence only through good work that can eliminate arbitrariness.

Several corporations have developed sophisticated complaints mechanisms. Adidas Groups has, for instance, developed the "Third Party Complaint Process for Breaches to the Adidas Group Workplace Standards or Violations of International Human Rights Norms".[114] The mechanism defines complaints as twofold: "(a) a violation by a supplier, licensee, agent or contractor of an element of the Workplace Standards relevant to that supplier, contractor or service provider" and "(b) any breach of an international human rights norm, whether related to an external service provider, supplier or to Adidas Group's own business operations, where these affect an outside party".[115] The complaint can be submitted by anyone who suffered violations or by organizations representing victims. The mechanism therefore functions on the basis of *actio popularis.*[116] The complaint mechanism envisaged several outcomes from settlement to submitting complaints to further mechanisms.[117] However, the most essential is to ensure remedies to the victims. Adidas argues that

112 CSR Europe, 'Assessing the Effectiveness of Company Grievance Mechanisms: CSR Europe's Management of Complaints Assessment (MOC-A) Results', December 2013, p. 38.

113 Barbara Linder, Karin Lukas and Astrid Steinkellner, 'The Right to Remedy: Extrajudicial Complaint Mechanisms for Resolving Conflicts of Interest between Business Actors and Those Affected by Their Operations', Vienna, April 2013, p. 86.

114 Adidas Group, 'Third Party Complaint Process for Breaches to the Adidas Group: Workplace Standards or Violations of International Human Rights Norms, p. 1.

115 Ibid.

116 Ibid., p. 2.

117 Ibid., pp. 7–8.

> where the adidas Group determines that it has caused or directly contributed to a violation it will undertake to cease or change the activity that is responsible, in order to prevent or mitigate the chance of the impact occurring or recurring. If an impact is occurring, the adidas Group will engage actively in its remediation, either directly or in cooperation with others.[118]

Moreover, Scotiabank provides that they have established that

> we have also developed our own mechanisms that enable employees, business partners and other stakeholders to raise concerns, including concerns arising out of human rights impacts. These mechanisms are listed in our Whistleblower Policy and Procedures and include a wide variety of complaint and escalation mechanisms. Employees can use internal support mechanisms to raise concerns and get them resolved. The resolution procedures also include an independent Ombudsman for customers and a Staff Ombudsman for employees.[119]

Further, Anglo American has developed a complex internal grievance procedure.[120] It notes that

> complaints and grievances are able to be submitted anonymously or via third parties and that at least one free means of submitting complaints and grievances is provided for. The centralised coordination of complaints and grievances is also recommended to ensure that they are managed in a consistent way. The selection of the most appropriate model should be determined by the volume and type of complaints and grievances being received, the nature of the relationship between the operation and its stakeholders (e.g. levels of trust and goodwill) and the wider context in the country of operation.[121]

However, the outcomes are so indeterminate, which sheds little light on the whole mechanism. Lukas et al. report that

> According to Anglo, the majority of grievances pertained to rather low-level issues ("housekeeping stuff") and did not touch upon serious rights violations. It acknowledges, however, that the potentially affected people are not yet well aware of the complaint mechanisms and don't make use of it regularly. Targets for the future are, therefore, to raise awareness of the

118 Ibid., p. 8.
119 Scotiabank, 'Human Rights Statement', 10 December 2016, p. 3.
120 AngloAmerican, 'Seat Toolbox: Socio-Economic Assessment Toolbox', Version 3, Tool 4A: Complaints and Grievance Procedure,
121 Ibid., p. 74.

> system, train the company staff who is in constant contact with communities to receive complaints and report on the progress and outcomes including internal auditing.[122] (footnotes omitted)

All in all, internal corporate mechanisms may provide another avenue for rights-holders for enforcing corporate accountability for socio-economic rights. However, they work best when coupled with some other mechanisms and provided that they follow principles of transparency, fairness and impartiality.

A bottom-up approach to access to justice

A bottom-up approach to access to justice refers to a socio-legal understanding of the access to justice, which *inter alia* includes social movements, pressures of civil society, protests, boycotts, consumer campaigns and other forms of pressure.[123] A bottom-up approach is usually employed where and when legal responses have not been functioning properly. However, they can be employed as a tool to pressure governments to reform their domestic system for corporate accountability for socio-economic rights. As for bottom-up norm creation, Levit observes that it "debunks the perceived hegemony of official, top-down international lawmaking – lawmaking that often occurs beyond the physical and metaphysical reach of its subjects – and showcases an alternative route to law that is inherently grounded and pluralist".[124] Some recent examples show that bottom-up lawmaking can be in some instances successful.[125] As for bottom-up approaches to accountability they mostly refer to protests. Peaceful assemblies of various groups such as trade unions, civil society groups, student and academic groups, and consumer groups have been often the most effective exercise of the bottom-up approaches to protect their rights and access justice in business and human rights. More specifically, the effective exercise of freedom of assembly is a key element of ensuring victims' access to justice.[126] Freedom of assembly protects the content and conceptual pluralism that is vital for a public debate and

122 Barbara Linder, Karin Lukas and Astrid Steinkellner, 'The Right to Remedy: Extrajudicial Complaint Mechanisms for Resolving Conflicts of Interest between Business Actors and Those Affected by Their Operations', p. 57.

123 Jernej Letnar Černič, 'Corporate Accountability for Human Rights: From a Top-Down to a Bottom-Up Approach', *in* Jena Martin, Karen E. Bravo (eds.), *The Business and Human Rights Landscape: Moving Forward, Looking Back*, Cambridge: Cambridge University Press (2016), pp. 193–218.

124 Janet Koven Levit, 'Bottom-Up International Lawmaking: Reflections on the New Haven School of International Law', 32 *Yale Journal of International Law* 393 (2007), p. 409. See also, Janet Koven Levit, 'A Bottom-Up Approach to International Lawmaking: The Tale of Three Trade Finance Instruments', 30 *Yale Journal of International Law* 125 (2005).

125 The Guiding Principles; 'Maastricht Principles on Extraterritorial Obligations of States in the area of Economic, Social and Cultural Rights', 28 September 2011.

126 *Baczkowski and others v Poland*, Application no. 1543/06 (European Court of Human Rights), 3 May 2007, para 61.

pressure of civil society in a democratic society.[127] It enables the exchange of different and contradictory positions on matters of private and public importance such as corporate accountability for socio-economic rights. States certainly have no right to absolutely prohibit the exercise of the freedom of assembly and of association and expression, but they must balance their actions with the simultaneous protection of the values of pluralism, human dignity, freedom and equality.

The right to free, prior and informed consent is the cornerstone of Indigenous peoples' rights and business, and has been a good example of a bottom-up approach to corporate accountability. ILO Convention 169 states that

> in cases in which the State retains the ownership of mineral or sub-surface resources or rights to other resources pertaining to lands, governments shall establish or maintain procedures through which they shall consult these peoples, with a view to ascertaining whether and to what degree their interests would be prejudiced, before undertaking or permitting any programmes for the exploration or exploitation of such resources pertaining to their lands.[128]

Similarly, the UN Declaration notes that

> States shall consult and cooperate in good faith with the indigenous peoples concerned through their own representative institutions in order to obtain their free and informed consent prior to the approval of any project affecting their lands or territories and other resources, particularly in connection with the development, utilization or exploitation of mineral, water or other resources.[129]

International human rights bodies have confirmed the importance of the right to free, prior, informed consent.[130] However, the legal nature of the rights is questionable, as is its application to the corporate conduct. Anaya has argued in 2009 that "the principles of consultation and consent are aimed at avoiding imposition of will of one party over the other and at instead striving for mutual understanding and consensual decision-making".[131] The right itself is divided into three parts.

127 *Fatma Akaltun Fırat v Turkey*, Application no. 34010/06 (European Court of Human Rights), 10 September 2013.
128 ILO, 'Indigenous and Tribal Peoples Convention', 1989 (No. 169), art. 15.
129 UN, General Assembly, 'Declaration on the Rights of Indigenous Peoples', UN Doc. A/RES/61/295, 2 October 2007, art. 32.2.
130 UN, Human Rights Committee, 'Concluding Observations: Suriname', UN Doc. CCPR/C/SUR/CO/3, 3 December 2015, paras 47–48; UN, Human Rights Committee, 'Concluding Observations: Namibia', UN Doc. CCPR/C/NAM/CO/2, 22 April 2016, paras 43–44.
131 UN, Human Rights Council, 'Report of the Special Rapporteur on the Situation of Human Rights and Fundamental Freedoms of Indigenous People, James Anaya', UN Doc. A/HRC/12/34, 15 July 2009.

First, corporations are obliged not to pressure Indigenous peoples when forming consent. Second, consent must be given prior to the project starting. Third, corporations and other investors are obliged to fully inform Indigenous peoples about the nature and scope of the project. All in all, bottom-up approaches could be viable options for rights-holders in two ways, first as a tool of persuasion of state elite to reform the domestic framework for socio-economic rights, and second in the case of failures of domestic judicial systems.

Challenges

Enforcement of corporate accountability for socio-economic rights is interwoven with many financial, legal and political obstacles.[132] Still, it is considered difficult to establish any form of corporate accountability for socio-economic rights violations. Only individual domestic legal orders have seen rare cases successful in finding corporate accountability for socio-economic rights. Victims usually face several difficulties in bringing cases. This sub-section addresses two of the most important challenges in domestic systems: *forum non conveniens* and separation of legal entities.

Forum non conveniens

Victims face a number of legal challenges when bringing claims against corporations. For instance, there are two main legal obstacles before English courts. First, English courts have discretion under the *forum non conveniens* (*forum non discretion*) doctrine (*forum*) to decide that the jurisdiction where the acts and injuries occurred (even if outside the United Kingdom) is the "appropriate" forum for the case to be heard. Under the doctrine of *forum non conveniens* a court can decline jurisdiction over the case if it holds that a more appropriate forum exists elsewhere. The current tenets of the doctrine are based upon Scottish principles,[133] which explain "*forum non conveniens*" as "appropriate" rather than the "convenient" forum.[134] In *Connelly v RTZ Corporation PLC and RTZ Overseas Ltd.*,[135] the House of Lords held that

132 UN, Human Rights Council, 'Improving Accountability and Access to Remedy for Victims of Business-Related Human Rights Abuse: Report of the United Nations High Commissioner for Human Rights', UN Doc. A/HRC/32/19, 10 May 2016, para 4.

133 *MacMaster v MacMaster* (1833) 11 S. 685, 11 Sess. Cas. 685, 687 (No. 280) (2nd Div. Scot.).

134 *Société du Gaz de Paris v La Société Anonyme de Navigation* 'Les Armateurs Français', [1926] S.C. 33, 35 (House of Lords). See also, *Spiliada Maritime Corporate v Cansulex Ltd.*, [1987,] A.C. 460, 474 (H.L.); *The Atlantic Star v Bona Spes*, [1974] A.C. 436, 442 (House of Lords). See, 'Limitations of Access at the National Level: Forum Non Conveniens', 9(2) *Gonzaga Journal of International Law* 119 (2006).

135 *Connelly v RTZ Corporation*, [1997] 3 WLR 373 (House of Lords), 24 July 1997.

whether "the court is satisfied that there is some other tribunal, having competent jurisdiction, in which the case may be tried more suitably for the interests of all the parties and for the ends of justice"[136] was in disagreement with the diction of Section 31 (1) (b) of the Legal Aid Act 1988 that artificially curtailed that the receipt by the plaintiff of legal aid should be considered.[137] In *Owusu v Jackons and others*[138] the European Court of Justice clarified the relationship between Article 2 of the Brussels Convention and the reach of the doctrine of *forum non conveniens* within the EU. The Court held that Article 2 was mandatory and applicable so as to confer jurisdiction on the English court in *Owusu* and held that the member states cannot apply *forum non conveniens* principles in order to decline jurisdiction conferred by Article 2.[139] Under the Owusu decision, pursuant to Article 2 of the Brussels Convention, EU member states can no longer rely on the *forum non conveniens* doctrine to refuse jurisdiction.

In this way, *Connelly v RTZ Corporation PLC and RTZ Overseas Ltd* demonstrate that corporations with headquarters in England are no longer able to use different standards concerning health and safety at home and *in Rome*. Socio-economic rights are not a source of tort in England and therefore domestic tort law has been the object of proceedings in cases against corporations. The civil litigation in the United Kingdom is of two-pronged importance. First, discussed cases establish that home states have an important role to ensure that actors under their control observe socio-economic rights. In this regard, it appears that "the use of identical, or comparable, health and safety standards would protect employees, residents and consumers in the foreign jurisdiction".[140] Second, the cases of *Connelly v Rio Tinto Zinc Corp. Plc*, *Lubbe and others v Cape Plc.* and *Thor Chemicals Holding Ltd.* represent clear evidence that proceedings may continue against corporations in England if litigation against their subsidiaries is not possible in their own jurisdictions. These cases raise expectations that victims of torts could proceed against English parent corporations in the English courts. However, it is still true that the case law does not necessarily create a precedent for cases in which human rights violations were committed by subsidiaries abroad without considerable involvement, control or knowledge of the parent company to proceed in the English Courts in the future. In this way, the impact of English

136 *Connelly v R.T.Z. Corporation*, [1998] A.C. 854 at 868-69; *Connelly v R.T.Z. Corp. Plc.*, [1998] A.C. 854 (House of Lords) (citing *Sim v Robinow*, 1892 Sess. Cas. (R.) 668 and *Spiliada Maritime Corp. v Cansulex Ltd.*, [1987] A.C. 460, 474).

137 Ibid. See for discussion, Alex Twanda Magaisa, 'Suing Multinational Corporate Groups for Torts in Wake of the Lubbe Case, Commentary', *Law, Social Justice and Global Development (LGD)*, 2001 (2), footnote 14. Connelly v R.T.Z. Plc., [1998] A.C. at 874.
Ibid. See also, *Lubbe and 4 Others v Cape plc*, [2000] 1 W.L.R. 1545 (House of Lords).

138 *Owusu v Jackson Case C-281/02*, [2005] ECR I-1383 (European Court of Justice).

139 Ibid., para 46.

140 Binda Sahni, 'Limitations of Access at the National Level: Forum Non Conveniens', 9(2) *Gonzaga Journal of International Law* 119, 144 (2006).

jurisprudence on the development of greater socio-economic rights protection should not be overestimated.

Confronting separation of legal entities in corporate structures

This section employs a victims-oriented approach in proving liability of a parent corporation for the acts of a subsidiary or agent. Where subsidiary corporations are involved in socio-economic rights violations, three avenues can be identified to tackle the conundrum of separation of legal entities. First, the doctrine of piercing (lifting) the corporate veil opens room for the responsibility of a parent corporation as a shareholder of its subsidiary corporations. The second approach concerns questions of whether a presumption can be established so that acts or omissions by subsidiaries can be attributed to a parent corporation as its own conduct. Alternatively, the third approach proposes the direct liability of the parent corporation for the act and omissions of corporations. Taken together, those approaches require that the parent corporations are identified in order to bring claims in the national legal order of the state of nationality of the parent (transnational) corporation. This section argues that where subsidiary corporations are found liable for socio-economic rights violations, the burden of proof should be placed on the parent corporation with a controlling interest in a subsidiary which would have to rebut the presumption that they are responsible for acts and omissions of its subsidiary. The argument here is that the responsibility of the parent corporation for the acts of a subsidiary or the direct involvement of the parent corporation can be established for alleged socio-economic violations by its subsidiary.

The doctrine of piercing the corporate veil[141] derives from common law legal traditions, where adjudication particularly relies on the facts. It is of particular interest in large corporate groups. The separate legal personality of a subsidiary cannot *eo ipso* exclude the possibility of attributing its conduct to the parent corporations. This is because treating a parent and subsidiary corporation as separate legal entities often does not reflect the reality of relationship in complex corporate relationships.[142] It may appear that there are no clear criteria which prevail when piercing the corporate veil.[143] In this light, the factual relationship has to be established that the parent corporations exercise control over the subsidiary corporation to be held liable for the acts and omissions of the subsidiary of corporations. In *Royal Dutch Shell v Wiwa*, the US court came to conclusion that Royal Dutch/Shell controlled Shell's Nigerian subsidiary and

141 See generally, Karen Vandekerckhove, *Piercing the Corporate Veil: A Transnational Approach*, The Hague: Wolters Kluwer (2007).

142 Oliver De Schutter, 'Extraterritorial Jurisdiction as a Tool for Improving the Human Rights Accountability of Transnational Corporations', 4 November 2006, p. 37.

143 Robert B. Thompson, 'Piercing the Corporate Veil: An Empirical Study', 76 *Cornell Law Review* 1036 (1991).

thus the activities of the subsidiary can be imputed to the parent company.[144] From this analysis, it becomes clear that piercing the corporate veil may embrace considerations that the parent corporation is responsible for the conduct of the subsidiary corporations if it exercises sufficient control over them. Hence, if a subsidiary has violated its obligation to observe socio-economic rights, then a parent corporation would have the burden of proof that a corporate form was not used to avoid its legal obligation. In this light, it would be required for a plaintiff to pierce the corporate veil of each intermediate company before it may reach the parent company.

Another approach for overcoming the separation of legal entities is the doctrine of integrated enterprise. The integrated enterprise doctrine argues for "the absolute presumption that the acts and omissions of the subsidiary can be attributed to the parent because of the interconnectedness of separate legal personalities".[145] In other words, legal rules apply also to large corporate groups which control several interconnected corporations.[146] For example, the 1990 American with Disabilities Act employs such an approach.[147] It prohibits discrimination against persons with disabilities, as committed by any employer, employment agency, labour organization or joint labour-management committee. With regards to the separation of legal entities, it creates a presumption that "if an employer controls a corporation whose place of incorporation is a foreign country, any practice that constitutes discrimination under this section and is engaged in by such corporation shall be presumed to be engaged in by such employer".[148] This means that US corporations are obliged to ensure that corporations under their control comply with prohibition of discrimination on the basis of the disability. The Act also includes set of factors which shall determine whether an employer controls the corporations. Decisive factors in this respect are the "interrelation of operations; the common management; the centralized control of labour relations; and the common ownership or financial control, of the employer and the corporation".[149] The underlying rationale for the integrated enterprise doctrine lies in the

144 *Wiwa v Royal Dutch Petroleum Co.*, No. 96 Civ. 8386(KMW), 2002 U.S. Dist. LEXIS. 3293, 20 February 2002, (S.D.N.Y.), pp. 77–78.

145 'Seminar of Legal Experts: Extraterritorial Legislation as a Tool to Improve the Accountability of Transnational Corporations for Human Rights Violations', (Brussels, 3–4 November 2006), Summary Report, p. 5.

146 Oliver De Schutter, 'Extraterritorial Jurisdiction as a Tool for Improving the Human Rights Accountability of Transnational Corporations', 4 November 2006, p. 39. See for application of this approach under ATSA, Scott Coye-Huhn, 'No More Hiding behind Forms, Factors and Flying Hats: A Proposal for a per se Piercing of the Corporate Veil for Corporations that Violate the Law of Nations under the Alien Tort Claims Statute', 72(2) *University Cincinnati Law Review* 743 (2003).

147 Americans with Disabilities Act of 1990 Pub. L. 101–336, title I, § 102, July 26, 1990, 104 Stat. 331; amended by Pub. L. 102–166, title I, § 109(b)(2), Nov. 21,1991, 105 Stat. 1077; 42 U.S.C. § 12112 (c)(2)(A) (1994).

148 42 U.S.C. § 12112 (c)(2)(B) (1994).

149 42 U.S.C. § 12112 (c)(2)(C) (1994).

presumption that the "controlling" parent company effectively affects the conduct of the subsidiary. This then justifies the attribution of the acts of the subsidiary to the parent corporation.

The third approach focuses on the direct liability of the parent corporation for the acts and omission of its subsidiaries. It may appear that a legal obligation exists to exercise control over the activities of the subsidiary to hold corporations liable. In this light, the direct liability of a parent corporation for failure to control the conduct of its subsidiaries may be difficult to establish, as a parent corporation is generally not legal liable for the acts of its subsidiaries due to the doctrine of limited liability.[150] Subsidiary corporations are often distinct legal entities incorporated under law of the country where they operate. This presumption can be rebutted where there is a direct or indirect involvement in the subsidiary's acts. For instance, the Court noted in *Bowoto et al. v Chevron Co* that "the fact that defendants were making abnormally frequent attempts to contact Nigeria on the third day of the Parabe incident is probative of defendants' involvement in the incident".[151] Nevertheless, subsidiary corporations have direct obligations and the responsibility to observe socio-economic rights also in the country where they operate. This section argues that an appropriate proposal would be to reverse the burden of proof. This would place the burden of proof on the parent companies with a controlling interest in a subsidiary which would have to rebut the presumption that they are responsible for the acts and omissions of its subsidiary.[152] Such a presumption could be rebutted if a parent company shows that it took reasonable measures to prevent the acts and omissions of its subsidiary.

This section has argued for the responsibility of the parent corporation for the acts of the subsidiary, including socio-economic rights violations by or involving subsidiary, where they exercise control over corporations. In contrast, this section has not argued that the parent corporation must control every decision of its subsidiaries for it to be held liable for its conduct. The argument, rather, is that they provide a business framework for subsidiaries' activities abroad. Without parent corporations' capital, they may not be able to finance their activities abroad and without insurance their risk may not be covered. Taken together, it appears that the support of a parent corporation plays an important role at least in the initial activities of subsidiaries. It appears that the approach is similar to the direct liability of a parent corporation and may be better suited to resolving challenges relating to separation of legal entities by suggesting policy objectives and then developing normative proposals aimed at implementing those objectives.

150 See for example, classic English case: *Salomon v Salomon & Co.* (1896), [1897] A.C. 22 (House of Lords).

151 *Bowoto et al. v Chevron Co. et al.*, June 5, 2007, Case 3:99-cv-02506-SI, Document 1628, p. 3, 5 June 2007 (States District Court, N.D. California).

152 See, Scott Coye-Huhn 'No More Hiding Behind Forms, Factors and Flying Hats: A Proposal for a per se Piercing of the Corporate Veil for Corporations that Violate the Law of Nations Under the Alien Tort Claims Statute', p. 758.

Holistic approach to accountability for socio-economic violations

In order to achieve effective corporate accountability for socio-economic rights in a broader sense, one has to employ all available strategies to enforce accountability for socio-economic rights violations.[153] All available strategies include concurrence of different actors, modes and levels of accountability in order to bring justice to victims for violations of their socio-economic rights by or involving corporations. Holistic approaches place in the centre the human dignity of rights-holders. This study has concentrated on corporate accountability; however holistic approach argues that the concurrence of different actors, modes and accountability is theoretically feasible and possible in order to guarantee at least some victims' access to justice. In some cases accountability could be established against different actors and at different levels at the same time. For instance, a holistic approach to business and socio-economic rights also includes individual and state responsibility. Concurrence follows the objective of enforcing the rights of victims concerning socio-economic rights. Different levels of accountability can be present at the same time side by side by arguing for concurrence of different levels of accountability, which enhances individual access to justice, which is often limited due to substantive and procedural hurdles, but also due to low-level respect for the rule of law in respective domestic legal environments. Daskalopoulou-Livada stated at the ICC Rome Conference there is no

> need for establishing the principle of criminal responsibility of legal persons under the Statute of the Court, not because Greek law did not provide for the criminal responsibility of such persons, but because there was no criminal responsibility which could not be traced back to individuals.[154]

Similarly, Kamminga observed that "individual responsibility under international law has not replaced . . . state responsibility for the same offences".[155] Several domestic systems allow for the concurrence of corporate and individual criminal law responsibility. The French Criminal Code states in Article 121 (2) that "the criminal liability of legal persons does not exclude that of natural persons".[156]

153 See for a detailed discussion, Jernej Letnar Černič, 'Corporate Accountability for Human Rights: From a Top-Down to a Bottom-Up Approach', *in* Jena Martin, Karen E. Bravo (eds.), *The Business and Human Rights Landscape: Moving Forward, Looking Back*, Cambridge: Cambridge University Press (2016).

154 UN, Diplomatic Conference of Plenipotentiaries on the Establishment of an International Criminal Court, 'Summary Records of the Meetings of the Committee as a Whole, United Nations', UN Doc. A/CONF.183/C.1/L.3 (Vol.II), 16 June 1998, p. 136 (para 57).

155 Menno T. Kamminga, 'Corporate Obligations Under International Law', *in Report of the 71st Conference of the International Law Association*, Berlin: International Law Association, pp. 442–427.

156 Criminal Code of the French Republic, Act no. 2000-647, 10 July, Art. 8, Official Journal, 11 July 2000, Article 121-2.

Further, Article 51(2) of the Criminal Code of the Netherlands allows, for example, for concurrence between corporate and individual criminal responsibility.[157] Similar examples are found at the international level. For instance, the UN Convention Against Transnational Organized Crime provides in Article 10 (3) that the liability of legal entities "shall be without prejudice to the criminal liability of the natural persons who have committed the offences".[158] In conclusion, the reason for arguing for a holistic approach to corporate accountability is to enhance victims' alternative to enforce violations of their socio-economic rights by or involving corporations through corporate, individual or state responsibility.

Conclusion

Victims have generally so far remained with weak rights to effective judicial, quasi-judicial and non-judicial protection in the event of socio-economic rights violations by corporate actors. This chapter has studied selected available judicial, quasi-judicial and non-judicial mechanisms for enforcing corporate accountability for socio-economic rights from domestic law to bottom-up approaches. It found that best effective mechanisms are still to be found, despite some deficiencies, in domestic systems. The international level at the moment only provides quasi-judicial mechanisms with limited reach, such as the National Contact Points under the OECD Guidelines. Rights-holders and their advocates therefore have to resort to either the domestic system (which is often plagued by legal hurdles and rule-of-law challenges, particularly in the domestic systems of Asian, African, South American, Central and Eastern European countries) or they have to resort to innovative quasi-judicial and non-judicial approaches (such as internal complaints mechanisms, arbitration or even bottom-up enforcement). However, as grim as the landscape may seem some new avenues are arising for rights-holders to protect their socio-economic rights and establish corporate accountability. Thus proposals for arbitration tribunals for business and human rights and the rise, despite of their weaknesses, of internal complaints procedures may provide hope for rights-holders. Further, the potential adoption of the Treaty on Business and Human Rights may provide an added value in improving the rights of victims in the field of business and human rights, and would have to be followed by further steps towards bringing justice closer to victims.[159] It is necessary that states improve the domestic systems by adopting binding statutes that would require corporations to take preventive measures, ensure liability of parent companies for the actions and omissions of their subsidiaries, and bolster civil, criminal and

157 Criminal Code of the Netherlands, art. 51(2). See also, The Australian Commonwealth Criminal Code Act, No. 12, 1995, Section 12.1.

158 UN, General Assembly, 'The United Nations Convention Against Transnational Organized Crime', UN Doc. A/RES/55/25, 15 November 2000, art. 10.

159 Jernej Letnar Černič, Nicolás Carrillo-Santarelli (eds.), *The Future of Business and Human Rights: Theoretical and Practical Considerations for a UN Treaty*. Cambridge; Antwerp; Portland: Intersentia (2018).

administrative liability of corporations. Domestic systems remain best equipped to deal with alleged socio-economic rights violations of rights-holders. However, challenges of procedural and substantial hurdles of bringing cases against corporations will remain both in home and host states. Among them, perhaps the most difficult are access to justice in extraterritorial cases and separation of legal personalities in complex corporate entities.

Bibliography

Books

Desierto, Diane, *Public Policy in International Economic Law: The ICESCR in Trade, Finance and Investment*, Oxford: Oxford University Press (2015).

Deva, Surya, *Regulating Corporate Human Rights Violations: Humanizing Business*, London: Routledge (2012).

Dupuy, Pierre-Marie, Petersmann, Ernst-Ulrich and Francioni, Francesco, *Human Rights in International Investment Law and Arbitration*, Oxford: Oxford University Press (2009).

Letnar Černič, Jernej, *Human Rights Law and Business: Corporate Responsibility for Fundamental Human Rights*, Groningen: Europa Law Publishing (2010).

Letnar Černič, Jernej and Van Ho, Tara, (eds.), *Human Rights and Business: Direct Corporate Accountability for Human Rights*, Oisterwijk: Wolf Legal Publishers (2015).

Letnar Černič, Jernej and Carrillo-Santarelli, Nicolás (eds.), *The Future of Business and Human Rights: Theoretical and Practical Considerations for a UN Treaty.* Cambridge; Antwerp; Portland: Intersentia (2018).

Lukas, Karin, Linder, Barbara, Kutrzeba, Astrid and Sprenger, Claudia, *Corporate Accountability: The Role and Impact of Non-Judicial Mechanisms*, Cheltenham and Northampton: Edward Elgar Publishing (2016).

Minkler, Lanse (ed.), *The State of Economic and Social Human Rights*, Cambridge: Cambridge University Press (2013).

Vandekerckhove, Karen, *Piercing the Corporate Veil: A Transnational Approach*, The Hague: Wolters Kluwer (2007).

Journal articles

Akintayo, Akinola E., 'A Good Thing from Nazareth? Stemming the Tide of Neo-Liberalism Against Socio-Economic Rights: Lessons from the Nigerian case of Bamidele Aturu v Minister of Petroleum Resources and Others', 15(2) *ESR Review: Economic and Social Rights in South Africa* 5 (2014).

Allen, Michael Thad, 'The Limits of Lex Americana: The Holocaust Restitution Litigation as a Cul-de-Sac of International Human-Rights Law', 17 *Widener Law Review* 1 (2011).

Baxi, Upendra, 'Human Rights Responsibility of Multinational Corporations, Political Ecology of Injustice: Learning from Bhopal Thirty Plus?', 1(1) *Business and Human Rights Journal* 21 (2016).

Coye-Huhn, Scott, 'No More Hiding Behind Forms, Factors and Flying Hats: A Proposal for a per se Piercing of the Corporate Veil for Corporations that Violate the

Law of Nations under the Alien Tort Claims Statute', 72(2) *University Cincinnati Law Review* 743 (2003).

Eide, Asbjørn, 'Realisation of Social and Economic Rights and the Minimum Threshold Approach', 10(2) *Human Rights Law Journal* 37 (1989).

Goldhaber, Michael D., 'Corporate Human Rights Litigation in Non-US Courts: A Comparative Scorecard', 3(1) *UC Irvine Law Review* 127 (2013).

Green, Michael Z., 'Measures to Encourage and Reward Post-Dispute Agreements to Arbitrate Employment Claims', 8 *Nevada Law Journal* 58 (2007).

Ibe, Stanley, 'Implementing Economic, Social and Cultural Rights in Nigeria: Opportunities and Challenges', 10 *African Human Rights Law Journal* 197 (2010).

Langford, Malcolm, 'Domestic Adjudication and Economic, Social and Cultural Rights: A Socio-Legal Review', 6(11) *Sur International Journal of Human Rights* 91 (2009).

Leader, Sheldon, 'Human Rights, Risks and New Strategies for Global Investment', 9(3) *Journal of International Economic Law* 657 (2006).

Letnar Černič, Jernej, 'Corporate Human Rights Obligations Under Stabilization Clauses', 11(2) *German Law Journal* 210 (2010).

Levit, Janet Koven, 'Bottom-Up International Lawmaking: Reflections on the New Haven School of International Law', 32 *Yale Journal of International Law* 393 (2007).

Levit, Janet Koven, 'A Bottom-Up Approach to International Lawmaking: The Tale of Three Trade Finance Instruments', 30 *Yale Journal of International Law* 125 (2005).

Magaisa, Alex Twanda, 'Suing Multinational Corporate Groups for Torts in Wake of the Lubbe Case, Commentary', *Law, Social Justice and Global Development (LGD)*, 2001 (2).

Saunders, Pammela Q., 'Rethinking Corporate Human Rights Accountability', 89 *Tulane Law Review* 603 (2014).

Sahni, Binda, 'Limitations of Access at the National Level: Forum Non Conveniens', 9(2) *Gonzaga Journal of International Law* 119 (2006).

Siegel, Jonathan R., 'A Theory of Justiciability', 86 *Texas Law Review* 73 (2007).

Thompson, Robert B., 'Piercing the Corporate Veil: An Empirical Study', 76 *Cornell Law Review* 1036 (1991).

Van den Herik, Larissa and Letnar Černič, Jernej, 'Regulating Corporations Under International Law: From Human Rights to International Criminal Law and Back Again', 8 *Journal of International Criminal Justice* 725 (2010).

Book chapters

Bohoslavsky, Juan Pablo and Letnar Černič, Jernej, 'Introduction', *in* Juan Pablo Bohoslavsky and Jernej Letnar Černič (eds.), *Making Sovereign Financing and Human Rights Work*, Oxford and Portland: Hart Publishing (2014), pp. 1–14.

Durojaye, Ebenezer, 'Litigating the Right to Health in Nigeria: Challenges and Prospects', *in* Magnus Killander (ed.), *International Law and Domestic Human Rights Litigation in Africa*, Pretoria: Pretoria University Law Press (2010), pp. 149–171.

Krygier, Martin, 'Rule of Law', *in* Michel Rosenfeld and András Sajó (eds.), *The Oxford Handbook of Comparative Constitutional Law*, Oxford: Oxford University Press (2012), pp. 233–249.

Langford, Malcolm, 'Judicial Review in National Courts: Recognition and Responsiveness', *in* Eibe Riedel, Gilles Giacca and Christophe Golay (eds.), *Economic, Social and Cultural Rights in International Law: Contemporary Issues and Challenges*, Oxford: Oxford University Press (2014), pp. 417–447.

Leader, Sheldon, 'Risk Management, Project Finance and Rights-Based Development', *in* Sheldon Leader and David Ong (eds.), *Global Project Finance, Human Rights and Sustainable Development*, Cambridge: Cambridge University Press (2011), pp. 107–141.

Letnar Černič, Jernej and Van Ho, Tara, 'Introduction', *in* Jernej Letnar Černič and Tara Van Ho (eds.), *Human Rights and Business: Direct Corporate Accountability for Human Rights*, Oisterwijk: Wolf Legal Publishers (2015), pp. 1–23.

Letnar Černič, Jernej, 'An Elephant in a Room of Porcelain: Establishing Corporate Responsibility for Human Rights', *in* Jernej Letnar Černič and Tara van Ho (eds.), *Human Rights and Business: Direct Corporate Accountability for Human Rights*, Oisterwijk: Wolf Legal Publishers (2015), pp. 131–158.

Letnar Černič, Jernej, 'Corporate Responsibility for Human Rights: Towards a Pluralist Approach', *in* Wouter Vandenhole (ed.), *Challenging Territoriality in Human Rights Law: Building Blocks for a Plural and Diverse Duty-Bearer Regime*, Abingdon: Routledge (2015), pp. 69–89.

Letnar Černič, Jernej, 'Corporate Accountability for Human Rights: From a Top-Down to a Bottom-Up Approach', *in* Jena Martin and Karen E. Bravo (eds.), *in The Business and Human Rights Landscape: Moving Forward, Looking Back*, Cambridge: Cambridge University Press (2016), pp. 193–218.

Treaty

UN, International Covenant on Economic, 'Social and Cultural Rights, G.A. res. 2200A (XXI), 21 U.N.GAOR Supp. (No. 16) at 49', UN Doc. A/6316 Treaty Series, vol. 993, 16 December 1966.

Legislation

Alien Torts Claims Act of 1789, 28 U.S.C. § 1350.

Americans with Disabilities Act of 1990 Pub. L. 101–336, title I, § 102, July 26, 1990, 104 Stat. 331; amended by Pub. L. 102–166, title I, § 109(b)(2), Nov. 21,1991, 105 Stat. 1077; 42 U.S.C. § 12112 (c)(2)(A) (1994).

Judiciary Act of 1789, ch. 20, § 11, 1 Stat. 73.

Torture Victims Protection Act of 1991.

Criminal Code of the French Republic, Act no. 2000-647, 10 July, Art. 8, Official Journal 11 July 2000.

Criminal Code of the Netherlands.

The Australian Commonwealth Criminal Code Act, No. 12, 1995.

Newspaper articles

Ceaux, Pascal and Follorou, Jacques, 'Total va indemniser ses accusateurs', *Le Monde*, 30 Novembre 2005.

Agence France Press, 'Belgium Reopens Myanmar Humanity Crimes Probe Against Oil Giant Total', 2 October 2007.

Le Monde.fr with Reuters, 'Total: la Belgique rouvre une enquête pour crimes contre l'humanité', *Le Monde*, 1 October 2007.

Ramasastry, Anita, 'A Swiss Court Allows Gypsies' Holocaust Lawsuit to Proceed: Case Questions Role of Corporate Giant IBM in World War II', *Find Law* columnist – *CNN.com*, 8 July 2004.

Official documents

UN, CESCR, 'General Comment No. 9: The Domestic Application of the Covenant', UN Doc. E/C.12/1998/24, 3 December 1998.

UN, CESCR, 'General Comment No. 24 (2017) on State Obligations Under the International Covenant on Economic, Social and Cultural Rights in the Context of Business Activities', UN Doc. E/C.12/GC/24, 10 August 2017.

UN, Diplomatic Conference of Plenipotentiaries on the Establishment of an International Criminal Court, 'Summary Records of the Meetings of the Committee as a Whole, United Nations', UN Doc. A/CONF.183/C.1/L.3 (Vol.II), 16 June 1998.

UN, General Assembly, 'The United Nations Convention Against Transnational Organized Crime', UN Doc. A/RES/55/25, 15 November 2000.

UN, General Assembly, 'Optional Protocol to the International Covenant on Economic, Social and Cultural Rights', UN. Doc. A/RES/63/117, 5 March 2009.

UN, Human Rights Council, Report of Special Representative of the Secretary-General on the Issue of Human Rights and Transnational Corporations and Other Business Enterprises, John Ruggie, 'Guiding Principles on Business and Human Rights: Implementing the United Nations "Protect, Respect and Remedy" Framework' ['The Guiding Principles'], UN Doc. A/HRC/17/31, 21 March 2011. UN, Human Rights Council, Improving Accountability and Access to Remedy for Victims of Business-related Human Rights Abuse, UN Doc. A/HRC/32/19, 10 May 2016.

UN, Human Rights Council, 'Improving Accountability and Access to Remedy for Victims of Business-Related Human Rights Abuse: Explanatory Notes for Guidance', UN Doc. A/HRC/32/19/Add.1, 12 May 2016.

UN, Report of the Working Group on the Issue of Human Rights and Transnational Corporations and other Business Enterprises, 'Access to Effective Remedies Under the Guiding Principles on Business and Human Rights: Implementing the United Nations Protect, Respect and Remedy Framework', UN Doc. A/72/162, 18 July 2017.

UN, General Assembly, 'Declaration on the Rights of Indigenous Peoples', UN Doc. A/RES/61/295, 2 October 2007.

UN, Human Rights Committee, 'Concluding Observations: Suriname', UN Doc. CCPR/C/SUR/CO/3, 3 December 2015.

UN, Human Rights Committee, 'Concluding Observations: Namibia', UN Doc. CCPR/C/NAM/CO/2, 22 April 2016.

UN, Human Rights Council, 'Report of the Special Rapporteur on the Situation of Human Rights and Fundamental Freedoms of Indigenous People, James Anaya', UN Doc. A/HRC/12/34, 15 July 2009.

UN, Human Rights Council, 'Improving Accountability and Access to Remedy for Victims of Business-Related Human Rights Abuse: Report of the United Nations High Commissioner for Human Rights', UN Doc. A/HRC/32/19, 10 May 2016.

Cases

Aguilar v Imperial Nurseries, No. 3-07-cv-193 (JCH) (Connecticut District Court), 28 May 2008.

Akpan v Royal Dutch Shell Plc, Case no. C/09/337005/HA ZA 09-1580 (District Court of The Hague), 30 January 2014.

Anvil Mining Ltd v *Association Canadienne contre l'Impunité*, QCCA 117 (Québec Court of Appeal) Canada), 20 January 2012.

Araya v Nevsun Resources Ltd., 2016 BCSC 1856 (Superior Court of British Columbia, Canada), 6 October 2016.

Association France-Palestine Solidarité v Société Alstom Transport SA (Case No. 11/05331), Versailles Court of Appeal, 22 March 2013.

Baczkowski and others v Poland, Application no. 1543/06 (European Court of Human Rights), 3 May 2007.

Bodner v Banque Paribas, 114 F Supp. 2d 117 (United States District Court for the Eastern District of New York), 31 August 2000.

Bowoto et al. v Chevron Co. et al., June 5, 2007, Case 3:99-cv-02506-SI, Document 1628, 5 June 2007 (States District Court, N.D. California).

Chandler v Cape plc, EWCA Civ 525 (Court of Appeal), 25 April 2012.

Choc v Hudbay Minerals, 2013 ONSC 1414 (Superior Court of Justice Ontario, Canada), 22 July 2003.

Connelly v RTZ Corporation, [1997] 3 WLR 373 (House of Lords), 24 July 1997.

Connelly v R.T.Z. Corp. Plc., [1998] A.C. 854 (House of Lords.)

Dagi v BHP (no. 2) [1997] 1 VR 428, (Supreme Court of Victoria – Australia), 12 June 1996.

Delhi Development Horticulture Employee's Union v Delhi Administration, AIR 1992 SC 789 (Supreme Court of India), 4 February 1992.

Fatma Akaltun Fırat v Turkey, Application no. 34010/06 (European Court of Human Rights), 10 September 2013.

Garcia v Tahoe Resources Inc., 2017 BCCA 39 (Superior Court of British Columbia, Canada), 26 January 2017.

Hulki Güneş v *Turkey*, Application no. 28490/95 (European Court of Human Rights), 19 June 2003.

In re Holocaust Victim Assets Litigation, 105 F. Supp. 2d 139 (United States District Court for the Eastern District of New York), 2 August 2000.

Jesner v Arab bank, PLC, 584 U.S. ___ (2018).

Judgment 50-12 SHOMU GEPPO 3444 (Niigata District Court, Japan), 26 March 2004.

Judgment 50-12 SHOMU GEPPO 3646 (Fukuoka High Court, Japan), 24 May 2004.

Judgment 51-12 SHOMU GEPPO (Hiroshima High Court, Japan), 19 January 2005.

Kiobel v Royal Dutch Petroleum Co, 569 U.S. 108 (2013) (Supreme Court of the United States).

Licea v Curacao Drydock Co., 584 F. Supp. 2d 1355 (Southern District of Florida), 31 October 2008.

Lubbe and 4 Others v Cape plc, [2000] 1 WLR 1545 (House of Lords), 20 July 2000.

Lungowe & Ors v Vedanta Resources Plc & Anor, EWCA Civ 1528 (Court of Appeal), 13 October 2017.

MacMaster v MacMaster (1833,) 11 S. 685, 11 Sess. Cas. 685, 687 (No. 280) (2nd Div. Scot.).

Mazibuko and Others v City of Johannesburg and Others, CCT 39/09 (Constitutional Court of South Africa), 8 October 2009.
Olga Tellis v Bombay Municipal Corporation, AIR 1986 SC 180 (Supreme Court of India), 10 July 1985.
Owusu v Jackson Case C-281/02, [2005] ECR I-1383 (European Court of Justice).
Prosecutor v Frans Van A, (2005) Case No. 09/751003-04, Judgment LJN: AU8685 (District Court of The Hague), 23 December 2005.
Recherches Internationales Quebec v Cambior Inc., QJ No. 2554 (Quebec Superior Court), 14 August 1998.
Sa Majesté La Reine v Les Pétroles Global Inc, Judgment 2013 QCCS 4262 (Superior Court of Quebec).
Salomon v Salomon & Co. (1896), [1897] A.C. 22 (House of Lords).
Société du Gaz de Paris v La Société Anonyme de Navigation 'Les Armateurs Français', [1926] S.C. 33, 35 (H.L.).
Spiliada Maritime Corporate v Cansulex Ltd., [1987,] A.C. 460, 474 (H.L.).
State v Golfview Mining (Pty) Ltd (Case No. 462/04/2009), Judgment ESH 82/11 (Ermelo Regional Court, South Africa).
The Atlantic Star v Bona Spes, [1974] A.C. 436, 442 (H.L.).
Union Carbide Corporation v Union of India, Order 15-02-1989 and Order 05-04-1989, in Civil Appeal No. 3187-89 (Supreme Court of India).
Wiwa v Royal Dutch Petroleum Co., No. 96 Civ. 8386(KMW), 2002 U.S. Dist. LEXIS. 3293, 20 February 2002, (S.D.N.Y.), *World Bank Group v Wallace* (Case No. 36315), Judgment [2016] SCC 15 (Supreme Court of Canada).
Yaiguaje v Chevron Corporation, 2015 SCC 42 (Supreme Court of Canada), 4 September 2015.

Websites

'National Fund of Republic of Austria for Victims of National Socialism', www.nationalfonds.org/home.html, (last accessed 19 January 2018).
'Status of Ratification International Human Rights Treaties (Interactive Dashboard)', http://indicators.ohchr.org/ (last accessed 19 January 2018).

Reports and miscellaneous

'Acacia Mining Remedial Programme at the North Mara Gold Mine', March 2015, https://business-humanrights.org/sites/default/files/documents/Acacia%20-%20Response%20to%20Raid%20-%20March%202015%20%282%29.pdf (last accessed 19 January 2018).
Amnesty International, 'Clouds of Injustice: Bhopal Disaster 20 Years on', 2004.
Amnesty International, 'UK:Threat of High Court Action Spurs Review of Corporate Conspiracy Claim', 20 November 2014.
AngloAmerican, 'Seat Toolbox: Socio-Economic Assessment Toolbox', Version 3.
Azarov, Valentina, 'Investigative or Political Barriers? Dutch Prosecutor Dismisses Criminal Complicity Case Against Riwal', *Rights as Usual Blog*, 29 May 2013.
Barrick, 'The Porgera Joint Venture: Remedy Framework', 1 December 2014, http://s1.q4cdn.com/808035602/files/porgera/Porgera-Joint-Venture-Remedy-Framework-Dec1-2014.pdf (last accessed 19 January 2018).

Business and Human Rights Centre, Corporate Legal Accountability, https://business-humanrights.org/en/corporate-legal-accountability (last accessed 19 January 2018).

Business and Human Rights Resource Centre, 'Cambior lawsuit (re Guyana)', http://business-humanrights.org/en/cambior-lawsuit-re-guyana (last accessed 19 January 2018).

Business and Human Rights Resource Centre, 'Anvil mining lawsuit (re Dem. Rep. of Congo)', http://business-humanrights.org/en/anvil-mining-lawsuit-re-dem-rep-of-congo (last accessed 19 January 2018).

Cronstedt, Claes, Thompson, Robert C., Chambers, Rachel, Margolis, Adrienne, Rönnegård, David and Tyler, Katherine, 'An International Arbitration Tribunal on Business and Human Rights: Enhancing Access to Remedy', (International Arbitration Proposal) Version 4, 10 November 2014.

Cronstedt, Claes, Eijsbouts, Jan and Thompson, Robert C., 'International Business and Human Rights Arbitration', (Proposal), 13 February 2017.

CSR Europe, 'Assessing the Effectiveness of Company Grievance Mechanisms: CSR Europe's Management of Complaints Assessment (MOC-A) Results', December 2013.

De Schutter, Oliver, 'Extraterritorial Jurisdiction as a Tool for Improving the Human Rights Accountability of Transnational Corporations', 4 November 2006.

Deva, Surya, 'Access to Effective Remedy: Taking Human Rights and Rights Holders Seriously', *Cambridge Core Blog*, 14 November 2017.

Dutch National Contact Point, 'Final Statement Former Employees of Bralima vs. Bralima and Heineken', 18 August 2017.

European Center for Constitutional and Human Rights, 'A Comparison of National Contact Points: Best Practices in OECD Complaints Procedures', Berlin, November 2011.

European Centre for Constitutional and Human Rights, 'Human Rights Inapplicable in International Investment Arbitration?' Berlin, July 2012.

ILO, 'Governing Body – Subcommittee on Multinational Enterprises', www.ilo.org/empent/Informationresources/WCMS_101252/lang-en/index.htm (last accessed 19 January 2018).

ILO, 'Indigenous and Tribal Peoples Convention', 1989 (No. 169).

ILO, 'Tripartite Declaration of Principles Concerning Multinational Enterprises and Social Policy', adopted at its 204th Session (1st Edition, 1977).

ILO, 'Tripartite Declaration of Principles Concerning Multinational Enterprises and Social Policy', adopted at its 279th Session (3rd Edition, 2001).

ILO, 'Tripartite Declaration of Principles Concerning Multinational Enterprises and Social Policy', adopted at its 295th Session (4th Edition, 2006).

ILO, 'Tripartite Declaration of Principles Concerning Multinational Enterprises and Social Policy', adopted at its 329th Session (5th Edition, 2017).

'International Arbitration Tribunal on Business and Human Rights: Reshaping Access to Remedy', Remarks by Claes Cronstedt, London, 29 September 2014.

Letnar Černič, Jernej, 'The 2011 Update of the OECD Guidelines for Multinational Enterprises', *ASIL Insights*, Vol. 4, Issue 4. 10 February 2012, https://www.asil.org/insights/volume/16/issue/4/2011-update-oecd-guidelines-multinational-enterprises (last accessed 19 January 2018).

Linder, Barbara, Lukas, Karin and Steinkellner, Astrid, 'The Right to Remedy: Extra-judicial Complaint Mechanisms for Resolving Conflicts of Interest between Business Actors and Those Affected by their Operations', Vienna, April 2013.

'Maastricht Principles on Extraterritorial Obligations of States in the Area of Economic, Social and Cultural Rights', 28 September 2011.

Menno T. Kamminga, 'Corporate Obligations Under International Law', *in Report of the 71st Conference of the International Law Association*, Berlin: International Law Association, pp. 442–427.

Nieuwenkamp, Roel, 'Outcomes from OECD National Contact Points Cases: More Remedy Than You May Think!' *Cambridge Core blog*, 10 November 2017.

OECD Guidelines for Multinational Enterprises, 2011 Edition.

Permanent Court of Arbitration, 'Optional Rules for Arbitration of Disputes Relating to the Environment and/or Natural Resources', 19 June 2001.

Ramasastry, Anita and Thompson, Robert C., 'Business and International Crimes Project: Assessing the Liability of Business Entities for Grave Violations of International Law: A Survey of Sixteen Countries', Fafo-report 536 (2006).

'Seminar of Legal Experts: Extraterritorial Legislation as a Tool to Improve the Accountability of Transnational Corporations for Human Rights Violations', (Brussels, 3–4 November 2006), Summary Report.

SOMO, 'The Patchwork of Non-Judicial Grievance Mechanisms: Addressing the Limitations of the Current Landscape', Somo Paper, November 2014.

Scotiabank, 'Human Rights Statement', 10 December 2016.

UK National Contact Point OECD Guidelines, 'Crude Accountability & KPO Consortium: Final Statement After Examination of Complaint', November 2017,

UK National Contact Point OECD Guidelines, 'Raid & ENRC: Final Statement After Examination of Complaint', February 2016.

US Chamber Institute for Legal Reform, 'Lawsuits Against Corporations Under the Alien Tort Statute', February 2016.

Part III

Corporate accountability for socio-economic rights and case studies

8 Corporate accountability concerning socio-economic rights in Cambodia

Introduction 195
Socio-economic and the rule-of-law environment and alleged human rights violations in Cambodia 198
Socio-economic environment and rule-of-law environment 198
Alleged corporate socio-economic rights violations 199
Cambodia's approach to human rights protection, business and socio-economic livelihoods 201
Domestic human rights protection 201
Cambodia's institutional approach to business and socio-economic rights 202
Regional influences benefiting Cambodia's approach to business and human rights? 203
Business and socio-economic rights in Cambodia's garment industry 206
Corporate legal accountability for socio-economic rights in Cambodia 210
Conclusion 214

Introduction

Cambodia is a very complex environment, like many other lower-middle income countries in the Global South. Most of the population struggles to survive each day by way of informal employment, while resting on the country's weak shoulders a handful of the elite leads extravagant lifestyles.[1] In contrast, the country enjoyed annual economic growth exceeding 7% in the period from 1994 to 2015 based primarily on foreign direct investment.[2] Most of Cambodia's inhabitants are below 30 years of age, giving the country remarkable momentum.

1 See for example, Global Witness, Hostile Takeover, 7 July 2016.

2 Asian Development Bank, 'Asian Development Outlook 2017: Transcending the Middle-Income Challenge', April 2017. See also, World Bank 2017 Overview Cambodia, www.worldbank.org/en/country/cambodia/overview (last accessed 19 January 2018).

This chapter explores corporate accountability for ensuring socio-economic rights are adhered to in Cambodia.

In the last few decades, Cambodia and South-East Asia have been witness to tremendous economic development, bringing better living standards to most of the population. The economic community of the Association of South-East Nations (ASEAN) represents a relatively recent yet growing regional market. However, in its 2015 briefing the Business and Human Rights Centre observed that "rapid economic integration in Southeast Asia – despite its huge potential to lift people out of poverty and create decent work – is currently accompanied by widespread human rights abuses: involving companies headquartered within the region and beyond".[3] It noted that "by far the highest number of approaches to companies was regarding alleged abuses in Myanmar (123 approaches), followed by Philippines (48), Cambodia (46), Indonesia (43) and Malaysia (11)".[4] The alleged abuses range from forced labour, political and civil rights oppression to land rights violations.[5]

More specifically, Cambodia faces particular difficulties in ensuring human rights in the garment industry and sectors impacting on land rights. Therefore, the Cambodian Centre for Human Rights notes that in Cambodia the "business sector is plagued with a myriad of human rights concerns".[6] In particular, the independence and impartiality of all three branches of government remains an unresolved issue. The former UN special rapporteur on the situation of human rights in Cambodia, Surya P. Subedi, observed in 2014 that

> the need for the independence of the national structures to promote and protect human rights, as well as greater transparency and participation in the way in which the country is governed. Ways must be found to adapt the multiple reforms under way to those needs.[7]

Moreover, the UN Human Rights Council recommended the Cambodian government under the 2nd Cycle of the Universal Periodic Review to "promote legislation on corporate social responsibility and the dissemination of guiding principles on business and human rights with a view to improving safety in the work place and working conditions for employees".[8] Yet such rhetorical declarations have yet to be

3 Business and Human Rights Resource Centre, 'Development for All, or a Privileged Few? Business & Human Rights in Southeast Asia', April 2015, p. 18.
4 Ibid., p. 7.
5 Ibid., pp. 8–18.
6 Cambodian Centre for Human Rights, 'Business and Human Rights Handbook for Cambodia', p. 8.
7 United Nations, General Assembly, 'Report of the Special Rapporteur on the Situation of Human Rights in Cambodia, Surya P. Subedi', A/HRC/27/70, 15 August 2014, para 80.
8 UN, Human Rights Council, 'Report of the Working Group on the Universal Periodic Review, Cambodia', UN Doc. A/HRC/26/16, 27 March 2014, para 118 and 127.

fully realized by the Cambodian government. Cambodia has been lagging behind in business and socio-economic rights debates and developments.

Like many countries, Cambodia suffers from various socio-economic and rule-of-law challenges.[9] The rule of law is defined in this chapter as the absence of any arbitrary interference by state and non-state actors in the fair, independent and impartial functioning of branches of state government.[10] At first glance, Cambodia is yet another lower-middle income country, facing difficulties coping with everyday life. However, lying in the background is an autocratic regime entailing a mix of totalitarian elements that control many dimensions of Cambodian society. Reports have emerged of individuals and families hoping to oppose the ruling Cambodian People's Party (CPP) being persecuted and imprisoned.[11] As the successor to the Red Khmers, the CPP controls all layers of Cambodian society, from the state electoral commission, made up entirely of its members, to the judicial branch of power. It is only the "Extraordinary Chambers for War Crimes", which prosecute those most responsible for genocide and crimes against humanity, that seem to operate fairly independently.[12] Yet the Chambers encounter constant pressure from the Cambodian government, which would like to stop their operations. Accordingly, today individuals only quietly criticize the functioning of the ruling elite since they are aware of the possible consequences of any loud or public criticism.

This chapter is divided into five sections. The interactions between the socio-economic environment, the rule-of-law environment and alleged human rights violations in Cambodia are outlined and explained in the second section. In the third section, Cambodia's approach to human rights protection is critically analyzed. In so doing, this section explores and examines Cambodia's approach to business and human rights. The fourth section thereafter analyzes business and socio-economic rights in the Cambodian garment industry, while the fifth section deals with corporate legal accountability in Cambodia. Equipped with this knowledge, the sixth section examines corporate legal accountability for socio-economic rights in Cambodia. All in all, the conclusion points to the need for a more rule of law–based approach to business and socio-economic development in Cambodia, one that both employs a holistic approach and accounts for all the different strategies available to ensure a healthier outlook for corporate accountability for socio-economic rights.

9 See for example, UN, OHCHR, 'Role and Achievements of the Office of the United Nations High Commissioner for Human Rights in Assisting the Government and People of Cambodia in the Promotion and Protection of Human Rights, UN Doc. A/HRC/36/32, 17 August 2017, para 25–37.

10 Martin Krygier, 'The Rule of Law', *in* Michel Rosenfeld and András Sajó (eds.), *Oxford Handbook of Comparative Constitutional Law*, Oxford: Oxford University Press (2012), pp. 233–249.

11 Ibid., paras 8–9.

12 See for a detailed discussion, Simon M. Meisenberg and Ignaz Stegmiller (eds.), *The Extraordinary Chambers in the Courts of Cambodia: Assessing Their Contribution to International Criminal Law*, The Hague: Asser Press (2016).

Socio-economic and the rule-of-law environment and alleged human rights violations in Cambodia

Socio-economic environment and rule-of-law environment

The socio-economic and rule-of-law environment has ever since the country was democratized been subjected to the corrupt practices of the elite surrounding the Hun Sen government.[13] In the last three decades, the country has made remarkable progress in the provision of socio-economic rights such as right to education, food, health, adequate housing and water. At the same time, it should be noted that it started from a very low starting point, making rapid progress no real surprise. However, economic development also requires equivalent development in socio-economic and civil and political rights. Although the Human Development Index in Cambodia has risen sharply in the last two decades, it remains below the average for the countries of South-East Asia. Globally, the Human Development Index puts Cambodia in 143rd place out of 187 countries.[14] Most of the population still lives close to poverty as a result of low incomes and the lack of access to health services and education. The World Bank states that

> while Cambodia has achieved the Millennium Development Goal . . . of halving poverty in 2009, the vast majority of families who escaped poverty were only able to do so by a small margin. Around 4.5 million people remain near-poor, vulnerable to falling back into poverty when exposed to economic and other external shocks.[15]

Life expectancy at birth in Cambodia from 1990 to 2013 rose by a staggering 53.6 years to 68.8 years.[16] Child mortality fell and primary school attendance increased. Basic education in recent years has become almost universal. Such a leap in primary school attendance is surprising in view of the fact that the Cambodian government dedicated, comparatively speaking, only a small portion of its budget to the provision of social services.[17] Likewise, progress has not been as successful in combating inequalities in society since this is also linked to the effective implementation of political and civil rights.[18]

13 See in detail for example, Peter Manning, *Transitional Justice and Memory in Cambodia: Beyond the Khmer Rouge*, London: Routledge (2017).

14 Human Development Index, Cambodia, 2016, http://hdr.undp.org/en/countries/profiles/KHM.

15 See also, World Bank, 2017 Overview, Cambodia.

16 Human Development Report 2016, 'Human Development for Everyone, Briefing Note for Countries on the 2016 Human Development Report', Cambodia, p. 3.

17 Only 3.5 of GDP, World Bank, 2008.

18 As a result of this growing inequality, ever more individuals are forced to leave the countryside and to try their luck, especially in Phnom Penh. Many people also illegally immigrate to the neighbouring, more developed countries of Thailand, Vietnam and Laos.

The transition from the agricultural to the industrial sector, which only began less than two decades ago, will certainly take a few more years. The rural-urban transition has been slower in Cambodia since in 2011 only 20% of the 15 million people were living in cities.[19] Most of the rural population still depends on agriculture and livestock. Phnom Penh is currently "only" a city of 2 million people. Today, almost half the population still works in agriculture. The informal sector of the economy in Cambodia and across the Global South is characterized by the exceptional entrepreneurial creativity needed to overcome the bureaucratic obstacles needed to maintain the position of the ruling elite.

Corruption in the country remains high, thus affecting confidence in fair business, in turn repelled any greater foreign investment, mainly from Europe, North America and the developed Asian countries. Koyangi observes that "due to pervasive corruption, few Cambodians trust either law enforcement or the judiciary to safeguard their rights and assets. Judges are basically in the pocket of the ruling Cambodian People's Party, while many lawyers work for whoever can pay the most".[20] Among the biggest investors are, of course, Chinese, Vietnamese, Japanese and Thai corporations. Asian Nikkei reported that "transparency International's Kol said Chinese companies and business people have an advantage in this area because their activities are not subject to such strict oversight back home".[21] European investment has not been seen very much. This is probably because of possible monitoring of operations of the European corporations back in their home markets. European investors are also discouraged by the volatile political environment, legal confusion and doubt that arises in the areas of fair business and concluding transactions. However, Neam and Everret argue that "the country's economic development has been driven in large part by exploitation of natural resources, which has brought Cambodia's elite into conflict over land rights with the less powerful".[22] Phnom Penh, the capital, is itself highly divided: different faces of poverty through to the immense wealth of local corrupt elite, the representatives of international governmental and non-governmental organizations and foreign business people.

Alleged corporate socio-economic rights violations

Beyond poverty, several socio-economic rights are alleged to have been committed by business corporations in Cambodia. They include alleged violations of workers' rights, including child labour, mostly in the garment industry in Cambodia, alleged violations of individuals' and communities' socio-economic rights

19 Index Mundi, Cambodia, 2016, www.indexmundi.com/cambodia/ (last accessed 19 January 2018).

20 Ken Koyanagi, 'Hollow Growth Leaves Cambodians Wanting More', *Nikkei Asian Review*, 16 March 2017.

21 Ibid.

22 Koy Neam and Silas Everett, 'Human Rights Protection in Modern Cambodia: Building on Unstable Grounds', 23 April 2014, Asia Foundation.

in terms of land rights violations and several breaches of civil and political rights due to the complicity of business with the government. The Cambodian Human Rights Centre refers to the

> factories and brands most related to where human rights abuses are taking place: companies holding economic land concessions that have had particularly drastic impacts on the communities, factories where strikes and working conditions are particularly problematic and brands related to those factories who are failing to adhere to human rights principles.[23]

It further stated that

> land is typically transferred to private companies for commercial development, often in violation of the Land Law. Land has also been appropriated for the construction of hydroelectric dams, which in addition to depriving and displacing communities, has severe long-term environmental and economic impacts on the affected areas.[24]

Such instances contribute to the low levels of the right to education, food, health, housing and water. The former UN special rapporteur observed in 2012 that he had

> consistently received information about the human rights issues related to land concessions, including forced evictions, poorly planned resettlement and relocation, environmental destruction and unsustainable exploitation of natural resources and threats to indigenous people's livelihood, culture and traditions, among others.[25]

Moreover, in 2009 the CESCR's "Concluding Observations on Cambodia" expressed concern

> about the reports that the rapid increase in economic land concessions in the last several years, even within the protected zones, is the major factor in the degradation of natural resources, adversely affecting the ecology and biodiversity, resulting in the displacement of indigenous peoples from their lands without just compensation and resettlement and in the loss of livelihood for rural communities who depend on land and forest resources for their survival.[26]

23 Cambodian Centre for Human Rights, http://cchrcambodia.org/index_old.php?url=project_page/project_page.php&p=project_profile.php&id=3&pro=BHRP (last accessed 19 January 2018).

24 Ibid.

25 UN, Human Rights Council, Report of the Special Rapporteur on the situation of human rights in Cambodia Surya P. Subedi to the Human Rights Council at its 21st Session, 'A human rights analysis of economic and other land concessions in Cambodia', UN Doc. A/HRC/21/63/Add.1/Rev.1, 11 October 2012, para. 2.

26 'Concluding observations of the Committee on Economic, Social and Cultural Rights', E/C.12/KHM/CO/1, 12 June 2009, para 15.

Overall, it is mostly the socio-economic rights of vulnerable groups such as women, children and Indigenous peoples that have been directly or indirectly affected by these business activities. Such violations intrinsically arise through general deficiencies in the rule-of-law situation and respect for civil and political rights, which create daily suffering and make the legal environment unpredictable for all individuals in Cambodia.

Cambodia's approach to human rights protection, business and socio-economic livelihoods

Domestic human rights protection

Article 31 of the Constitution of the Kingdom of Cambodia provides that "the Kingdom of Cambodia shall recognize and respect human rights as stipulated in the United Nations Charter the Universal Declaration of Human Rights, the covenants and conventions related to human rights, women's and children's rights".[27] It directly and indirectly protects rights, including socio-economic ones of citizens.[28] For instance, Article 38 states that the "the law protects the life, honor and dignity of citizens".[29] Further, Article 36 provides that "Khmer citizens of either sex shall enjoy the rights to choose any employment according their ability and to the needs of the society".[30] All provisions of the Constitution also apply to legal entities. Moreover, Cambodia has ratified most UN human rights treaties, with the exception of the First Optional Protocol to the International Covenant on Civil and Political Rights and the Second Optional Protocol to the International Covenant on Civil and Political Rights, aiming at abolition of the death penalty.[31] Cambodia has also ratified all of eight fundamental ILO Conventions.[32] International human rights treaties form part of the Cambodian legal system and are directly applicable.[33] The Cambodian legal system also includes strict protections in domestic national legislation on labour law and land law. The state therefore has acquired both national and international obligations to respect, protect and fulfil all human rights of individuals, minorities and Indigenous peoples in its territory, including with regard to the activities of transnational corporations.

27 Constitute Project, 'Cambodia's Constitution of 1993 with Amendments Through 2008'.

28 Ibid., see especially, arts 65–75.

29 Ibid., art. 38 (2).

30 Ibid., art. 36 (1).

31 UN, OHCHR, Ratification Status for Cambodia, http://tbinternet.ohchr.org/_layouts/TreatyBodyExternal/Treaty.aspx?CountryID=29&Lang=EN (last accessed 19 January 2018).

32 ILO, 'Information System on International Labour Standards', Ratifications for Cambodia, www.ilo.org/dyn/normlex/en/f?p=1000:11200:0::NO:11200:P11200_COUNTRY_ID:103055 (last accessed 19 January 2018).

33 Business and Human Rights Resource Centre, 'Business and Human Rights in ASEAN A Baseline Study', Cambodia, April 2013, pp. 71–94. See also, Decision of the Constitutional Council No. 092/003/2007, 10 July 2007, on the status of international law in the legal system of Cambodia, Ibid., p. 76.

The Cambodian state has to do whatever is possible, including taking steps to prevent, investigate, punish and redress business-related human rights abuses through effective policies, legislation, regulations and adjudication to achieve the maximum level of protection of socio-economic and all human rights. For instance, in the context of land rights, the former UN special rapporteur on the situation of human rights in Cambodia noted that "greater scrutiny of the history and background of business enterprises and their investment proposals' viability should be implemented by the relevant authorities in order to screen investors before granting a land concession".[34] Standing to one side is not an option; it appears that the Cambodian government has to show it has exercised diligence in controlling private actors. Moreover, corporations operating in Cambodia are obliged to observe socio-economic rights of individuals.

Cambodia's institutional approach to business and socio-economic rights

The Cambodian government has so far neither adopted nor drafted a national action plan to implement the UN Guiding Principles on Business and Human Rights. It does not have a full-fledged policy to promote business and human rights, including socio-economic rights. Several domestic sources of law in the Cambodian legal system provide for business and human rights obligations.[35] In 2012, the former UN special rapporteur on Cambodia noted that international

> standards on business and human rights are directly relevant to Cambodia through their international legal commitments and domestic law . . . . all businesses involved in land concessions in Cambodia (the host State), including business operations from foreign countries (the home States) bear the responsibility to protect against human rights violations.[36]

He also argued that

> there are practical, operational and logistical reasons for incorporating these requirements into business and development activities and many governments have incorporated these standards into their national laws and policies and companies into their standard operations.[37] (footnote omitted)

34 UN, Human Rights Council, Report of the Special Rapporteur on the Situation of Human Rights in Cambodia Surya P. Subedi to the Human Rights Council at its 21st Session, 'A Human Rights Analysis of Economic and Other Land Concessions in Cambodia', para 208.

35 Business Human Rights Resource Centre, 'Business and Human Rights in ASEAN. A Baseline Study', Cambodia, pp. 81–83.

36 Report of the former UN Special Rapporteur on the situation of human rights in Cambodia Surya P. Subedi to the Human Rights Council at its 21st session, 'A human rights analysis of economic and other land concessions in Cambodia', A/HRC/21/63/Add.1/Rev.1, 11 October 2012, para 74.

37 Ibid., para. 80. See also, paras. 217 and 218.

Moreover, a 2003 report notes that "Cambodia has not provided any guidance to business enterprises on how to respect human rights throughout their operations, but all business licenses and contracts with the government require all businesses to comply with existing laws in force".[38] However, those recommendations have so far not been met.

This is despite the considerable foreign aid provided to produce several civil society reports on Business and Human Rights in Cambodia.[39] Greater efforts, even though scarce, have been seen at the regional level. Such unwillingness to adopt instruments in the area of business and human rights has much to do to with the state of the rule of law in Cambodia where government elite and big business, particularly investors from China and Vietnam, have built a spider web of connected business and political interests, thereby largely inhibiting any more binding domestic initiatives. Therefore, there is a lack of any initiatives in the area of corporate accountability regarding socio-economic rights.

Regional influences benefiting Cambodia's approach to business and socio-economic rights?

Could regional influences impact business and socio-economic rights in Cambodia? Individuals in Cambodia and elsewhere in Asia cannot yet take advantage of the regional system of human rights protection. This does not mean that in the Asian states the protection of human rights is completely absent, but that it is implemented differently than in the European system. So why has the Asian region still not developed a system for the protection of human rights? Asia is a large and varied continent in which few common elements are shared by its different parts.[40] ASEAN member states impose different policies to justify the protection of national sovereignty.[41] Equally important is the fact that the deficient protection of human rights is not the only area in which Asian countries strongly converge. Yet the picture is hardly black and white, as many countries are known to protect human rights, for example, by very effectively protecting labour rights and fighting corruption. Many Asian countries have ratified some of the nine founding UN human rights protections treaties, although the ratification of some is delayed, such as the Convention on the Protection of the Rights of All Migrant Workers and Members of Their Families. Moreover, all South-Asian countries participate in the Universal Periodic Review before the

38 See for example, Business and Human Rights Resource Centre, 'Business and Human Rights in ASEAN: A Baseline Study', Cambodia, p. 86.

39 Ibid., pp. 71–94; Cambodian Centre for Human Rights, 'Business and Human Rights in Cambodia: Constructing the Three Pillars', November 2010.

40 Tan Hsien-Li, *The ASEAN Intergovernmental Commission on Human Rights: Institutionalising Human Rights in Southeast Asia*, Cambridge: Cambridge University Press (2011), pp. 60–71.

41 Attilio Pisanò, 'Human Rights and Sovereignty in the ASEAN Path Towards a Human Rights Declaration', 15 *Human Rights Review* 391 (2014).

UN Council for Human Rights. Asian governments often stress the importance of community values taking precedence over the protection of individual rights and freedoms. The stability, security and homogeneity of society are supported by important values such as rights and freedoms. This position is especially present in most developed Asian countries. Their governments ask: Why insist on the full implementation of political rights if the standard of living of our inhabitants is growing and they have extensive socio-economic rights? Do we really need a full-fledged democracy and the rule of law to effectively protect civil and political rights?

Article 14 of the Charter of ASEAN provides for the establishment of an ASEAN Human Rights Body.[42] The drafters initially even foresaw this body having the possibility to adopt "individual messages" along the lines of the Human Rights Committee of the United Nations. However, the member states of ASEAN established in 2009 the Intergovernmental Commission for the protection of human rights.[43] Although an intergovernmental commission cannot accept individual complaints against the member states, it may promote the protection of human rights by organizing various fora and other activities. The intergovernmental commission is also currently more focused on the promotion of human rights than on protecting them. Moreover, on 18 November 2012 ASEAN adopted a declaration on the protection of human rights.[44] This is a remarkable document using modern wording to protect both civil and political rights, as well as some of the newer rights.[45] In addition to protecting human rights, Article 6 highlights everyone's obligation to the society and state, which includes the already mentioned communitarian values. Unfortunately, there have been problems enforcing it in domestic settings.[46]

ASEAN has traditionally been supportive of policies facilitating the functioning of a market economy in the South-Asian market.[47] Its member states have

42 Association of Southeast Asian Nations (ASEAN), Charter of the Association of Southeast Asian Nations, 20 November 2007, http://www.refworld.org/docid/4948c4842.html (accessed 19 January 2018).

43 Tan Hsien-Li, 'The ASEAN Intergovernmental Commission on Human Rights as a Tool for Social Justice', *in* Ida Lintel, Antoine Buyse and Brianne McGonigle Leyh (eds.), *Defending Human Rights: Tools for Social Justice: Volume in Honour of Fried van Hoof on the Occasion of his Valedictory Lecture and the 30th Anniversary of the Netherlands Institute of Human Rights*, Antwerp: Intersentia (2012), pp. 35–40.

44 ASEAN Human Rights Declaration, Association of Southeast Asian Nations, Human Rights Declaration (adopted at the 21st ASEAN Summit, Phnom Penh, Cambodia, Nov. 18, 2012).

45 Nicholas Doyle, 'The ASEAN Human Rights Declaration and the Implications of Recent Southeast Asian Initiatives in Human Rights Institution-Building and Standard Setting', 63 *International and Comparative Law Quarterly* 67 (2014).

46 Mathew Davies, 'ASEAN Synthesis: Human Rights, Non-Intervention, and the ASEAN Human Rights Declaration (Forum: The Integration of Regions)', 14 *Georgetown Journal of International Affairs* 51 (2013), pp. 51–57.

47 Delphia Lim and Geetanjali Mukherjee, 'Business and Human Rights Challenges in ASEAN: The Role and Modalities of the State', *in* Mahdev Mohan and Cynthia Morel (eds.), *Business and Human Rights in Southeast Asia: Risk and the Regulatory Turn*, Cambridge: Cambridge University Press (2015), pp. 30–56.

traditionally defended the pillars of a free economy based on the rule of law.[48] ASEAN's approach to business and human rights is multi-layered. In this way, it has not developed any official policies on business and human rights.[49] However, some workshops and events have been organized to promote business, sustainable development and human rights in ASEAN countries.[50] ASEAN has therefore not been leading the way in promoting the responsibilities of businesses with respect to human rights.[51] Like elsewhere in Asia, with few exceptions ASEAN has not actively participated in discussions on business and human rights, with not many individuals and non-governmental organizations actively working in the field. Its approach may be characterized by a lack of interest and capacity despite some steps having been taken and rhetorically.[52]

ASEAN members, present at the UN Human Rights Council in June 2011, voted for the adoption of the UN Guiding Principles on Business and Human Rights.[53] However, like most states, ASEAN countries have been very passive[54] in developing their national plans and strengthening their national systems to ensure greater corporate human rights accountability; a situation far removed from the consensus seen when adopting the UN Guiding Principles.[55] So far, of all ASEAN members not one has developed a National Action Plan under the UN Guiding Principles on Business and Human Rights, albeit Malaysia has taken some initial steps to adopt a national action plan.[56]

Despite the slow development of human rights protection and business on the Asian continent, one should not be too critical. ASEAN member states clearly

48 Joel Ng, 'Rule of Law as a Framework within the ASEAN Community', 5 *Journal of East Asia and International Law* 327 (2012).

49 Asian Forum for Human Rights and Development (FORUM-ASIA), 'Corporate Accountability in ASEAN: A Human Rights-Based Approach', 2013.

50 See for example, Asia-Europe Foundation, 14th Informal ASEM Seminar on Human Rights on the topic 'Human Rights and Businesses', 18–20 November 2014, Hanoi, Vietnam.

51 Euston Quah and Tan Tsiat Siong, 'Sustaining Growth, Climate Change, and Meeting Environmental Obligations: What can ASEAN Governments Do?' *in* Ilan Kelman, Robert Kibugi, Rose-Liza and Eisma Osorio (eds.), *Adaptation to Climate Change: ASEAN and Comparative Experiences*, Singapore: World Scientific (2016), pp. 231–256.

52 Business and Human Rights Resource Centre, 'Business and Human Rights in ASEAN: A Baseline Study', Cambodia.

53 UN, Human Rights Council, Report of Special Representative of the Secretary-General on the Issue of Human Rights and Transnational Corporations and Other Business Enterprises, John Ruggie, 'Guiding Principles on Business and Human Rights: Implementing the United Nations "Protect, Respect and Remedy" Framework', UN Doc A/HRC/17/31, 21 March 2011.

54 ASEAN CSR Network.

55 See also recent developments in Switzerland, Corporate Justice, 'Swiss Parliament Motion for Mandatory Human Rights Due Diligence Narrowly Turned Down Conservative Backlash Blocks Increased Corporate Accountability', 13 March 2015.

56 UN, OHCHR, 'State National Action Plans', www.ohchr.org/EN/Issues/Business/Pages/NationalActionPlans.aspx (last accessed 19 January 2018).

and publicly advocate the effective protection of human rights.[57] Greater progress depends on the simultaneous development of various other areas of socio-economic life.[58] In this light, it is necessary to promote the effective protection of human rights in domestic systems and assist those Asian countries which are not ASEAN members. It is beyond doubt that the typical person in most Asian countries is becoming increasingly aware that the government cannot arbitrarily interfere with their rights and freedoms. Additionally, the regional influence could impact the conduct of the government and corporate actors in Cambodia by persuading them that the protection of community values should not serve as an excuse for the daily abuse of state or corporate power.

Business and socio-economic rights in Cambodia's garment industry

The Cambodian economy is largely based on textile industry exports, an area that has been operating successfully due to free-trade agreements with the European Union, the United States, Canada and Australia.[59] In 2016 it exported EUR 3,394 billion in textile products to the European Union.[60] It has particularly benefited from the EU Generalized Scheme of Preferences, resulting, for instance, in a positive balance for Cambodia of almost EUR 4 billion in 2016.[61]

The garment industry most frequently sees violations of labour rights, the rights of safety and health at work, equal treatment, and the prohibition on forced and child labour. International textile corporations operate in a very competitive environment, making the cost of labour an important issue. In so doing, American, European, Canadian and other transnational textile corporations chiefly operate with corporations from countries that hold preferential trade agreements with these countries. These countries of the Global South should primarily control their own textile factories at home themselves, but too often turn a blind eye as part of a desperate desire to attract foreign direct investment. The question is: How would these workers find themselves if global companies decided to withdraw from the state due to the high cost of their labour?

Do global corporations have an obligation to ensure that minimum human rights standards are protected in their global supply chains? What level and extent

57 Gerard Clarke, 'The Evolving ASEAN Human Rights System: The ASEAN Human Rights Declaration of 2012', 11 *Northwestern University Journal of International Human Rights* 1 (2012).

58 Hao Duy Phan, 'Promoting Compliance: An Assessment of ASEAN Instruments Since the ASEAN Charter', 41 *Syracuse Journal of International Law and Commerce* 379 (2014). Attilio Pisanò, 'Towards an ASEAN Human Rights Mechanism: The ASEAN Commission on the Promotion and Protection of the Rights of Women and Children', 20 *The International Journal of Human Rights* 321 (2016).

59 Cambodia's Free Trade Agreements, https://aric.adb.org/fta-country (last accessed 19 January 2018).

60 European Union, Trade in Goods with Cambodia, 2016, p. 2.

61 Ibid., p. 3.

Picture 8.1 Garment factories district, Canadian Industrial Park, Phnom Penh, April 2015

(Source: the author)

Picture 8.2 Garment factories district, Canadian Industrial Park, Phnom Penh, April 2015

(Source: the author)

of diligence should they show? The domestic law of most European countries does not include provisions stating that corporations have an extraterritorial obligation to provide a degree of diligence to ensure that their suppliers and suppliers comply with minimum standards.[62] The suburbs of Phnom Penh are home to many local textile factories that are suppliers to some of the best known global brands, from Adidas to H&M. In these factories mainly young women work, toiling at least six days a week, ten hours or more a day. From the inside and outside the textile factories are tastefully furbished and can only be visited under close supervision. Such should be the requirements for transnational corporations, which are not always present.

Their representatives conduct supervisory visits of local suppliers every few months. Most of the factory workers are employed under fixed-term contracts, if they are sick and absent for a while, the days they miss are deducted from their wages or they must do overtime. If a worker does not accept an expedited procedure, they are terminated and a more flexible worker is engaged.[63] Due to the judicial system that could otherwise effectively protect workers' rights not functioning properly, factory owners can afford to directly infringe workers' rights.

Factories are carefully protected and sealed off under the fastidious eyes of their security services. One cannot visit these factories without permission. For the Cambodian government, this situation is quite suitable since it allegedly personally and symbiotically has links with the owners of the textile factories. This was shown in January 2014 when the Cambodian authorities cracked down on workers protesting for better pay in a bloody way.[64] At that time, the authorities killed five workers. There was excessive use of force, but no one was prosecuted. After the protests, workers' pay rose.[65] It is noted that the Cambodian authorities do not fulfil their positive obligation to protect the human rights of workers in textile factories. Regular periodic inspections are not carried out.

According to research by local non-governmental organizations, in the last few years the government has only fined ten textile factories for non-compliance with labour legislation, even though there are a few hundred textile factories

62 Justine Nolan, 'Business and Human Rights: The Challenge of Putting Principles into Practice and Regulating Global Supply Chains', 42 *Alternative Law Journal* 42 (2017). See also, André Campos, Mariëtte van Huijstee and Martje Theuws, 'From Moral Responsibility to Legal Liability? Modern Day Slavery Conditions in the Global Garment Supply Chain and the Need to Strengthen Regulatory Frameworks: The Case of Inditex-Zara in Brazil', 2015.

63 Ludo Cuyvers and Tim De Meyer, 'Market-Driven Promotion of International Labour Standards in Southeast Asia: The Corporatization of Social Justice', *in* Axel Marx, Miet Maertens, Johan Swinnen and Jan Wouters (eds.), *Private Standards and Global Governance: Economic, Legal and Political Perspectives*, Cheltenham: Edward Elgar (2012), pp. 114–149.

64 Prak Chan Thul, 'Cambodia Protesters Call off Rally After Bloody Crackdown', *Reuters*, 4 January 2014.

65 The Economist, *The Cambodian Government Threatens Labour Rights*, Phnom Penh: The Economist, 26 October 2017.

on the outskirts of Phnom Penh.[66] It is clear that it is not in the government's interest to ensure restrictive and careful monitoring since that would lead to the discovery of many anomalies. Also questionable is its institutional capacity to deal with or to supervise the work in textile factories. Government officials are unmotivated and poorly paid, making them vulnerable to pressure from textile factory owners. Yet a more crucial issue is: If everything is in transnational companies' hands in terms of their contracts with local suppliers and businesses, then these companies should be there every day, via their representatives, at least once a week to monitor the work process in textile factories, but the latter do so only once a month. Similarly: Should all transnational companies be required to disclose lists of their suppliers so that effective control can be exercised at least by civil society groups?

In 2001, the ILO established the "Better factories" initiative. It aims to "improve working conditions in Cambodia's export garment factories. It combines independent monitoring with finding solutions (through suggestions to management), training, advice and information".[67] The 33rd Synthesis Report on the programme notes that "the top ten non-compliance issues remain the same as in the previous year including issues related to occupational safety in the workplace, overtime and temperature levels in the factory".[68] It is hard to expect transnational corporations to voluntarily do more than the window-dressing policies of corporate social responsibility. Global textile corporations usually do not own subsidiaries in countries of the Global South. In practice, they mostly conduct business with different local suppliers and producers to whom they send orders which these companies must fulfil according to relevant quality standards. Only a few corporations such as H&M publish information on their website concerning with which local suppliers in Phnom Penh and elsewhere they are working.[69] Yet, as recognized by the head of their sustainable development department, this company, which is supposed to be a model for everyone else, does not control the local suppliers' factories on a daily basis, at the very least only once a month.[70] On the contrary, some other corporations have lately been avoiding disclosing information on where their clothing was made.

66 Human Rights Watch, '"Work Faster or Get Out", Labor Rights Abuses in Cambodia's Garment Industry', 2015, p. 16.

67 ILO, 'Better Factories Cambodia', www.ilo.org/asia/projects/WCMS_099340/lang—en/index.htm (last accessed 19 January 2018).

68 Better Factories, 'BFC's 33rd Synthesis Report Finds that Garment Factory Working Conditions Improve yet the Top-Ten Issues Remain Constant', 1 July 2016.

69 HM, Sustainabiltiy, 'Supplier Factory List', http://sustainability.hm.com/en/sustainability/downloads-resources/resources/supplier-list.html (last accessed 19 January 2018). See also: Jernej Letnar Černič, 'Moving Towards Protecting Human Rights in Global Business Supply Chains', 35 *Boston University International Law Journal* 101 (2018), p. 109.

70 Lars Åke Bergqvist, 'UN Forum on Business and Human Rights Session: Beyond Auditing: Effective Ways to address Human Rights Violations in Garment Supply Chains', 18 November 2015.

Transnational textile corporations are obliged to ensure that all companies in their corporate structure, no matter where they are registered, as well as their suppliers and business partners, protect human rights. They have a duty of care to monitor its corporate chain. It is more difficult to establish the extent of their duty of care. Should they be liable for any breach in the factories in Phnom Penh under the obligation to protect, as a result, or just the obligation of conduct? In judicial practice and theory, the considered view is that transnational corporations cannot be held responsible for all violations caused by their subsidiaries, but are obliged to endeavour that violations do not occur. To fulfil such obligations, rhetorical slogans are insufficient but the administration of transnational corporations must demonstrate that the management system regularly and systematically supervises the operation of the subsidiaries through visits and periodic reviews. Monitoring must be carried out carefully and effectively, sanctions must be available and there must be a possibility of filing internal complaints.

Vulnerable workers in textile factories in Cambodia do not have sufficient social power themselves to bring about changes within the bottom-up system. These must come from top to bottom from civil society, which already partially supervises the garment industry worldwide.[71] When the first dominoes of positive change in the global supply chains of textile corporations start to fall, they will be followed by others, down to the smallest supplier. Equally difficult is the question of what this will mean for foreign direct investment in countries like Cambodia. The hope is that global textile companies will more effectively implement human rights protection, while at the same time looking for a competitive advantage that will continue to help further the economic and social development of the countries of the Global South. Any further divergence in the commercial interests of global textile enterprises and the individual rights of an ordinary person from the South should be avoided and a balance between the frequently conflicting objectives must be found.

Corporate legal accountability for socio-economic rights in Cambodia

Corporate legal accountability in Cambodia faces the problems of legitimacy, justice and transparency. In the last few decades, it has therefore been ineffective due to the hurdles in its domestic legal system, which lacks fairness, independence and impartiality. Observers note that victims' options when it comes to bringing claims for human rights violations are limited or even non-existent not only in the business and socio-economic rights context, but also generally in other areas of human rights. It seems that the current rule-of-law environment does not support claims being made against corporations and the linked governmental elite. It is difficult to talk about the separation of powers in Cambodia as all three

71 Fashion Transparency Index 2017, http://fashionrevolution.org/about/why-transparency-matters/ (last accessed 19 January 2018).

branches are under the influence of the ruling party. International observers have for many years been expressing their concerns about the rule-of-law situation. For instance, in 2014 the former special rapporteur on the situation of human rights in Cambodia, Surya P. Subedi, expressed his concern:

> that the laws adopted by Parliament contain certain provisions that are detrimental to the principle of the separation of powers. The laws give the Ministry of Justice undue influence over the court system and the judiciary . . . The Supreme Council of Magistracy is the guardian of the independence of the judiciary in that it decides on all issues related to the appointment, transfer and promotion of judges. The Supreme Council also receives complaints and takes disciplinary actions against judges. The executive should have no role to play in such matters . . . the Special Rapporteur had previously recommended that judges and prosecutors should not be active members of a political party . . . and had hoped that the law on the status of judges and prosecutors would spell out a requirement to that effect much more explicitly.[72]

This means the right to a fair, impartial and independent trial practically does not exist. Subedi argued in his 2015 article that

> corruption seemed to be widespread at all levels in the judiciary. Because no laws needed to protect the judges were in place, the judges were treated as civil servants and seemed to rely on patronage and political protection rather than on the law for the security of their jobs. This had resulted in individual judges' and prosecutors' compromising their independence.[73]

Victims have often been left voiceless before the Cambodian judiciary in the face of systematic and general socio-economic rights violations. Such developments have not gone unnoticed by international human rights bodies. The UN Human Rights Committee in 2015 reminded the Cambodian government that it "has an obligation to investigate all cases of past human rights violations . . ., in particular violations of Article 6 of the Covenant, prosecute the perpetrators and, where appropriate, punish them and provide compensation to the families of the victims".[74] What is more, the current special rapporteur on the situation of human rights in Cambodia, Rhona Smith, has urged "the Cambodian authorities to review and revise a number of laws to strengthen the protection of human

72 UN, Human Rights Council, 'Report of the Special Rapporteur on the Situation of Human Rights in Cambodia, Surya P. Subedi', UN Doc. A/HRC/27/70, 15 August 2014, para 37.

73 Surya P. Subedi, 'The UN Human Rights Special Rapporteurs and the Impact of Their Work: Some Reflections of the UN Special Rapporteur for Cambodia', 6(1) *Asian Journal of International Law* 1 (2015), pp. 5–6.

74 UN, Human Rights Committee, 'Concluding Observations: Cambodia', UN Doc. CCPR/C/KHM/CO/2, 27 April 2015, para 11.

rights and called for judges to publish reasoning for all decisions in order to strengthen both real and perceived judicial independence".[75]

Therefore, most cases for alleged corporate and even state human rights abuses have so far been brought outside Cambodia. For example, on 7 October 2014 victims sent a communication to the Office of the Chief Prosecutor of the International Criminal Court concerning claims of crimes against humanity in the context of the widespread and systematic land grabbing by members of Cambodia's government elite.[76] Moreover, in 2003 victims filed complaints against several corporations concerning land grabbing in the Koh Kong sugar plantation lawsuits.[77] Both cases are ongoing. What is striking is that the state appears to have been unwilling to curtail corporate conduct that infringes on socio-economic human rights.

The most prominent case against corporations operating in Cambodia and regarding abuses is currently pending before the Ombudsman Advisory Mechanism of the International Financial Corporation of the World Bank. The complaint is directed against Dragon Capital, a Vietnamese equity fund, partly owned by the International Finance Corporation (IFC) which, among others, has invested in the Vietnamese Hoang Anh Gia Lai (HAGL) that is alleged to have illegally acquired land occupied by several Indigenous peoples in Cambodia's Ratanakiri province.[78] The victims alleged they

> have suffered serious harm as a result of the activities of a Vietnamese company, Hoang Anh Gia Lai (HAGL), operating through a number of subsidiaries in Cambodia. Among HAGL's investors is Dragon Capital Group Ltd (DCGL), which invests in HAGL through Vietnamese Enterprise Investments Ltd (VEIL), a fund that it established and manages. According to Summary Project Information (SPI), IFC invested in DCGL/VEIL in 2002 and again in 2003.[79] (footnotes omitted)

They claimed that "as a result of HAGL's operations, the complainants have experienced losses of both a communal and household nature".[80] Further, they claim that

75 UN, OHCHR, 'Time to Move on – UN Expert Urges Cambodia to Fully Implement Rights and Freedoms at Every Level', 20 October 2015 www.ohchr.org/en/NewsEvents/Pages/DisplayNews.aspx?NewsID=20718&LangID=E#sthash.b47LITAm.dpuf (last accessed 19 January 2018).

76 Business and Human Rights Resource Centre, 'Cambodian Villagers', *Intl. Criminal Court Complaint* (re land grabbing)'.

77 Ibid. Business and Human Rights Resource Centre, 'Koh Kong Sugar Plantation Lawsuits (re Cambodia)'.

78 Inclusive development international, 'World Bank Group Implicated in Illegal Seizures of Indigenous Land in Cambodia and Laos, Communities call for Bank's Help to Get Their Land Back', Phom Penh, 10 February 2014.

79 CAO, Complaint concerning IFC investment in Dragon Capital Group and VEIL (Project no. 10740 and 20926), 10 February 2014, para 4.

80 Ibid., para 10.

> the extensive loss of critical natural resources has had a severe impact on livelihoods. It has led to a decrease in income and in some cases significant reductions in quality, diversity and quantity of food consumption. Communities have relied heavily on natural resources as a food source and are now forced to purchase more food from the market, but cannot always afford to do so.[81]

All in all, they raised allegations relating to several socio-economic rights.

The above Ombudsman Advisory Mechanism is not strictly judicial in nature, but may be described as a quasi-judicial process that is closer to alternative dispute resolution and mediation. Thereafter, the Compliance Advisor Ombudsman produced an assessment report[82] whereby it did not examine the complaint of the victims on its merits but facilitated meditation and agreement between local communities and the relevant corporation.[83] This form of mediation between villagers from seventeen villages and the HAGL Corporation appears to have been successful, since in May 2015 they concluded an agreement on the "Ground rules on Dispute Resolution Process between HAGL Company and its subsidiaries and 17 affected villagers" which stipulates the procedural rule of alternative dispute settlement.[84] This conciliation process appears to have started off successfully as six joint statements have so far been delivered, although their impact on the ground must be scrutinized before making any final assessment. For instance, the sixth joint statement notes that

> the parties confirm that the lands of customary use of the villages of Kachout and Ket are now located outside the boundaries of HAGL's current ELC. HAGL and the villages of Ket and Kachout are continuing discussions, through the CAO-facilitated mediation, in relation to other agreements made in Siem Reap in September 2015, including on the issues of preparation and restoration of damaged roads, bridges and affected water sources; agreement on a long-term grievance mechanism; and to support these communities in their request to obtain communal land title.[85]

81 Ibid., para 12.

82 The Compliance Advisor Ombudsman [CAO] defines assessment as:

> Assessment of the issues and provide support to stakeholders in understanding and "determining whether they would like to pursue a consensual solution through a collaborative process convened by CAO's Dispute Resolution function, or whether the case should be handled by CAO's Compliance function to review IFC's/MIGA's environmental and social due diligence."

83 CAO Assessment, 'Complaint Concerning IFC Investment in Dragon Capital Group and VEIL', (Project no. 10740 and 20926), May 2014.

84 CAO, 'Ground Rules on Dispute Resolution Process Between HAGL Company and Its Subsidiaries and 17 Affected Villagers', 12 January 2015.

85 CAO, 'Joint Statement Dispute Resolution Process Between HAGL Company and Its Subsidiaries and Representatives of Ket Village, and Kachout Village Banlung, Ratanakiri Province, Kingdom of Cambodia', 27 July 2016.

Finally, the CAO report notes that at the beginning of the mediation process "HAGL publicly apologized to the indigenous communities for its impacts on their traditions".[86] Thereafter, several meetings and visits between the local people and HAGL were held in order to secure land titles of Indigenous peoples,[87] although the process is still ongoing. In July 2017, an agreement was reached between villagers and Vietnamese corporations "to return nearly 20 community 'Spirit Mountains', restore streams filled or polluted by its activities and repair roads and bridges".[88] Nonetheless, it still needs to be approved by the government.

However, it remains unclear how effective the process has really been in practice for the socio-economic livelihood of the local Indigenous population given the general state of the rule of law in Cambodia. This is particularly because there is a lack of independent reports from the ground to confirm the statements and conclusions of the ombudsman advisory mechanism. Moreover, victims' voices are missing from the process. The role of governmental institutions is unclear concerning their obligation to protect socio-economic rights; therefore doubts are expressed given the unsatisfactory rule-of-law situation in Cambodia. The case is continuing and it remains to be seen what the general positive consequences and impact on the rule-of-law environment in Cambodia will be, if any. On the other hand, if one cannot point to some positive outcomes of the ombudsman advisory procedures, this might indicate the bleak future of such mechanisms. What is the added value of a mechanism that is unable to enforce victims' rights in practice? Therefore, this case is illustrative of the challenges victims face in enforcing their socio-economic rights.

Conclusion

Cambodia's approach to corporate accountability for socio-economic rights has been so far deficient. Although Cambodia has made steady progress in the level of its socio-economic rights and human rights in general, corporate accountability for socio-economic rights in Cambodia remains ineffective and underdeveloped. First, difficulties in enforcing corporate responsibility in Cambodia are apparent and not only arise from the inefficient domestic legal system. The vagueness of the institutional and regulatory framework for regulating corporations is also evident. Second, there is a clear lack of knowledge about the role and content of business and human rights, including socio-economic rights. To this end, the government should take more concrete steps entailing deadlines to adopt the National Action Plan under the UN Guiding Principles and translate it into the domestic legal system. However, a considerable share of the developments also

86 CAO Progress Report Cambodia: VEIL II-01/Ratanakiri Province, July 2016, page 3.
87 Ibid.
88 Phak Seangly and Martin de Bourmont, 'Vietnam Rubber Firm Reaches Accord with Ratanakkiri Ethnic Villages', *Phnom Penh Post*, 27 July 2017.

depends on regional pressure, especially from ASEAN. Third, the lack of capacity and knowledge in the field is overwhelming.

Special educational programmes should be organized for a range of stakeholders to familiarize them with issues and dilemmas concerning business and human rights, particularly targeting businesses and public officials at all levels of the judicial, legislative and executive branches of government. Government should aim to strengthen civil society, not curtail it. Fourth, courses on business and human rights should also be placed at the heart of undergraduate and graduate study programmes in economics, law, natural sciences and other disciplines at universities in Cambodia so that it accompanies young graduates from the start through to the end of their careers, whether in the public or private sector. Finally, businesses should take on a more proactive role in promoting the values and rule of business and socio-economic rights. All in all, Cambodia should strengthen its effort to improve victims' access to justice. On the other hand, it should insist that their foreign investors incorporate socio-economic rights into their business operations and those of their business partners, contractors and suppliers through a broad array of preventive measures. The Cambodian government has positive obligations to prevent corporations from interfering in the socio-economic rights and livelihoods of individuals residing in the country.

Bibliography

Books

Manning, Peter, *Transitional Justice and Memory in Cambodia: Beyond the Khmer Rouge*, London: Routledge (2017).

Meisenberg, Simon M. and Stegmiller, Ignaz (eds.), *The Extraordinary Chambers in the Courts of Cambodia: Assessing Their Contribution to International Criminal Law*, The Hague: Asser Press (2016).

Tan, Hsien-Li, *The ASEAN Intergovernmental Commission on Human Rights: Institutionalising Human Rights in Southeast Asia*, Cambridge: Cambridge University Press (2011), pp. 60–71.

Journal articles

Clarke, Gerard, 'The Evolving ASEAN Human Rights System: The ASEAN Human Rights Declaration of 2012', 11 *Northwestern University Journal of International Human Rights* 1 (2012).

Davies, Mathew, 'ASEAN Synthesis: Human Rights, Non-Intervention and the ASEAN Human Rights Declaration (Forum: The Integration of Regions)', 14 *Georgetown Journal of International Affairs* 51 (2013).

Doyle, Nicholas, 'The ASEAN Human Rights Declaration and the Implications of Recent Southeast Asian Initiatives in Human Rights Institution-Building and Standard Setting', 63 *International and Comparative Law Quarterly* 67 (2014).

Letnar Černič, Jernej, 'Moving Towards Protecting Human Rights in Global Business Supply Chains', 35 *Boston University International Law Journal* 101 (2018).

Ng, Joel, 'Rule of Law as a Framework within the ASEAN Community', 5 *Journal of East Asia and International Law* 327 (2012).

Nolan, Justine, 'Business and Human Rights: The Challenge of Putting Principles into Practice and Regulating Global Supply Chains', 42 *Alternative Law Journal* 42 (2017).

Phan, Hao Duy, 'Promoting Compliance: An Assessment of ASEAN Instruments Since the ASEAN Charter', 41 *Syracuse Journal of International Law and Commerce* 379 (2014).

Pisanò, Attilio, 'Human Rights and Sovereignty in the ASEAN Path Towards a Human Rights Declaration', 15 *Human Rights Review* 391 (2014).

Pisanò, Attilio, 'Towards an ASEAN Human Rights Mechanism: The ASEAN Commission on the Promotion and Protection of the Rights of Women and Children', 20 *The International Journal of Human Rights* 321 (2016).

Subedi, Surya P., 'The UN Human Rights Special Rapporteurs and the Impact of Their Work: Some Reflections of the UN Special Rapporteur for Cambodia', 6(1) *Asian Journal of International Law* 1 (2015).

Book chapters

Cuyvers, Ludo and De Meyer, Tim, 'Market-Driven Promotion of International Labour Standards in Southeast Asia: The Corporatization of Social Justice', *in* Axel Marx, Miet Maertens, Johan Swinnen and Jan Wouters (eds.), *Private Standards and Global Governance: Economic, Legal and Political Perspectives*, Cheltenham: Edward Elgar (2012), pp. 114–149.

Hsien-Li, Tan, 'The ASEAN Intergovernmental Commission on Human Rights as a Tool for Social Justice', *in* Ida Lintel, Antoine Buyse and Brianne McGonigle Leyh (eds.), *Defending Human Rights: Tools for Social Justice: Volume in Honour of Fried van Hoof on the Occasion of His Valedictory Lecture and the 30th Anniversary of the Netherlands Institute of Human Rights*, Antwerp: Intersentia (2012), pp. 35–40.

Krygier, Martin, 'The Rule of Law', *in* Michel Rosenfeld and András Sajó (eds.), *Oxford Handbook of Comparative Constitutional Law*, Oxford: Oxford University Press (2012), pp. 233–249.

Lim, Delphia and Mukherjee, Geetanjali, 'Business and Human Rights Challenges in ASEAN: The Role and Modalities of the State', *in* Mahdev Mohan and Cynthia Morel (eds.), *Business and Human Rights in Southeast Asia: Risk and the Regulatory Turn*, Cambridge: Cambridge University Press (2015), pp. 30–56.

Quah, Euston and Siong, Tan Tsiat, 'Sustaining Growth, Climate Change and Meeting Environmental Obligations: What Can ASEAN Governments Do?' *in* Ilan Kelman, Robert Kibugi, Rose-Liza and Eisma Osorio (eds.), *Adaptation to Climate Change: ASEAN and Comparative Experiences*, Singapore: World Scientific (2016), pp. 231–256.

Newspaper and magazine articles

Koyanagi, Ken, 'Hollow Growth Leaves Cambodians Wanting More', *Nikkei Asian Review*, 16 March 2017.

Seangly, Phak and de Bourmont, Martin, 'Vietnam Rubber firm Reaches Accord with Ratanakkiri Ethnic Villages', *Phnom Penh Post*, 27 July 2017.

The Economist, 'The Cambodian Government Threatens Labour Rights', *Phnom Penh: The Economist*, 26 October 2017.
Thul, Prak Chan, 'Cambodia Protesters Call off Rally After Bloody Crackdown', *Phnom Penh: Reuters*, 4 January 2014.

Official documents

2015 Business and Human Rights Forum, 16-18 November 2015, Palais des Nations, Geneva, Switzerland, http://www.ohchr.org/EN/Issues/Business/Forum/Pages/2015ForumBHR.aspx ((accessed 19 January 2018).
Association of Southeast Asian Nations (ASEAN), Charter of the Association of Southeast Asian Nations, 20 November 2007, http://www.refworld.org/docid/4948c4842.html (accessed 19 January 2018).
ASEAN Human Rights Declaration, Association of Southeast Asian Nations, Human Rights Declaration (adopted at the 21st ASEAN Summit, Phnom Penh, Cambodia, Nov. 18, 2012).
Asia-Europe Foundation, 14th Informal ASEM Seminar on Human Rights on the topic 'Human Rights and Businesses', 18–20 November 2014, Hanoi, Vietnam.
UN, Human Rights Council, Report of Special Representative of the Secretary-General on the Issue of Human Rights and Transnational Corporations and Other Business Enterprises, John Ruggie, 'Guiding Principles on Business and Human Rights: Implementing the United Nations "Protect, Respect and Remedy" Framework' ['The Guiding Principles'], UN Doc. A/HRC/17/31, 21 March 2011.
UN, Human Rights Council, 'Report of the Special Rapporteur on the situation of human rights in Cambodia, Surya P. Subedi', UN Doc. A/HRC/27/70, 15 August 2014.
UN, Human Rights Council, Report of the Special Rapporteur on the Situation of Human Rights in Cambodia Surya P. Subedi to the Human Rights Council at its 21st Session, 'A Human Rights Analysis of Economic and Other Land Concessions in Cambodia', UN Doc. A/HRC/21/63/Add.1/Rev.1, 11 October 2012.
UN, Human Rights Committee, 'Concluding observations: Cambodia', UN Doc. CCPR/C/KHM/CO/2, 27 April 2015.
UN, Human Rights Council, 'Report of the Working Group on the Universal Periodic Review, Cambodia', Un Doc. A/HRC/26/16, 27 March 2014.
UN, OHCHR, 'Role and Achievements of the Office of the United Nations High Commissioner for Human Rights in Assisting the Government and People of Cambodia in the Promotion and Protection of Human Rights', UN Doc. A/HRC/36/32, 17 August 2017.
UN, CESCR, 'Concluding Observations of the Committee on Economic, Social and Cultural Rights: Cambodia', UN Doc. E/C.12/KHM/CO/1, 12 June 2009.

Cases

CAO, 'Complaint Concerning IFC Investment in Dragon Capital Group and VEIL (Project no. 10740 and 20926)', 10 February 2014.
CAO Assessment, 'Complaint Concerning IFC investment in Dragon Capital Group and VEIL (Project no. 10740 and 20926)', May 2014.

CAO, 'Ground Rules on Dispute Resolution Process Between HAGL Company and Its Subsidiaries and 17 Affected Villagers', 12 January 2015.
CAO, 'Joint Statement Dispute Resolution Process Between HAGL Company and Its Subsidiaries and Representatives of Ket Village and Kachout Village Banlung, Ratanakiri Province, Kingdom of Cambodia', 27 July 2016.
CAO, 'Progress Report Cambodia: VEIL II-01/Ratanakiri Province', July 2016.
'Decision of the Constitutional Council No. 092/003/2007', 10 July 2007.

Websites

ASEAN CSR Network, http://asean-csr-network.org/c/participation/participating-organizations (last accessed 19 January 2018).
Cambodian Centre for Human Rights, http://cchrcambodia.org/index_old.php?url=project_page/project_page.php&p=project_profile.php&id=3&pro=BHRP (last accessed 19 January 2018).
Cambodia's Free Trade Agreement, https://aric.adb.org/fta-country (last accessed 19 January 2018).
Fashion Transparency Index 2017, http://fashionrevolution.org/about/why-transparency-matters/ (last accessed 19 January 2018).
HM, 'Sustainabiltiy, Supplier Factory List', http://sustainability.hm.com/en/sustainability/downloads-resources/resources/supplier-list.html (last accessed 19 January 2018).
ILO, 'Better Factories Cambodia', www.ilo.org/asia/projects/WCMS_099340/lang-en/index.htm (last accessed 19 January 2018).
ILO, 'Information System on International Labour Standards', Ratifications for Cambodia, www.ilo.org/dyn/normlex/en/f?p=1000:11200:0::NO:11200:P11200_COUNTRY_ID:103055 (last accessed 19 January 2018).
Index Mundi, Cambodia, 2016, www.indexmundi.com/cambodia/ (last accessed 19 January 2018).
UN, OHCHR, 'Ratification Status for Cambodia', http://tbinternet.ohchr.org/_layouts/TreatyBodyExternal/Treaty.aspx?CountryID=29&Lang=EN (last accessed 19 January 2018).

Reports and miscellaneous

Asian Development Bank, 'Asian Development Outlook 2017: Transcending the Middle-Income Challenge', April 2017.
Asian Forum for Human Rights and Development (FORUM-ASIA), 'Corporate Accountability in ASEAN: A Human Rights-Based Approach', 2013.
Better Factories, 'BFC's 33rd Synthesis Report Finds that Garment Factory Working Conditions Improve Yet the Top-Ten Issues Remain Constant', 1 July 2016.
Business and Human Rights Resource Centre, 'Business and Human Rights in ASEAN: A Baseline Study', Cambodia, April 2013.
Business and Human Rights Resource Centre, 'Cambodian Villagers', *Intl. Criminal Court complaint* (re land grabbing)'.
Business and Human Rights Resource Centre, 'Development for All, or a Privileged Few? Business & human rights in Southeast Asia', April 2015.
Business and Human Rights Resource Centre, 'Koh Kong Sugar Plantation Lawsuits (re Cambodia)'.

Cambodian Centre for Human Rights, 'Business and Human Rights in Cambodia: Constructing the Three Pillars', November 2010.

Cambodian Centre for Human Rights, 'Business and Human Rights Handbook for Cambodia'.

Campos andré, van Huijstee, Mariëtte and Theuws, Martje, 'From Moral Responsibility to Legal Liability? Modern Day Slavery Conditions in the Global Garment Supply Chain and the Need to Strengthen Regulatory Frameworks: The Case of Inditex-Zara in Brazil', 2015.

Constitute Project, 'Cambodia's Constitution of 1993 with Amendments Through 2008'.

Corporate Justice, 'Swiss Parliament Motion for Mandatory Human Rights Due Diligence Narrowly Turned Down Conservative Backlash Blocks Increased Corporate Accountability', 13 March 2015.

European Union, 'Trade in Goods with Cambodia', 2016.

Global Witness, 'Hostile Takeover', 7 July 2016.

Human Development Report 2016, 'Human Development for Everyone, Briefing Note for Countries on the 2016 Human Development Report', Cambodia.

Human Rights Resource Centre, 'Business and Human Rights in ASEAN A Baseline Study', Cambodia, April 2013.

Human Rights Watch, '"Work Faster or Get Out", Labor Rights Abuses in Cambodia's Garment Industry', 2015.

Inclusive Development International, 'World Bank Group Implicated in Illegal Seizures of Indigenous Land in Cambodia and Laos, Communities Call for Bank's Help to Get Their Land Back', Phom Penh, 10 February 2014.

Lars Åke Bergqvist, 'UN Forum on Business and Human Rights Session: Beyond Auditing: Effective Ways to Address Human Rights Violations in Garment Supply Chains', 18 November 2015.

Neam, Koy and Everett, Silas, 'Human Rights Protection in Modern Cambodia: Building on Unstable Grounds', 23 April 2014, Asia Foundation.

UN, OHCHR, 'State National Action Plans', www.ohchr.org/EN/Issues/Business/Pages/NationalActionPlans.aspx (last accessed 19 January 2018).

UN, OHCHR, 'Time to Move on – UN Expert Urges Cambodia to Fully Implement Rights and Freedoms at Every Level', 20 October 2016 www.ohchr.org/en/NewsEvents/Pages/DisplayNews.aspx?NewsID=20718&LangID=E#sthash.b47LITAm.dpuf (last accessed 19 January 2018).

World Bank, 2017, 'Overview Cambodia', www.worldbank.org/en/country/cambodia/overview (last accessed 19 January 2018).

9 Corporate accountability concerning socio-economic rights in China

Introduction 220

Socio-economic and the rule-of-law environment in China 222

Business and socio-economic human rights in China 224

The domestic normative framework for corporate accountability for socio-economic rights in China 225

China's approach to corporate accountability for socio-economic rights in China at the international level 228

Extraterritorial obligations under socio-economic rights of Chinese state-owned and private corporations when doing business abroad 229

Access to justice for socio-economic rights 236

Conclusion 241

Introduction

China has in recent decades become one of the few economic power houses in the world. Its economic growth has been in recent decades impressive. It has orchestrated a successful move from economy based primarily on agriculture to one on the advanced technology based on exports industry.[1] Recently it has been, due to its increased production capacity, searching for the new markets outside its national territory. Most of the largest corporations in China such as Sinopec Group, China National Petroleum and China State Construction Engineering are, despite a flourishing private sector, state owned, which also raises the question of state obligations and responsibility to ensure that state-owned corporations comply with socio-economic rights.[2] Some commentators have described China as a totalitarian state and others as authoritarian, as the rule of law is generally absent or subject to the questionable interpretation of government elite

1 See generally, Arthur R. Kroeber, *China's Economy: What Everyone Needs to Know*, Oxford: Oxford University Press (2016).

2 Ibid., p. 89. See also, Fortune 500, http://fortune.com/global500/ (last accessed 19 January 2018).

gathered around the Communist Party. Even though China's economic growth has been staggering in recent decades, it has not been coupled in equal increase in human development, increase of well-being of its population, and in decreasing inequality and increasing human capabilities. The rule of law has never been fully exercised and has been substituted by the rule by law formed by various political and economic elites.[3]

China has been described by many terms from being non-liberal, dictatorial to totalitarian state. But perhaps is the most appropriate definition put forward by Kroeber. He describes China as "a bureaucratic, authoritarian, one party state that in principle is run by a centralized command structure in Beijing, but in practice is often highly decentralized-necessarily so because of the country's great size and population".[4] Human rights protections have long been in China considered as anti-theme,[5] as it has long resisted to take up the values and protection of liberal democracies such as the rule of law. Rather, it has subscribed to the rule by law. As Liao observes:

> China's Constitution provides for the freedoms of speech, the press and association, among others. It also calls for judicial independence. Of course, even liberal democracies limit the exercise of such constitutionally guaranteed freedoms – but in China; the limits can seem to overshadow the rights themselves.[6]

China has put much emphasis on the enjoyment of socio-economic rights, whereas civil and political rights have been less frequently in focus. Moreover, its population has in recent years grown particularly sensitive as far as the implementation of socio-economic rights goes. Juan Pablo Bohoslavsky, United Nations independent expert on the effects of foreign debt, has therefore observed that "there is a growing awareness within Chinese governmental, business and lending institutions about the need to have more robust social and environmental safeguard policies in place".[7] Some corporations based in China that are reported to be Chinese state-owned corporations have been allegedly involved in committing socio-economic violations abroad.[8]

3 Minxin Pei, *China's Trapped Transition. The Limits of Developmental Autocracy*, Cambridge, MA: Harvard University Press (2008).

4 Arthur R. Kroeber, *China's Economy: What Everyone Needs to Know*, Oxford: Oxford University Press (2016), pp. 23–24.

5 See for instance, Stephen C. Angle, *Human Rights and Chinese Thought: A Cross-Cultural Inquiry*, Cambridge: Cambridge University Press (2002).

6 Rebecca Liao, 'Judicial Reform in China', *Foreign Affairs*, 2 February 2017.

7 Juan Pablo Bohoslavsky, 'End of Mission Statement China', 6 July 2015, www.ohchr.org/EN/NewsEvents/Pages/DisplayNews.aspx?NewsID=16203&LangID=E (last accessed 19 January 2018).

8 See, Business and Human Rights Resource Centre, 'Time for Action: Business & Human Rights in Greater China', 26 August 2014.

The balance of this chapter examines China's approach to corporate accountability for socio-economic rights. It finds that China has been trying to remodel its approach to business and socio-economic rights and obliging its corporations to comply not only with socio-economic rights, but all human rights, not only in China, but also abroad. The second section describes the socio-economic and rule-of-law environment in China, thereby giving foundations for an analysis of the business and socio-economic normative framework. The third section deals with business and socio-economic rights in China. First, it studies the domestic normative framework for business and socio-economic rights within China, and second, the international level – China's approach to business and human rights within the United Nations. The fourth section critically examines attempts of various Chinese societies and organizations to improve regulation of China-based corporations doing business beyond its borders in order to improve how individuals obtain effective access to judicial fora against Chinese corporations for alleged human rights violations. Finally, the fifth section deals with access to justice for socio-economic rights. All in all, the conclusion argues that China has to improve corporate accountability for socio-economic rights by creating a legal basis for effective access to justice by ensuring effective, fair, impartial and independent proceedings where victims would be able to bring their claims.

Socio-economic and the rule-of-law environment in China

China has made a huge leap forward in recent decades. It is now the largest economy in the world. In recent decades it has recorded growth on average by 10%, although growth has in recent years decreased to single digits. Its growth has created millions of jobs and has thereby increased socio-economic standards of living of the population and concurrently caused immense social inequality, particularly between urban and rural areas.[9] Therefore, the World Bank still lists China as a developing country.[10] It states that "98.99 million people still lived below the national poverty line of RMB 2,300 per year at the end of 2012".[11] China ranks 90th with index of 0.738 on the UN Human Development Index,[12] whereas some of its disputed territories such as Hong Kong and Taiwan rank substantially higher, in the top 20 of the world's most socio-economic developed countries.[13]

9 Arthur R. Kroeber, *China's Economy: What Everyone Needs to Know*, Oxford: Oxford University Press (2016), p. 196. Christoph Lakner and Branko Milanovic, 'Global Income Distribution: From the Fall of the Berlin Wall to the Great Recession', (The World Bank Development Research Group Poverty and Inequality Team) Policy Research Working Paper 6719 (2013).

10 World Bank in China, Overview, 28 March 2017.

11 Ibid.

12 UN, Human Development Indicators 2016, China, http://hdr.undp.org/en/countries/profiles/CHN (last accessed 19 January 2018).

13 Ibid.

In 2016 the Gini coefficient reached 0.465 points,[14] although Alston observes that "independent research suggests a Gini coefficient of 0.61 in 2010 and 0.6 in 2014, which would make it one of the most unequal countries on earth".[15] Moreover, China has also subscribed to the Sustainable Development Goals, which are known for not having developed binding sanctions and enforcement mechanisms.[16]

However, mainland China has in recent decades achieved remarkable results. Phillip Alston, special rapporteur on extreme poverty and human rights, stated in his 2017 report following his mission to China that

> in 2003, only 10 per cent of the population had health insurance. By 2013, some 95 per cent were covered, including most of the rural poor and the vulnerable urban groups. In 2009, only 240 million people were covered by pension schemes and 58 million were actually receiving pensions. By 2014, coverage was up to 842 million and recipients up to 229 million.[17]

The same author, nonetheless, admits, "the great progress that China has made in poverty alleviation has been accompanied by the emergence of very high levels of inequality".[18] However, what is certainly true that income inequality in China has reached staggering heights.[19] Therefore, socio-economic situation in China has been far from ideal. Human Rights Watch reported that in 2014

> the government censors the press, the Internet, print publications and academic research and justifies human rights abuses as necessary to preserve "social stability". It carries out involuntary population relocation and rehousing on a massive scale and enforces highly repressive policies in ethnic minority areas in Tibet, Xinjiang and Inner Mongolia. Though primary school enrolment and basic literacy rates are high, China's education system discriminates against children and young people with disabilities.[20]

14 Statista, 'Gini Coefficient in China: Inequality of Income Distribution in China from 2005 to 2016'.

15 UN, Human Rights Council, 'Report of the Special Rapporteur on Extreme Poverty and Human Rights on His Mission to China: Philip Alston', UN Doc. A/HRC/35/26/Add.2, 28 March 2017, para 24 quoting Martin King Whyte, 'Soaring Income Gaps: China in Comparative Perspective', 143(2) *Daedalus* 39, 41 (2014).

16 Delia Paul, 'China Releases National Plan to Implement SDGs', IISD / SDG Knowledge Hub, 17 October 2016. See for a detailed discussion Jernej Letnar Černič, 'Sustainable Development, Corporate Social Responsibility and Business in the People's Republic of China: A Tale of three worlds?', *in* Paolo Davide Farah (ed.), *China and the Good Governance of the Markets in the Light of the Economic Development*, Abingdon: Routledge (2018).

17 Philip Alston's 2017 UN report on China, para 13.

18 Ibid., para 23.

19 Gabriel Wildau and Tom Mitchell, 'China Income Inequality Among World's Worst', *Shanghai and Beijing: Financial Times*, 14 January 2016. See also, Sara Hsu, 'High Income Inequality Still Festering in China', *Forbes*, 18 November 2016.

20 Human Rights Watch, 'Country Summary: China', January 2014, https://www.hrw.org/world-report/2014/country-chapters/china-and-tibet (last accessed 19 January 2018).

Nonetheless, National Human Rights Action Plan of China (2016–2020) provides that China will aim to "comprehensively safeguarding citizens' economic, social and cultural rights" and

> will improve the people's standard of living and quality of life; upgrade the public service system and ensure more people have equal access to such services; spare no effort in poverty alleviation to lift the entire population who live under the current poverty line out of poverty.[21]

However, that plan only includes few socio-economic rights such as right to work, right to basic living standards, right to social security, right to health and right to education, thereby excluding some other seminal rights.[22] Nonetheless, one can concur with Sen that "economic growth can make a very large contribution to improving people's lives; but single-minded emphasis on growth has limitations that need to be clearly understood".[23] However, it appears that China has recently subscribed to the holistic understanding of development.

Business and socio-economic human rights in China

Business and human rights in China is not without historical background and precedent. Fairness, transparency, honesty and integrity in business practices can be followed in the "culture of diligence, honesty and charity among businessmen" at the time of Ming and Qing Dynasties.[24] As such, an edict issued in 1731 by an emperor of the Qing Dynasty states that "the ideal way for a wealthy household to perpetuate itself included the need to be constantly vigilant, even in peacetime, in dispensing relief and aid to the poor".[25] Such historical examples are often reciprocated in values of Confucius doctrine and its modern concretization in the form of "harmonious society".[26] As for socio-economic rights, Chinese academics have attempted to explain them in the line with social harmony.[27] All in all, business and socio-economic rights interact normatively in China in two ways: through domestic and international frameworks (see Figure 9.1).

21 The State Council of the People's Republic of China, 'National Human Rights Action Plan of China (2016–2020)', August 2016.

22 Ibid.

23 Amartya Sen, 'Quality of Life: India vs. China', *The New York Review of Books*, 12 May 2011.

24 Li-Wen Lin, 'Corporate Social Responsibility in China: Window Dressing or Structural Change', 28(1) *Berkeley Journal of International Law* 64, 85 (2010).

25 Teemu Ruskola, 'Conceptualizing Corporations and Kinship: Comparative Law and Development Theory in a Chinese Perspective', 52(6) *Stanford Law Review* 1599 (2000), quoted in Li-Wen Lin, 'Corporate Social Responsibility in China', 28(1) *Berkeley Journal of International Law* 64, 76 (2010).

26 See for instance, John Delury, '"Harmonious" in China', 148 *Policy Review* 35 (2008).

27 See for a short overview of their arguments, Larry Catá Backer, 'Realizing Socio-Economic Rights Under Emerging Global Regulatory Frameworks: The Potential Impact of Privatization and the Role of Companies in China and India', 45(4) *The George Washington International Law Review* 615 (2013).

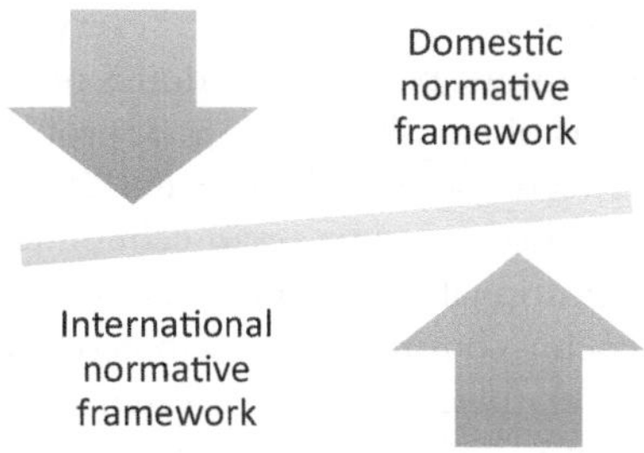

Figure 9.1 Corporate accountability for socio-economic rights in China
(Source: author's own work)

The domestic normative framework for corporate accountability for socio-economic rights in China

The domestic framework for business and socio-economic rights has been far from perfect. CESCR has noted in this respect its concern "about the lack of adequate and effective measures adopted by the State party to ensure that Chinese companies, both State-owned and private, respect economic, social and cultural rights, including when operating abroad".[28] Therefore, it recommended China to "establish a clear regulatory framework for companies operating in the State party to ensure that their activities promote and do not negatively affect the enjoyment of economic, social and cultural human rights" and to "adopt appropriate legislative and administrative measures to ensure the legal liability of companies and their subsidiaries operating in or managed from the State party's territory regarding violations of economic, social and cultural rights in the context of their projects abroad".[29] In spite of increase in the scope of socio-economic rights due the economic developments, its protections as it follows from the above have been still lacking.

The primary obligation to protect socio-economic rights on its territory is surely borne by China, which must enable all inhabitants to have dignified living and working conditions and strive for them to be realized by all private entities on their territory. Article 33 of its Constitution notes that "the State respects and preserves human rights".[30] The majority of national constitutions provide protection for human rights; however the PRC Constitution is somehow different, as it places rights and duties on equal footing. Article 33 of the Constitution

28 UN, CESCR, 'Concluding Observations: China, including Hong Kong, China, and Macao', UN Doc. E/C.12/CHN/CO/2, 13 June 2014, para 13.

29 Ibid.

30 'Constitution of the People's Republic of China, adopted at the 5th Session of the 5th National People's Congress', 4 December 1982. See also, Thomas Kellogg, 'Constitutionalism with Chinese Characteristics? Constitutional Development and Civil Litigation in China', 7(2) *International Journal of Constitutional Law* 215 (2009).

provides for both individual rights and duties: "every citizen is entitled to the rights and at the same time must perform the duties prescribed by the Constitution and other laws".[31] It is obviously *primae facie* problematic that constitution imposes rights only on citizens, not on all residents. Constitution in the following articles provides for protection of some socio-economic rights.[32] Legal persons are also bound by constitutional provisions.[33] However, it appears that China employs scattered approach to business and socio-economic rights as protections are included in different statues,[34] which are often difficult to find. However, one may note that realization of socio-economic rights falls within progressive obligations and may in the future present backbone for realization of civil and political rights.[35]

Corporate accountability for socio-economic rights in China indirectly derives from various domestic sources of law that can be found in civil/company law, criminal law and administrative law areas. PRC Company Law states in Article 5 that "when engaging in business activities, a company shall abide by laws and administrative regulations, observe social morality and business ethics, act in good faith, accept supervision by the government and the public and bear social responsibilities".[36] One can argue that at least corporate accountability to respect for socio-economic rights falls within "social morality and business ethics". More specifically, Article 17 notes that companies should promote "the legitimate rights and interests of its staff members, conclude labor contracts with them, participate in the social insurance system and reinforce the labor protection for them so as to achieve safe production".[37] More relevant for socio-economic rights, it asks companies to "improve vocational education and on-the-job training among their staff and workers so as to enhance their quality".[38] Several

31 Ibid.

32 Constitution of the People's Republic of China, arts 42–48.

33 Qi Yuling v Chen Xiaoqi and Chen Kezheng, Reply of the Supreme People's Court to the Shandong High Court, 13 August 2001, quoted in Surya Deva, 'Access to Justice: Human Rights Abuses Involving Corporations – The People's Republic of China', *International Commission of Jurists* 10 (2010).

34 See for a comprehensive overview, Larry Catá Backer, 'Realizing Socio-Economic Rights Under Emerging Global Regulatory Frameworks': The Potential Impact of Privatization and the Role of Companies in China and India', 45(4) *The George Washington International Law Review* 615 (2013).

35 Larry Catá Backer, 'China's Corporate Social Responsibility with National Characteristics: Coherence and Dissonance with the Global Business and Human Rights Project', *in* Jena Martin and Karen E. Bravo (eds.), *The Business and Human Rights Landscape: Moving Forward, Looking Back*, New York: Cambridge University Press (2016), pp. 530–558.

36 Company Law of the People's Republic of China, adopted on 29 December 1993 and last revised on 28 December 2013, http://www.fdi.gov.cn/1800000121_39_4814_0_7.html (last accessed 19 January 2018), art. 5. See, Minkang Gu, *Understanding Chinese Company Law*, Hong Kong: Hong Kong University Press (2006).

37 Company Law of the People's Republic of China, art. 17.

38 Ibid. See also, arts 20 and 65. See, arts 21(1), 148 and 149 concerning directors' duties. Surya Deva, 'Sustainable Development: What Role for the Company Law?', 8 *International and Comparative Corporate Law Journal* 76 (2011), p. 95.

other statutes, including labour legislations,[39] refer to corporations and socio-economic rights.[40] What is more, corporations are strictly monitored as to their compliance with the labour law, whereas the right to freedom of association in the form of trade unions has still not been recognized. Several provisions are also found in criminal law, which allows for individual and corporate criminal liability for criminal offences. Criminal Law states in Article 30 that "any company, enterprise, institution, State organ, or organization that commits an act that endangers society, which is prescribed by law as a crime committed by a unit, shall bear criminal responsibility".[41] A number of relevant provisions are also found in administrative law.[42] Further, the developments in voluntary initiatives of Chinese corporations are evident. Liang Xiaohui observed that "international conventions are being translated into Chinese law and the enforcement of these laws is becoming more stringent. Chinese companies must comply, either voluntarily or involuntarily".[43] Furthermore, he states, "after a decade of promoting business and human rights in China, the concept of CSR and sustainability is now commonly braced by the Chinese government and businesses".[44] Its domestic legal system provides for several sources that

39 See for a comprehensive overview, Surya Deva, 'Access to Justice Human Rights Abuses Involving Corporations – The People's Republic of China', *International Commission of Jurists* 10 (2010), pp. 11–15. See also, Dana C. Nicholas, 'China's Labour Enforcement Crisis: International Intervention and Corporate Social Responsibility', 11 *St. Mary's Law Review on Minority Issues* 155 (2009). Marisa Anne Pagnattaro, 'Is Labour Really "Cheap" in China? Compliance With Labour and Employment Laws', 10 *San Diego International Law Journal* 357 (2009).

40 Law of the People's Republic of China on Safety in Mines, adopted on 7 November 1992 and last revised on 31 August 2014, http://www.npc.gov.cn/englishnpc/Law/2007-12/12/content_1383872.htm (last accessed 19 January 2018); and the Law of the People's Republic of China on Work Safety, adopted on 29 June 2002 and last revised on 31 August 2014, http://www.npc.gov.cn/englishnpc/Law/2007-12/06/content_1382127.htm (last accessed 19 January 2018).

41 Criminal Law of the People's Republic of China, adopted on 1 July 1979 and last revised on 14 March 1997, http://www.fmprc.gov.cn/ce/cgvienna/eng/dbtyw/jdwt/crimelaw/t209043.htm (last accessed 19 Janaury 2018), art. 30.

42 Environmental Protection Law of the People's Republic of China, adopted on 26 December 1989, http://www.china.org.cn/english/environment/34356.htm (last accessed 19 January 2018), establishes in article 6 that:

"All units and individuals shall have the obligation to protect the environment and shall have the right to report on or file charges against units or individuals that cause pollution or damage to the environment."

See, Business and Human Rights Resource Centre, 'Time for Action: Business & Human Rights in Greater China', 26 August 2014.

43 Liang Xiaohui at the meeting: Global Business Initiative, 'Business Executives Conference – Sustainable Business and Investment in the Global Context: Rights, Risks and Responsibilities', Beijing, 16 April 2013, quoted in Business and Human Rights Resource Centre, 'Time for Action: Business & Human Rights in Greater China', 26 August 2014, p. 5.

44 Solveig Marie Igesund, 'Promoting Business and Human Rights in China', Norwegian Human Rights Centre, 13 May 2015. See also, Motoko Aizawa, '"Going Out" in Search of Oil and Gas: How Should Chinese Companies Investing Abroad Tackle Human Rights Challenges?' Institute for Human Rights and Business, 24 March 2015.

illustrate that corporations are obliged to observe socio-economic rights. They derive from different sources of law, scattered from company law and criminal law to administrative and environmental law. Domestic sources, apart from the constitution, therefore refer only indirectly to socio-economic rights as they employ different terminology, which may despite the rhetoric of commitments pose concrete problems in practice.

China's approach to corporate accountability for socio-economic rights in China at the international level

China has ratified seven of the major international human rights treaties.[45] As for socio-economic rights, it signed ICESCR on 27 October 1997 and ratified it on 27 March 2011.[46] On the other hand, China has been more or less passive concerning recent developments on business and human rights at the United Nations. China voted in June 2011 in the UN Human Rights Council for resolution of the adoption of the UN Guiding Principles on Business and Human Rights.[47] It has so far not drafted nor adopted a national action plan for implementation of the UN Guiding Principles in their national system. However, some Chinese state-owned enterprises have recently started to engage with the UN Guiding Principles and corporate social responsibility issues in general.[48] What is more interesting, China voted in June 2014 in the Human Rights Council for two opposing resolutions. More specifically, it has voted for Norway's resolution supporting the implementation of the UN Guiding Principles[49], but it also has endorsed Ecuador's resolution for a business and human rights treaty,[50] which illustrates its traditionally pragmatic approach in the international arena. However, China has so far not been very engaged in all three sessions of the open-ended intergovernmental working group on a legally binding instrument on

45 Office of the High Commissioner (OHCHR), 'Ratification Status for China', http://tbinternet.ohchr.org/_layouts/TreatyBodyExternal/Treaty.aspx (last accessed 19 January 2018).

46 University of Minnesota Human Rights Library, 'Ratification of International Human Rights Treaties – China', http://hrlibrary.umn.edu/research/ratification-china.html (last accessed 19 January 2018).

47 UN, Human Rights Council, Report of Special Representative of the Secretary-General on the Issue of Human Rights and Transnational Corporations and Other Business Enterprises, John Ruggie, 'Guiding Principles on Business and Human Rights: Implementing the United Nations "Protect, Respect and Remedy" Framework' ['The Guiding Principles'], UN Doc. A/HRC/17/31, 21 March 2011.

48 Tracktwo, 'CSR Training Programme for Chinese Central State-Owned Enterprises', October 2014.

49 UN, Human Rights Council, 'Human rights and Transnational Corporations and Other Business Enterprises', UN Doc. A/HRC/26/L.1, 23 June 2014.

50 UN, Human Rights Council, 'Elaboration of an International Legally Binding Instrument on Transnational Corporations and Other Business Enterprises with Respect to Human Rights (Bolivia (Plurinational State of), Cuba, Ecuador, South Africa, Venezuela (Bolivarian Republic of): Draft Resolution', A/HRC/26/L.22/Rev.1, 25 June 2014, para 1.

transnational corporations and other business enterprises with respect to human rights.[51]

Extraterritorial obligations under socio-economic rights of Chinese state-owned and private corporations when doing business abroad

States have a positive obligation to protect individuals against infringements of private entities and to exercise control over companies that are allegedly involved in human rights violations. States in which corporations are registered should endeavour to prevent violations within and outside their territory. There is an emerging legal basis in international law to enforce responsibility of states and transnational corporations for violations committed outside their home territory.

China has been over at least the past three decades changing the outlook of the global economy. Its economy has brought prosperity and well-being not only to its own populations, but also beyond its borders. However, some commentators do not share an opinion about the sustainability of such economic expansion.[52] Nonetheless, expansion of Chinese investment has been felt in almost every corner of the world, but particularly in Asia, Africa, Central and Eastern Europe, and Latin America. Thousands of Chinese corporations have invested in almost every state in the world[53] by mostly targeting extractive and financial industries and large infrastructure projects.[54] Chinese private and state-owned corporations have brought about economic growth, infrastructure, and technology, as well as an increase in the well-being of local populations in developed countries, but also in the Global South. They have in this way improved socio-economic livelihoods of many individuals across many countries in the Global South by building transport infrastructure, hospitals, and schools, as well as advancing agriculture technology, thereby ensuring water and food provision.

Apart from positive impacts, there have been also negative consequences to the rule of law, human rights and the environment.[55] Negative impact has been

51 See, Draft report on the third session of the open-ended intergovernmental working group on transnational corporations and other business enterprises with respect to human rights, 23–27 October 2017.

52 See for instance, Pankaj Ghemawat and Thomas Hout, 'Can China's Companies Conquer the World? The Overlooked Importance of Corporate Power', 95(2) *Foreign Affairs* 86 (2016).

53 Global Business Initiative on Human Rights, Global Compact Network China, Institute for Human Rights and Business, Peking University and Tracktwo, 'The China Responsible Business Forum, Corporate Responsibility in the Era of the UN Guiding Principles', 2014, p. 5.

54 See for example, James Thuo Gathii, 'Beyond China's Human Rights Exceptionalism in Africa: Leveraging Science, Technology and Engineering for Long-Term Growth', 51 *Columbia Journal of Transnational Law* 664 (2013).

55 See, Business and Human Rights Resource Centre, Chinese investment overseas, https://www.business-humanrights.org/en/chinese-investment-overseas?page=34&dateorder=dateasc (last accessed 19 January 2018).

mostly felt in Asia and on the African continent.[56] For example, Business and Human Rights Resources Centre observes that Chinese corporations have been allegedly complicit in "abuses most frequently occurred were Myanmar (Burma) (24%), Cambodia (9%), India (9%) and Democratic Republic of Congo (6%)".[57] Additionally, Bohoslavsky notes that Chinese corporations "have contributed in several countries to serious violations of human rights, including forced evictions, arbitrary detention and violations of the right to life".[58] He adds that "Chinese companies and lending institutions appear occasionally to have been difficult to approach or insensitive to respond to concerns raised"[59] and that "lack of an open and responsive dialogue with persons protesting against development projects can frequently be a seed for larger trouble, enhance social tensions and generate additional conflict".[60] Some recent domestic and international documents suggest that China has extraterritorial obligations to control corporations.[61]

Different Chinese organizations have in recent years adopted a number of guidelines. For instance, the Chinese governmental body for state-owned corporations, SASAC, in 2008 adopted a general document for state-owned enterprises when doing business abroad, "SASAC 2008 Guidelines to the State-owned Enterprises Directly under the Central Government on Fulfilling Corporate Social Responsibilities".[62] They provide in Section 6 that

> CSOEs should enhance the awareness of CSR; actively implement CSR, setting example in legal and honest business operation, resource-saving and environment protection. CSOEs should also the model in building human-oriented and harmonious enterprise and become the backbone of China not only in economy but also in CSR.[63]

It is notable that they refer to CSR and strictly avoid the language of human rights by always referring to harmonious society or enterprise. Nonetheless,

56 See for example, Timothy Webster, 'China's Human Rights Footprint in Africa', 51 *Columbia Journal of Transnational Law* 626 (2013).

57 Business and Human Rights Resource Centre, 'Time for Action: Business & Human Rights in Greater China', 26 August 2014, p. 4.

58 Juan Pablo Bohoslavsky, 'End of Mission Statement China', 6 July 2015, www.ohchr.org/EN/NewsEvents/Pages/DisplayNews.aspx?NewsID=16203&LangID=E (last accessed 19 January 2018).

59 Ibid.

60 Ibid.

61 'Maastricht Principles on Extraterritorial Obligations of States in the Area of Economic, Social and Cultural Rights', (adopted in 2011), principle 9.

62 State-owned Assets Supervision and Administration Commission of the State Council (SASAC) of the People's Republic of China, 'Guidelines to the State-Owned Enterprises Directly Under the Central Government on Fulfilling Corporate Social Responsibilities', 2008.

63 Ibid., section 6.

Chinese state-owned enterprises are obliged to comply with the "a legal and honest way in business operation".[64]

This means compliance "with regulations and laws, public ethnics and commercial conventions and trade rules" and fulfilment of "their tax obligations, undertake the interests of investors and creditors, protect intellectual property rights, keep business creditability, oppose improper competition and eradicate corruption in commercial activities".[65] The SASAC Guidelines however do not provide any legal basis for binding corporate obligations concerning socio-economic rights, nor do they provide access to justice to those affected individuals beyond borders of China in the case of allegations of socio-economic rights violations.[66] However, from our conversations with Chinese officials, those and similar guidelines provide almost binding reference for Chinese state-owned corporations when doing business abroad.[67] However, it seems that a detailed theoretical and empirical research is necessary to assess the added value of the guidelines.

Moreover, different professional societies have adopted several sector-specific guidelines for corporations involved in that sector. The Chinese Chamber of Commerce and Minerals, Metals and Chemical Importers and Exporters (CCCMC) has adopted a document titled "Guidelines for Social Responsibility in Outbound Mining Investments" of the Chinese Chamber of Commerce of Minerals, Metals and Chemical Importers and Exporters (CCCMC).[68] Those guidelines provide in Article 2.3 that corporations "respect the human rights of all individuals and groups associated with its products, services and business relations, including respect and protect the rights and interests of its employees as well as employees of its partners along the supply chain".[69] Even though the guidelines again do not directly refer to corporate obligations concerning socio-economic rights, they nonetheless indirectly require them to respect and protect them. In other words, corporations have negative and positive obligations to uphold socio-economic rights. They also have an obligation of conduct to ensure that their subsidiaries and business partners do not infringe on socio-economic rights. In other words, the latter provisions recognize that mining corporations have an obligation of conduct to control their supply chains.

Further, they appear to recognize socio-economic rights of vulnerable groups such as Indigenous peoples by obliging corporation to "protect the rights for free, prior and informed consent of local communities including indigenous

64 Ibid., section 8.

65 Ibid.

66 Sophie Richardson, 'China: Quashing Criticism at Home and Abroad, Human Rights Watch', Oxford University China Africa Network (Blog), 27 May 2014.

67 Sun Lihui, Interview, 2016 Business and Human Rights Forum, 15 November 2016.

68 China Chamber of Commerce of Metals, Minerals & Chemicals Importers & Exporters (CCMCC), 'Guidelines for Social Responsibility in Outbound Mining Investments' (2014).

69 Ibid. art. 2.3.

peoples"[70]. The legal nature of the guidelines is non-binding; however they provide illustration of emerging obligations of corporations for socio-economic rights. Hathaway, for instance, argues that "declarations of rights . . . are not easily defined and measured . . .".[71] The Guidelines have created "a formal grievance mechanism which includes third party involvement",[72] which "shall be legitimate, accessible, predictable, equitable, transparent and rights-compatible"[73] and "shall allow for anonymous complaints to be raised in a safe environment".[74] Such commitments aim to improve access to justice for victims of socio-economic and other human rights violations. They also provide for the following non-binding measures: "providing trainings, workshops, exchanges and other measures to strengthen the capacities of companies",[75] assessing "social responsibility according to the principles and requirements outlined in these Guidelines",[76] and "evaluation of CSR performance of Chinese companies engaged in outbound mining investments according to these Guidelines and disseminate best practice".[77] The CESCR asked China in June 2014 to

> adopt a human rights-based approach to its policies of international cooperation, by: (a) Undertaking a systematic and independent human rights impact assessment prior to making funding decisions; (b) Establishing an effective monitoring mechanism to regularly assess the human rights impact of its policies and projects in the receiving countries and to take remedial measures when required; (c) Ensuring that there is an accessible complaint mechanism for violations of economic, social and cultural rights in the receiving countries.[78]

The CESCR also noted "the lack of adequate and effective measures adopted by the State party to ensure that Chinese companies, both State-owned and private, respect economic, social and cultural rights, including when operating abroad".[79] It therefore asked China to "establish a clear regulatory framework for companies operating in the State party to ensure that their activities promote and do not negatively affect the enjoyment of economic, social and cultural human rights";[80] and to

70 Ibid. art. 3.4.3.
71 Oona A. Hathaway, 'Do Human Rights Treaties Make a Difference?', 111 *Yale Law Journal* 1935, 2023 (2002).
72 CCMCC, 'Guidelines for Social Responsibility in Outbound Mining Investments', art. 4.8.4.
73 Ibid.
74 Ibid.
75 Ibid., art. 4.2.
76 Ibid., art. 4.3.
77 Ibid., art. 4.4.
78 UN, CESCR, 'Concluding Observations: China, including Hong Kong, China, and Macao', para 12.
79 Ibid., para 13.
80 Ibid.

> adopt appropriate legislative and administrative measures to ensure the legal liability of companies and their subsidiaries operating in or managed from the State party's territory regarding violations of economic, social and cultural rights in the context of their projects abroad.[81]

The language of the CESCR in the concluding observations has been quite straightforward and direct. Similarly, Bohoslavsky has argued that

> international human rights standards and guidelines are in particular relevant when China provides funding for projects in countries with high risks, experiencing internal armed conflicts, weak governance structures or a lack of effective enforcement of national and international law by national authorities.[82]

He further submitted that corporations based in China are in "need for guidance on how to operate in difficult political and social environments in full respect for human rights and in compliance with applicable national and international laws in the respective host country".[83]

The China Chamber of Commerce of Metals, Minerals & Chemicals Importers & Exporters thereafter in 2016 drafted and adopted Chinese Due Diligence Guidelines for Responsible Mineral Supply Chains.[84] The objective of the guidelines is to provide

> guidance to all Chinese companies which are extracting and/or are using mineral resources and their related products and are engaged at any point in the supply chain of minerals to identify, prevent and mitigate their risks of contributing to conflict, serious human rights abuses and risks of serious misconduct, as well as to observe the UN Guiding Principles on Business and Human Rights during the entire life-cycle of the mining project.[85]

As for socio-economic rights, the Guidelines note in Section 7.3.2 that

> before disengaging, considering the potential socio-economic impacts on mining communities, such as the risk of extensive and/or sustained loss of livelihoods in or near the sites of mineral extraction, or loss of economic activity essential to the welfare of communities in or near extraction sites is highly encouraged.[86]

81 Ibid.

82 Juan Pablo Bohoslavsky, 'End of Mission Statement China', 6 July 2015, www.ohchr.org/EN/NewsEvents/Pages/DisplayNews.aspx?NewsID=16203&LangID=E (last accessed 19 January 2018).

83 Ibid.

84 China Chamber of Commerce of Metals, Minerals & Chemicals Importers & Exporters (CCMCC), 'Due Diligence Guidelines for Responsible Mineral Supply Chains' (2015).

85 Ibid., p. 8.

86 Ibid., section 7.3.2.

Moreover, for instance, the China Chamber of Commerce of Metals, Minerals & Chemicals Importers & Exporters at the 2017 UN Business and Human Rights Forum confirmed its commitment to improving transparency and due diligence in the supply chains of Chinese corporations.[87] Further, there exist also Guidelines on Environmental Protection in Foreign Investment and Cooperation, which

> advise Chinese companies doing business abroad to respect host country environmental protection laws, religions and customs and ensure rights and interests of workers; in addition, they suggest that companies follow established principles and practices of international organizations and multilateral financial institutions.[88]

As SASAC guidelines, they can also be only described as recommendations. China has in recent years adopted a number of guidelines. The problems with some of the above guidelines have been that they can be described as a private initiative and it is doubtful to which extent and scope they reflect the official position of the Chinese government. However, those guidelines nonetheless represent some authoritative commitments that corporations active in various industries, for example in the extractive industry sector, have to comply with.

A few observations can be made. First, it appears that much of the regulation in the Chinese business and socio-economic field derives from private regulation and not state/government regulation. Backer aptly observes that

> in China . . . the government apparatus remained very much in the background as large multinational enterprises and supra-national monitoring systems engaged in the formulation and remediation of adverse human rights consequences of social and economic rights . . . These entities remain accountable to the state for violations of law, but to each other and their transnational stakeholders for the violation of rights developed and adopted through private systems that supplement state regulations.[89] (footnote omitted)

However, when and if government regulation is absent, one can ask oneself: How effective is the private regulation, as is the case in China, in ensuring corporate accountability for socio-economic rights? Nonetheless, it seems that Chinese corporations are now slowly moving to the contestations that they have to observe socio-economic rights when doing business. They have both negative obligations

87 Sun Lihui, Presentation, 2017 Business and Human Rights Forum, 28 November 2017.

88 Ibid.

89 Larry Catá Backer, 'Realizing Socio-Economic Rights under Emerging Global Regulatory Frameworks': The Potential Impact of Privatization and the Role of Companies in China and India', 45(4) *The George Washington International Law Review* 615 (2013), p. 670.

to refrain from violations of socio-economic rights and positive obligations to control their supply chains in order to not endanger the socio-economic livelihoods of individuals.[90] States are also obliged to prevent and investigate violations, bring to justice and punish the perpetrators, and provide reparations for violations caused.

The previously mentioned documents of the Chinese government and various private organizations appear to suggest that they recognize that with the privilege and power of investing comes also responsibility and accountability to respect, protect and fulfil socio-economic livelihoods of local populations. Similarly, Bohoslavsky argues that

> the obligation of China to ensure that Chinese business enterprises respect human rights in their overseas investments is commeasurable to the relevant human rights risks of a particular operation in a particular country; for example, in conflict-affected areas, the host State may be unable to protect human rights adequately owing to a lack of effective control.[91]

As China moves into the group of developed and industrialized states, it in doing so also takes up the role of duty-bearers of obligations of "international assistance and co-operation", as this derives from the practices of international human rights bodies. This is particularly so relating to how their state-owned companies do business abroad, where they certainly have obligations to respect, protect and fulfil socio-economic rights. Further, some recent examples illustrate that Chinese corporations are well equipped with addressing challenges in ensuring socio-economic rights.[92] For instance, Sino-American Petroleum Development Peru Inc. (SAPET), a subsidiary of China National Petroleum Corporation, has managed to accommodate the rights of Indigenous peoples relating to oil extraction in Peru.[93]

Chinese corporations are therefore obliged to conduct due diligence when embarking on new projects in order to ensure that their business partners do not negatively affect the reasonable minimum core of economic and social rights. However, as everywhere, differences occur between formal obligations and their

90 UN, International Human Rights Instruments, 'Compilation of General Comments and General Recommendations Adopted by Human Rights Treaty Bodies', UN Doc. HRI/GEN/1/Rev.1, 29 July 1994.

91 UN, Human Rights Council, 'Report of the Independent Expert on the Effects of Foreign Debt and Other Related International Financial Obligations of States on the Full Enjoyment of All Human Rights, Particularly Economic, Social and Cultural Rights on His Mission to China: Juan Pablo Bohoslavsky', UN Doc. A/HRC/31/60/Add.1, 1 March 2016, para 26.

92 Ibid., paras 73–76.

93 See for example, Adina Matisoff, 'Going Beyond Compliance to Mitigate Risks: CNPC's Engagement with Indigenous Federations in Peru', *in* Tao Hu and Yiting Wang (eds.), Washington: *Environmental and Social Risk Management of Chinese Transnational Corporations*, Yale and WWF Workshop (2014), p. 11.

applications in practice. For Chinese corporations it is essential to maintain their global presence, the fact that they respect and protect individual human dignity, and possibly also that they attempt to improve daily socio-economic livelihoods of individuals.

Access to justice for socio-economic rights

In spite of a high standing of socio-economic rights or their substance in China, their enforcement has been lacking in recent years. They have not been upgraded to constitutional or even statutory basis.[94] CESCR has noted that ICESCR has not been translated in the domestic system and more importantly that its contents "are therefore not directly applicable by national courts and tribunals".[95] It therefore advised the Chinese government to

> guarantee the direct applicability of all rights under the Covenant in its domestic legal order. The Committee also recommends that the State party raise awareness of the content of the Covenant rights and their justiciability, in particular among judges, lawyers and law enforcement officials, as well as the members of the National People's Congress and other actors responsible for the implementation of the Covenant and among rights holders.[96]

Does the judiciary in China comply with the principle of the rule of law in order to curtail sometimes arbitrary powers of the executive branch? Are domestic ordinary courts competent and justified to control whether procedures were conducted in ways compliant to the principle of the rule of law? The judiciary in China does not fulfil the fundamental notions of independence, impartiality and fairness. Vested and private interests have been informally influencing the Chinese judiciary. Clearly, the Chinese Communist Party has been exerting the most influence on the judicial decision-making, thereby making judges directly dependable and possibly accountable to local, regional and central elites.[97] Sen has therefore observed that there is "a serious fragility in any authoritarian system of governance, since there is little recourse or remedy when the government

94 Sanzhuan Guo, 'Implementation of Human Rights Treaties by Chinese Courts: Problems and Prospects', 8(1) *Chinese Journal of International Law* 161 (2009). See also, Hanqin Xue and Qian Jin, 'International Treaties in the Chinese Domestic Legal System', 8(2) *Chinese Journal of International Law* 299 (2009). See also, Wim Muller, 'Beyond History and S: China and the Future of International Law', Ph.D Thesis, Florence: European University Institute (2013).

95 UN, CESCR, 'Concluding Observations: China, Including Hong Kong, China, and Macao', para 9.

96 Ibid.

97 Ling Li, 'The Chinese Communist Party and People's Courts: Judicial Dependence in China', 64(1) *American Journal of Comparative Law* 37 (2016). See also, Zhu Suli, 'Political Parties in China's Judiciary', 17(2) *Duke Journal of Comparative & International Law* 533, (2007).

leaders alter their goals or suppress their failures".[98] Grimheden once submitted that there is a need for reform of the Chinese judiciary.[99] He nonetheless acknowledged that the Chinese judiciary has been moving towards "enhanced professionalization, stature and independence" whereby concluding, "reform in the future is likely to continue along these same".[100] However, those reforms have not changed the culture of unfairness, dependence and partiality in judicial decision-making.[101]

Individuals can best enforce their socio-economic rights in domestic courts. However, this possibility exists only theoretically. The Chinese judiciary has been internally plagued by corruption, networks of vested interests and non-transparency. The principle of the rule of law has still not been internalized on a theoretical normative level or on a practical level. The objective of the rule of law in any system is to curtail the power of the most influential elite, whether political, corporate, governmental or other, which are all eager to subject government to their private, mostly financial interests. Moreover, Kroeber argues that the "fundamental cause of corruption in modern China is a system in which weak rule of law is institutionalized by the insistence that the Communist Party hold a monopoly on political power and be exempt from legal processes that apply to everyone else".[102]

The regulation of business and socio-economic rights in China has been so deficient due to systematic and general problems with the functioning of the rule of law in any facet of society. An individual's best bet in China is therefore to use obscure domestic statutes in labour, administrative and environmental law. Nonetheless, the Constitution of the People's Republic of China states in Article 41 that

> citizens have the right to make to relevant State organs complaints or charges against, or exposures of, any State organ or functionary for violation of law or dereliction of duty; but fabrication or distortion of facts for purposes of libel or false incrimination is prohibited.[103]

It further provides that "citizens who have suffered losses as a result of infringement of their civic rights by any State organ or functionary have the right to

98 Amartya Sen, 'Quality of life: India vs. China'.

99 Jonas Grimheden, 'Themis v. Xiezhi: Assessing Judicial Independence in the People's Republic of China Under International Human Rights Law', Ph.D Thesis, Lund: University of Lund (2004).

100 Jonas Grimheden, 'The Reform Path of the Chinese Judiciary: Progress or Stand-Still?', 30(4) *Fordham International Law Journal* 1000, 1013 (2006).

101 Keith Hand, 'Resolving Constitutional Disputes in Contemporary China', 7(1) *University of Pennsylvania East Asia Law Review* 51, 113 (2011).

102 Arthur R. Kroeber, *China's Economy: What Everyone Needs to Know*, Oxford: Oxford University Press (2016), p. 209.

103 Constitution of the People's Republic of China, art. 41.

compensation in accordance with the provisions of law".[104] Further, Article 90 of Legislation Law provides in its paragraph 2 that

> where any state organ and social group, enterprise or non-enterprise institution or citizen . . ., deems that an administrative regulation, local decree, autonomous decree or special decree contravenes the Constitution or a national law, it may make a written proposal to the Standing Committee of National People's Congress for review and the office of operation of the Standing Committee shall study such proposal and where necessary, it shall distribute such proposal to the relevant special committees for review and comments.[105]

It is questionable what is the added value of such complaint procedure, which is also known as "letters and visits" (xinfang) or a "petitioning" procedure.[106] Nonetheless, Peerenboom argues that

> given the weak powers of the courts, shortcomings in the legal framework particularly with respect to individual remedies and the lack of resources to address systemic socioeconomic claims, cooperation with government agencies to resolve the immediate case is often the best, if not the only, option.[107]

Therefore, several claims have been brought against foreign corporations before foreign courts, particularly in the United States.[108] More specifically, victims have brought claims under the Alien Torts Claims Act against China Construction Bank, Cisco System, ConocoPhilips, Nike and Yahoo! for alleged violations that took place in China.[109] Several cases have been brought also in Japan concerning forced labour violations during the Second World War.[110] More specifically, the settlement was reached concerning the Nishimatsu lawsuit about the forced labour of Chinese workers during the Second World War. The settlement provided for establishing "a trust fund of ¥250 million to compensate the Chinese workers (or their descendants) . . . The company issued an

104 Ibid.

105 Legislation Law of the People's Republic of China, 3th Session of the 9th National People's Republic of China, 15 March 2000.

106 Lianjiang Li, Mingxing Liu and Kevin J. O'Brien, 'Petitioning Beijing: The High Tide of 2003–2006', 210 *China Quarterly* 313 (2012).

107 Randall Peerenboom, 'Economic and Social Rights: The Role of Courts in China', 12 *San Diego International Law Journal* 303, 306 (2011).

108 See for example, *Wang Xiaoning v. Yahoo! Inc.*, Case No. C07-02151 CW/JCS, 13 November 2007.

109 Business and Human Rights Resource Centre, 'Corporate Legal Accountability'.

110 Business and Human Rights Resource Centre, 'Nishimatsu Lawsuit (re World War II forced labour)'.

apology under the 'Settlement Terms' and has promised to erect a memorial at the site of the power plant".[111] Nonetheless, Alston observed concerning access to justice that he

> was informed by the relevant official at the National People's Congress that out of perhaps 100 communications received (for a population exceeding 1.3 billion), he could recall only a couple of instances over the past few years in which action had formally been taken upon the receipt of a written suggestion . . . not much progress appears to have been made with regard to the regularization of this accountability mechanism. It remains as untransparent and discretionary as before.[112]

He added that "the current Chinese approach . . . denies individuals meaningful access to accountability mechanisms for violations of their economic and social rights" and "contradicts the country's international human rights treaty obligations".[113] He further submitted that it is

> for the Government, working together with civil society actors and individual citizens, . . . to develop meaningful avenues for complaints about rights violations that fit within the Chinese domestic context and to enable individuals to hold all levels of government to account when individual rights are violated.[114]

However, the right to fair trial has not been equally applied to all individuals in China. Alston highlights "very rapidly shrinking space for the expression of views that differ from those of the Party" and that "President Xi Jinping has emphasized the importance of ensuring the accountability of Party and Government officials. This accountability needs to extend also to situations in which human rights are violated by those same officials".[115]

Victims of alleged violations of socio-economic rights violations in China face a number of obstacles. They have very low chances with succeeding with their individual claim against corporations, particularly state owned. However, there have been some successful efforts when collective pressure has been exercised on corporations. Such has been the case of the melamine-affected baby milk products produced by Sanlu Group where several thousand victims have received

111 Ibid.

112 UN, Human Rights Council, 'Report of the Special Rapporteur on Extreme Poverty and Human Rights on His Mission to China: Philip Alston', para 71.

113 Ibid., para 75.

114 Ibid.

115 Philip Alston, 'Oral Statement at the 35th session of the Human Rights Council', 7 June 2017, www.ohchr.org/EN/NewsEvents/Pages/DisplayNews.aspx?NewsID=21772&LangID=E (last accessed 19 January 2018).

compensations from the corporation[116] and several officials have been removed from their posts.[117] Several cases relate to socio-economic violations arising from the mine, construction and factory accidents.[118] Moreover, Wu, argues that

> environmental class action lawsuits are on the rise, as China confronts major environmental problems. In addition, with increased worries about product safety, Chinese consumers are likely to seek greater enforcement of consumer protection laws. A narrow textualist interpretation of the new Company Law suggests that the Company Law's veil piercing provisions may not cover all such litigation.[119]

Several reasons can be found for China's record in the failures of judiciaries to ensure fair, impartial and independent proceedings[120] and the presence of corruption and involvement of politics.[121] Minzner has argued "the authorities have sought to close down rhetoric (constitutionalism), channels (court trials) and social forces (lawyers) that activists had used to mobilize greater changes".[122] The Chinese system can be therefore described as composed of authoritarian mentality, formalism, submissiveness, political correctness, and even the judges' self-censorship, prosecution of human rights defenders and problems relating to company law enforcement.[123] Moreover, there has been a lack of knowledge about socio-economic rights. The reasons for poor implementation of the ICESCR in China's legal order cannot just be found in the normative system, but also in the judiciary's deficient knowledge of socio-economic rights. Appropriate measures, such as awareness and law enforcement, should be applied.

116 Supreme People's Court of the People's Republic of China, 'Judicial News – China's Top Legislature Decides to Remove Milk Scandal Official Form Deputy Post', Beijing, 27 June 2009.

117 Surya Deva, 'Access to Justice Human Rights Abuses Involving Corporations – The People's Republic of China', *International Commission of Jurists* 10, 59–62 (2010).

118 See for example, the most recent incident: China Labour Bulletin, 'Zhejiang Shoe Factory Collapse Kills At least 12 Workers, Injures 33 Others', 6 July 2015.

119 Mark Wu, 'Piercing China's Corporate Veil: Open Questions from the New Company Law', 117(2) *Yale Law Journal* 329, 334 (2007).

120 David C. Buxbaum, 'China: Litigation Without a Law of Evidence, Oral Testimony, Witnesses, and a Transparent Judiciary', *in* Dennis Campbell (ed.), *Comparative Law Yearbook of International Business,* Alphen aan den Rijn: Wolters Kluwer (vol. 34, 2012), pp. 37–55.

121 Guanghua Yu, *The Roles of Law and Politics in China's Development*, Berlin: Springer (2014).

122 Carl Minzner, 'China at the Tipping Point? The Turn Against Legal Reform', 24(1) *Journal of Democracy* 65 (January 2013), p. 69.

123 See for a comprehensive study, Surya Deva, 'Access to Justice Human Rights Abuses Involving Corporations – The People's Republic of China', *International Commission of Jurists* 10, 34–50 and 51–55 (2010). See also, article on prosecution of the lawyers: Jennifer Duggan, 'China Targets Lawyers in New Human Rights Crackdown', Shanghai: *The Guardian*, 13 July 2015.

Conclusion

China has done much in recent years to raise awareness of corporate accountability for socio-economic rights. However, it is also valid that it started from very low levels. There are several levels of challenges of enforcing socio-economic rights against corporations in China. First, in general, most of socio-economic rights are not explicitly protected in the domestic system and only indirectly derive from statutory sources of law through the concept of a "harmonious society". Second, most regulations of corporate conduct of Chinese corporations are only voluntary and non-binding, thereby making it difficult for victims of alleged violations to bring cases before the court of law. Further, the regulatory framework for corporations in China is extremely vague, ineffective and inefficient. Third, lack of progress in corporate accountability for socio-economic rights in China suffers systematic and structural problems that have plagued the Chinese judiciary, namely how to ensure its fairness, impartiality and independence. Therefore, reforms in business and socio-economic rights areas in China are very much dependent on the reform of the rule of law in China. However, it seems that in China there is no real will to cleanse and pursue the protection of human rights and to ensure impartial, independent and fair judicial proceedings. More importantly, the state should have at its disposal robust institutions of the rule of law that are aware that their primary task is to protect the dignity of ordinary people. But because institutions are people dependent, it may be necessary to internalize values of the socio-economic rights, which may take time.

All in all, it seems that the Chinese national system offers growing support for corporate accountability for socio-economic rights in increasing fields of law. What is clear is that legal cultures have not yet followed the developments in the formal sources of law, thereby explaining few cases being brought against corporations. Nonetheless, there exists the formal legal basis being brought against corporations. Notwithstanding these developments, the prospects of bringing claims against a corporation in China for the violation of socio-economic human rights remain relatively low. A prosecution on the basis of the individual liability of corporate managers appears a more viable option with less danger of becoming a futile exercise. Moreover, several documents suggest that Chinese corporations, when doing business abroad, are to respect and protect socio-economic rights of individuals.

Bibliography

Books

Angle, Stephen C., *Human Rights and Chinese Thought: A Cross-Cultural Inquiry*, Cambridge: Cambridge University Press (2002).

Gu, Minkang, *Understanding Chinese Company Law*, Hong Kong: Hong Kong University Press (2006).

Kroeber, Arthur R., *China's Economy: What Everyone Needs to Know*, Oxford: Oxford University Press (2016).

Pei, Minxin, *China's Trapped Transition: The Limits of Developmental Autocracy*, Cambridge, MA: Harvard University Press (2008).

Yu, Guanghua, *The Roles of Law and Politics in China's Development*, Berlin: Springer (2014).

Journal articles

Backer, Larry Catá, 'Realizing Socio-Economic Rights Under Emerging Global Regulatory Frameworks: The Potential Impact of Privatization and the Role of Companies in China and India', 45(4) *The George Washington International Law Review* 615 (2013).

Delury, John, '"Harmonious" in China', 148 *Policy Review* 35 (2008).

Deva, Surya, 'Sustainable Development: What Role for the Company Law?', 8 *International and Comparative Corporate Law Journal* 76 (2011).

Gathii, James Thuo, 'Beyond China's Human Rights Exceptionalism in Africa: Leveraging Science, Technology and Engineering for Long-Term Growth', 51 *Columbia Journal of Transnational Law* 664 (2013).

Ghemawat, Pankaj and Hout, Thomas, 'Can China's Companies Conquer the World? The Overlooked Importance of Corporate Power', 95(2) *Foreign Affairs* 86 (2016).Guo, Sanzhuan, 'Implementation of Human Rights Treaties by Chinese Courts: Problems and Prospects', 8(1) *Chinese Journal of International Law* 161 (2009).

Grimheden, Jonas, 'The Reform Path of the Chinese Judiciary: Progress or Stand-Still?', 30(4) *Fordham International Law Journal* 1000 (2006).

Hand, Keith, 'Resolving Constitutional Disputes in Contemporary China', 7(1) *University of Pennsylvania East Asia Law Review* 51 (2011).

Hathaway, Oona A., 'Do Human Rights Treaties Make a Difference?', 111 *Yale Law Journal* 1935 (2002).

Kellogg, Thomas, 'Constitutionalism with Chinese Characteristics? Constitutional Development and Civil Litigation in China', 7(2) *International Journal of Constitutional Law* 215 (2009).

Li, Lianjiang, Liu, Mingxing and O'Brien, Kevin J., 'Petitioning Beijing: The High Tide of 2003–2006', 210 *China Quarterly* 313 (2012).

Li, Ling, 'The Chinese Communist Party and People's Courts: Judicial Dependence in China', 64(1) *American Journal of Comparative Law* 37 (2016).

Lin, Li-Wen, 'Corporate Social Responsibility in China: Window Dressing or Structural Change', 28(1) *Berkeley Journal of International Law* 64 (2010).

Minzner, Carl, 'China at the Tipping Point? The Turn Against Legal Reform', 24(1) *Journal of Democracy* 65 (January 2013).

Nicholas, Dana C., 'China's Labour Enforcement Crisis: International Intervention and Corporate Social Responsibility', 11 *St. Mary's Law Review on Minority Issues* 155 (2009).

Pagnattaro, Marisa Anne, 'Is Labour Really "Cheap" in China? Compliance with Labour and Employment Laws', 10 *San Diego International Law Journal* 357 (2009).

Peerenboom, Randall, 'Economic and Social Rights: The Role of Courts in China', 12 *San Diego International Law Journal* 303 (2011).

Ruskola, Teemu, 'Conceptualizing Corporations and Kinship: Comparative Law and Development Theory in a Chinese Perspective', 52(6) *Stanford Law Review* 1599 (2000).

Suli, Zhu, 'Political Parties in China's Judiciary', 17(2) *Duke Journal of Comparative & International Law* 533 (2007).

Webster, Timothy, 'China's Human Rights Footprint in Africa', 51 *Columbia Journal of Transnational Law* 626 (2013).

Whyte, Martin King, 'Soaring Income Gaps: China in Comparative Perspective', 143(2) *Daedalus* 39 (2014).

Wu, Mark, 'Piercing China's Corporate Veil: Open Questions from the New Company Law', 117(2) *Yale Law Journal* 329 (2007).

Xue, Hanqin and Jin, Qian, 'International Treaties in the Chinese Domestic Legal System', 8(2) *Chinese Journal of International Law* 299 (2009).

Book chapters

Buxbaum, David C., 'China: Litigation Without a Law of Evidence, Oral Testimony, Witnesses and a Transparent Judiciary', *in* Dennis Campbell (ed.), *Comparative Law Yearbook of International Business*, Alphen aan den Rijn: Wolters Kluwer (vol. 34, 2012), pp. 37–55.

Backer, Larry Catá, 'China's Corporate Social Responsibility with National Characteristics: Coherence and Dissonance with the Global Business and Human Rights Project', *in* Jena Martin and Karen E. Bravo (eds.), *The Business and Human Rights Landscape: Moving Forward, Looking Back*, New York: Cambridge University Press (2016), pp. 530–558.

Letnar Černič, Jernej, 'Sustainable Development, Corporate Social Responsibility and Business in the People's Republic of China: A Tale of three worlds?', *in* Paolo Davide Farah (ed.), *China and the Good Governance of the Markets in the Light of the Economic Development*, Abingdon: Routledge (2018).

Newspaper and magazine articles

Aizawa, Motoko, '"Going Out" in Search of Oil and Gas: How should Chinese companies investing abroad tackle human rights challenges?' *Institute for Human Rights and Business*, 24 March 2015.

Duggan, Jennifer, 'China Targets Lawyers in New Human Rights Crackdown', Shanghai: *The Guardian*, 13 July 2015.

Liao, Rebecca, 'Judicial Reform in China', *Foreign Affairs*, 2 February 2017.

Sara Hsu, 'High Income Inequality Still Festering in China', *Forbes*, 18 November 2016.

Sen, Amartya, 'Quality of Life: India vs. China', *The New York Review of Books*, 12 May 2011.

Wildau, Gabriel and Mitchell, Tom, 'China Income Inequality Among World's Worst', Shanghai and Beijing: *Financial Times*, 14 January 2016.

Official documents

Company Law of the People's Republic of China, adopted on 29 December 1993 and last revised on 28 December 2013, http://www.fdi.gov.cn/1800000121_39_4814_0_7.html (last accessed 19 January 2018).

Constitution of the People's Republic of China, adopted at the 5th Session of the 5th National People's Congress, 4 December 1982.

Criminal Law of the People's Republic of China, adopted on 1 July 1979 and last revised on 14 March 1997, http://www.fmprc.gov.cn/ce/cgvienna/eng/dbtyw/jdwt/crimelaw/t209043.htm (last accessed 19 Janaury 2018), art. 30.

Environmental Protection Law of the People's Republic of China, adopted on 26 December 1989, http://www.china.org.cn/english/environment/34356.htm (last accessed 19 January 2018).

Law of the People's Republic of China on Safety in Mines, adopted on 7 November 1992 and last revised on 31 August 2014, http://www.npc.gov.cn/english npc/Law/2007-12/12/content_1383872.htm (last accessed 19 January 2018).

Law of the People's Republic of China on Work Safety, adopted on 29 June 2002 and last revised on 31 August 2014, http://www.npc.gov.cn/englishnpc/Law/2007-12/06/content_1382127.htm (last accessed 19 January 2018).

Legislation Law of the People's Republic of China, adopted at the 3th Session of the 9th National People's Republic of China, 15 March 2000.

UN, CESCR, 'Concluding Observations: China, Including Hong Kong, China and Macao', UN Doc. E/C.12/CHN/CO/2, 13 June 2014.

UN, Human Rights Council, Report of Special Representative of the Secretary-General on the Issue of Human Rights and Transnational Corporations and Other Business Enterprises, John Ruggie, 'Guiding Principles on Business and Human Rights: Implementing the United Nations "Protect, Respect and Remedy" Framework' ['The Guiding Principles'], UN Doc. A/HRC/17/31, 21 March 2011.

UN, Human Rights Council, 'Elaboration of an International Legally Binding Instrument on Transnational Corporations and Other Business Enterprises with Respect to Human Rights (Bolivia (Plurinational State of), Cuba, Ecuador, South Africa, Venezuela (Bolivarian Republic of): draft resolution', A/HRC/26/L.22/Rev.1, 25 June 2014.

UN, Human Rights Council, 'Report of the Independent Expert on the Effects of Foreign Debt and Other Related International Financial Obligations of States on the Full Enjoyment of All Human Rights, Particularly Economic, Social and Cultural Rights on His Mission to China: Juan Pablo Bohoslavsky', UN Doc. A/HRC/31/60/Add.1, 1 March 2016.

UN, Human Rights Council, 'Report of the Special Rapporteur on Extreme Poverty and Human Rights on His Mission to China: Philip Alston', UN Doc. A/HRC/35/26/Add.2, 28 March 2017.

UN, International Human Rights Instruments, 'Compilation of General Comments and General Recommendations Adopted by Human Rights Treaty Bodies', UN Doc. HRI/GEN/1/Rev.1, 29 July 1994.

Cases

Qi Yuling v Chen Xiaoqi and Chen Kezheng, Reply of the Supreme People's Court to the Shandong High Court, 13 August 2001.

Wang Xiaoning v. Yahoo! Inc., Case No. C07-02151 CW/JCS, 13 November 2007.

Websites

Business and Human Rights Resource Centre, Chinese investment overseas, https://www.business-humanrights.org/en/chinese-investment-overseas?page=34&dateorder=dateasc (last accessed 19 January 2018).

Fortune 500, http://fortune.com/global500/ (last accessed 19 January 2018).

Office of the High Commissioner (OHCHR), 'Ratification Status for China', http://tbinternet.ohchr.org/_layouts/TreatyBodyExternal/Treaty.aspx (last accessed 19 January 2018).

University of Minnesota Human Rights Library, Ratification of International Human Rights Treaties – China, http://hrlibrary.umn.edu/research/ratification-china.html (last accessed 19 January 2018).

Reports and miscellaneous

Alston, Philip, 'Oral Statement at the 35th Session of the Human Rights Council', 7 June 2017, www.ohchr.org/EN/NewsEvents/Pages/DisplayNews.aspx?NewsID=21772&LangID=E (last accessed 19 January 2018).

Bohoslavsky, Juan Pablo, 'End of Mission Statement China', 6 July 2015, www.ohchr.org/EN/NewsEvents/Pages/DisplayNews.aspx?NewsID=16203&LangID=E (last accessed 19 January 2018).

Business and Human Rights Resource Centre, 'Corporate Legal Accountability'.

Business and Human Rights Resource Centre, 'Nishimatsu lawsuit (re World War II forced labour)'.

Business and Human Rights Resource Centre, 'Time for Action: Business & Human Rights in Greater China', 26 August 2014.

China Chamber of Commerce of Metals, Minerals & Chemicals Importers & Exporters (CCMCC), 'Due Diligence Guidelines for Responsible Mineral Supply Chains', 2015.

China Chamber of Commerce of Metals, Minerals & Chemicals Importers & Exporters (CCMCC), 'Guidelines for Social Responsibility in Outbound Mining Investments', 2014.

China Labour Bulletin, 'Zhejiang Shoe Factory Collapse Kills At least 12 Workers, Injures 33 Others', 6 July 2015.

Deva, Surya, 'Access to Justice: Human Rights Abuses Involving Corporations – The People's Republic of China', International Commission of Jurists, 2010.

'Draft Report on the Third Session of the Open-Ended Intergovernmental Working Group on Transnational Corporations and Other Business Enterprises with Respect to Human Rights', 23–27 October 2017.

Global Business Initiative on Human Rights, Global Compact Network China, Institute for Human Rights and Business, Peking University and Tracktwo, 'The China Responsible Business Forum, Corporate Responsibility in the Era of the UN Guiding Principles', 2014.

Grimheden, Jonas, 'Themis v. Xiezhi: Assessing Judicial Independence in the People's Republic of China Under International Human Rights Law', Ph.D Thesis, Lund: University of Lund, 2004.

Human Rights Watch, 'Country Summary: China', January 2014, https://www.hrw.org/world-report/2014/country-chapters/china-and-tibet (last accessed 19 January 2018).

Igesund, Solveig Marie, 'Promoting Business and Human Rights in China', Norwegian Human Rights Centre, 13 May 2015.

Lihui, Sun, Interview, 2016, 'Business and Human Rights Forum', 15 November 2016.

Lihui, Sun, Presentation, 2017, 'Business and Human Rights Forum', 28 November 2017.

Lakner, Christoph and Milanovic, Branko, 'Global Income Distribution: From the Fall of the Berlin Wall to the Great Recession', (The World Bank Development

Research Group Poverty and Inequality Team) Policy Research Working Paper 6719, 2013.
'Maastricht Principles on Extraterritorial Obligations of States in the area of Economic, Social and Cultural Rights', (adopted in 2011).
Matisoff, Adina, 'Going Beyond Compliance to Mitigate Risks: CNPC's Engagement with Indigenous Federations in Peru', *in* Tao Hu and Yiting Wang (eds.), *Environmental and Social Risk Management of Chinese Transnational Corporations*, Washington: Yale and WWF Workshop, 2014.
Muller, Wim, 'Beyond History and Sovereignty: China and the Future of International Law', Ph.D Thesis, Florence: European University Institute, 2013.
Paul, Delia, 'China Releases National Plan to Implement SDGs', IISD/SDG Knowledge Hub, 17 October 2016.
Richardson, Sophie, 'China: Quashing Criticism at Home and Abroad, Human Rights Watch', Oxford University China Africa Network (Blog), 27 May 2014.
State-owned Assets Supervision and Administration Commission of the State Council (SASAC) of the People's Republic of China, 'Guidelines to the State-owned Enterprises Directly under the Central Government on Fulfilling Corporate Social Responsibilities', 2008.
Statista, 'Gini Coefficient in China: Inequality of Income Distribution in China from 2005 to 2016'.
Supreme People's Court of the People's Republic of China, 'Judicial News – China's Top Legislature Decides to Remove Milk Scandal Official from Deputy Post', Beijing, 27 June 2009.
The State Council of the People's Republic of China, 'National Human Rights Action Plan of China (2016–2020)', August 2016.
Tracktwo, 'CSR Training Programme for Chinese Central State-owned Enterprises', October 2014.
UN, Human Development Indicators 2016, China, http://hdr.undp.org/en/countries/profiles/CHN (last accessed 19 January 2018).
World Bank in China, Overview, updated 28 March 2017.
Xiaohui, Liang at the meeting: Global Business Initiative, 'Business Executives Conference – Sustainable Business and Investment in the Global Context: Rights, Risks and Responsibilities', Beijing, 16 April 2013.

10 Corporate accountability concerning socio-economic rights in Colombia

Introduction 247
Business, human rights and socio-economic environment in Colombia 249
Business and socio-economic environment 249
Business and socio-economic rights in Colombia 251
Colombian transitional justice process and the role of corporations 252
Access to justice in Colombia 255
Enforcing cases against corporations doing business in Colombia in foreign courts 256
Enforcing cases against corporations doing business in Colombia in domestic courts 259
The Colombian Constitutional Court, socio-economic rights and corporations 259
Colombian ordinary courts 262
The Inter-American Human Rights System 263
The Colombian Peace Accord and how to move forward in business and human rights in Colombia? 267
Conclusion 270

Introduction

This chapter studies how far corporate accountability for socio-economic rights extends in Colombia. The Colombian government has been more or less committed to business and human rights.[1] Therefore, the field has been advancing more progressively than in other countries in the region. However, the Colombian's government public policies have so far included only voluntary initiatives. They have not aimed to effectively address the responsibility of alleged perpetrators and to improve the rights of the victims. Colombia has been chosen as a

1 Lina M. Céspedes Báez and Angélica María Gutiérrez, 'La Responsabilidad Civil por Actividades Peligrosas: una Forma de Establecer el Nexo entre Personas Jurídicas Privadas y Violaciones de Derechos Humanos en Colombia', 125 *Vniversitas* 149 (2012).

case study of this book due to the many socio-economic challenges and violations involving domestic and foreign corporate actors, and due to the immersive inequality in the provision of socio-economic rights. Colombia has suffered from the widening socio-economic inequality, deriving also from various indicators.[2] Whereas few fortunate individuals and families have enjoyed the highest levels of socio-economic rights, the majority of the population has on a daily basis encountered difficulties in satisfying their socio-economic needs in order to develop their capabilities.[3]

Violations of some socio-economic rights have been especially large in number.[4] Businesses in Colombia have so far indirectly contributed to the violations of several socio-economic rights.[5] Several hundred thousand individuals have been forcibly displaced during the civil war, thereby foregoing their right to housing and decreasing their access to other socio-economic rights such the right to food, water, health and education, as most of them had to move to vulnerable suburbs of large urban cities such as Bogotá and Medellín.[6] OHCHR observers witnessed a "disparity in enjoyment of economic, social and cultural rights between rural and urban areas and within urban areas" and that the following socio-economic issues affect rural areas:

> limited local State presence and capacity; ineffective national-local coordination; armed conflict; limited access to justice; corruption; insufficient integration of rights into public policy planning, implementation and evaluation; insufficient measurement of progressive realization; and limited accountability.[7]

Such features have contributed to the several challenges to guarantee socio-economic rights on different levels. This chapter argues that both government and businesses are obliged to work to increase the level of the provisions of socio-economic rights, thereby also improving victims' (both individuals and

2 Carlos Alberto López Cadena, 'Pobreza y Derechos en Colombia', 24 *Revista Derecho del Estado* 9 (2010). See also, Jernej Letnar Černič, *Nevidne reči*, Ljubljana: IDH (2016).

3 Silvia Blanco, 'La Desigualdad Social Lastra el Crecimiento Económico de Colombia', Bogotá: El País, 29 May 2014.

4 Felipe Gómez Isa, 'Justicia, Verdad y Reparación en el Proceso de Paz en Colombia', 33 *Revista Derecho del Estado* 35 (2014).

5 Felipe Alejandro Galvis Castro, 'Activismo Judicial y Emancipación Social: Notas a Partir de la Justiciabilidad de los Derechos Económicos, Sociales y Culturales en Colombia y Argentina', http://biblioteca.clacso.edu.ar/ar/libros/becas/2007/cultura/galvis.pdf (last accessed 19 January 2018).

6 Beatriz Eugenia Sánchez Mojica, 'A City Torn Apart: Forced Displacement in Medellin, Colombia', 1(22) *Colombia International Law: Revista Colombiana de Derecho Internacional* 179 (2013). Felipe Gómez Isa, 'El Desplazamiento Forzado de los Pueblos Indígenas en Colombia', 30 *Anuario Español* de Derecho Internacional 431 (2014).

7 UN, Human Rights Council, 'Annual Report of the United Nations High Commissioner for Human Rights on the situation of human rights in Colombia', UN Doc. A/HRC/34/3/Add.3, 23 March 2017, para 46.

Indigenous peoples) access to justice. The UN Human Rights Committee in 2016 observed that

> the State party should continue and intensify its efforts to prevent violations of Covenant rights and to give effect to the rights of victims of the armed conflict to truth, justice and full reparation. It should, in particular, ensure that: . . . perpetrators of such violations are brought to justice and held accountable for their acts.[8]

Apart from the Constitutional Court, few ordinary Colombian courts have emphasized the accountability of corporations for socio-economic rights violations.

Corporate accountability for socio-economic rights in Colombia is important from at least two perspectives. First, it is seminal to remedy the violations by corporate actors and compensate suffering incurred by victims and bring perpetrators to accountability. Second, it is essential to send clear language of binding obligations and accountability to potential domestic and foreign investors which would want to invest in previously inaccessible territories rich in natural resources and controlled by guerrilla groups and paramilitaries, which would presumably be opened for foreign investments. This chapter therefore proceeds in five subsections which dissect the functioning of the business and socio-economic environment in Colombia. The second section describes and analyzes the business, human rights and socio-economic environment in Colombia, whereas the third section studies the Colombian transitional justice process and the role of corporations. The fourth section examines access to justice in Colombia by: first, analyzing enforcement of cases against corporations doing business in Colombia in foreign courts; second, dissecting enforcement cases against corporations doing business in Colombia in domestic courts; and third, studying the Inter-American Human Rights System. Finally, the fifth section presents and analyzes the Colombian Peace Accord and how to move forward with corporate accountability for socio-economic rights in Colombia.

Business, human rights and socio-economic environment in Colombia

Business and socio-economic environment

Colombia has been, despite the armed conflict, a front-runner in South America in attracting foreign investment and persuading foreign corporations to invest.[9] Its government has been among the few governments that have promoted liberal regulation of the market economy without any severe government

8 UN, Human Rights Committee, 'Concluding observations: Colombia', UN Doc. CCPR/C/COL/CO/7, 17 November 2016, para 9.

9 World Bank, 'Global Economic Prospects – Forecasts – Colombia'. See also, Mauricio Romero Vidal (ed.), *La Economía* de los Paramilitares: Redes de Corrupción, Negocios y Política, Bogotá: Debate (2011).

interference. Such liberal policies have attracted much-needed investment, jobs, and growth, and have assisted in counter-balancing the negative effects of civil war.[10] Annual economic growth has been in recent years between four and six percentage points.[11] However, only about 40% of the population has also been engaged in formal employment, as all others work in the various forms of the informal economy.[12] Further, there exist exceptional natural resources in its territory, ranging from various minerals to water resources. Therefore, Colombia should not have too much difficulty in ensuring a dignified living standard for its population. However, most Colombian cities and villages show a diametrically opposite picture from favourable economic indicators. In 2014, the Gini coefficient, measuring the level of social inequality, in Colombia was 0.535,[13] making it one of the most unequal societies in the world. As far as the UN Human Development Index goes, it is ranked 97th.[14]

One can attribute responsibility for the existing situation in the Colombian society to the armed conflict which ended only recently and went on for five decades continuously between different actors, especially in rural areas. More specifically, the armed conflict took place mostly between the Colombian military, the left-wing guerrillas, the right-wing paramilitaries and organized criminal groups involved in the production of illicit substances. Additionally, the armed conflict also brought together a number of domestic and transnational corporations. It caused a loss of over two hundred thousand lives, mostly civilians, and displaced almost six million rural residents.[15] A 2013 report by the Colombian Center for Historical Memory entitled "Enough!" ("Basta ya!") has clearly and accurately described the scale of systematic human rights violations since 1958.[16] Several millions had to leave their local rural environments due to daily violence and systematic violations, and seek refuge in the outskirts of large cities where extreme poverty and inequality prevail. Several decades of the armed conflict have not only resulted in a number of human rights violations, but they have caught society in an endless and vicious cycle of violence, impunity, inequality, and political and economic instability.[17] Several domestic

10 Carlos Alberto López Cadena, 'Pobreza y Derechos en Colombia', 24 *Revista Derecho del Estado* 9 (2010).

11 World Bank, 'Global Economic Prospects – Forecasts – Colombia', year 2015.

12 Alexandra Jolly, 'UN vs Under-employed: A Look at Colombia's Massive Informal Labor Sector', Colombia Reports, 21 May 2014, http://colombiareports.com/informal-workforce/ (last accessed 19 January 2018).

13 World Bank, 'Global Economic Prospects – Forecasts – Colombia', year 2013.

14 UN Human Development Report 2015, p. 48.

15 UNCHR, 'Global Trends 2015'.

16 Grupo de Memoria Histórica, *¡Basta ya! Colombia: Memorias de Guerra y Dignidad*, Bogotá: Imprenta Nacional (2013).

17 Isabelle Joumard and Juliana Londoño Vélez, 'Income in Equality and Poverty in Colombia. Part 1: The Role of the Labour Market', OECD Economics Department Working Papers No. 1036 (2013); Isabelle Joumard and Juliana Londoño Vélez, 'Income in Equality and Poverty in Colombia. Part 2: The Redistributive Impact of Taxes and Transfers', OECD Economics Department Working Papers No. 1037 (2013).

and foreign transnational corporations have also operated in Colombia during the armed conflict. Most of them exploited natural resources in rural areas and have been often accused of being complicit in the systematic violation of human rights, including socio-economic rights of the local population, especially of Indigenous peoples. These peoples have opposed the arrival of foreign corporations on their ancient territory, but mostly in vain. In some regions, organized criminal organizations have taken over all democratic and the rule-of-law institutions, including the judiciary. The democratic institutions have in this way become completely paralyzed.

Business and socio-economic rights in Colombia

Latin America has been generally slow to take up recent development in business and human rights. The UN Working Group has rightly observed that

> the region needs jobs as well as social and economic inclusiveness. The UN Guiding Principles provide a solid platform to align business activities with human rights and sustainable development. Latin American culture has never questioned human rights. The region has a unique opportunity to become a champion on business and human rights, bolster its competitiveness in the global market and respond to social needs.[18]

The constitution of Colombia, which applies to natural and legal persons, includes several provisions on fundamental rights[19] and socio-economic rights,[20] whereas some socio-economic provisions such as the right to education,[21] health[22] and social security[23] directly bind private actors. Further, its domestic legal system provides vaguely for the right of Indigenous peoples to free, prior and informed consent which protects the socio-economic livelihood of Indigenous peoples, as Decree 1320 of 1998 "provides for consultation with indigenous and black communities, prior to the exploitation of renewable natural resources in the areas they inhabit".[24]

Colombia has been, nonetheless, one of the frontrunners in adopting National Action Plans. It adopted its National Action Plan under the UN Guiding Principles on Human Rights and Business[25] as one of the first states outside Europe. Its

18 Regional Forum in Medellín, 'The Impact of Businesses on Human Rights in Latin American and the Caribbean – First Regional Debate', 26 August 2013.

19 Constitution of Colombia (Constitución Política de Colombia, 1991), chapter 1.

20 Ibid., chapter 2.

21 Ibid., art. 69.

22 Ibid., art. 49.

23 Ibid., art. 48.

24 Decree 1320 of 1998, Diario Oficial No 43.340, 15 July 1998, Article 2.

25 Gobierno de Colombia, Plan Nacional de Acción sobre Derechos Humanos y Empresas, 2015. See also, The Office of the Presidential Advisor for Human Rights of the Republic of Colombia, 'National Action Plan on Human Rights and Business, Report on advancements

National Action Plan reflects the divisive content of the UN Guiding Principles. It has a main objective of "guaranteeing that state of Colombia adequately protects human rights and that business activities respect human rights and contribute to the sustainable development of the country".[26] In this way, the Colombian government has set the following priorities in business and human rights: "It will generate a culture of human rights and peace building in the business sector"; "It will promote and guide the implementation of due diligence mechanisms"; "It will generate incentives in both large, medium, small and micro entrepreneurs so that human rights become a competitive advantage"; and "It will coordinate the actions of Corporate Social Responsibility (CSR) to generate greater impact, by proposing an agenda in which human rights are the common conceptual framework for the alliance between the State and the private sector".[27] However, as highlighted by various NGOs, more emphasis should be placed on effective supervision and implementation of the National Action Plan.[28] Moreover, CESCR recently noted "that the Plan does not incorporate appropriate measures clearly establishing the principle of human rights due diligence in order to identify, prevent and mitigate the risk of violation of Covenant rights".[29] One of the objections against Colombia's state policy on business and human rights has been that it favours voluntary initiatives and disregards binding. Nonetheless, Mrs Gaviria Betancur, a human rights commissioner of Colombia, argued in a 2016 UN Business and Human Rights Forum that the private sector should and will be held accountable for human rights violations in Colombia.[30] However, it seems that more coherent efforts are required in Colombia to prosecute and remedy business and human rights–related abuses and to address the increasing gap between top-down and bottom-up approaches to business and human rights.

Colombian transitional justice process and the role of corporations

The Colombian congress adopted in July 2012 the legal framework for peace ("El marco jurídico para la paz"), which provides in Article 1 that the government will "ensure at the highest possible level, the rights of victims to truth, justice and reparation".[31] It is notable that the legal framework establishes

in implementation', May 2017, http://www.derechoshumanos.gov.co/observatorio/publicaciones/Documents/2017/170602_InformeAnualEmpresa_English.pdf (last accessed 19 January 2018).

26 Ibid., p. 8.

27 Ibid., p. 17.

28 ICAR and De justicia, 'Assessment of the Colombian National Action Plan (NAP) on Business and Human Rights', September 2016, pp. 29–30.

29 UN, Committee on Economic, 'Social and Cultural Rights (CESCR), Concluding Observations: Colombia', UN Doc. E/C.12/COL/CO/6, 19 October 2017, para 12.

30 Paula Gaviria Betancur, 2016 UN Business and Human Rights Forum, Geneva, 14 November 2016.

31 Legislative Act 1/2012, Legal Framework for Peace, 31 July 2012. See also, Section 5 of this Chapter.

obligations of conduct and result, which means that the state is under direct obligation to protect the rights of victims and provide them with reparations. Such wording of the legal framework therefore leaves much to be desired and achieved. States are obliged to prosecute and punish responsible individuals for genocide, crimes against humanity and war crimes. Some commentators have argued that the state can narrow such obligations during transition periods if they introduce objective, equitable and fair criteria.[32] However, there are several disagreements as to how far such an obligation reaches. In contrast such policies can turn into *de facto* amnesties for those responsible. It has been generally accepted in international law that amnesties for genocide, crimes and war crimes are not acceptable or allowed. For crimes of lesser gravity amnesties may be employed under strict conditions. The same applies for the companies and their directors and employees who have been reported to be involved in the crimes.

Such an approach in the legal framework also makes it difficult for cases not only against individuals responsible but also against corporations to succeed. However, as Uprimny argues,

> the pardon of the perpetrators is only justifiable when it constitutes the only existing measure to achieve peace and reconciliation and when it is proportional to the seriousness of the acts committed by the accused and the contributions made by justice.[33]

However, peace cannot justify impunity for the commission of or complicity in grave crimes. Accordingly, the Constitutional Court of Colombia argued in its seminal decision C-370/2006 that

> peace does not justify everything. The value of peace cannot be given absolute scope, since it is also necessary to guarantee the materialization of the essential content of the value of justice and the right of the victims to justice, as well as the other rights of the victims.[34]

The Colombian Constitutional Court therefore tried to develop some minimum criteria where the state would be absolved from prosecutions:

> (i) transparency of the selection and prioritization process; (ii) a serious, impartial, effective investigation, carried out within a reasonable time and with its participation; (iii) the existence of an appeal to contest the decision on the selection and prioritization of his case; (iv) specialized advice; (v) the

32 See, Ibid., 2.

33 Rodrigo Uprimny Yepes, 'Las Enseñanzas del Análisis Comparado: Procesos Transicionales, Formas de Justicia Transicional y el Caso Colombiano', *in* Catalina Botero Marino, María Saffon Sanín and Rodrigo Uprimny Yepes (eds.), *¿Justicia Transicional sin Transición? Verdad, Justicia y Reparación para Colombia*, Bogotá: DeJusticia (2006), pp. 17–44, p. 28.

34 Judgment C-370/06 (Constitutional Court of Colombia), 18 May 2006, para 5.5.

> right to truth, so that when a case has not been selected or prioritized, it is guaranteed through non-criminal and extrajudicial judicial mechanisms; (vi) the right to integral reparation and; (vii) the right to know where the remains of their relatives are located.[35]

Those criteria appear to be reasonable, particularly points (iv), (v) and (vii), which give the victims the right to full compensation and, most importantly, the right to know where the remains of their relatives are located and the guarantee of non-criminal and extra-judicial mechanisms. If proposed measures cannot be guaranteed, the state amnesties turn null and void.[36] The Court noted that there should be priority in prosecuting crimes against humanity, genocide and war crimes. It seems the violations were pragmatically chosen by the Colombian Constitutional Court; nonetheless the list appears to include mostly international crimes. Even so, the list also includes a number of crimes in which corporations have been allegedly involved such as extrajudicial executions, torture, forced disappearances, war crimes and crimes against humanity. Do socio-economic rights also fall under the most heinous crimes? They could at least indirectly fall in this category. Nonetheless, such a closed-ended list may be explained by the complexity of transitional justice contexts in Colombia. Some authors describe such an approach as a "minimalist model" in contrast with a "maximalist model".[37] It is not clear that such an approach is pursuing the interest of justice, but may be only possible in a transitional context. However, the Court's reasoning has not stopped here, as it moved from subject-matter jurisdiction to individual criminal responsibility, which can be by analogy also relevant for corporations.

The Court noted that

> the concentration of responsibility on top officials does not imply that all lesser crimes against humanity, genocide and war crimes committed in a systematic manner are not investigated but would allowed to be imputed only to those who played an essential role in their commission.[38]

It defined the most responsible person as the

> that person who has an essential role in the criminal organization for the commission of each crime, that is to say, that it has: directed, controlled or financed the commission of crimes against humanity, genocide and war crimes committed in a systematic manner.[39]

35 Judgment C-579-13 (Constitutional Court of Colombia), 28 August 2013, para 9.9.1.
36 See also, ibid., para 9.9.4.
37 Diana María Salcedo López, 'Género, Derechos de las Víctimas y Justicia Transicional: Retos en Colombia', 6 *Revista de Paz y Conflictos* 124 (2013).
38 Judgment C-579-13, para 9.6.
39 Ibid., para 8.2.3.

Some commentators note that such definition of persons responsible does not leave much room for impunity for the most atrocious crimes.[40] However, such a position is debatable. Do directors and employees of transnational corporations and their subsidiaries fall in this category? It would be difficult to advance such an argument as the previous cases and examples show that in most cases they are alleged that they have been "only" complicit in the commission of crimes together with paramilitary groups. It would have to be clarified whether the category of "most responsible" includes not only direct commission of the most atrocious crimes but also of direct and indirect participation in the most atrocious crimes.

One can argue that the prosecution of the most atrocious crimes must also be advanced against transnational corporations, subsidiaries and people behind the veil provided that there exists probable cause for such actions. Prosecutions of transnational corporations in Colombia may open the doors for justice to be delivered for individuals who have suffered the most. Particularly, as the financial and economic actors are ones which are most important for sustaining the regimes and groups that systematically violate human rights, a transitional justice process in Colombia needs to ensure that individuals have the right to be heard and finally get compensated for the rights violated, including by or involving transnational corporations and their subsidiaries. If the contrary practice prevails, this would amount to informal amnesty. However, domestic prosecutions face many difficult challenges. First, it may appear that the Colombian courts apply higher standards than those applied in similar criminal cases. Second, it appears that much rests on the political will of those in power, in spite of the insistence of the international community that there can be no lasting peace without justice. There will always be those who argue that prosecutions are a hindrance to, rather than a foundation for, reconciliation between different groups in society. However, the answer might be that both peace and justice are possible and necessary; the question is not *if* but *when* justice should be pursued.

Access to justice in Colombia

This section studies victims' access to the judiciary when enforcing cases concerning socio-economic against corporations doing business in Colombia. Access to the judiciary and its fairness, transparency, independence and impartiality are still problematic in the Colombian judiciary.[41] It is not surprising

40 Felipe Gómez Isa, 'Justicia, Verdad y Reparación en el Proceso de Paz en Colombia'.

41 See for example, Luis Antonio Restrepo Arango, Proceso Histórico de los Derechos Humanos en Colombia, Medellín: Ediciones Unaula (2nd Edition, 2011); Ingrid Betancourt, *No Silence Has an End*, New York: Penguin (2010); Jorge Cardona, *Diario del Conflicto: de las Delicias a la Habana (1996–2013)*, Bogotá: Ediciones Uniandes – Random House Mondadori (2013); Nicolás Gómez Dávila, *Escolios a un Texto Implícito*, Bogotá: Villegas Editores (2001); Rafael Guarín, *Paz Justa: En Contra de la Impunidad y a Favor de las Víctimas, la Justicia y la Paz*, Bogotá: Corporación Pensamiento Siglo XXI – Konrad Adenauer Stiftung (2012).

that it is still struggling and it is faced with countless hurdles to bringing justice to victims of human rights violations. However, it is still noticeable that most allegations concerning human rights, including socio-economic rights against corporations, involve foreign corporations. Some claim the contrary; however we were not able to find several substantial cases against corporations before the Colombian courts. The Inter-American Human Rights Commission recently at a public hearing discussed the alleged arbitrary practices of Canadian corporations in Latin America.[42] The discussion illustrated several human rights problems of Canadian extractive companies in doing business in Latin America.[43] This section therefore first examines selected cases against corporations alleged of human rights violations in foreign courts, mostly before US courts under the Aliens Tort Statute. Thereafter, it analyzes enforcing corporate accountability in Colombian domestic courts, and finally it examines some cases before the Inter-American Commission and the Inter-American Court of Human Rights.

Enforcing cases against corporations doing business in Colombia in foreign courts

The Business and Human Rights Resource Centre lists eight lawsuits against the multinational corporations BP, Chiquita, Coca Cola, Drummond, DynCorp, Nestlé and Occidental for alleged human rights violations in Colombia.[44] Most of those cases relate to complicity in abuses of the right to life and cases of forced disappearances; however they indirectly also concern socio-economic rights of individuals and Indigenous peoples.

First, let us consider the case against Chiquita Brands Inc. concerning its alleged complicity in human rights violations during the armed conflict in Colombia.[45] Victims have brought several actions alleging that the corporation has been involved in human rights violations, including of socio-economic rights of the local population.[46] Most of the claims have been brought before the courts in the United States.[47] What is telling is that one criminal complaint was settled in 2007 by Chiquita admitting "that it made payments from 1997 to 2004 to the United Self-Defences Forces of Colombia" and "agreed to pay a $25 million

42 Comisión Interamericana de Derechos Humanos (CIDH), Public Hearing, 153 Period of Sessions, 28 October 2014. See, CIDH, 'Canadá: Impacto de empresas mineras canadienses en A. Latina', www.youtube.com/watch?v=OWYue8FP9ZY (last accessed 19 January 2018).

43 Ibid.

44 Business and Human Rights Resource Centre, Corporate Legal Accountability.

45 Chiquita, www.chiquita.com (last accessed 19 January 2018). See also, Jernej Letnar Černič, 'Corporate Responsibility for Human Rights: Towards a Pluralist Approach', *in* Wouter Vandenhole (ed.), *Challenging Territoriality in Human Rights Law: Building Blocks for a Plural and Diverse Duty-Bearer Regime*, Abingdon: Routledge (2015), pp. 69–89.

46 See, Business and Human Rights Resource Centre, 'Chiquita Lawsuits (re Colombia)'.

47 Ibid.

fine".[48] Another complaint submitted that the corporation "throughout the late 1980s to the mid-1990s" aided "terrorist organizations in Colombia in their campaign of terror against the civilian population of the Urabá region, in order to maintain its profitable control of Colombia's banana growing region. Plaintiffs are family members".[49] The complaint has further claimed that "Chiquita funded, armed and otherwise supported the FARC" and was involved in "serious human rights violations".[50] The US District Court allowed the plaintiffs in 2016 to continue with the class action under the Torture Victim Protection Act.[51] Victims and their relatives have in May 2017 also brought complaint against responsible executives of Chiquita to the prosecutor of the International Criminal Court.[52] Finally, victims have in 2007 brought another complaint under the Antiterrorism Act, whereas the US District Court recently denied Chiquita's motion for summary judgment.[53]

Second, the European Center for Constitutional and Human Rights (ECCHR) on 5 March 2012 brought against Nestlé a complaint before the court in Zug alleging its complicity in the murder of a member of a trade union, Luciano Romero, in Nestlé's Colombian subsidiary, Cicolac.[54] The complaint was dismissed in 2014, as the case was barred due to the statute of limitations.[55] The Centre also brought complaint in the same matter before the European Court of Human Rights against Switzerland, alleging that it breached its procedural obligations under the right to life (Article 2) and the right to an effective remedy (Article 13) of the European Convention for the Protection of Human Rights and Fundamental Freedoms.[56] The European Court of Human Rights declared in 2015 that the complaint as inadmissible due to the non-exhaustion of domestic remedies.[57]

Third, another claim against the transnational corporations was brought in July 2001 against two subsidiaries of Coca Cola – Bebidas y Alimentos and Pan-American Beverages, Inc. (Panamco) – before the US federal court. It alleged that "the companies hired, contracted with or otherwise directed paramilitary security forces that murdered and tortured the leaders of Sinaltrainal (which represents workers at the bottlers' facilities)".[58] This case falls in the category

48 Ibid.
49 Does 1 through 254 v Chiquita Brands International Inc, 17 March 2011, para 1.
50 Ibid.
51 See, Business and Human Rights Resource Centre, 'Chiquita Lawsuits (re Colombia)'.
52 FIDH, 'Human Rights Coalition Calls on ICC to Investigate Role of Chiquita Executives in Contributing to Crimes Against Humanity', 18 May 2017.
53 Case No. 08-M -01916- 3 January 2018. (United States District Court, Southern District of Florida).
54 See, Business and Human Rights Resource Centre, 'Chiquita Lawsuits (re Colombia)'.
55 Ibid.
56 European Center for Constitutional and Human Rights (ECCHR), 'Nestlé precedent case: Murder of trade unionist Romero in Colombia', 18 December 2014.
57 See, Business and Human Rights Resource Centre, 'Chiquita Lawsuits (re Colombia)'.
58 Ibid.

of cases against transnational corporations conducting business operations in Colombia for violations of the physical integrity of trade union leaders. The US Court of Appeals for the Eleventh Circuit on 11 August 2009 confirmed the dismissal of the claim and it concluded that "the war crimes exception to the state action requirement is not applicable to the plaintiffs because the alleged murder and torture was not committed in the course of a civil war".[59] Such reasoning may be US specific; however, in a wider human rights context, it is not very acceptable. It is not very clear why US courts often lose themselves in the explanation of whether the "state action" exception was applicable or not. It would be more advisable for the courts to employ human rights terminology and hear complaints.

Most of the cases against corporations that have been brought against the subsidiaries of transnational corporations have been registered under Colombian law. That opens the questions: Do transnational corporations have positive human rights obligations in a global business environment? What are obligations of the parent company to protect socio-economic rights within corporate groups?[60] Accordingly, its secretary-general, José Rafael Unda, expressed his preferences towards a voluntary approach to business and human rights.[61] He emphasized that access to justice for victims should be improved, but not only in business and human rights, as the Colombian justice system is generally very weak and non-effective.[62] He is not aware of any cases against Colombian companies; however there are many previous consultations procedures involving Indigenous communities.[63]

Accordingly, CESCR recommended in its 2016 "Concluding Observations on Canada" that "that the State party strengthen its legislation governing the conduct of corporations registered or domiciled in the State party in their activities abroad, including by requiring those corporations to conduct human rights impact assessments prior to making investment decisions"[64] and that "the State party introduce effective mechanisms to investigate complaints filed against those corporations and adopt the legislative measures necessary to facilitate access to justice before domestic courts by victims of the conduct of those corporations".[65] The access to justice in Colombia is very much connected to the wider transitional justice processes. There have been allegations that several Colombian and transnational corporations have been for decades cooperating with the paramilitaries either voluntarily or forcibly. In this way, it is alleged that they have been

59 Case No. 06-15851, D. C. Docket No. 01-03208-CV-JEM (United States Court of Appeal), 11 August 2009, p. 26.
60 See, Chapter 5.
61 Interview with José Rafael Unda, Bogota, 7 February 2014.
62 Ibid.
63 Ibid.
64 UN, CESCR, Concluding observations: Canada, UN Doc. E/C.12/CAN/CO/6, 23 March 2016, para 16.
65 Ibid.

also involved in several systematic human violations, including complicity in war crimes, crimes against humanity and displacements. The number of victims of the armed conflict has been staggering and can now be found closer to seven million victims. States have a clear legal obligation under both treaty and customary international law to investigate and prosecute grave breaches of the Geneva Conventions (and Additional Protocol I) and other serious violations of international humanitarian law.[66] Equally, there is a state obligation to provide reparations for war crimes and crimes against humanity, as well as to ensure the right to an adequate remedy under human rights law.[67]

Enforcing cases against corporations doing business in Colombia in domestic courts

The Colombian Constitutional Court, socio-economic rights and corporations

The Colombian Constitutional Court has been famed in comparative practice as one of the most creative of the highest domestic constitutional courts. Its decisions have been particularly impressive in the field of socio-economic rights, as the Colombian everyday life illustrates the necessity for their effective management and provision.[68] The Constitution of Colombia provides in the first paragraph of Article 86 that everyone can bring before the ordinary courts a constitutional complaint (tutela) in order to protect their rights against acts or omissions of public authorities. The right to bring a constitutional complaint for alleged human rights violations has almost been completely democratized in the absence of strict procedural rules. In practice, however, access to the Constitutional Court is still ineffective for the most vulnerable groups, which have been often paralyzed in the protection of their rights due to their social exclusion. Notably, it is difficult and almost impossible only through the use of tutela to combat systemic and structural obstacles to the protection of socio-economic rights.[69]

66 See, Geneva Convention I (GCI), 12 August 1949, art. 49; Geneva Convention II (GCII), 12 August 1949, art. 50; Geneva Convention III (GCIII), 12 August 1949, art. 129; Geneva Convention IV (GCIV), 12 August 1949, art. 146; Additional Protocol I (API), 8 June 1977, arts 11 and 85.

67 See, Hague Convention IV, 18 October 1907, art. 3; GCI, art. 51; GCII, art. 52; GCIII, art. 131; GCIV, art. 148; API, art. 91. See also, Dinah Shelton, *Remedies in International Human Rights Law*, Oxford: Oxford University Press (3rd Edition, 2005).

68 Rodrigo Uprimny Yepes and Mauricio García Villegas, 'Corte Constitucional y Emancipacion Social en Colombia', *in* Boaventura de Sousa Santos and Mauricio Garcia Villegas (eds.), *Emancipacion Social y Violencia en Colombia*, Bogotá: Grupo Editorial Norma (2004), pp. 255–288.

69 Hernán Alejandro Olano García, 'El cumplimiento de los fallos de tutela de la corte constitucional colombiana', 2(1) *Estudios Constitucionales* 255 (2004).

The Colombian Constitutional Court receives annually from five hundred to a thousand tutelas.[70] It has also reaffirmed in several cases the necessity of protections of human dignity of vulnerable groups.[71] The role of the Constitutional Court has been, in its opinion, to protect the rights of the most vulnerable groups in society and enable them to equal participation in society.[72] The Court has so far in its jurisprudences protected several socio-economic rights,[73] including the right to health,[74] adequate housing,[75] social security[76] and water,[77] including against private providers of such rights.[78] Further, the Constitutional Court has been particularly effective in enforcing the right to prior, free and informed consent.[79] More specifically, it has suspended mining "in certain areas of high altitude ecosystems".[80] Further, the Colombian Constitutional Court noted concerning the right of Indigenous peoples to free, prior and informed consent that

> it is necessary . . . that formulas for concerted action or agreement with the community are put forward and, finally, that the community declares, through their authorized representatives, either their consent or their dissatisfaction in relation with the project and the way in which their ethnic, cultural, social and economic identity is affected.[81]

70 Constitutional Court of Colombia, Statistics 2015.

71 Judgment T-016/07 (Constitutional Court of Colombia), 22 January 2007. See also, Daniel Felipe Riveros Pardo, 'Los Derechos Económicos, Sociales y Culturales Como Derechos Subjetivos: Una Visión Estructural', 24 *Revista Derecho del Estado* 29 (2010).

72 Interview with judge Jorge Ivan Palacio Palacio, Bogota, February 2014. Liliana Carrera Silva, 'La Acción de Tutela en Colombia', V(27) *Revista IUS* 72 (2011).

73 Julieta Lemaitre, 'El Coronel sí tiene quien le Escriba: la Tutela por Mínimo Vital en Colombia', *SELA (Seminario en Latinoamérica de Teoría Constitucional y Política) Papers* 43 (2005).

74 Judgment T-859/03 (Constitutional Court of Colombia), 25 September 2003. See also, Judgment T-760/08 (Constitutional Court of Colombia), 31 July 2008.

75 Judgment T-423/92 (Constitutional Court of Colombia), 24 June 1992; Judgment T-495/10 (Constitutional Court of Colombia), 16 June 2010; Judgment T-375/17 (Constitutional Court of Colombia), 9 June 2017.

76 Judgment T-615/02 (Constitutional Court of Colombia), 8 August 2002.

77 Judgment T-406/92 (Constitutional Court of Colombia), 5 June 1992.

78 Judgment T-495/10 (Constitutional Court of Colombia), 16 June 2010; Judgment T-375/17 (Constitutional Court of Colombia), 9 June 2017.

79 See for example, María Mónica Monsalve S., 'La Consulta Previa que les Llegó a los Nasas Diez Años Tarde', *El Espectador*, 10 September 2017.

80 Luis E. Juvinao Navarro, 'Judicial Activism, the De Facto Regulator of Colombian Mining', *Global Risk Insights*, 17 May 2016.

81 Judgment SU-039/97 (Constitutional Court of Colombia), 21 February 1997, para 3.3., translated in Roque Roldán Ortega, *Indigenous Peoples of Colombia and the Law: A Critical Approach to the Study of Past and Present Situations*, London: Gaia Foundation; Bogotá: COAMA; San José: ILO, (2000), p. 104. See for a detailed analysis, José Parra, 'The Role of Domestic Courts in International Human Rights Law: The Constitutional Court of Colombia and Free, Prior and Informed Consent', 23(3) *Journal on Minority and Group Rights* 355 (2016). See also Judgment C-035/16 (Constitutional Court of Colombia), 8 February 2016.

Therefore, the Constitutional Court has described Decree 1320 of 1998 as "contrary to the Constitution and to the standards incorporated into national legislation through Act No. 21 of 1991".[82] The Court has also emphasized that if the effective protection of civil and political rights has been necessary for the fair functioning of a democracy and the rule of law, the protection of social and economic rights is necessary to ensure a reasonable level of decent life.[83]

In its case law, the Constitutional Court has developed the doctrine of "constitutional and international standards" (el bloque de constitucionalidad), which refers to minimum constitutional and international human right obligations. In doing so, the Court has become the guardian of the rights of ordinary people.[84] The Constitutional Court often selects and jointly considers increasing number of tutelas, which illustrated the urgent structural, systematic and widespread difficulties in individuals' exercising their rights.[85] If the complaint has not achieved the status of urgency (threatening the survival of the individual), the Constitutional Court does not take it into consideration. In doing so, the Court may include the state institutions and agencies which could assist in eliminating specific problems. Tutela has been a very affordable, quick and effective means of redress.[86] The Court can thereby directly influence the design of public policies on social protection, education, health and the provision of basic essential goods. It has in its case law advised authorities on how much funding should be allocated to improve the situation in individual areas of social and economic rights. Nevertheless, the Constitutional Court is fully conscious of its role in the broader social context, which requires it to actively address the acute and systemic problems.[87] In this way, the Constitutional Court allowed individuals

82 Judgment T-652/98 (Constitutional Court of Colombia), 10 November 1998, at 4, quoted in IKV Pax Christi, 'Free, Prior and Informed Consultation in Colombia: The Case of the Expansion of the Cerrejón Project', January 2012.

83 Luis Ricardo Gómez Pinto, 'El Control Constitucional en Colombia: Sobre el Inhibicionismo de la Corte Constitucional en los 100 Años del Control de la Acción Pública', 122 *Vniversitas* 169 (2011).

84 See, Nelson Camilo Sánchez and Rodrigo Uprimny Yepes, 'Transitional Justice Without Transition? The Colombian Experience in the Implementation of Transition Measures', *in Inter-American Institute of Human Rights, Contribution of Truth, Justice, and Reparation Policies to Latin American Democracies*, San José: IIHR (2011) pp. 121–152; Rodrigo Uprimny Yepes and Mauricio García Villegas, 'Corte Constitucional y Emancipacion Social en Colombia', *in* Boaventura de Sousa Santos and Mauricio Garcia Villegas (eds.), *Emancipacion Social y Violencia en Colombia*, Bogotá: Grupo Editorial Norma (2004); Rodrigo Uprimny Yepes, 'Las Enseñanzas del Análisis Comparado: Procesos Transicionales, Formas de Justicia Transicional y el Caso Colombiano', *in* Catalina Botero Marino, María Saffon Sanín and Rodrigo Uprimny Yepes (eds.), *¿Justicia Transicional sin Transición? Verdad, Justicia y Reparación para Colombia*, Bogotá: DeJusticia (2006).

85 Catalina Botero Marino, *La Acción de Tutela en el Ordenamiento Constitucional Colombiano*, Bogotá: Escuela Judicial Rodrigo Lara Bonilla, Consejo Superior de la Judicatura (2006).

86 Constitution of Colombia, art. 86 (4).

87 Manuel José Cepeda-Espinoza, 'Social and Economic Rights and the Colombian Constitutional Court', 89 *Texas Law Review* 1699 (2011).

to bring tutela also against non-state actors in the case of business activities by expressly mentioning the UN Guiding Principles on Business and Human Rights.[88] For instance, the Court asked "the company to undertake preventative measures in relation to the possible harm that it may cause to houses that are found in the same situation as that of the applicant".[89] The Court has already earlier emphasized the possibility in the contexts where public corporations exercise their public functions.[90]

The Constitutional Court has thereby brought access to justice closer to individuals and groups living in the most vulnerable situations. It has taken up a role of active promoter of socio-economic reforms. Tutela, of course, has not been without drawbacks, as its ultimate success depends primarily on whether there are available budgetary resources for guaranteeing a certain level of socio-economic rights. The Court has taken this progressive approach to indirectly emancipate vulnerable individuals and groups and crushed some taboo topics and issues. Tutela has in recent decades completely democratized the Colombian judiciary by making it accessible and effective. The Colombian Constitutional Court occupies among the highest domestic courts a special place and performs its role in the specific situation in the country where it operates.[91] Justiciability of socio-economic rights in Colombian society also contributes to its development (both of individuals and society), but also to the protection of civil and political rights. The protection of both is the basis for the functioning of a modern democratic state based on the rule of law.

Colombian ordinary courts

Colombian ordinary courts have addressed violations mostly through criminal law lenses by prosecuting responsible individuals within corporations who are most responsible for violations. There have been quite a few successful cases of bringing those responsible to justice either on the basis of the individual or corporate responsibility. In the case of *Urapalma SA concerning oil palm business in northern Colombia*, Juzgado Quinto Penal del Circuito Especializado de Medellín, a district court in Medellín, found responsibility of over twenty employees of oil corporations connected to right-wing militia AUC for

88 Judgment T-732/16 (Constitutional Court of Colombia), 19 December 2016. See for a detailed discussion, Nicolás Carrillo-Santarelli and Carlos Arévalo-Narváez, 'The Discursive Use and Development of the Guiding Principles on Business and Human Rights in Latin America', 30 *Colombia International Law: Revista Colombiana de Derecho Internacional* 61 (2017).

89 Judgment T-732/16, decision. See also, paras 53 and 64.

90 See, Judgment T-254/93 (Constitutional Court of Colombia), 30 June 1993; Judgment T-202/12 (Constitutional Court of Colombia), 14 March 2012.

91 Antonio Barreto-Rozo and Jorge González-Jácome, 'The Colombian Constitutional Court at the Crossroads of Peace', *International Journal of Constitutional Law Blog*, 25 August 2017.

forced displacement of the members of the Afro-Colombian communities of Curvaradó and Jiguamiandó in the Department of Chocó, and thereby affecting socio-economic livelihood of those communities.[92] The Court asked for "reparation for members of the communities and the restitution of communal lands".[93] The sentence has so far not been enforced.[94] It appears that only a few cases have resulted in final judgments. However, the Attorney General's Office has created a special task group investigating corporate involvement in the armed conflict. The Pax therefore argues that "how much progress is made in holding corporate actors accountable overcoming years, both in the transitional justice system and the ordinary justice system, will largely depend on the work carried out by this group".[95] Further, CESCR observed in 2017 that Colombian authorities should "strengthen existing mechanisms to investigate complaints against companies and take effective measures to ensure victims access to effective remedies and to reparation or compensation".[96] It remains to be seen how the Special Jurisdiction for Peace will deal with cases involving corporations and their responsible persons.[97]

The Inter-American Human Rights System

The most prominent case deriving from Colombia concerning business and socio-economic rights has been the case of *Santo Domingo Massacre v Colombia.* The Santo Domingo massacre refers to one of the many grave massacres in Colombia. On 13 December 1998, the Colombian Air Force started to bombard the Santo Domingo village in Arauca. In doing so it caused the death of seventeen civilians and a further twenty-seven were injured.[98] It seems

> probable that, following the explosion, the survivors and injured were machine-gunned from a helicopter when they tried to assist the injured and to flee the village "thereby resulting" in the displacement of the population of Santo Domingo, after which the empty homes were sacked or pillaged.[99]

92 Juzgado Quinto Penal del Circuito Especializado de Medellín. Decision No. 54, Sentencia Rad. No. 201101799 de 30 de octubre de 2014. See in detail, Laura Bernal-Bermúdez, 'Urapalma case', *in PAX, Peace, Everyone's Business!* May 2017, pp. 143–149, p. 143.

93 Ibid.

94 Ibid., p. 147.

95 Ibid., p. 126.

96 UN, CESCR, 'Concluding Observations: Colombia', UN Doc. E/C.12/COL/CO/6, 19 October 2017, para 13 (c).

97 Sandra Botero, 'Colombia's Special Criminal Tribunal: Justicia Especial para la Paz', *International Journal of Constitutional Law Blog*, 15 October 2017.

98 *Santo Domingo Massacre v Colombia* (Inter-American Court of Human Rights), 30 November 2012, para 3.

99 Ibid.

This massacre would have fallen under the ambit of state obligations of Colombia had it not been for the involvement of several companies. Accordingly, the representatives of the victims alleged that crimes were committed

> with air support from the Colombian Air Force and United States personnel at the service of a foreign company, associated with security and surveillance work for a multinational company that exploited an oilfield in the area and with resources provided by another company, under a contractual relationship with State institutions.[100]

The companies involved in the massacre were Occidental Petroleum Corporation and Ecopetrol S.A.[101] The Inter-American Commission recommended Colombia to "conduct an impartial and exhaustive investigation within a reasonable time to prosecute and punish all those responsible for the facts; investigate the connections between State agents and the extractive company that operates in the area where the facts occurred" and "make adequate reparation", both pecuniary and non-pecuniary for the violations declared, including the establishment and dissemination of the truth about the events.[102] However, as the Court later noted, none of these steps were seen through. It called upon Colombia to "continue the administrative and judicial investigations and proceedings underway and open any more that are appropriate in order to determine the facts and responsibilities".[103] The Inter-American Court adequately further noted that:

> the Colombian State did not have an adequate legislative framework that truly developed the obligation to protect human rights in relation to the activities of multinational corporations on its territory.[104]

Eventually, the Court found that Colombia:

> is responsible for the violation of the right to life, recognized in Article 4(1) of the Convention, in relation to Article 1(1) thereof, to the detriment of the persons who died as well as the right to personal integrity, contained in Article 5(1) of the Convention, in relation to Article 1(1) of this instrument, to the detriment of the persons who were injured, as well as of the next of kin of all of them and of the right to measures of protection for children.[105] (footnotes omitted)

100 Ibid., para 5.
101 Ibid., para 55.
102 Ibid., para 135.
103 Ibid., para 297.
104 Ibid., para 185.
105 Ibid., para 247. Compare, *Kaliña and Lokono Peoples v Suriname* (Inter-American Court of Human Rights), 25 November 2015, paras 225–226. See for example, Nicolás Carrillo-Santarelli and Carlos Arévalo-Narváez, 'The Discursive Use and Development of the

It remains unclear whether the judgment was finally executed in the Colombia legal order and the victims remedied. However, the Court did not, due to the lack of jurisdiction, address the issue of the corporate responsibility of the allegedly involved companies for violations. Therefore, victims brought a case under ATS in the federal court in California against Occidental Petroleum (Oxy) and Airscan, Inc., which was contracted to provide security at the mining site.[106] The plaintiff claimed that Occidental "was complicit in extrajudicial killing, torture, crimes against humanity and war crimes".[107] Plaintiffs argued that "Occidental wields such enormous power and influence in Colombia that it would not be possible for them to obtain meaningful justice against the company in Colombia".[108] The United States District Court for the Central District in California noted that:

> The Colombian courts have shown themselves willing to vindicate Plaintiffs' legitimate claims against that country's government for its military's acts and the government has proven itself both willing and able to hold the individuals responsible for the bombing to account, as the Galvis Gelves and Romero Pradilla litigation show.[109]

Thereafter, the federal appeals court dismissed the claims, as there was no direct connection of alleged violations with US territory and on the basis of the political question doctrine.[110] The judicial process in the United States presented one of the few opportunities for the victims to obtain compensation. Reports from Colombian courts concerning this case are scattered. *El Tiempo* has reported that a court in Bogotá convicted three pilots of Colombian military forces for the death of seventeen civilians in the Santo Domingo massacre.[111] The relatives' victims were also apparently awarded USD 700,000 for the crimes committed.[112] However, this is not end of the story, as a judge in Auraca delivered in 2011 another judgment establishing responsibility of the paramilitary group FARC for crimes committed.[113] As explained previously, the Colombian courts

Guiding Principles on Business and Human Rights in Latin America', 30 *Colombia International Law: Revista Colombiana de Derecho Internacional* 61 (2017).

106 See, Business and Human Rights Resource Centre, 'Occidental lawsuit (re Colombia)'.

107 Ibid.

108 *Luis Alberto Galvis Mujica, et al., v Occidental Petroleum et al*, 3 August 2010, p. 12.

109 *Luis Alberto Galvis Mujica, et al. v Airscan Inc. and Occidental Petroleum Corporation* (United States Court for Appeals for the Ninth Circuit), D.C. No. 2:03-cv-02860- GW-JWJ, 12 November 2014, pp. 72–73.

110 See, Jonathan Stempel, 'U.S. Court Refuses to Hold Occidental Liable in Colombia Bombing', *Reuters*, 12 November 2014.

111 Redacción El Tiempo, 'Condena de 6 años a Pilotos de FAC por Caso Santo Domingo', *El Tiempo*, 22 September 2007.

112 El Colombiano, 'El Estado Tendrá que Pagar 700.000 Dólares por Caso Santo Domingo, Arauca', www.elcolombiano.com/historico/olac_condenasantodomingo_efe_ana_25052004-CVEC_AO_4264615 (last accessed 19 January 2018).

113 Juan David Laverde Palma, 'Dos Sentencias Contrarias', *El Espectador*, 21 March 2012.

have already in the past established state responsibility for the massacre in Santo Domingo. What is curious, as *El Espectador* reports, is that "the sentence of Judge Rodrigo Rodriguez Barragán was delivered on 31 January 2011, that is, almost 14 months ago and nobody appealed it?".[114] The lawyer of the three accused military pilots noted that "It was a surprise . . . we found it inadvertently; a Google search led us to the document".[115]

It seems that of different types of responsibility (state, individual and corporate), only corporate responsibility was missing in this case. No corporations or directors have ever been prosecuted for crimes committed in Santo Domingo, even though responsibility of corporations is well documented. There are seemingly several reasons for this. First, the most obvious of the reasons, is that Colombia as a country belongs to a civil law family, which means that enforcing corporate criminal liability for any kind offences is not a possibility nor it is very common. Corporations in the Colombian legal system cannot be held liable for crimes committed; only individuals within corporations can be held individually responsible for crimes committed. Second, there is reluctance against bringing cases against corporations or their employees. The government maintains a very investment-friendly environment that is very open for foreign corporations to do business and that attracts investments. Such polices can be welcomed, as they provide jobs and growth for the local economy. On the other hand, it means that the Colombian administrative and judicial authorities are very reluctant to employ any measures against foreign corporations that would be perceived by them as "hostile" or limiting investment opportunities. In such way, the government appears to prioritize transnational corporations and indirectly disregards the rights enjoyed by ordinary people.

In the case of the Santo Domingo massacre, nobody in the management of the largest corporations was prosecuted for complicity in the crimes committed. In short, the Colombian system seems to be unwilling to prosecute such abuses. Apart from the latter, the Colombian system also might not be able to proceed with such complex cases of corporate complicity which involve issues such as parent-subsidiary relationships. Judges might not be properly trained to hear such cases, nor prosecutors to bring such cases. All in all, these reasons make it that no corporation, nor its directors or employees, was criminally prosecuted for complicity in crimes committed, even though corporations were allegedly involved in their commission. Three soldiers who were convicted for throwing a cluster bomb on the village of Santo Domingo hardly were the only ones responsible for the deaths of seventeen villagers. They most likely received orders from their superiors, who were not prosecuted for crimes and who allegedly worked in closed cooperation with the security personnel of transnational corporation Unictral, whose helicopter took part in the atrocities. In other words, only "small fishes" have been prosecuted and indeed convicted, whereas the most responsible

114 Ibid.
115 Ibid.

have not been dealt with properly. However, such a conclusion cannot be only made in the context of business and human rights, as it is also possible in other areas of the judiciary and transitional justice in Colombia. Victims only rarely get their day in court, as there are, it seems, too many cases of human rights violations and injustices to be remedied. The legal framework admittedly mentions the prosecutions of those most responsible for crimes committed; however it remains to be seen if the most responsible will be indeed prosecuted and if they will include among them also those most responsible.[116] Therefore, a solution for corporate responsibility must be also found in the legal framework for corporate responsibility and the Special Jurisdiction for Peace in Colombia.

The Colombian Peace Accord and how to move forward in business and human rights in Colombia?

Post-conflict societies often have difficulties establishing judicial mechanisms after the conflict has ended for the enforcement of responsibility of the alleged perpetrators. Colombian President Juan Manuel Santos and the leader of the leftist guerrilla movement FARC-EP Rodrigo Londoño Echeverry signed on 23 September 2015 in Havana the Final Agreement to End the Armed Conflict and Build a Stable and Lasting Peace that ended armed conflict in Colombia.[117] The Agreement was in 2017 incorporated into the constitutional system of Colombia.[118] It also established a Special Jurisdiction for Peace (Acuerdo de creación de una Jurisdicción Especial para la Paz) which has jurisdiction to prosecute the alleged perpetrators from all sides of the armed conflict.[119]

The Agreement states in Section 2 that the parties are committed to the realization of victims' rights and the process of transitional justice, including the establishment of a commission for truth, coexistence, and prevention of the repetition of crimes and systematic human rights violations.[120] The agreement then in Section 3 foresees the creation of a Special Jurisdiction for Peace which will consist of two parts: the judicial departments (Salas de Justicia) and Court of

116 See also, Laura Bernal-Bermudez, 'The Power of Corporations and the Power of People: Understanding Remedy and Accountability for Human Rights Violations – Colombia 2000–2014', Thesis, Oxford: University of Oxford, 2017.

117 Government of Colombia and FARC-EP, 'Final Agreement to End the Armed Conflict and Built a Stable Lasting Peace', 24 November 2017.

118 Legislative Act No. 01, 4 April 2017.

119 Joint Communiqué # 60 regarding the Agreement for the Creation of a Special Jurisdiction for Peace (Comunicado Conjunto # 60 sobre el Acuerdo de Creación de una Jurisdicción Especial para la Paz), Havana, 23 September 2015.

120 Ibid. See also, Nicolás Carrillo-Santarelli, 'An Assessment of the Colombian-FARC "Peace Jurisdiction" Agreement', *EJIL: Talk!* 29 September 2015. See also, Fernando Sarmiento Santander (ed.), *Lecciones Para la Paz Negociada. Retrospectiva Histórica en Colombia*, Bogotá: CINEP (2011). Compare, Final Agreement to End the Armed Conflict and Build a Stable and Lasting Peace, chapter 5.1.2.

Peace (Tribunal para la Paz).[121] Their objective is to

> realize the victims' right to justice, offer truth to the Colombian society, protect victims' rights, contribute to achieving a stable and lasting peace and take decisions that offer full legal certainty to those who participated directly or indirectly in the internal armed conflict with regard to acts committed in the context of and during said conflict and which represent serious breaches of international humanitarian law and serious violations of human rights.[122]

It is encouraging that the authorities of the special jurisdiction can theoretically prosecute alleged perpetrators, both on the government side as well as on the rebel side of the armed conflict.[123] Such an arrangement is difficult to achieve in any post-conflict society. Whether the commitment will be put into practice, only time will tell.[124] For instance, the highest structures of the Colombian army have been so far strongly opposed to prosecutions of the alleged perpetrators on the government side. The agreement does not explicitly include or exclude corporations and other private actors from accountability process. However, it seems unlikely that corporations will be prosecuted before the Special Jurisdiction for Peace.[125] Perhaps some cases could centre on responsible persons within corporations for alleged violations during the civil war. Further, socio-economic rights violations could be prosecuted against private actors on the basis of "serious violations of human rights". However, in reality in seems more likely that corporate negative impacts on socio-economic rights could be prosecuted only indirectly through civil and political rights violations.

In conflict and post-conflict societies, it is difficult to agree on how to move from war to post-war regimes. All too often the actors involved request amnesties from prosecution for war crimes, crimes against humanity, genocide and systematic human rights violations. The Colombian agreement is one of the few exceptions, as its jurisdiction does not exclude the three most serious crimes. Moreover, Section 4 provides that only less severe political offences can be subject to amnesties. The agreement does not exclude only the three worst crimes from amnesty, but also other "serious crimes such as kidnapping or other serious forms of deprivation of liberty, torture, forced displacement, forced disappearances, extrajudicial executions and sexual violence".[126] All these forms of human

121 Joint Communiqué # 60 regarding the Agreement for the Creation of a Special Jurisdiction for Peace, Havana, Cuba, 23 September 2015, section 3.
122 Ibid., section 2.
123 Ibid., section 5.
124 UN, Doc. A/HRC/34/3/Add.3, para 21–30.
125 See for detailed discussion, PAX, Peace, everyone's business!, May 2017, pp. 120–139.
126 Joint Communiqué # 60 regarding the Agreement for the Creation of a Special Jurisdiction for Peace, section 4. Compare, Final Agreement to End the Armed Conflict and Build a Stable and Lasting Peace, paras 40–41 of chapter 5.1.2.

rights violations have been committed directly or indirectly by various actors in the last few decades in Colombia, including corporations, thereby making it necessary and appropriate that they also be prosecuted.

A Special Jurisdiction for Peace provides for two procedures. The first is for those alleged perpetrators who accept their responsibility and another is for those who will not accept it or who will do so at a later stage.[127] The individual responsibility of the latter will be determined in adversarial criminal proceedings.[128] In the case of voluntary recognition of criminal responsibility, the maximum penalties provided for is five to eight years of imprisonment.[129] However, if the Court finds individuals criminally responsible, the maximum penalty will be up to twenty years in prison.[130] The agreement stipulates that "the essential aim of punishment is to satisfy the rights of victims and to consolidate peace, which must pursue corrective and restorative functions of restitution".[131]

The agreement summarizes the latest developments in the field of international human rights law and international criminal law. Its content seems of higher quality and wider than those of the Legal Framework for Peace (Marco jurídico para la paz). The latter was acknowledged also by the chief prosecutor of the International Criminal Court in her statements after the signing of the agreement.[132] The Special Jurisdiction, of course, will not only prosecute the alleged perpetrators or allow for their conviction, but it will also create a symbolic collective memory in Colombian society of the atrocities committed. Of course, the path from the signing of the agreement to the establishment and initial operation of the Special Jurisdiction has already been long. The question is: Who will investigate crimes and detain the alleged perpetrators to be dealt with by jurisdiction if we know that the soldiers of the Colombian army committed a series of crimes and most of them continue to avoid any form of criminal responsibility, and that the most responsible members of the rebel groups are located deep in the Colombian rainforest? Whereas the Colombian justice system is now formally and theoretically fair, impartial and independent, the continuity of the old and the organized crime groups associated with various political stakeholders may indicate that there are structural and practical barriers to a fair trial and the rule of law. Therefore, the agreement still has a long way to go to ensure effective protection of victims' rights and the eradication of the culture of fear of Colombian society.

127 Ibid., section 6.
128 Ibid.
129 Ibid., section 7.
130 Ibid.
131 Ibid.
132 Redacción El Tiempo, 'Gobierno pide no especular en debates sobre acuerdo con las Farc', *El Tiempo*, 24 September 2015.

Conclusion

Colombia has been on a daily basis facing several challenges in guaranteeing socio-economic rights. Corporate accountability for socio-economic rights in Colombia illustrates that it is often difficult to establish a binding legal framework for socio-economic rights and thereafter to enforce violations of socio-economic and other human rights by corporate actors. Colombian authorities appear to be committed to business and human rights, including socio-economic rights, and have already adopted National Action Plans on business and human rights. Additionally, the Colombian constitutional framework for protection of socio-economic rights has been theoretically strong and the Constitutional Court of Colombia has developed rich jurisprudence on socio-economic rights, not only against the state, but also against corporations. However, its ordinary courts have so far still struggled to ensure corporate accountability for socio-economic rights, as most of the claims have been brought outside Colombia. However, the analysis illustrates how difficult it is to assert the accountability of foreign transnational corporations for the violations caused by their subsidiaries in third countries, such as Colombia. These are, as a rule, registered in the legal order where they operate, so the process of establishing relationships between parent companies and subsidiaries is complicated and time-consuming, and victims have therefore little chance of success. Relations between parent companies and subsidiaries are intentionally very diverse and very difficult to prove. All in all, Colombia has developed a multi-layered domestic framework for the advancement of business and human rights; however it needs to now put it into practice in order to more efficiently protect the socio-economic rights of ordinary people. Such a framework needs to be complemented with the robust prosecutions of corporations and businessmen who were actively involved in violations during the armed conflict. Clearly, state authorities in Colombia and corporations are obliged to work together to greater acceptance of both state and corporate obligations to guarantee socio-economic rights of individuals and Indigenous peoples.

Bibliography

Books

Betancourt, Ingrid, *No Silence Has an End*, New York: Penguin (2010).

Botero Marino, Catalina, *La Acción de Tutela en el Ordenamiento Constitucional Colombiano*, Bogotá: Escuela Judicial Rodrigo Lara Bonilla, Consejo Superior de la Judicatura (2006).

Cardona, Jorge, *Diario del Conflicto: de las Delicias a la Habana (1996–2013)*, Bogotá: Ediciones Uniandes and Random House Mondadori (2013).

Gómez Dávila, Nicolás, *Escolios a un Texto Implícito*, Bogotá: Villegas Editores (2001).

Guarín, Rafael, *Paz Justa: En Contra de la Impunidad y a Favor de las Víctimas, la Justicia y la Paz*, Bogotá: Corporación Pensamiento Siglo XXI and Konrad Adenauer Stiftung (2012).

Letnar Černič, Jernej, *Nevidne reči*, Ljubljana: IDH (2016).
Restrepo Arango, Luis Antonio, *Proceso Histórico de los Derechos Humanos en Colombia*, Medellín: Ediciones Unaula (2nd Edition, 2011).
Roldán Ortega, Roque, *Indigenous Peoples of Colombia and the Law: A Critical Approach to the Study of Past and Present Situations*, London: Gaia Foundation; Bogotá: COAMA; San José: ILO (2000).
Romero Vidal, Mauricio (ed.), *La Economía de los Paramilitares: Redes de Corrupción, Negocios y Política*, Bogotá: Debate (2011).
Shelton, Dinah, *Remedies in International Human Rights Law*, Oxford: Oxford University Press (3rd Edition, 2005).

Journal articles

Carrera Silva, Liliana, 'La Acción de Tutela en Colombia', V(27) *Revista IUS* 72 (2011).
Carrillo-Santarelli, Nicolás and Arévalo-Narváez, Carlos, 'The Discursive Use and Development of the Guiding Principles on Business and Human Rights in Latin America', 30 *Colombia International Law: Revista Colombiana de Derecho Internacional* 61 (2017).
Cepeda-Espinoza, Manuel José, 'Social and Economic Rights and the Colombian Constitutional Court', 89 *Texas Law Review* 1699 (2011).
Céspedes Báez, Lina M. and Gutiérrez, Angélica María, 'La Responsabilidad Civil por Activades Peligrosas: una Forma de Establecer el Nexo entre Personas Jurídicas Privadas y Violaciones de Derechos Humanos en Colombia', 125 *Vniversitas* 149 (2012).
Gómez Isa, Felipe, 'El Desplazamiento Forzado de los Pueblos Indígenas en Colombia', 30 *Anuario Español de Derecho Internacional* 431 (2014).
Gómez Isa, Felipe, 'Justicia, Verdad y Reparación en el Proceso de Paz en Colombia', 33 *Revista Derecho del Estado* 35 (2014).
Gómez Pinto, Luis Ricardo, 'El Control Constitucional en Colombia: Sobre el Inhibicionismo de la Corte Constitucional en los 100 Años del Control de la Acción Pública', 122 *Vniversitas* 169 (2011).
López Cadena, Carlos Alberto, 'Pobreza y Derechos en Colombia', 24 *Revista Derecho del Estado* 9 (2010).
Olano García, Hernán Alejandro, 'El cumplimiento de los fallos de tutela de la corte constitucional colombiana', 2(1) *Estudios Constitucionales* 255 (2004).
Parra, José, 'The Role of Domestic Courts in International Human Rights Law: The Constitutional Court of Colombia and Free, Prior and Informed Consent', 23(3) *Journal on Minority and Group Rights* 355 (2016).
Riveros Pardo, Daniel Felipe, 'Los Derechos Económicos, Sociales y Culturales Como Derechos Subjetivos: Una Visión Estructural', 24 *Revista Derecho del Estado* 29 (2010).
Salcedo López, Diana María, 'Género, Derechos de las Víctimas y Justicia Transicional: Retos en Colombia', 6 *Revista de Paz y Conflictos* 124 (2013).
Sánchez Mojica, Beatriz Eugenia, 'A City Torn Apart: Forced Displacement in Medellin, Colombia', 1(22) *Colombia International Law: Revista Colombiana de Derecho Internacional* 179 (2013).

Book chapters

Letnar Černič, Jernej, 'Corporate Responsibility for Human Rights: Towards a Pluralist Approach', *in* Wouter Vandenhole (ed.), *Challenging Territoriality in Human Rights Law: Building Blocks for a Plural and Diverse Duty-Bearer Regime*, Abingdon: Routledge (2015), pp. 69–89.

Sánchez, Nelson Camilo and Uprimny Yepes, Rodrigo, 'Transitional Justice Without Transition? The Colombian Experience in the Implementation of Transition Measures', *in* Inter-American Institute of Human Rights (ed.), *Contribution of Truth, Justice and Reparation Policies to Latin American Democracies*, San José: IIHR (2011), pp. 121–152.

Uprimny Yepes, Rodrigo and García Villegas, Mauricio, 'Corte Constitucional y Emancipacion Social en Colombia', *in* Boaventura de Sousa Santos and Mauricio Garcia Villegas (eds.), *Emancipacion Social y Violencia en Colombia*, Bogotá: Grupo Editorial Norma (2004), pp. 255–288.

Uprimny Yepes, Rodrigo, 'Las Enseñanzas del Análisis Comparado: Procesos Transicionales, Formas de Justicia Transicional y el Caso Colombiano', *in* Catalina Botero Marino, María Saffon Sanín and Rodrigo Uprimny Yepes (eds.), *¿Justicia Transicional sin Transición? Verdad, Justicia y Reparación para Colombia*, Bogotá: DeJusticia (2006), pp. 17–44.

Legislation

Additional Protocol I to the Geneva Conventions (API), 8 June 1977.

Constitution of Colombia (Constitución Política de Colombia, 1991).

Decree 1320 of 1998, Diario Oficial No 43.340, 15 July 1998.

Geneva Convention I (GCI), 12 August 1949.

Geneva Convention II (GCII), 12 August 1949.

Geneva Convention III (GCIII), 12 August 1949.

Geneva Convention IV (GCIV), 12 August 1949.

Gobierno de Colombia, Plan Nacional de Acción sobre Derechos Humanos y Empresas, 2015.

Government of Colombia and FARC-EP, Final Agreement to End the Armed Conflict and Built a Stable Lasting Peace, 24 November 2017.

Hague Convention IV, 18 October 1907.

Legislative Act 1/2012, Legal Framework for Peace, 31 July 2012.

Legislative Act No. 01, 4 April 2017.

Newspaper articles

Blanco, Silvia, 'La Desigualdad Social Lastra el Crecimiento Económico de Colombia', Bogotá: *El País*, 29 May 2014.

El Colombiano, 'El Estado Tendrá que Pagar 700.000 Dólares por Caso Santo Domingo, Arauca', www.elcolombiano.com/historico/olac_condenasantodomingo_efe_ana_25052004-CVEC_AO_4264615 (last accessed 19 January 2018).

Laverde Palma, Juan David, 'Dos Sentencias Contrarias', *El Espectador*, 21 March 2012.

Monsalve S., María Mónica, 'La Consulta Previa que les Llegó a los Nasas Diez Años Tarde', *El Espectador*, 10 September 2017.

Redacción El Tiempo, 'Condena de 6 años a Pilotos de FAC por Caso Santo Domingo', *El Tiempo*, 22 September 2007.
Redacción El Tiempo, 'Gobierno pide no especular en debates sobre acuerdo con las Farc', *El Tiempo*, 24 September 2015.
Stempel, Jonathan, 'U.S. Court Refuses to Hold Occidental Liable in Colombia Bombing', *Reuters*, 12 November 2014.

Official documents

UN, CESCR, 'Concluding Observations: Colombia', UN Doc. E/C.12/COL/CO/6, 19 October 2017.
UN, CESCR, 'Concluding Observations: Canada;, UN Doc. E/C.12/CAN/CO/6, 23 March 2016.
UN, CESCR, 'Concluding Observations: Colombia', UN Doc. E/C.12/COL/CO/6, 19 October 2017.
UN, Human Rights Committee, 'Concluding Observations: Colombia', UN Doc. CCPR/C/COL/CO/7, 17 November 2016.
UN, Human Rights Council, 'Annual Report of the United Nations High Commissioner for Human Rights on the Situation of Human Rights in Colombia', UN Doc. A/HRC/34/3/Add.3, 23 March 2017.

Cases

Case No. 06-15851, D. C. Docket No. 01-03208-CV-JEM (United States Court of Appeal), 11 August 2009.
Case No. 08-M -01916-, 3 January 2018. (United States District Court, Southern District of Florida).
Does 1 through 254 v Chiquita Brands International Inc, 17 March 2011.
Judgment C-370/06 (Constitutional Court of Colombia), 18 May 2006.
Judgment C-579-13 (Constitutional Court of Colombia), 28 August 2013.
Judgment C-035/16 (Constitutional Court of Colombia), 8 February 2016.
Judgment T-652/98 (Constitutional Court of Colombia), 10 November 1998.
Judgment T-016/07 (Constitutional Court of Colombia), 22 January 2007.
Judgment T-859/03 (Constitutional Court of Colombia), 25 September 2003.
Judgment T-760/08 (Constitutional Court of Colombia), 31 July 2008.
Judgment T-423/92 (Constitutional Court of Colombia), 24 June 1992.
Judgment T-495/10 (Constitutional Court of Colombia), 16 June 2010.
Judgment T-375/17 (Constitutional Court of Colombia), 9 June 2017.
Judgment T-615/02 (Constitutional Court of Colombia), 8 August 2002.
Judgment T-406/92 (Constitutional Court of Colombia), 5 June 1992.
Judgment T-495/10 (Constitutional Court of Colombia), 16 June 2010.
Judgment T-375/17 (Constitutional Court of Colombia), 9 June 2017.
Judgment T-732/16 (Constitutional Court of Colombia), 19 December 2016.
Judgment T-254/93 (Constitutional Court of Colombia), 30 June 1993.
Judgment T-202/12 (Constitutional Court of Colombia), 14 March 2012.
Kaliña and Lokono Peoples v Suriname (Inter-American Court of Human Rights), 25 November 2015.
Luis Alberto Galvis Mujica v Occidental Petroleum, 3 August 2010.

Luis Alberto Galvis Mujica, et al. v Airscan Inc. and Occidental Petroleum Corporation (United States Court for Appeals for the Ninth Circuit), D.C. No. 2:03-cv-02860-GW-JWJ, 12 November 2014,

Judgment SU-039/97 (Constitutional Court of Colombia), 21 February 1997.

Santo Domingo Massacre v Colombia (Inter-American Court of Human Rights), 30 November 2012.

Websites

Chiquita, www.chiquita.com (last accessed 19 January 2018).

Reports and miscellaneous

Barreto-Rozo, Antonio and González-Jácome, Jorge, 'The Colombian Constitutional Court at the Crossroads of Peace', International Journal of Constitutional Law Blog, 25 August 2017.

Laura Bernal-Bermudez, 'The Power of Corporations and the Power of People: Understanding Remedy and Accountability for Human Rights Violations – Colombia 2000–2014', Thesis, Oxford: University of Oxford, 2017.

Bernal-Bermúdez, Laura, 'Urapalma case', *in* PAX, *Peace, Everyone's Business!* May 2017, pp. 143–149.

Botero, Sandra, 'Colombia's Special Criminal Tribunal: Justicia Especial para la Paz', *International Journal of Constitutional Law Blog*, 15 October 2017.

Business and Human Rights Resource Centre, 'Chiquita Lawsuits (re Colombia)'.

Business and Human Rights Resource Centre, 'Coca Cola Lawsuits (re Colombia)'.

Business and Human Rights Resource Centre, 'Occidental lawsuit (re Colombia)'.

Business and Human Rights Resource Centre, 'Legal Case Map'.

Carrillo-Santarelli, Nicolás, 'An Assessment of the Colombian-FARC "Peace Jurisdiction" Agreement', *EJIL: Talk!* 29 September 2015.

Comisión Interamericana de Derechos Humanos (CIDH), 'Public Hearing, 153 Period of Sessions', 28 October 2014.

Constitutional Court of Colombia, 'Statistics', 2015.

CIDH, 'Canadá: Impacto de empresas mineras canadienses en A. Latina', www.youtube.com/watch?v=OWYue8FP9ZY (last accessed 19 January 2018).

European Center for Constitutional and Human Rights (ECCHR), 'Nestlé Precedent Case: Murder of Trade Unionist Romero in Colombia', 18 December 2014.

FIDH, 'Human Rights Coalition Calls on ICC to Investigate Role of Chiquita Executives in Contributing to Crimes against Humanity', 18 May 2017.

Galvis Castro, Felipe Alejandro, 'Activismo Judicial y Emancipación Social: Notas a Partir de la Justiciabilidad de los Derechos Económicos, Sociales y Culturales en Colombia y Argentina', http://biblioteca.clacso.edu.ar/ar/libros/becas/2007/cultura/galvis.pdf (last accessed 19 January 2018).

Gaviria Betancur, Paula, 2016 UN Business and Human Rights Forum', Geneva, 14 November 2016.

Grupo de Memoria Histórica, *¡Basta ya! Colombia: Memorias de Guerra y Dignidad*, Bogotá: Imprenta Nacional (2013).

ICAR and De justicia, 'Assessment of the Colombian National Action Plan (NAP) on Business and Human Rights', September 2016, pp. 29–30.

IKV Pax Christi, 'Free, Prior and Informed Consultation in Colombia: The Case of the Expansion of the Cerrejón Project', January 2012.

Interview with judge Jorge Ivan Palacio Palacio, Bogota, February 2014.

Joint Communiqué # 60 regarding the Agreement for the Creation of a Special Jurisdiction for Peace (Comunicado Conjunto # 60 sobre el Acuerdo de Creación de una Jurisdicción Especial para la Paz), Havana, 23 September 2015.

Joumard, Isabelle and Londoño Vélez, Juliana, 'Income in Equality and Poverty in Colombia. Part 1: The Role of the Labour Market', OECD Economics Department Working Papers No. 1036 (2013).

Joumard, Isabelle and Londoño Vélez, Juliana, 'Income in Equality and Poverty in Colombia. Part 2: The Redistributive Impact of Taxes and Transfers', OECD Economics Department Working Papers No. 1037, (2013).

Jolly, Alexandra, 'UN vs Under-Employed: A look at Colombia's Massive Informal Labor Sector', *Colombia Reports*, 21 May 2014, http://colombiareports.com/informal-workforce/ (last accessed 19 January 2018).

Juvinao Navarro, Luis E., 'Judicial Activism, the De Facto Regulator of Colombian Mining', *Global Risk Insights*, 17 May 2016.

Lemaitre, Julieta, 'El Coronel sí tiene quien le Escriba: la Tutela por Mínimo Vital en Colombia', *SELA (Seminario en Latinoamérica de Teoría Constitucional y Política) Papers* 43 (2005).

Regional Forum in Medellín, 'The Impact of Businesses on Human Rights in Latin American and the Caribbean – First regional debate', 26 August 2013.

The Office of the Presidential Advisor for Human Rights of the Republic of Colombia, 'National Action Plan on Human Rights and Business, Report on advancements in implementation', May 2017, http://www.derechoshumanos.gov.co/observatorio/publicaciones/Documents/2017/170602_InformeAnualEmpresa_English.pdf (last accessed 19 January 2018).

UN Human Development Report 2015.

World Bank, Global Economic Prospects – Forecasts – Colombia.

Part IV

Proposals for reform

11 Conclusions and recommendations

The primacy of protecting the human dignity of rights-holders 280
Corporate obligations concerning socio-economic rights 281
Access to justice 282
Case studies 283
Recommendations 284

Businesses have at times maintained contradictory relationships with human rights. At the rhetorical level, they appear to support the enjoyment of human rights, yet when it comes to agreeing on binding obligations, they generally seem to oppose it. With civil and political rights, some agreement can still be reached that businesses should support the protection they afford, largely since they create negative obligations, which is not entirely correct. Further, their involvement in socio-economic rights violations is already proverbial. However, socio-economic rights generally require corporations to take positive steps, and this is where their commitment tends to evaporate. This book examined corporate accountability for socio-economic rights. It is claimed that corporations violate socio-economic rights on a daily basis.[1] The focus herein has departed from the position of rights-holders of socio-economic rights and victims of violations of socio-economic rights, and has moved on to the question of duty-bearers of socio-economic rights as an inherent component of human dignity or even the rule-of-law concept. Thus, the historical and theoretical pillars of the concept were first investigated based on the values of human dignity, equality and sustainable development. Protecting the human dignity of rights-holders lies at the core of any discourse on human rights and fundamental freedoms. Corporations are among actors such as states, international organizations, organized criminal groups and others (see Figure 11.1) that, depending on the context, are duty-bearers of socio-economic rights.

1 See, Chapter 1.

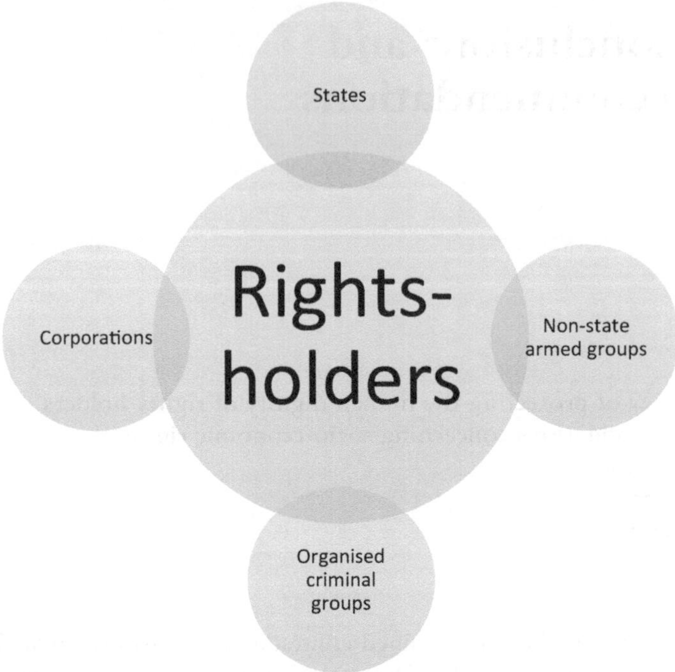

Figure 11.1 The primacy of protecting the human dignity of rights-holders
(Source: author's own work)

The primacy of protecting the human dignity of rights-holders

Human dignity is the essence of the existence of every human being. The excursion into history showed the idea of businesses infringing human rights is far from new and that several individuals, but also corporations, have been (indirectly) prosecuted for violations they have committed. This book then looked at existing and emerging corporate obligations concerning socio-economic rights in domestic and international settings in general, along with a specific focus by studying the rights to education, food, health, adequate housing and water that are essential for developing an individual's "capabilities" and self-realization in life. How to measure the socio-economic livelihood of an individual? Nussbaum states that, "traditionally deprived people may be satisfied with a low living standard, believing that this is all they have any hope of getting".[2] Sen argues that "the central well-being is the ability to achieve valuable functioning".[3] Nonetheless,

2 Martha C. Nussbaum, 'Women and Equality, the Capabilities Approach', 138(3) *International Labour Review* 227, 240 (1999).
3 Amartya Sen, 'Well-Being, Agency and Freedom: The Dewey Lectures 1984', 82(4) *The Journal of Philosophy* 169, 200 (1985).

one can answer this challenge by concentrating on the individual's capabilities not only to meet his/her basic needs in given socio-economic rights, but to also satisfy the higher objective of enabling their self-realization. More specifically, this enables the individual to attain the individual freedom for self-realization through their civil and political rights. Wiles argues that socio-economic rights "are rights that protect the necessities of life and provide for the foundations of an adequate quality of life" and "the conditions for the pursuit of human dignity and equal opportunities"[4] (footnotes omitted). In order to guarantee the human dignity of such an individual, all actors, including states, international organizations, corporations and others are obliged to work together to ensure dignity is both an individual and a collective value. Corporations also derive their obligations from the fact that human dignity is a collective value that belongs to all individuals in society.

Corporate obligations concerning socio-economic rights

Perhaps this book's key finding is that the obligations of corporations regarding socio-economic rights stem from several domestic systems, international frameworks and the internal commitment of corporations themselves. Several sources reveal that corporations are required in domestic law and indirectly also in international (human rights) law to respect human rights.[5] Corporate obligations mostly derive from constitutional and statutory provisions in domestic settings. They may derive also from their good practices.[6] However, it is the case that such obligations are traditionally sometimes vague and ambiguous, with their source concealed in statutes of criminal, civil and administrative law, depending on the state. Therefore, more clarity is required to identify corporate obligations concerning socio-economic rights, particularly the obligations to protect and fulfil. Or perhaps one has to rethink the traditional concept of sources of law or international law, thus far accepted as unbiased fact in the academic community. The socio-economic rights of rights-holders are shaped in the horizontal and mutually reinforcing relationship with the obligations of duty-holders such as corporations (see Figure 11.2).

This study investigated corporate obligations pertaining to five socio-economic rights due to both their seminal importance and for space reasons, namely the rights to education, food, health, adequate housing and water. In this way, it maintains that corporations hold both negative obligations (obligation to respect) and positive obligations (obligations to protect and fulfil) concerning socio-economic rights. On one hand, it argued that corporations have at a

4 Ellen Wiles, 'Aspirational Principles or Enforceable Rights? The Future for Socio-Economic Rights in National Law', 22(1) *American University International Law Review* 35, 64 (2006).

5 Jernej Letnar Černič and Tara Van Ho (eds.), *Human Rights and Business: Direct Corporate Accountability for Human Rights*, Oisterwijk: Wolf Legal Publishers (2015).

6 See chapter 4.

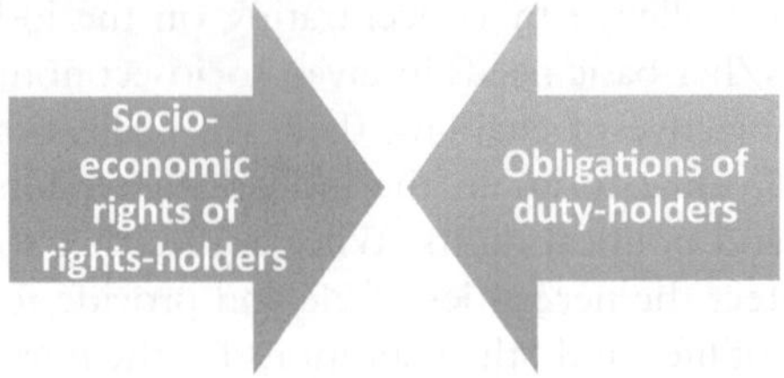

Figure 11.2 Socio-economic rights of rights-holders versus obligations of duty-holders (Source: author's own work)

minimum the obligation not to interfere with an individual's socio-economic livelihood, which is an obligation of result. On the other hand, it suggested that the obligations to protect and fulfil are more obligations of conduct and corporations should seek to ensure at least the reasonable core of socio-economic rights. Further, it was argued that corporations must conduct effective, rapid, impartial and independent supervisions of their supply chains to make sure that their business partners like suppliers and contractors do not breach the reasonable core of socio-economic rights. Finally, corporations have emerging obligations to fulfil socio-economic rights, particularly in limited local contexts, where they can satisfy them by ensuring at least the minimum rights to education, food, health, adequate housing and water, even though several obstacles appear to imposing such obligations on private actors. Of course, these obligations may at this stage only be on an ethical or moral level, but sustainable development nevertheless encourages corporations to contribute financial resources to the provision of socio-economic rights, and certain corporations already have done this.

Access to justice

Prosecuting socio-economic rights violations in both the Global North and South depends on several factors largely beyond the power of the victims. Even when all objective conditions are met, victims or relatives must be able to gather the courage to pursue the accountability of all perpetrators of the violations and compensation for the suffering caused. The enforcement of human rights violations should certainly not be a luxury of just a few, but should be accessible to all affected by a violation. How can rights-holders most effectively enforce corporate accountability for socio-economic rights?

Domestic systems generally do not fully permit the enforcement of corporate accountability for socio-economic rights for acts or omissions by corporations at home and in third countries, which requires victims to often resort to ineffective and reluctant domestic courts in Asia, Africa, Central and Eastern Europe, and South America. Another growing challenge is that socio-economic rights are not always enforceable. In recent years, progress has only been made in a few jurisdictions, especially in the English legal system. Nonetheless, socio-economic rights can be protected against corporate actors through, for example, civil and political rights. This book concentrated on rights-holders' access to remedies when their socio-economic rights have been violated. It analyzed the various judicial, quasi-judicial and non-judicial fora to which victims may have resort. This book contends that victims should have access to various possibilities in business and socio-economic rights to bring cases against different responsible actors. In this way, this would not only include corporate accountability, but also individual and state accountability. It has therefore argued for a holistic, inclusive and pluralistic approach to ensuring access to justice. The findings reveal that the domestic systems of corporations' home states, typically in the Global North, are still the best option for victims to succeed with their claims. The case studies of Cambodia, China and Colombia show that most cases against corporations were brought outside their domestic system, whereas at least in the case of Colombia the Constitutional Court has in the past protected socio-economic rights, especially against state-owned corporations.[7]

The study has called for a broad concept of access to justice, which includes a range of possible alternatives available to rights-holders for enforcing corporate accountability. It identified the gap found in bringing cases against corporations concerning socio-economic abuses. While some domestic and international quasi-judicial mechanisms already exist for enforcing corporate accountability for socio-economic rights, they are few and far between. Therefore, the existing mechanisms need to be remodelled or newly developed to effectively protect the human dignity and socio-economic rights of rights-holders. Enforcing accountability also leads to social change. Backer et al. observed that "catalysing litigation produces empowerment among the most neglected group of human rights stakeholders. . .: it serves to remedy individual wrongs and it provides a powerful venue for participation of traditionally excluded groups".[8] It has thus developed tripartite frameworks that are built on the socio-economic rights of rights-holders, corporate obligations for socio-economic rights and access to remedies (see Figure 11.3).

Case studies

Finally, the last part studied three domestic challenges in identifying and enforcing socio-economic rights in the three different legal settings of Cambodia, China and Colombia. Excursions into these fora encountered several difficulties regarding business and socio-economic rights. The first issue was the legal recognition of socio-economic rights, the second was justiciability before the domestic

7 See, chapters 8, 9 and 10.

8 Larry Catá Backer, Nabih Haddad, Tomonori Teraoka and Keren Wang, 'Democratizing the Global Business and Human Rights Project by Catalyzing Strategic Litigation from the Bottom Up', *in* Jena Martin and Karen E. Bravo (eds.), *The Business and Human Rights Landscape*, Cambridge: Cambridge University Press (2016), pp. 254–287, p. 265.

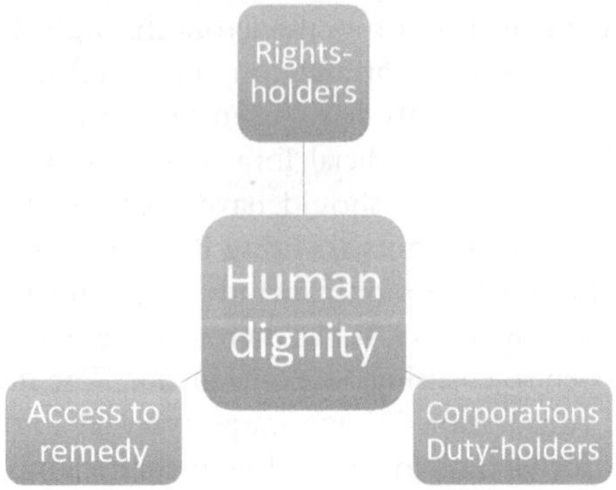

Figure 11.3 Tripartite framework of corporate accountability for socio-economic rights

(Source: author's own work)

courts and the third one related to their enforcement against corporations. In addition, several domestic systems, including the three that were studied, have seen several challenges to the rule of law not necessarily connected to business and socio-economic rights, but to general circumstances in the country. This is closely connected to how the rule of law functions in many domestic legal systems, where widespread distrust has created an inviolable deadlock in which public institutions are often used to foster private financial and other interests. It appears that the rule of law has not been fully been put in place and is subject to the interests of various elites, which interpret it as meaning the protection of its private, too often financial interests. Both sets of human rights – socio-economic rights and civil and political rights in business – have suffered as a result. It seems that it has not been easy to translate liberal values in the institutions of several states. Those case studies demonstrate, if anything, the local elite's resistance to liberal values like the rule of law and the protection of human rights.

Recommendations

The current model of corporate socio-economic obligations and accountability is vague and unclear. The examination showed the need for a holistic, pluralistic and inclusive approach to corporate obligations and accountability concerning socio-economic rights. The recommendations listed below are not utopian since they are based on the current domestic and international framework's foundations for regulating corporate accountability for socio-economic rights. What seems necessary is an elucidation of the existing normative structures at the domestic and international levels and internalization of human dignity among all actors. That is why the bulk of the book analyzed the current normative frameworks. Moreover, reforms are therefore required in domestic and international arrangements in order to bolster rights-holders' access to justice. This study therefore makes ten recommendations for developing and remodelling corporate accountability for socio-economic rights and developing the normative framework *de lege ferenda*:

- Place the human dignity of individual rights-holders in the centre of socio-economic rights.
- Support the initiative for the UN Treaty on Business and Human Rights, which could motivate domestic systems to proceed with reforms.
- The need for greater clarity of the nature and scope of socio-economic obligations, particularly the scope of positive obligations. To this effect, draft guidelines on corporations and socio-economic rights should be drafted at the UN level, perhaps within the mandate of the UN Working Group on Business and Human Rights. States should clarify the socio-economic obligations in National Action Plans under the UN Guiding Principles to improve their national legal framework and improve victims' access to justice.
- Clarify the corporate obligations to protect and fulfil socio-economic rights. Although corporations have both negative and emerging positive obligations in their global supply chains, what is needed is a better explanation of their nature and scope in those supply chains.
- The business sector should also adopt more general or sectoral voluntary regulations aimed at enhancing their position in terms of commanding greater respect within society.
- Domestic and international judicial and non-judicial fora for enforcing corporate accountability for socio-economic rights must be improved in order for socio-economic rights to be enforced against corporations not only indirectly, but also directly. There is a need for a rights-specific forum on socio-economic rights due to their particularities and the sensitivity of their nature because many domestic systems do not allow for the judicial realization of socio-economic rights even for vulnerable groups.
- Improve the rule-of-law environment in host and home states in order to give victims a better chance of enforcing their rights, including enhancing protections of the right to a fair trial.
- A holistic, inclusive and pluralistic approach to access to justice including corporate, state and individual accountability and giving support to bottom-up approaches to business and socio-economic rights.
- Improve the functioning of the National Contact Points under the OECD Guidelines and make them more savvy to socio-economic rights in order to provide victims with more effective access to protection in the event of violations; equally, enhance the procedure under the ILO Tripartite Declaration.
- Establish a global financial fund for victims of corporate violations along the lines of the example of the trust fund of the International Criminal Court.[9]

9 Trust Fund of the International Criminal Court, www.trustfundforvictims.org/en/home (last accessed 19 January 2018).

These recommendations are needed to place the individual at the centre of the business and human rights discourse and to support their self-realization. The individual's self-realization is only enabled by ensuring the provision of fundamental socio-economic rights, thereby also giving the individual access to civil and political rights. A holistic and inclusive approach to corporate accountability for socio-economic rights has yet to develop, while attempts made in this regard in the human rights and business context can only be described as partly successful. The current normative structures at all levels are not equipped to deal with cases concerning corporate violations of socio-economic rights, thereby leaving rights-holders in legal oblivion. Accordingly, it is essential to develop legal structures for examining cases against corporations concerning socio-economic violations, preferably at the domestic levels, with some kind of supervisory mechanisms at the international level. Nolan and Taylor therefore correctly observed that

> while the proliferation of soft and, more occasionally, hard law mechanisms to hold corporations accountable for violations of ESC rights have been incrementally effective in legitimizing the inclusion of such rights within a company's sphere of responsibility, accountability for the violation of such rights remains limited.[10]

This becomes increasingly difficult when one considers that evidentiary problems are more acute in a civil dispute due to the intentional avoidance of regulatory measures and the lack of liability in most situations. All in all, it may appear that transparent rules are required for determining when the rules of company law should be set aside for the benefit of human dignity and when the doctrine of the separation of legal entities does not apply.

It is domestic judiciaries that are the primary protectors of socio-economic rights and their values against negative corporate behaviours. To this end, it seems necessary for officials and judges to internalize the value of human dignity and socio-economic rights protections. States should show greater interest in systematically training the government officials, lawyers and especially judges who are expected to apply such socio-economic rights in the local system on a daily basis. Accordingly, all branches of government within a state should organize special training programmes to educate stakeholders and make them aware of the use of case law. Socio-economic rights should be applied on a day-to-day basis at all levels of the judicial, legislative and executive branches of government. This practice would help avoid the situation of being overlooked and ignored to the benefit of corporate projects. Especially important is the awareness of lawyers, as they are the most important protagonists here. The topic should be included in the core of university study programmes so that corporate accountability under socio-economic rights can be studied and later monitored by young graduates.

10 Justine Nolan and Luke Taylor, 'Corporate Responsibility for Economic, Social and Cultural Rights: Rights in Search of a Remedy?', 87(2) *Journal of Business Ethics* 433, 454 (2009).

In conclusion, corporations and their responsible persons must internalize the values of human dignity and socio-economic rights, while placing the individual at the centre of business and socio-economic rights.

Bibliography

Books

Letnar Černič, Jernej and Van Ho, Tara (eds.), *Human Rights and Business: Direct Corporate Accountability for Human Rights*, Oisterwijk: Wolf Legal Publishers (2015).

Journal articles

Nolan, Justine and Taylor, Luke, 'Corporate Responsibility for Economic, Social and Cultural Rights: Rights in Search of a Remedy?', 87(2) *Journal of Business Ethics* 433 (2009).

Nussbaum, Martha C., 'Women and Equality, the Capabilities Approach', 138(3) *International Labour Review* 227 (1999).

Sen, Amartya, 'Well-Being, Agency and Freedom: The Dewey Lectures 1984', 82(4) *The Journal of Philosophy* 169 (1985).

Wiles, Ellen, 'Aspirational Principles or Enforceable Rights? The Future for Socio-Economic Rights in National Law', 22(1) *American University International Law Review* 35 (2006).

Book chapter

Backer, Larry Catá, Haddad, Nabih, Teraoka, Tomonori and Wang, Keren, 'Democratizing the Global Business and Human Rights Project by Catalyzing Strategic Litigation from the Bottom Up', *in* Jena Martin and Karen E. Bravo (eds.), *The Business and Human Rights Landscape*, Cambridge: Cambridge University Press (2016), pp. 254–287.

Websites

Trust Fund of the International Criminal Court, www.trustfundforvictims.org/en/home (last accessed 19 January 2018).

Index

access to justice 3, 6, 12, 13, 15, 16, 23, 55, 60, 99, 112, 153, 155, 156, 169, 172, 175, 182, 184, 215, 220, 222, 231, 232, 236, 239, 247–249, 255, 258, 262, 279, 282, 283, 285
access to medicines 73
access to remedy/remedies 16, 155, 156, 159, 171, 283, 284
added value 59, 71, 79, 109, 141, 169, 183, 214, 231, 238
adequate housing (right to) 4, 15, 64, 74, 75, 87, 111, 116, 125, 139–143, 146, 198, 280–282
Adidas 173, 174, 208
Africa 7, 22, 23, 35, 43, 49, 229, 282
African Commission on Human and Peoples' Rights 125
Agent Orange case 34
Aguirre, Daniel 6
Alston, Philip 6, 88, 92, 223, 239
amnesty 255, 268
Anglo American 9, 35, 73, 75, 174
apartheid 22, 35, 36
arbitral decisions 50
arbitration 15, 153, 155, 157, 159, 169–172, 183
armed conflict/conflicts 233, 248–251, 256–259, 263, 267, 268, 270
armed groups 280
Asia 22, 43, 46, 61, 77, 196, 198, 203, 205, 229, 230, 282
Asian countries 45, 199, 203, 204, 206
Association of South-East Nations (ASEAN) 196, 203–206, 215
AstraZeneca 73, 74
Azim Premji 70
Australia 99, 162
Austria 163
Availability, accessibility, acceptability and quality (of socio-economic rights) 134, 136
Awochi case 33

Backer, Larry 91, 234, 283
Bangladesh 77, 111, 154
Bangladesh Accord 111
Belgium 162
Bhopal case 134, 161
BHP Billiton 7
bilateral investment 48, 170
Bill and Melinda Gates Foundation 70
Bogotá 248
Bohoslavsky, Juan Pablo 221, 230, 233, 235
Bolivia 130
bottom-up approach 153, 175, 176
bottom-up enforcement 12, 183
bottom-up system 210
Brazil 7, 8, 71, 76, 136
Brussels Convention 178
burden of proof 179–181
Business and Human Rights Resource Centre 256

Cambodia 14, 15, 159, 195–203, 206, 208, 210–212, 214, 215, 230, 283
Canada 23, 99, 162, 206, 258
CARE 77
Carrillo-Santarelli, Nicolas 96
Central and Eastern Europe 229, 282
Chandler case 109
Chevron case 181
Chile 145
China 14, 15, 45, 78, 159, 164, 203, 220–241, 283

China Construction Bank 238
China National Petroleum 220, 235
China State Construction 220
Chinese Chamber of Commerce of Metals Minerals & Chemicals Importers & Exporters (CCCMC) 231
Chiquita 256, 257
Cisco System 238
Citigroup 71
civil claims 163, 172
civil society 6, 10, 58, 65, 66, 74, 75, 91, 136, 175, 176, 203, 209, 210, 215, 239
Clapham, Andrew 51, 97, 138
Coca Cola 77, 256, 257
collective value 51, 125, 281
Colombia 14, 15, 154, 159, 247, 248–259, 262–267, 269, 270, 283
Colombian Peace Accord 247, 249, 267
colonialism 21, 22
complicity 23, 24, 30, 106, 200, 253, 256, 257, 259, 266
Congo, Democratic Republic of 77, 95, 145, 230
ConocoPhilips 238
consent 176, 177, 251, 260; (local communities) 106, 231
Constitutional Courts: Colombian 144, 247, 249, 253, 254, 259–262, 270, 283; German 94
Constitutions: Bolivia 130; Colombia 251, 259, 261; Ecuador 130; Kenya 93; Kingdom of Cambodia 201; Lao People's Democratic Republic 143; Mexico 139; People's Republic of China 221, 225, 226, 228, 237, 238; Portugal 140; Republic of Slovenia 93; Republic of South Africa 93, 130, 140, 143; Russian Federation 140
corporate complicity 23, 266
corporate criminal liability 266
corporate group 112, 129, 135, 137, 142, 147
corporate social responsibility (CSR) 10, 196, 209, 227, 228, 230, 232, 252
corporate veil 179, 180
corruption 67, 199, 203, 211, 231, 237, 248; anti-corruption 50
Costa Rica 154
crimes against humanity 23, 24, 26, 27, 29, 30, 96, 197, 212, 253, 254, 259, 265, 268
criminal customary international law 259
criminal liability 30, 96, 182, 266
criminal prosecutions 172
criminal responsibility 26, 33, 34, 36, 182, 227, 254, 269
customary international law 259

Daimler Mercedes 111
decision-making 158, 176, 236
De Schutter, Olivier 94, 102, 104, 109, 131
Deutsche Bank 23
Deva, Surya 44, 156
developed countries 41, 43, 45, 46, 57, 58, 229
developing countries 58, 69, 115
domestic judicial mechanisms 153, 156, 159
domestic law 95, 100, 183, 202, 208, 281
domestic non-judicial mechanisms 153, 165
Dresdner Bank 29, 30
due diligence 66, 95, 102, 106–110, 112, 116, 129, 133, 135, 137, 142, 147, 233–235, 252
duty-bearer 13, 80, 91
duty-holder 6, 13

Ecopetrol 264
Ecuador 8, 71, 130
education (right to) 4, 43, 64, 65, 69–71, 104, 106, 114, 125–129, 198, 200, 224
EdX 70
employment 27, 45, 54, 71, 95, 108, 168, 180, 195, 201, 250
enforcement 3, 4, 6, 12, 13, 25, 79, 88, 96, 153, 155, 159, 160, 164, 165, 167, 168, 169, 170, 177, 183, 199, 223, 227, 233, 236, 240, 249, 267, 282, 284
England 178
entities: legal entities 127, 153, 177, 179, 180, 181, 183, 201, 286; private entities 57, 113, 114, 225, 229
equality 4, 40, 50–52, 54, 56, 176, 279; inequality 42, 52, 54, 139, 164, 221, 222, 223, 248, 250
European Center for Constitutional and Human Rights (ECCHR) 257
European Convention for the Protection of Human Rights and Fundamental Freedoms 127, 257
European Court of Human Rights 257

European Court of Justice 178
European Union 111, 206
extraterritorial obligations 145, 208, 220, 229, 230

Fafo 33, 161
fairness 132, 175, 210, 224, 236, 241, 255
Farben case 24, 26–28, 32, 34
Farha, Leilani 139, 141
FIDH 7
Flick case 24–26, 34, 38
food (right to) 4, 49, 50, 57, 59, 64, 71, 125, 126, 128, 130, 131, 133, 135, 138, 248
Ford 111
foreign direct investment 41, 47, 48, 49, 206, 210
forum non conveniens 153, 161, 177, 178
France 77, 95, 162
free, prior and informed consent 176, 231, 251, 260

garment factory/factories 72, 207, 209
garment industry 73, 195–197, 199, 206, 210
Geneva Conventions 259
genocide 23, 197, 253, 254, 268
Germany 24–27, 29
Ghana 71, 75
Gini coefficient 223, 250
globalization 15, 40, 40–45, 49, 59
Global partnership for Sustainable Development 53, 55, 58, 115
Goldmann Sachs 76
good practices 64, 65, 66, 67, 68, 69, 71, 72, 73, 76, 78, 79, 80
Gsk 74

HAGL 212–214
hard law 286
health (right to) 4, 64, 72–74, 110, 125, 126, 132, 134, 136–138, 198, 224
High-Risk Areas 108
H&M 208, 209
holistic approach 10, 11, 15, 36, 155, 156, 172, 182, 183, 197
Holocaust 162
human dignity 10, 40, 41, 50, 51, 56, 64, 79, 111, 125, 126, 176, 182, 236, 260, 279, 280, 281, 283–287, 286, 287
humanitarian law 158, 268
human rights abuses 156, 159, 196, 200, 202, 212, 223, 233
human rights impact assessment/ assessments 66, 106, 115, 232, 258
Human Rights Watch 223

IBM 162
ICSID 145, 170
Ikea 112
ILO Convention No. 169 176
ILO Tripartite Declaration of Principles concerning Multinational Enterprises and Social Policy 153, 166–169, 285
India 22, 23, 45, 76, 77, 154, 161, 230
Indigenous peoples 8, 100, 176, 177, 200–202, 212, 231, 235, 249, 251, 256, 260, 270
Indonesia 23, 71, 196
inequality 42, 52, 54, 139, 164, 221, 222, 223, 248, 250
Inter-American Commission of Human Rights 256, 264
Inter-American Court of Human Rights 136, 256, 264
Inter-American Human Rights System 98, 247, 249, 263
International Commission of jurists 91
International Council on Mining and Minerals 75
International Covenant on Civil and Political Rights 101, 201
International Covenant on Economic, Social and Cultural Rights 5, 6, 70, 87, 96, 101, 126, 127, 131, 140, 154, 228, 236
International Labour Organization (ILO) 101, 133
investment 3, 40, 41, 46–50, 59, 106, 133, 134, 141, 145, 170, 199, 202, 206, 210, 229, 234, 249, 250, 258, 266
investor/investors 46–50, 66, 139, 141, 177, 199, 202, 203, 212, 215, 231, 249
Ivory Coast 71

Jägers, Nicola 138
Japan 163, 238
Joseph, Sarah 12
judicial, quasi-judicial and/or non-judicial: enforcement 159; fora/ forums 155, 283; mechanisms 3, 12; remedies 13
judicial independence 212, 221
jurisdiction 24, 26, 99, 108, 136, 156, 163, 177, 178, 254, 263, 265, 267–269

Kellogg 101, 132
Kenya 9
Khulumani case 35
Kiobel case 164
Krauch case 26, 28
Kroeber, Arthur R. 221, 237
Krupp case 24, 28, 29, 34

Langford, Malcom 88, 154, 164
Lebanon 77
legal obligation/obligations 13, 65, 67, 68, 79, 90, 97, 180, 181, 259
legitimacy 92, 173, 210
Lego 70
Liberia 75
limitation/limitations 94, 166, 224
litigation/litigations 34, 155, 163
local communities 4, 23, 75, 102, 106, 114, 116, 129, 135–138, 142, 147, 231

Macklem, Patrick 91
Mahindra Rural Housing Finance 76
Malawi Tea 2020 Programme 72
Malaysia 196, 205
management 29, 54, 59, 66, 71, 77, 109, 110, 113, 180, 209, 210, 259, 266
maximum available resources 5
McCruden, Christopher 51
McDonald's 132
Medellín 144, 248, 262
Merck 73
Mexico 71, 139
Microsoft 71
Millennium Development Goals (MDGs) 53
Minzner, Carl 240
multinational corporations 68, 256, 264
multinational enterprises 98, 109, 145, 153, 166–169, 234
Myanmar 196, 230

NAFTA 49
national law 15, 30, 108, 169, 238, 281
national legal orders 4, 159
natural resources 58, 199, 200, 213, 249–251
Nazi 24, 26, 30
Nepal 154
Nestlé 8, 70, 71, 77, 256, 257
Netherlands 99, 162, 183
Netherlands Temporary Court Martial 33
Newmont 70, 75
Nigeria 78, 125, 181
Nike 238
Nippon Mining Company 33
Nishimatsu lawsuit 238
Nolan, Justine 88, 92, 286
non-governmental organization (NGO) 54, 77, 136, 159, 199, 205, 208
non-state actors 3, 57, 97, 101, 127, 197, 262
Norway 53
Novartis 73
Nussbaum, Martha C. 47, 53, 126, 280

obligation to fulfil 87, 113–116, 129, 134, 135, 137, 141–143, 147
obligation to protect 64, 87, 106, 108, 109, 110, 111, 112, 128, 129, 133, 135, 137, 138, 141, 142, 146, 147, 208, 210, 214, 225, 229, 253, 264
obligation to respect 87, 89, 98, 105–107, 128, 129, 133, 135, 137–139, 142, 145, 147, 281
OECD Guidelines for Multinational Enterprises 98, 109, 145, 153, 166, 167, 183, 285
OECD National Contact Points (UK) 145
Olga Tellis Case 160
Ombudsman 174; Compliance Advisor Ombudsman of the International Finance Corporation of the World Bank 166, 213; Ombudsman Advisory Mechanism 212–214
Organisation for Economic Cooperation and Development (OECD) 59, 108, 109, 113, 166, 167
Oxfam 65, 66

pacta sunt servanda 172
Pakistan 154
Papua New Guinea 162
parent company/companies/corporations 110, 178, 179–181, 183, 258, 270; (and subcontracting) 95, 109
parent-subsidiary relationships 266
PepsiCo 78, 100
Permanent Court of Arbitration 170, 171
Peru 145, 235
Philippines 196
Phnom Penh 199, 207–210
pluralistic approach 283, 285
poverty 41–44, 49, 53–56, 58, 59, 65, 69, 76, 164, 196, 198, 199, 222–224, 250

privacy 140, 165
private actors 24, 57, 87, 92, 93, 100, 106, 128, 146, 202, 251, 268, 282
private companies 200
private entities 57, 113, 114, 225, 229
private hospitals and clinics 72
private merchants 22
private sector 58, 59, 76, 108, 136, 140, 141, 146, 215, 220, 252
Procter & Gamble 78
public good 45

Qualcomm 71

Rafael Unda, José 258
Rana plaza disaster 72, 111
regulatory framework 33, 36, 99, 127, 214, 225, 232, 241
remedy/remedies 3, 12, 13, 16, 36, 97, 105, 109, 112, 117, 129, 135, 137, 142, 143, 147, 155, 156, 158, 159, 164, 165, 167, 169, 171, 173, 236, 238, 249, 252, 257, 259, 263, 283, 284
reparation 35, 158, 249, 252, 254, 263, 264
risk 108, 109, 181, 233, 252
Rome Statute of the International Criminal Court (ICC) 182
Ruggie, John 7, 45, 49
rule of law 7, 46, 48, 50, 55, 56, 60, 92, 156, 182, 197, 203–205, 214, 220, 221, 229, 236, 237, 241, 261, 262, 269, 284

sanctions 35, 101, 223
Sanlu Group 239
Santa Domingo Massacre case 263, 265, 266
Scheinin, Martin 5
Scotiabank 174
Second World War 21–23, 30, 33, 34, 36, 238
Sen, Amartya 4, 51, 52, 56, 224, 236, 280
shareholders 79
Shelton, Dinah 44
Siemens 70
Sinopec Group 220
slavery 23, 26, 29, 95, 96, 133
slave trade 21, 22, 23, 36
Slovenia 93
socio-economic environment 15, 40, 41, 46, 50, 53, 57, 59, 195, 198, 247, 249
soft law 97
South Africa 75, 93, 113, 130, 140, 143
South African Truth and Reconciliation Commission 35, 36
Sri Lanka 154
stakeholders 48, 60, 67, 77, 107, 111, 129, 135, 137, 142, 147, 170, 172, 174, 213, 234, 269, 283, 286
standards: educational standards 70; international standards 90, 101, 202, 261; living standards 4, 41, 42, 56–58, 168, 196, 224; minimum standard 49, 65; socio-economic standards 47, 50, 139, 222
state obligation/obligations 90, 100, 102, 113, 139, 144, 145, 220, 259, 264
State-owned Assets Supervision and Administration Commission of the State Council (SASAC) 230, 231, 234
state-owned corporation/corporations 7, 102, 103, 128, 133, 146, 160, 221, 229, 231
state responsibility 15, 44, 97, 182, 183, 266
Stiglitz, Joseph 42
subsidiary/subsidiaries 8, 28, 69, 95, 109, 110, 112, 162, 178–181, 183, 209, 210, 213, 225, 231, 233, 235, 255, 257, 266, 270
Suez Environment 77
supplier/suppliers 13, 69, 71, 73, 74, 77, 103, 107, 110–113, 128, 132, 173, 208–210, 215, 282
supply chain 69, 71, 108, 109, 110–113, 132, 133, 231, 233
Supreme Courts: Chile 145; India 134, 144, 160, 161; Israel 94; US 34, 164; Victoria (Australia) 162
sustainability 49, 53, 66, 71, 77, 78, 132, 227, 229
Sustainable Development Goals (SDGs) 54, 55, 57–59, 65, 66, 76, 115, 223
sustainable livelihood 126
Switzerland 257

Tanzania 8
Taylor, Luke 286
terrorist organizations 257
Tiffany & Co. 66
Tomaševski, Katarina 104
torture 258, 265, 268
Torture Victim Protection Act 257
Total 76
trade union/unions 175, 227, 257, 258

transitional justice 247, 249, 252, 254, 255, 267
transnational corporations 7, 9, 12, 43, 44, 57, 64, 76, 159, 163, 210, 229, 250, 251, 255, 257, 258, 266, 270
transparency 73, 95, 109, 175, 196, 199, 210, 224, 234, 253, 255; non-transparency 237
trust fund 238, 285
tutela 259, 261, 262

UN Business and Human Rights Forum 49, 234, 252
UNCITRAL 172
UN Commission on International Trade Law (UNCITRAL) 170
UN Committee on Economic, Social and Cultural Rights (CESCR) 5, 52, 69, 95, 99, 104, 115, 127, 132, 136, 144, 154, 200, 225, 232, 233, 236, 252, 258, 263
UN Committee on the Rights of the Child (CRC) 99, 132
UN Convention on the Protection of the Rights of All Migrant Workers and Members of Their Families 203
UN Declaration on the Rights of Indigenous Peoples 129
UN Global Compact 98
UN Global Compact – CEO Water Mandate 76, 77, 146
UN Guiding Principles on Business and Human Rights 105, 108, 144, 156, 196, 202, 205, 228, 233, 262
UN Habitat 77
UN Human Development Index 52, 198, 250
UN Human Rights Council 97, 196, 205, 228
UN International Covenant on Civil and Political Rights 101, 201, 211, 249, 252
UN International Covenant on Economic, Social and Cultural Rights (ICESCR) 5, 6, 70, 87, 101, 126, 127, 131, 140, 154, 165, 228, 236
United Kingdom 93, 99, 177, 178
United Kingdom Modern Slavery Act (2015) 96, 109
United States 24, 26, 43, 49, 70, 95, 161, 163, 164, 206, 264, 265
Universal Declaration of Human Rights 101, 132, 133, 201
UN Millennium Declaration 57
UN Office of the High Commissioner for Human Rights 50, 74, 165
UN "Protect, Respect and Remedy" framework 105
UN Treaty on Business and Human Rights 98, 171, 172, 183, 285
UN Working Group on Business and Human Rights 12, 67, 90, 97, 251, 285
Urbaser case 145
US Alien Tort Statute (ATS) 163, 164, 265
US Nuremberg Military Tribunal 24, 26, 28

value chain 77
Vandenhole, Wouter 40, 44, 90, 105
Vedanta case 8
Venezuela 7
Vietnam War 22, 34
violations (human rights) 21, 36, 44, 109, 111, 129, 135, 137, 142, 147, 153, 156, 158, 159, 163, 169, 172, 178, 195, 197, 198, 210, 211, 222, 229, 230, 232, 252, 256, 257, 259, 267, 268; (socio-economic rights) 3, 4, 15, 21, 30, 36, 95, 107, 112, 153, 155, 156, 159, 165, 179, 181–184, 199, 211, 235, 239, 249, 268, 270, 279, 282, 286
vulnerable groups 139–141, 201, 231, 259, 260, 285

Walmart 71
war crimes 23, 24, 26, 27, 29–32, 197, 253, 254, 258, 259, 265, 268
water (right to) 64, 76–78, 93, 101, 125–127, 130, 143–147, 250
Wiwa case 179
worker/workers 7, 9, 27, 28, 32–35, 72, 73, 108, 111, 140, 168, 199, 203, 206, 208, 210, 226, 234, 238, 257
World Bank 166, 198, 212, 222

Yahoo! 238
Yeshanew, Sisay Alemahu 12, 133

Zambia 8, 9, 40
Zyklon B Case 30

For Product Safety Concerns and Information please contact our EU representative GPSR@taylorandfrancis.com Taylor & Francis Verlag GmbH, Kaufingerstraße 24, 80331 München, Germany